THE 1956 PRESIDENTIAL CAMPAIGN

The 1956
PRESIDENTIAL CAMPAIGN

By

CHARLES A. H. THOMSON

FRANCES M. SHATTUCK

GREENWOOD PRESS, PUBLISHERS
WESTPORT, CONNECTICUT

Library of Congress Cataloging in Publication Data

Thomson, Charles Alexander Holmes, 1913-
 The 1956 Presidential campaign.

 Reprint of the ed. published by the Brookings Institu-
tion, Washington, D. C.
 Includes bibliographical references.
 1. Presidents--United States--Election--1956.
I. Shattuck, Frances M., joint author. II. Title.
[E837.5.T49 1974]   329'.023'730921   74-11990
ISBN 0-8371-7707-3

Originally published in 1960 by The Brookings Institution,
Washington

Reprinted with the permission of The Brookings Institution

Reprinted in 1974 by Greenwood Press,
a division of Williamhouse-Regency Inc.

Library of Congress Catalog Card Number 74-11990

ISBN 0-8371-7707-3

Printed in the United States of America

Foreword

This volume is a pioneering attempt to study the election process as a whole for the presidential election of 1956. It grew out of the five-volume study, *Presidential Nominating Politics in 1952*, by Paul T. David, Malcolm Moos, and Ralph M. Goldman, which was conducted under the auspices of the American Political Science Association. That volume, however, concluded with the political conventions.

The purpose of the study is to clarify the major interests, values, and activities that are combined in such a campaign and to explore the role of communications, organization, and goal-oriented behavior. These are of interest to both the social scientist and the political practitioner.

A related purpose of the analysis is to show what could be done with limited resources to provide the kinds of data on which judgments and classifications of candidates, statements on issues, and party behavior might be made. The study stands as a first trial, a model on which others may improve. Methods and access need refinement. Richer results will reward more sustained and sophisticated efforts. It is hoped that the present study may indicate some of the avenues worth exploring and represent an American counterpart of the British studies of general elections sponsored by Nuffield College, Oxford.

In a very real sense the book is a collaborative effort. The first and last chapters were drafted jointly by both authors. Miss Shattuck took main responsibility for drafting the chapters detailing the course of events up to the preliminaries of the Democratic and Republican National Conventions. Mr. Thomson took main responsibility for drafting the remaining chapters. Each author received detailed comment and criticism from the other; the main points of interpretation and analysis are in large part shared.

The authors have had the advantage of comment and criticism

from an Advisory Committee composed of Paul T. David, Angus Campbell, Avery Leiserson, Malcolm Moos, and E. E. Schattschneider; and from George A. Graham, Director of Governmental Studies at Brookings.

Brookings wishes to record its gratitude to the authors for this contribution, to A. Evelyn Breck for editing the manuscript, and to the Ford Foundation, whose grant for general support helped to finance the study.

ROBERT D. CALKINS
President

April 1960

Authors' Preface

Two temptations constantly beset us in executing our design. One was to reject interpretation not fully supported by logic and data, such as is considered necessary underpinning for effective work in fields relating to human behavior. The other was to quote copiously from speeches of candidates and campaigners in the dual hope of giving an authentic flavor to the account and of providing some basis for the analyst of the future to analyze not the words of the authors but those of the actors as reported. Had we succumbed to the first temptation, we would have had a tiny manuscript indeed. Had we succumbed to the second, we would have provided a book too thick and too repetitive, and one that might have missed its objective of authenticity because any selection would have so warped context as to make rigorous analysis inappropriate.

A third temptation was also resisted—to respond to the substance of political discussion rather than to its varying shape and intensity. We undertook to do a history of a political campaign, not a history of an epoch in which political campaigning took place. It has been impossible for us to take time or space to put all the arguments into objective context. To do so would have required books on agriculture, defense, foreign policy, immigration, education, and many other topics that figured in the debate of the campaign. Readers must supply much of their own background on the subjects referred to and their own estimates of which candidate, if either, was right in the matter. Our own preferences have undoubtedly influenced the account, although our mutually divergent political biases have reduced this risk.

A number of people have given us the benefit of their criticism—George A. Graham, Paul T. David, Richard C. Bain, Ralph M. Goldman, Stanley E. Kelley, Jr.; and for particular mention, Bertram E. Benedict, who read the manuscript in two drafts with meticulous care and contributed much to its organization and clarity of statement. David Butler, author of the later volumes on the British elections, sat in conference with us and gave us the benefit of his advice and experience. We owe a special debt to Paul David's unwavering belief that the project was worth carrying out.

We have levied toll on a variety of sources, not the least of which have been various staff members of the Democratic and Republican National Committees. We have discussed developments with a number of participants—candidates, party managers, convention delegates, party workers. The senior author attended both party conventions in 1956, and was able to view the preliminary activities of both—of platform committees, rules committees, etc.—in some degree at first hand. Television helped fill the gaps in personal observation.

Even a cursory examination of the pages that follow will indicate the overwhelming debt we owe to the American press. Faced with the intellectual necessity of bringing under review a many-faceted enterprise in which numerous developments were proceeding contemporaneously, the press—both pen and pencil and electronic—served as an extension of eyes, ears, and judgment. We found little in our private conversations with various participants that could not be documented, or fairly inferred, from press coverage. The chief difficulties of using the press as a guide to convention and campaign behavior were those of richness of detail and nicety of interpretation, not to mention those of a fair recapture of mood and feeling after the passage of time.

We also used various memoirs and other book-length statements of role and intention produced by participants or their biographers. The *Western Political Quarterly* gave both an overview of the election as seen in the West and provided a state-by-state viewpoint as well. The work of Richard M. Scammon, underlying the voting analyses, was very valuable. We had hoped to match Republican analyses of the vote with Democratic counterparts; but the state of the literature did not permit this. We have been assured, however, that the Democrats have accepted the Republican research as authoritative. This is without prejudice to the differences in interpretation and lessons for action to be drawn by each party. We regret that the survey research done with finesse and care by the Survey Research Center at Ann Arbor was not published in time to take full advantage of it in our own judgments and analyses. On image of the candidates and ticket splitting the Survey Research Center's analyses remain unique for the nation as a whole.

Campaigns are worth studying. They bring together a variety of interests, values, and activities that are fundamental to political life and political science. These are often studied under the separate foci of communications, organization, and goal-oriented behavior. It has seemed to us that it is worth while to locate such studies within the integrated context of efforts to win votes, fix political images, and influence public decisions. We hope that our contribution will indicate some of the potentials for gain.

CHARLES A. H. THOMSON
FRANCES M. SHATTUCK

Contents

1

The Years of Preparation

ANY ACCOUNT OF THE Presidential election of 1956 must begin with a look backward to the most salient aspects of the election of 1952, and to the intervening political developments that played a role in the 1956 decision. Personalities, issues, party image, and performance all played their role in the developing context of political events.

Personalities

In 1952 two new personalities emerged into full view on the American political scene—Dwight D. Eisenhower and Adlai E. Stevenson. Eisenhower, to be sure, had been on the American scene, but chiefly as a military figure, an officer rocketed into world fame and endowed with many imputed characteristics that had to be revalued in a political personage. Stevenson was known to some as a minor official in wartime Washington, who had played a role in the birth of the United Nations in San Francisco; he was better known as a new figure in the politics of Illinois. By the time radio, television, and the other mass media had reported the campaign of 1952, both were shaped into new and different personalities in the public mind. In Eisenhower many people found a figure somewhat less rigidly military than they had thought a Supreme Commander would be—a figure above the turmoil of politics and partisan quarrels, who in his public distaste for sharp controversy and in his hate for petty misdoing fitted well the image of the benign yet judging father. In Stevenson they found diffidence curiously combined with urbanity, an unexpected ease in discussing the complex political issues of the day, a contrast to the image of "cronyism" and loose political practices imputed to the Truman regime. Both were favorably regarded on many personality traits; but voters did not seem to credit Stevenson with weighty experience in public affairs, particularly in the foreign field.[1]

The national vote in 1952 did much to fix the relative positions of the men in the public mind. Eisenhower's 34 million votes, well beyond the performance of his party as shown by the congressional races, established him as a near-unbeatable. Stevenson's 27 millions were less clearly a vote of national confidence, yet they gave him national force and the chance to be a titular leader with more than a title.

The course of the conventions and the campaign further fixed important points in these images. Both candidates were leaders chosen by factions from outside their ranks. Both had the blessing of the titular leaders: Eisenhower from Thomas E. Dewey, and Stevenson (receiving his with less grace) from Truman. Both triumphed over determined opposition in the conventions, and had to repair the resulting rifts. What they did to pull their parties together had much to do with the way the public came to perceive them. Eisenhower made peace with Senator Robert A. Taft on September 12, 1952, to the consternation of the more liberal Republicans, who did not yet realize the depths of Eisenhower's conservatism. They were troubled further by his failure to confront the Republican extremist right with clear opposition to the personal conduct, if not the principles, of Senator Joseph R. McCarthy. The Republican right, in its turn, was troubled by Eisenhower's hospitality to the internationalist principles and acceptance of the welfare measures of the New Deal and Fair Deal. The Republican middle, however, persisted in its near worshipful estimate of Eisenhower—an estimate shared by many in other political faiths. Stevenson, for his part, kept Truman at some

[1] For details on these images, as revealed in panel studies, see Ithiel de Sola Pool, "TV: A New Dimension in Politics," in Eugene L. Burdick and Arthur J. Brodbeck, eds., *American Voting Behavior* (1959), pp. 242-61. See also Department of Marketing, Miami University, *The Influence of Television on the 1952 Elections* (1954), pp. 46 ff; and Angus Campbell and Associates, *The Voter Decides* (1954), pp. 52-68.

distance as a means of coping with the issues of corruption and too-long Democratic tenure of office, while maintaining close enough relations with him and his followers to gain from their support. Whatever his image, Eisenhower was the more successful in getting unstinting efforts from Republican organizations. Stevenson in 1952 as in 1956 found that those aspects of his personality and candidacy that appealed to the New Deal intellectuals were liabilities in his relations with old-line party organizations.

As to the vice-presidential personalities of 1952, Senator John J. Sparkman left little if any residue that was of significance for public opinion in 1956. But Richard M. Nixon was another story. He established himself as a young man, filled with an ambition to rise that would drive him to attacks on opponents both within and without his party and would make him appear willing to espouse causes and principles mainly for reasons of political gain. His victories over intraparty enemies, his overcoming of the Eisenhower disposition to rid the ticket of a candidate possibly compromised in the public mind, and the tremendous immediate public vindication of his television explanation about why he had accepted special financial aid from ultraconservative backers, gave him a sense of independence and power that counted heavily in party councils.[2]

While he thus established himself as a courageous campaigner, he showed enormous skill in political innuendo. The text would not read exactly that way, but Democrats emerged as pinks, traitors, or worse in the minds of many hearers after Nixon got through talking about them. The effect on those observing Nixon at work in this fashion varied with the needs and values of the observer. For those he served, Nixon was a Roman tribune warring against evil. For victims of his technique, Nixon was a deadly and slippery enemy. In the minds of a great many not so closely engaged in this infighting, Nixon left a great uneasiness—regarding both the ends to which such techniques were used and the state of American politics that could be hospitable and rewarding to such tactics.

[2] For the details of the handling of the Nixon fund in political communications within the Republican party, see Earl Mazo, *Richard Nixon: A Political and Personal Portrait* (1959), pp. 101-21.

Issues

In regard to issues, the Republicans concentrated in 1952 on corruption, communism, and Korea. Thus they translated generalized feelings about twenty years of Democratic tenure and its attendant weaknesses into "the mess in Washington." They focused uneasiness about foreign policy and the apparent impotence of the United States on the world scene into concrete complaints about weakness, indecision, and suffering in Korea. And through near-explicit statement and subtler innuendo they noised it about that "twenty years of treason" had caused our sorry state abroad and had raised threats to security within. Eisenhower had no part of the innuendo; but by promising to go to Korea (and later in achieving a truce that was never his to force but was for the Communists to give), he dramatized the prospect of stronger actions by a fresh administration. Although later published surveys showed that communism as such had little to do with the final vote,[3] the more ardent believers within the Republican party thought it did. The Democrats showed themselves defensive against it, and in the interplay of party "gamesmanship" the issue took stature.

Parties

As for the parties, the returns suggested that the Democrats were stronger than the Republicans, although the triumph of Eisenhower, promptly and widely interpreted as a personal victory, undoubtedly masked to some extent the natural strength of the Republicans as a presidential party. Both parties demonstrated their characteristic splits—the Republicans between the conservative, Middle Western Taft wing and the relatively liberal, internationalist Eastern wing; and the Democrats between their liberal Northern and Western segments and their conservative Southern

[3] See Campbell and Associates, *The Voter Decides*, p. 52.

bloc. Republican inroads into the electoral college vote in the South left a question about how much the party had gained in strength there and how much the vote was an index of discontent by Southern Democrats with the rest of their party. Out of the ambiguity of this situation came opportunities for the Republican party in the South and pause for any third-party enthusiasts among Southern Democrats incensed over civil rights or other manifestations of Northern liberalism.

The election not only left the Republicans in command of the Executive Branch and with a tiny majority in the Congress, but it created a nucleus of political strength inside and outside of the administration that was loyal more to the President than to a party and eager to find its political future by operating through his position and his leadership. Here were men with backgrounds in the Dewey faction, in the business community, in the Citizens for Eisenhower—men who had opted early and powerfully for the General, and who felt it a matter of public duty to see that Taft, his men, and his policies not be allowed to dominate the executive. In the Cabinet, there was an admixture of Taft people —and of others designed to keep all factions happy. And there were those few, like Secretary of State John Foster Dulles, who were broadly acceptable to all factions in the party, and dedicated to a particular form of public service.[4]

In Congress, Taft and Speaker Joseph W. Martin, Jr., ruled at the outset; while the Eisenhower aura precluded direct confrontations, the President could not look to key men at the Capitol for tight organizational support. And his treatment of the Republicans of the far right who were soon flouting his authority was emasculated by his notions of governmental correctness and personal

[4] See Richard H. Rovere, *The Eisenhower Years* (1956), pp. 64 ff, for a contemporary appraisal. Rovere called Dulles a "breathing, talking symbol of party unity." Charles E. Wilson was non-factional, but congenial to the business community. Arthur Summerfield and Douglas McKay were also agreeable to them, although raising the issue of overrepresentation of General Motors. Rovere says that Dulles and Herbert Brownell were the only ones clearly from the Dewey wing, while Sinclair Weeks and Ezra Taft Benson were equally clearly from the Taft wing. Martin Durkin, the "plumber in a cabinet of millionaires," was anathema to Taft; George M. Humphrey was politically and geographically satisfactory, but resented by Taft because Taft had not been consulted on an Ohioan's appointment in advance.

unwillingness to risk a brawl. Those who did support his legislative program in Congress soon found him less than a doughty champion either in legislative chambers or on the hustings. This marred the image of the President as a man devoted to highest principle and willing to back up those who espoused his views. Taft's death in the summer of 1953 robbed the President of powerful support and shrewd advice; and during the remaining months of the first term, congressional Republicans often practiced the habits of opposition learned during twenty years as members of the out-party.

The tone of politics and the course of events in Washington after 1952 turned to a considerable extent on the political education of the President: his perception of the nature of political parties; his conception of the governmental system; his canons of correct behavior as politician and statesman; and above all his choice of companions and colleagues. Insisting on competence in government appointments, he took as chief talisman for competence high accomplishment in the sphere of business.

A central line of fission divided those in his official family who, like Secretary of the Treasury George M. Humphrey, believed that domestic economic strength and budgetary conservatism came first; and some, like John Foster Dulles, who believed that international strength was the main goal, without which domestic prosperity would be of no value.[5] The President characteristically gave comfort to both factions. On balance, he emphasized fiscal solidity and pushed as rapidly as seemed feasible toward a balanced budget, making yeoman efforts to reduce defense outlays while claiming more defense per dollar. A slight recession in 1953 disturbed the financial and business community and raised again the specter of hard times under Republicans. But with a righting of the economic indices and the imposition of firm checks on

---

[5] This split appeared first during the conference aboard the cruiser *Helena* on which the President-elect and a small group of his closest advisers conferred as he returned in secret from his mission to Korea—in late November, 1952. See Joseph and Stewart Alsop, *The Reporter's Trade* (1959), pp. 191, 199. General Omar Bradley, Chairman of the Joint Chiefs of Staff, Cabinet designees Dulles, Wilson, Humphrey, Brownell, McKay, and advisers Lucius Clay, Joseph M. Dodge, C. D. Jackson, and Emmet Hughes composed the contingent.

inflation, the fundamental causes for broad economic concern receded into the background, steadying Republican political prospects. Only the farm problem raised political doubts, as the long-term trends worked to put pressure on farmers' income and to move population out of full-time farming.

The Republican National Committee also had some uncertain moments as the new administration got under way. Two were capital: what to do about the chairmanship, and what to do about organization. National Chairman Arthur E. Summerfield, who had managed the President's victorious election campaign, resigned the chairmanship when he became Postmaster General. His successor was C. Wesley Roberts of Kansas, who was elected on January 18, 1953. He was well known in the Middle West as a former state party chairman and an early Eisenhower supporter. Within a month, however, Roberts was in trouble over charges growing out of a fee he had received in 1951: he claimed the money was given him for work as a public relations counsel, but his opponents asserted it was for lobbying although he was not a registered lobbyist. Eventually there was an investigation by a state legislative committee; Roberts called it a plot to destroy his usefulness. The President at first expressed himself satisfied with Roberts' defense; but when the legislative probe was begun, Eisenhower made it clear that he expected the chairman to resign if the committee found his conduct improper. This was indeed the finding, and Roberts resigned on March 27.

For the next National Chairman many voices were raised in behalf of Leonard W. Hall, a New York State lawyer who had just completed seven terms in the United States House of Representatives and in November 1952 had been elected a surrogate judge. While in Congress he had served part of the time as chairman of the National Republican Congressional Committee; thus it was not surprising that his selection for National Chairman was urged by Speaker Martin and many other Representatives. New York State political figures came to his support: ex-Governor Dewey, National Committeeman J. Russel Sprague, National Committeewoman Mrs. Charles W. Weis, Jr., and State Chairman W. L. Pfeiffer. President Eisenhower conferred with Hall on

April 4; and when Senator Taft three days later joined those favoring the New Yorker, Hall's election was considered certain. At the National Committee meeting on April 10, the choice was unanimous and Leonard Hall took command.

And take command he did. Loyal lieutenant to Eisenhower, he reorganized the National Committee staff on the lines that it maintained throughout the 1956 campaign. He raised money for it; he kept it at more than normal between-campaigns strength; he readied it to serve the midterm elections and the preparations for 1956 with unswerving service to the team.

The verdict of 1952 nearly shattered the Democratic organization on the national level, but it retained vigor in its main state and local strongholds. The campaign had left the party with a deficit of more than $800,000 and with strained interfactional relations, due in part to the tensions between the men of the Stevenson camp and those who had given primary loyalty to other circles. Stephen A. Mitchell maintained control for the liberal Stevenson forces as the National Committee's chairman; but the party organization at national headquarters was sharply reduced. Stevenson, seizing the opportunities offered by organizational decline, decided to make what he could of the office of titular leader, both in terms of personal growth and political leadership.[6]

Within the party Stevenson took over major tasks of financial repair and general reconstruction, speaking at numerous dinners and other fund-raising occasions. He traveled widely abroad and reported on his travels. For those who were watching—and he enjoyed some fairly prominent platforms from which to report—he appeared as a man with improved contacts and increased grasp of current world realities. Planned or no, this role was responsive to one of the gaps in public perception of him in 1952—as a man with little world experience and hence of little potency to deal with the key figures and issues of world politics.

The Democratic party emerged from the 1952 defeat dismayed at the size of the Eisenhower landslide and disorganized by his inroads into the Solid South. The Republicans had won the elec-

[6] Adlai E. Stevenson, *What I Think* (1956), pp. ix-x.

toral votes of all but nine states and had amassed 55.1 per cent of the popular vote. Stevenson had won no electoral vote outside the Southern or border states, and Florida, Tennessee, Texas, and Virginia had gone for Eisenhower—the first Southern states to vote for a Republican presidential candidate since 1928.

The 1952 convention fight over the loyalty oath had left scars, and the party "old line" regulars were dissatisfied with some of the new leadership. There were mutterings against National Chairman Stephen A. Mitchell. And the Democratic leaders in Congress, who had come off victorious in their own contests, naturally felt that their claim to speak for the party had more solid foundation, though regional or local, than that of a defeated national candidate.

The Democratic congressional leaders were to some degree more willing than was Stevenson to compromise the party position on issues by their receptivity to much of the Eisenhower program. Eisenhower was acceptable to them as a man above party; his principles, they perceived more quickly than did some of the Republicans, were really congenial to the position of the Republican-Democratic conservatives. Impressed not only by his margin of votes but also by the spate of comment picturing Eisenhower as a man who could do no political wrong, many Democrats took care to see that their legislative positions might permit a ride on Eisenhower coattails come 1954, thereby adding further credibility to the President's reputation for political power.

The Midterm Elections: Democratic Campaign

As the Democrats moved into the 1954 elections, they had in their own way to negotiate the shoals as well as to profit by the cross-currents set up by McCarthyism. This phenomenon split both the Republican and the Democratic parties; and it is impossible to say which one was hurt or gained the more. Stevenson capitalized on Eisenhower's failure to speak out against the junior senator from Wisconsin by charging that the administration had accepted McCarthyism, and the Democrats took full comfort from the sight of Republicans tearing at Republicans during the hearings that involved Secretary of the Army Robert T. Stevens and his counsel on the one side, with McCarthy assistants Roy M. Cohn and G. David Schine on the other. Yet the Democrats had their McCarthyites too, both in office and in the nation at large, and the non-McCarthyites had to move carefully so that opposition to the crusading Right would not seem to lend substance to McCarthy charges or otherwise provide targets for attacks rooted in the emotionalism of the times.

After the Maine election, promptly interpreted by Democrats as presaging a national trend, they moved into high gear, although many of the party's national figures were preoccupied otherwise. But Adlai Stevenson undertook to match the efforts of Nixon and Eisenhower. He probably played a larger role than any president or titular leader had previously done in an off-year election.

The Midterm Elections: Republican Campaign

Most of the 1954 contests turned on local issues and local personalities. But the Republicans, especially after they brought General Eisenhower into play, agitated the issues they thought had helped bring them victory nationally in 1952—Korea, communism, and corruption. Basic, however, was the argument that Eisenhower had to have a Republican Congress, else government in Washington would become, in the President's words, a "cold war." The Democrats used Defense Secretary Wilson's expressed preference for bird dogs (the employed) over kennel dogs (the baying unemployed) to dramatize their image of Republicans as the heartless party of big business, and their image of themselves as the party with a care for the jobless. Unemployment, though spotty, was the Democrats' top issue. Second was public power, in which the cries against the allegedly infamous private power development contract with Dixon-Yates were first voiced. Third was farm prices, in which Democrats lashed out against "flexible" price supports and pointed to the sag in farm income.

Both Republicans and Democrats claimed tax revisions as a reason for voting Republican or Democratic. The Republicans pointed to benefits for the whole nation, claiming the greatest peacetime tax reduction in history. Democrats countered that these gains had gone only to the corporations and to the wealthy.

The Republican campaign had stretched between two poles: Eisenhower and McCarthy. Early in 1954 McCarthy announced that he would deliver nine Lincoln Day speeches on a West Coast tour, with "twenty years of treason" as the theme. Democrats reacted violently to this announcement. Privately Nixon did what he could to keep McCarthy within the bounds of the Nixon-Chotiner formula for political probity.[7] Publicly Eisenhower advised Republicans to temper their political attacks; but Republican congressmen, faced with an election in the fall and seeing plenty of mileage in the issue of communism, were cool to this advice.

Eisenhower had spoken to his advisers about the need for electing a Republican Congress in 1954 even before his inauguration in January 1953 and had stated in October 1953 his intention to take no part in the campaign. This intention he restated in February 1954. As the year advanced and Republican prospects appeared more in doubt, the President retreated from his announced intention. By April he was saying that he had no detailed plan for speeches, but he liked to visit and expected to move around and talk about his program and about the government. In June he expressed his belief that the President's party should control Congress, and therefore he backed the election of Republican candidates. Before long he was posing for campaign photographs with candidates of his party and wavering between backing only those Republicans who had supported his program and endorsement of all Republican candidates.

The latter course appeared to have won out by late summer when Vice President Nixon assured a closed meeting of the Republican National Committee that the White House would back every Republican nominee over every Democrat. The September elections in Maine clinched the matter. For the first time

---

[7] See Mazo, *Richard Nixon*, pp. 140-48.

since 1935 Maine elected a Democratic governor, and though Senator Margaret Chase Smith and the three Republican Representatives won re-election, it was by noticeably reduced margins.

Once involved, the President stepped up his efforts, concentrating in later stages on the West. He stumped for more candidates than had any sitting President before him, climaxing his efforts with a one-day airplane sortie into four critical areas and a chain-phone-call gimmick designed to get out the Republican vote. Possibly because the President was not trying to purge recalcitrant members of his own party, he did not appear as a factionalist, but he failed to bring home a Republican majority of senators or representatives.

The Midterm Elections: Results

In 1954 the Democrats took the Senate, 48 to 47, with one former Republican—Wayne Morse—going independent. The Democrats moved from their 1952 minority position in the House (215 Democrats to 219 Republicans, with one independent) to a clear majority of 232 to 203. They took eight governorships from the Republicans, gaining a 27 to 21 margin. A possible result of the President's intervention—and of the late-generated heat of the campaign as a whole—was an unprecedented off-year turnout of better than 44 million votes.[8] Another and more certain result was that the leading Eisenhower backers of 1952 met at the White House just before Christmas 1954 to plan action for 1956.

As for the image of the candidates, the 1954 elections showed again that the President could be both within politics and above politics. To the politically involved, he undoubtedly became more of a man of politics as time wore on. To the mass of voters, he was not a politician. Whatever the evidence, the functions of selective perception preserved the notion that Eisenhower was not really a party man.

[8] This was a gain of some 5 per cent over the 1950 total, while the population of the country had increased about 8 per cent. *Congressional Quarterly Almanac* (1954), p. 712.

The 1954 elections revivified and fixed the image of Nixon as a none too generous or scrupulous exploiter of the issues of communism and corruption.

Despite the over-all returns, the Democrats noted with some misgiving that they had trailed by some 165,000 votes in the total cast in all races for national office outside of the South. Averell Harriman's victory in New York improved his availability for 1956, but like New York Governors before and after him, he said he would concentrate on the affairs of his state; and he voiced support for Stevenson.

On to 1956: Republican Preparations

The first nine months of 1955 saw a great acceleration of activity in connection with the 1956 presidential election. The Republican National Committee, meeting in early January, gave tentative approval to plans for a late convention and a short election campaign, on the stated assumption that Eisenhower would be the nominee and thus not need the public build-up that a lesser known man would. Many Lincoln Day speeches centered around renomination, and many groups and individuals spoke out in favor of drafting Eisenhower if necessary.

Whatever doubts may have been in the President's mind, or whatever family pressures may have been brought on him to serve but one term, the official party organization never wavered in its outspoken demand that he should run. At a luncheon meeting with the President in February, the Republican National Committee adopted a motion of confidence in his leadership. Republican National Chairman Leonard Hall at every opportunity reiterated his certainty that the President would be renominated and re-elected. Ex-Governor Dewey and Vice President Nixon voiced their hopes that Eisenhower would be the candidate.

The President played a role of cautious formal correctness and calculated ambiguity. Queries on his intentions from pressmen or politicians brought no direct answers. Most of his public comments during the first half of the year discouraged prospects of his renomination, but he never entirely closed the door. He expressed a longing for freedom and a desire to live on his farm. He indicated that neither his approval of a late convention nor his preference for San Francisco as the convention site meant that he intended to be the nominee. He derided the idea of an indispensable man, asserting that the Republican party could win with any worthy candidate and program. Yet when Senator Margaret Chase Smith told the National Conference of Republican Women that she hoped the President would run but doubted that he would, the President replied at his news conference that he did not know where Mrs. Smith had formed the impression that he would not run. At a press conference in late May, Eisenhower commented on his growing liking for the job and also declared that a presidential nominee should have a voice in selecting the vice-presidential nominee.

The chorus favoring an Eisenhower renomination grew so loud that it nearly drowned out the few efforts to speak up for other candidates, in case the President chose not to run again. Even so, sufficient sentiment was voiced in favor of Chief Justice Earl Warren so that in mid-April he found it advisable to issue a formal statement expressing his embarrassment at talk of his possible candidacy and taking himself out of such consideration. Senator William F. Knowland of California, the Republican leader in the Senate, while not avowing himself as a candidate for the nomination, nevertheless gave ground during two TV interviews for speculation that he was considering the possibility. Moreover, his inheritance of Senator Taft's mantle in the Senate and his acceptability to the Taft wing of the Republican party made it all the more likely that he nurtured covert hopes of a candidacy.

In June the President made a short tour in New England and gave the impression that he was enjoying himself immensely. His speeches were brief and felicitous. He talked like a candidate, but on his return to Washington he again adroitly parried leading questions. A month later an Ohio delegation urged him to run, and he mentioned the strain of the office on a man of his age and indicated a wish to see younger men brought to the fore.

During this period of formal indecision, the party organization continued to expand and perfect its tactics. At the same time, National Chairman Hall pursued his efforts to pin the President down. He used party fetes and gatherings for the purpose—most notably in the case of the three-day campaign school in Washington, D.C., for Republican state chairmen, held in early September. This school was important for more ends than just an opportunity to get the President to declare himself; with Hall as director, Murray Chotiner as associate director, and Richard Nixon a featured speaker, the school did much to fix the tone of the campaign to come.[9]

Nixon, fresh from a personal conference with Eisenhower in Denver, expressed confidence that the President would run and counseled the chairmen on how to use hard-hitting campaign tactics.

The state chairmen wired the President assurance of their support, but feared to offend him by urging him explicitly to run. At the conclusion of the school, however, Hall flew the whole group to Denver for a personal conference with the President—to find him intentionally equivocal as before. He urged them not to pin their hopes on one man and pointed to the party as overshadowing every individual member of it. However disappointed the state chairmen may have been, Chairman Hall nevertheless continued on the firm assumption that the President would be the candidate whatever he was saying.

Two weeks later, on September 24, President Eisenhower suffered a coronary thrombosis at Denver. Many people assumed that this development would automatically lead him to decide against being a candidate for renomination and a second term. It was reported that his family, already opposed to a second term

[9] Little has been published about the school, which was an off-the-record operation. Jack Redding did publish the gist of a paper prepared by Murray Chotiner, Nixon's former political associate, in his book *Inside the Democratic Party* (1958); and Stanley Kelley, Jr., discusses its philosophy of campaigning in his forthcoming Brookings book, entitled *Political Campaigning*. The heart of the advice given by Chotiner and echoed elsewhere in the school discussions was to wage a hard-hitting campaign, deflating the opposition before it got a chance to get started, and replying to opposition charges only when necessary, based on the folk wisdom that "nice guys finish last."

before the attack, would bring added pressure on him to retire. Dr. Paul Dudley White, a Boston heart specialist, called in as a consultant on the case, at first said that a second term would be physically possible, but later was less positive. The President himself was understandably silent, but inasmuch as some of his comments on retirement earlier in the year had communicated genuine longing rather than political byplay, it was certain that any such longing was intensified by the turn of events.

The uncertainty loosed a flood of statements, speculation, and predictions, with a few trial balloons launched to see if the winds were favorable. Hall, except for a hesitant day or so of "no comment," insisted that the party would go ahead with its plans unchanged and almost immediately he expressed his preference for an Eisenhower-Nixon ticket. Political commentators promptly enumerated other possible candidates: Vice President Nixon, Chief Justice Earl Warren, Governor Goodwin Knight, Senator William Knowland, all of California; Secretary of the Treasury George M. Humphrey of Ohio; Harold E. Stassen, the President's disarmament adviser, now of Pennsylvania; Governor Christian A. Herter of Massachusetts; the President's brother, Milton Eisenhower; banker, lawyer, diplomat, and administrator John J. McCloy. Mr. Stassen, in a television interview, said he would take the nomination if the President wished; Mr. Humphrey refused to answer a similar question at a news conference; Ambassador Henry Cabot Lodge, asked about his availability, replied that this was no time to talk politics.

The actions and reactions of the California four were perhaps the most extensive and the most interesting.

The Vice President found himself in a most delicate situation. If the President were to die before the end of his term, Mr. Nixon would succeed to the office and be in a strong position to obtain the nomination. If Mr. Eisenhower recovered to finish out his term but did not wish the nomination for a second term, Mr. Nixon might well be a likely choice if Eisenhower designated a successor so long as he retained Eisenhower's good will. Excessive eagerness to rule during the President's illness might turn the President against him. Moreover, Nixon's many enemies, both inside and outside of his own party, were determined to prevent his nomination and election and were ready to exploit any false move on his part. Therefore he stepped carefully; as soon as it had been decided that there would be no delegation of the President's powers, he receded into the background except for a brief visit to Denver when key members of the administration began going out one by one to see their chief. This, however, did not deter Nixon's backers from offstage maneuvering.

Chief Justice Warren maintained complete silence, although various polls showed his continuing popularity with the party and the electorate, and a number of politicians expressed personal preference for him.

Governor Knight suffered from no inhibitions in the matter; he spoke out early and often, starting less than two weeks after the President was stricken. He made it plain that he intended to head the California delegation to the Republican National Convention; that he would back Eisenhower if the President wished the nomination; that if Eisenhower decided to retire, the Californian would be a favorite son candidate; that he would support Nixon only on the recommendation of the President.

Senator Knowland was somewhat more restrained in language but also more determined not to let events get away from him. A few days after Mr. Eisenhower's attack he called the discussion of plans premature but at the same time emphasized that he had always expected that the President would communicate his decision by the end of January. Two weeks later, in Seattle, he derided the notion that there was an "heir apparent." By the end of October he was suggesting that the President announce his plans soon. Again in December he made it clear that he intended to announce his own candidacy for the nomination if Eisenhower had not declared an intention to run by the end of January. In mid-January Knowland extended the deadline to February 15 but made no retreat from his plan to become a candidate.

All of this activity made it clear that if Eisenhower were not a candidate for renomination, the fight for the spot would be waged as furiously as it had been in 1952. Public demands that the President should or should not name his successor or reveal his decision at an early date were strongly colored by the position in the party occupied by the speaker, and by his perception of his own position and prospects. From the standpoint of the inner White House group, delay in announcing a decision offered two advantages: it would give time in which to show the President how much the presidency could be eased of burdensome routine so that a second term need not be too onerous; and if the President decided to retire anyway, it would give an opportunity to agree on a substitute candidate.

To those in other camps, time seemed of the essence. No one else could declare himself a candidate for the nomination until the President bowed out publicly. Any other candidate needed time to build up a national reputation. Furthermore, the states with presidential primaries required filing and various other formalities well in advance of the primary dates.

For the party as a whole, there was also a potential danger that, while affairs continued in a state of uncertainty, too little would be done toward organizing the next year's campaign, while the Democrats appeared to be moving full steam ahead on the strength of their hope that they could win against anyone but Eisenhower. Another worry for the Republicans was the fear that only Eisenhower could carry the presidential vote of any Southern state. Their worries were not abated by the results of scattered local elections on November 8, 1955. Most spectacular of these was the election by a three-to-two margin of Democrat Richardson Dilworth as mayor of Philadelphia over Republican W. Thacher Longstreth. This was an election the Republicans had made special efforts to win—not just to show a comeback from their sharp losses in 1954 that had cost them the governorship and three House seats, but also to show a "trend" toward the GOP as a prelude to 1956.

Brighter than bye-elections for the President's immediate supporters were his apparent steady recovery and his refusal despite pressure to say definitely that he would retire. By mid-November he was well enough to come back for a moment to the seat of government in Washington, and then to go on to his Gettysburg farm for convalescence. His doctors announced that not until late

January or February could they make a firm judgment as to his ability to hold up under a second term.

Whatever the faith and hopes of the inner group, the political commentators sharply discounted the possibilities of a second term. On November 12, 1955, a poll of Washington newspaper correspondents showed that 88 per cent of them thought the President would not run again, and that the Republican ticket would consist of Richard Nixon and Christian Herter. A week later the Associated Press' Managing Editors Association forecast four to one that the President would not run; they considered Nixon the leading candidate for the nomination, with Warren as his most probable chief rival.[10]

Eisenhower Decides to Run

Once the President arrived in Gettysburg, a steady flow of news about his work, his health, and his recreation quickly demonstrated that it would be wrong to discount the probability of his running again. Eisenhower undertook an accelerated program of activities. Within the first two weeks, he met with one after another of his advisers, conferred with Republican congressional leaders, and held full-scale meetings of the National Security Council and the Cabinet. He also met with National Chairman Hall just before the National Committee gathered in Chicago at the beginning of December to make plans for the convention. Hall told newsmen after the meeting that he had never seen the President look better and that, although the question of a second term had not been discussed, he was "very much encouraged" and thought Eisenhower would run if he felt able.

The Chicago meeting was both party rally and business session. Its general theme was peace and prosperity under a Republican administration, that would enable any Republican presidential candidate to win in 1956. The keynote slogan was: "Everything is booming but the guns." The meeting received a long message

[10] *New York Times,* Nov. 12, 18, 1955.

from the Vice President and heard speeches by Ambassador Henry Cabot Lodge and three Cabinet secretaries, Benson, Weeks, and Mitchell. The official call was issued for the Republican National Convention to open "in San Mateo County, California, at 11 o'clock a.m. on Monday, August 20, 1956."

Nevertheless, the thought of the convalescing President pervaded the atmosphere of the whole meeting. On the second day Chairman Hall read the President's personal message to the committee: "You have a splendid record to submit to the voters. . . . I shall do everything in my power . . . to help you report the record accurately and fully to the country." This calculated ambiguity caused considerable speculation: Was Eisenhower promising to run if he felt physically fit? Or did he mean only that he would exert all possible influence in behalf of another candidate? At least he had not completely closed the door to renomination.

This situation continued for the next three months. The President eased back into his duties, under the careful scrutiny and supervision of his doctors. From Gettysburg Mr. Eisenhower went to Florida for more outdoor exercise, then returned to Washington to take up the "full duties" of the Presidency, reduced by his aides to the scope of a six-hour work day. At all his press conferences reporters probed the President for his second-term decision. He answered many of their questions at length, but gave few clear clues as to the inner workings of his mind. He told the press that his health was improved, and the doctors found his clinical record good; but he would make his own assessment on the basis of his own feelings, for only he knew the demands and the emotional strains of the Presidency, and he had to be convinced that he could carry on the job "efficiently" and for the good of the United States. His family, he said, did not object to his running. He would announce his decision as soon as it was firmly fixed in his mind; but he wanted to consider all the factors, and he wanted to confer with trusted advisers.

In great secrecy, on January 13, twelve men met with the President.[11] Each spoke his mind on whether the President should

---

[11] This account is based on Robert J. Donovan, *Eisenhower: The Inside Story* (1956), pp. 393-96. Four of the men were members of his Cabinet: Attorney General Herbert Brownell; Secretary of State John Foster Dulles; Secretary of the Treasury George M. Humphrey; and Postmaster General Arthur E. Summerfield.

run. Milton Eisenhower spoke last to sum up arguments pro and con, aside from the health question. But the arguments were all pro. They centered mainly on two points. As President, Eisenhower could do his best—and more than any other leader—to work for world peace and to unify the American people. Second, he was the only Republican certain to win the Presidency and gain the time still needed to modernize and unify the Republican party. Only his brother mentioned that another four years would be burdensome to a man who had already spent more than forty years in the service of the American people. Apparently most of those present, including the President himself, emerged from the meeting with the view that the affirmative had won hands down.

During these months of uncertainty Eisenhower and his managers had to consider how to deal with presidential primaries in states with early filing dates. In most of them, written consent of a presidential candidate was not required, and the local politicians arranged to enter Eisenhower's name or slates of delegates pledged to him, without any formal notice from the President. For the record, however, an exception was made for New Hampshire. There the statute requires formal notification to a prospective candidate that his name has been entered and that any request for withdrawal from the ballot must be made within ten days. In a carefully composed reply the President said on January 19:

> I do not feel that I should interpose any objection to such entry. However, because I must make clear to all that lack of objection cannot be construed as any final decision on my part relative to a candidacy for a second term in office I now hold, I hope that all who vote in the Republican primaries in 1956 will carefully weigh all the possibilities and personalities that may be involved.

Then followed an expression of his belief in the right of citizens to select their own candidates for office and of his hope that his illness would not interfere with their choice of presidential candidate. He continued with this warning:

Five were present or past presidential assistants: Sherman Adams, the Assistant to the President; James C. Hagerty, Press Secretary; Major General Wilton B. Persons, Deputy Assistant; Howard Pyle, Administrative Assistant; and Thomas E. Stephens, former Appointment Secretary. The other three were Henry Cabot Lodge, Leonard W. Hall, and Dr. Milton Eisenhower.

It would be idle to pretend that my health can be wholly restored to the excellent state in which the doctors believed it to be in mid-September. At the same time, my doctors report to me that the progress I am making toward a reasonable level of strength is normal and satisfactory. My future life must be carefully regulated to avoid excessive fatigue. My reasons for obedience to the medical authorities are not solely personal; I must obey them out of respect for the responsibilities I carry.

He closed with the promise to render a final decision "as soon as it is firmly fixed in my own mind."[12]

By mid-February the President had undergone the four or five weeks of a full work load the doctors considered essential before making "a medical estimate as to the ability of his heart to stand the work." A full battery of tests was administered, and six doctors made a complete examination, then issued a medical report, saying that the President had "made a good recovery from the attack of coronary thrombosis." Dr. Paul Dudley White added his own summary statement, with the conclusion: "Now, as to the future, after weighing very carefully all available evidence, including our own experience, and fully aware of the hazards and uncertainties that lie ahead, we believe that medically the chances are that the President should be able to carry on an active life satisfactorily for another five to ten years." Asked if he would vote for Eisenhower, Dr. White replied, "If he runs."[13]

These results, of course, made it nearly impossible for Eisenhower to refuse to run for reasons of health. Nonetheless, he still wanted to satisfy himself as to his stamina. For this test he went to Treasury Secretary George M. Humphrey's Georgia plantation in mid-February, where he hunted for quail and wild turkey, and played more golf than his doctors' plans envisaged. Ten days of these pursuits gave him final reassurance.

On February 29, 1956, the President said he would seek renomination. He made his announcement in the morning press conference. In the evening he amplified it in a nationwide radio-television address. He told the American people that although he felt as well as before his heart attack, his future life must be "a regime of ordered work activity, interspersed with regular

[12] *New York Times,* Jan. 20, 1956.
[13] *Ibid.,* Feb. 15, 1956.

amounts of exercise, recreation and rest." He would have to watch his weight, "take a short mid-day breather," "retire at a reasonable hour," and "eliminate many of the less important social and cere- monial activities." But he assured them that "as of this moment, there is not the slightest doubt that I can now perform as well as I ever have all of the important duties of the Presidency."

These duties he defined as "the making of important decisions, the formulation of policy through the National Security Council and the Cabinet, cooperation with the Congress . . . [and] a con- tinuous burden of study, contemplation and reflection" on the international position of the United States, the nation's economy, the role of the Federal government in the life of the people, the operations and adequacy of the armed forces. He listed items of less importance that could be decreased. These included public speeches, many office appointments, ceremonial dinners, recep- tions, and some parts of his correspondence. To these he added extensive traveling, with the specific condition that "neither for renomination nor re-election would I engage in extensive travel- ing and in whistle-stop speaking, normally referred to as barn- storming."

If the delegates to the Republican convention in August pre- ferred a presidential nominee who would campaign more actively, it was their right and even duty to select such a nominee. He was determined also "that every American shall have all available facts concerning my personal condition and the way I am now conducting the affairs of this office" so that at the November election there should be "a full understanding of both the record of this Administration and of how I propose to conduct myself in the future."[14]

On to 1956: Democratic Preparations

What of the Democratic preparations? After the 1954 elections, various readjustments were in order. Stevenson announced plans for less political activity. Hinting he might retire from public life, he resumed the practice of law. Democratic National Chairman

[14] *Ibid.*, Mar. 1, 1958.

Mitchell let it be known that he would resign before the end of the year, whereupon names of possible successors were tossed into the hat: Paul M. Butler, Indiana National Committeeman; Senator Earle C. Clements of Kentucky, Senate Democratic whip; former Price Administrator Michael DiSalle of Ohio; Elbert Carvel, ex-governor of Delaware, who had been a co-nominator of Stevenson at the 1952 convention; Archibald Alexander, treasurer of the state of New Jersey; James A. Finnegan, secretary of the Commonwealth of Pennsylvania and former Democratic chairman of Philadelphia; and F. Joseph Donohue, former Commissioner of the District of Columbia. Mitchell's choice for successor was Paul Butler, who was reportedly opposed by Truman. Finnegan was the candidate of Mayor David Lawrence of Pittsburgh. By the time the National Committee met in New Orleans at the beginning of December, Butler seemed to be in the lead, but the opposition to him was so intense that it was proposed to keep Mitchell in the post in order to avoid a split and Speaker Sam Rayburn urged that the choice be delayed. In the end the election went forward as scheduled, and Butler defeated DiSalle, Finnegan, and Donohue. Butler, accepting, promised impartiality among candidates, and a few days later he declared that Stevenson would have to fight for the 1956 nomination and named as other potential candidates Senators Estes Kefauver of Tennessee and Richard B. Russell of Georgia; Governors Frank J. Lausche of Ohio and G. Mennen Williams of Michigan, and Governors-elect Averell Harriman of New York and George M. Leader of Pennsylvania. Truman and Butler pledged cooperation, although Truman's close associate, National Committee Treasurer Stanley Woodward, resigned immediately following Butler's election.

With the coming of 1955 the presidential election of 1956 began to command increasing attention from would-be Democratic candidates and kingmakers, from newspapers, radio, and television. In view of Eisenhower's tremendous vote-getting power shown in 1952 and his continued popularity in opinion polls, candidates showed an understandable reluctance—prior to the President's heart attack in September—to take positive positions.

Their supporters were more willing. Speaking at one time or

another in behalf of Stevenson were Mrs. Franklin D. Roosevelt, Senator Herbert H. Lehman, ex-President Truman, and former Secretary of State Dean Acheson. Also backing Stevenson was Governor Harriman, who said that he himself was occupied full-time with New York State affairs, that he expected to continue in that job, and that his only aim was re-election to the governorship. But this did not prevent statements of Harriman support by Democratic State Chairman Richard H. Balch, New York State Secretary of State Carmine DeSapio, and Michael H. Prendergast who was elected new state chairman early in July. Senator Kefauver in a television interview at the end of May said that he was not a candidate, but when this was interpreted as a withdrawal from the race, he hastily explained: "I did not mean to imply that because I don't consider myself a candidate now I might not be one when the time comes."[15]

During the spring and summer, Mr. Truman, interviewed in Cleveland, predicted victory for the Democrats, renewed his support for Stevenson, but added that he would support whoever was nominated. Governor Robert B. Meyner of New Jersey let it be known that he was not committed to Stevenson or to anyone else; Representative John W. McCormack of Massachusetts, the House Democratic whip, predicted an open convention and thought it quite possible that Stevenson would not be the presidential candidate.

The annual Governors' Conference in Chicago during the second week of August offered an opportunity for pursuit of presidential politics in both parties, and it also gave Democratic governors the chance to visit Stevenson at his farm near Chicago. Twenty of the twenty-five Democratic governors present seized the opportunity; five Southern governors did not. A *New York Times* analyst reported that Stevenson had advanced from a "slight edge" for the nomination at the beginning of the conference to what both Democratic and Republican governors considered a "commanding lead" by the end. However, several of them conceded privately that the President's chances looked better in their states than did Stevenson's. This comparative strength

[15] *New York Times,* June 5, 1955.

of the President made for hesitation on the part of younger men who preferred to wait for the 1960 election when they would be assured of not having to run against Eisenhower. At mid-week Stevenson held a press conference in Chicago and promised to announce his decision on whether he would run for the nomination "not later than the end of November."[16]

In the wake of the Governors' Conference, Truman's support for Stevenson wavered more and more. Within a few days he was promising his backing for Stevenson or the convention nominee. Ten days later when asked in an interview about his views on Stevenson, he replied that it was the business of the party convention to select a candidate, that he wanted someone who could be elected. On the following day he managed both to reiterate support for Stevenson and to characterize Governor G. Mennen Williams of Michigan as a "wonderful man." (This interview took place at Mackinac Island, on Williams' home ground.) The next day brought a statement from former National Democratic Chairman Frank E. McKinney that he and Truman had discussed six or seven potential candidates.

Meanwhile Carmine DeSapio and Michael Prendergast continued to beat the drums for Harriman, and Harriman himself no longer said Stevenson was his choice but parried questions as to his own candidacy, while Governor George Bell Timmerman, Jr., and Senator J. Strom Thurmond of South Carolina suggested a possible Southern bolt to a third party unless the Democratic nominee were someone acceptable like Senator Richard Russell or Senator Lyndon Johnson.

For the first month or six weeks after President Eisenhower's heart attack in late September, Democrats cherished great hopes for victory in 1956. Additional moves toward tentative candidacies were made; this was about the time for them in any event. In early October Averell Harriman accepted November speaking engagements to help "old friends" in three northwestern states and to address an Iowa Democratic conference of twelve midwestern states. Ex-President Truman appeared at a New York State Democratic rally with Harriman, and on the following day he held a

---

[16] *Ibid.*, Aug. 14, 1955.

news conference. With Harriman seated beside him, Truman described the New York Governor as a "genius" and a "man with all the qualifications for the Presidency"; he declared he had not said he would back Stevenson, and he predicted an open convention.

A day later in a TV interview Harriman himself, while denying he was a candidate and praising Stevenson, said that he was not too old to run, that he was not "morally bound" to support Stevenson, and that Truman's backing "would be of tremendous value." Carmine DeSapio, after a short trip to California, reported Harriman strength in that state, although the Tammany leader insisted he had not made the trip to boom his candidate. Stevenson conferred in New York City with Senator Lehman, who after talking with Governor Harriman, DeSapio, and Mayor Robert F. Wagner of New York City, reiterated his preference for Stevenson. Senator Kefauver made two speeches in Pennsylvania, warning Democrats against over-optimism and stressing the importance of the votes of women and young people; later in Michigan he attacked Republican concern for special interests.

Truman, visiting Chicago late in October, had a private forty-five-minute talk with Adlai Stevenson from which even their aides were excluded. At its conclusion they held a joint news conference; reporters described Stevenson as "grim-faced and curt." Truman told the press that he "did not promise to support anyone before the convention. . . . If Governor Stevenson is nominated in the convention this coming summer, of course I will support him: I have been urging him to announce his candidacy."[17] Stevenson made a brief formal speech of welcome for the former President, and then hurried away to catch a plane while Truman remained with the newsmen for an additional half hour. In answer to further questions on his attitude toward the three most-talked-of candidates, Truman replied: "I will not take a public stand on any individual between now and the convention. Any man has the right to run for President."

Stevenson meanwhile was on his way to speak at a Minnesota Democratic rally honoring Representative John A. Blatnik, Sena-

[17] *Ibid.*, Oct. 30, 1955.

tor Hubert H. Humphrey, and Governor Orville L. Freeman. On the following day the Minnesota Democratic Central Committee adopted without debate a resolution urging Stevenson "to become a candidate for the Presidency of the United States and to enter the Minnesota primary election" and naming Senator Humphrey, Governor Freeman, and Lieutenant Governor Karl Rolvaag as delegates-at-large pledged to Stevenson. Stevenson in reply reiterated his promise to announce his intention in November. On the same day Governor George M. Leader of Pennsylvania, appearing on a TV program, backed Stevenson as "the right man in the right place at the right time for 1956 for the Democratic party." And Mayor Wagner of New York City strongly implied his support for Stevenson in a radio speech.[18]

Stevenson Decides to Run

Mid-November had been selected by the Democratic party for a $100-a-plate dinner and party rally in Chicago, in connection with a meeting of the National Committee to discuss preliminary plans for the 1956 campaign. Stevenson prepared to announce his candidacy at that time. Two well-placed observers report that his decision to run had been made in the spring of 1955, and he had been biding his time to make a formal announcement. Concerned over the decay in America's world position under the Republicans, he felt the country was wasting time and opportunity while grave problems mounted up at home and abroad; and he felt that if he were to continue to wield political influence, he had to accept the challenge of candidacy in 1956. The only question, according to them, was the timing of the formal announcement. Beset by divided counsel, Stevenson decided to make it at the November meeting of the National Committee.[19] A differing report from another observer declares that Stevenson did not make his decision until after Labor Day. During the earlier months of

[18] Ibid.

[19] Introduction by Arthur Schlesinger, Jr., and Seymour E. Harris to *The New America*, by Adlai Stevenson (1957), p. xiii.

1955, he paid especially close attention to the development of public opinion. He carefully weighed his probable support at the time of the Governors' Conference. Not until reassured by these trends and by the counsel of his sons did he make his formal announcement.[20]

Kefauver waited another month before making his formal entry; but he also, no doubt, had made up his mind some time previously. His entry, and his penchant for primaries, served to cast the race into two major phases, both arduous: a series of primary fights leading up to the convention; and for the victor the campaign proper.

Stevenson's announcement thus moved the Democratic competition for the presidential nomination from a phase of latency into a stage of open contest, not to be resolved until the party convention in August 1956.

[20] Kenneth Davis, *Prophet in His Own Country* (1957), pp. 444-45.

2

Democratic Preconvention Activities

THE DEMOCRATS DURING THE preconvention period
suffered all the normal disadvantages of the party out of power
when opposed to a popular incumbent President who is eligible
for re-election. They also had to contend with the uncertainty
brought about by Mr. Eisenhower's physical condition: first the
aftermath of the heart attack, and later the ileitis operation. Democrats who did not care to try for the Presidency against Eisenhower were likely to be more interested in their party's nomination at those times when either the President's inclination or his
state of health pointed to a different Republican candidate. Other
Democrats were determined to try their fortunes in any event,
but they had to devise varying strategies to meet varying contingencies.

Adlai Stevenson's announcement of candidacy in November
1955 inaugurated a stage of open contest that was not resolved
until he received the Democratic nomination the following
August. The several candidates for the nomination had to compete for convention delegates in both primary and nonprimary
states. Campaign issues had to be selected, providing explosive
possibilities for widening the split between northern liberals and
southern conservatives. The search for both a candidate and a
platform (particularly the plank on civil rights) could end in a
Southern bolt and a third-party threat.

The preconvention period fell into several phases: preparations for the campaign, carrying through January; increased campaign tempo, with Stevenson as front runner, abruptly ended by
Kefauver's surprise victory in Minnesota on March 20; the appearance of the "new" Stevenson, taking the offensive and regaining
the lead with primary victories in Florida and California; and

Harriman's late active bid, terminated in effect by Kefauver's withdrawal in late July, but persisting to the convention and the balloting.

Opening Moves in the Contest

Long before the would-be nominees began tossing their hats into the ring, the site and time of the convention had been decided on. Without consultation with the Republicans, early in 1955 Democratic national headquarters selected Chicago and scheduled their meeting for August 13, 1956.[1] It seems to have been assumed that this move would force the Republicans also to select Chicago (which had put in a bid for both conventions) and to meet at an earlier date than that selected by the Democrats. This turned out not to be the case. Despite objection from the radio-TV networks over the expensive duplication of facilities, the Republicans decided on San Francisco, beginning August 20. So for the first time since 1940 the Democrats were to meet in a different city from the Republicans; and for the first time since 1888 the Democratic convention was scheduled ahead of the Republican.

The later convention dates were intended to produce a shorter general election campaign and to prevent a drop in voter interest in the interval between the conventions and the campaign opening. In 1956 a shorter campaign looked feasible because of nationwide television and speedier transportation, and because the likely presidential nominees were men already well known to the voters.

CANDIDATES

There were three outstanding contenders for the Democratic presidential nomination, plus a sizable number of others men-

[1] This was the date finally decided on after it was assured that five states (Connecticut, Iowa, Massachusetts, Ohio, and South Dakota) would change their election laws requiring earlier certification of presidential and vice-presidential nominees for absentee ballots.

tioned as possibilities. Adlai Stevenson made his formal announcement on November 15, 1955; Estes Kefauver followed suit on December 16; Averell Harriman did not take the formal step until June 9, 1956, but nobody took his previous "inactive" status very seriously. Others who figured with less prominence were: Senators Lyndon Johnson of Texas, Stuart Symington of Missouri, Richard Russell of Georgia, Paul Douglas of Illinois, Harry F. Byrd of Virginia; Governors Frank Lausche of Ohio, G. Mennen Williams of Michigan, A. B. Chandler of Kentucky, Robert B. Meyner of New Jersey; and Speaker Sam Rayburn of Texas.

Stevenson had assembled a campaign organization of a more professional cast than he had in 1952. At the top was James A. Finnegan of Pennsylvania, holder of various state and party posts. Other members were: Hyman B. Raskin, Chicago attorney and former deputy chairman of the Democratic National Committee; former National Committee Chairman Stephen A. Mitchell; Wilson Wyatt, Stevenson's personal manager in 1952; Harry Ashmore of the *Arkansas Gazette;* Roger Tubby, former assistant press secretary to President Truman; and William McCormick Blair, Jr., Stevenson's law associate.

Kefauver's campaign manager was F. Joseph (Jiggs) Donohue, Washington lawyer and former commissioner of the District of Columbia. Associated with him were: A. Bradley Eben, Chicago attorney; Lincoln M. Polan, a West Virginia industrialist; William A. Roberts, a lawyer, of Washington, D.C., and J. Howard McGrath, former U.S. Attorney General.

Watching out for Harriman's interests were Carmine DeSapio, who was not only the state Secretary of State but also New York's Democratic National Committeeman and head of Tammany Hall, and State Chairman Michael Prendergast.

PRESIDENTIAL PRIMARIES

In large measure the character of the preconvention campaign was shaped by the choice of primaries by the two chief participants. The dates of these primaries, fixed by the individual states, suggested the timing of campaign tours within their borders, and the issues to be stressed were geared to the dominant interest of the locality or of the particular audience, although most major speeches ranged over a variety of outstanding issues.

Presidential primaries were scheduled in nineteen states (including Alabama, where only the Democrats hold one), Alaska, and the District of Columbia. Some, such as California, would yield firmly committed delegates. Some, such as New York, were for election of delegates only, with no formal commitment possible. Some held separate balloting on presidential candidates, with the results only advisory to the delegates selected. The number of delegate votes varied from six for Alaska and the District of Columbia to ninety-eight for New York.[2] There were many other possibilities, but these illustrations will suggest somewhat the range of variation and the kinds of choices to be made by a potential candidate.

Stevenson had not been entered in any primaries in 1952 and had no taste for battling it out in that fashion in 1956; but Kefauver's entry into the race left him no choice, and he reluctantly entered the contest. He and his advisers carefully chose a minimum number of elections, strategically spaced in the various sections of the country, where he would fight to show his capabilities in that direction; and there were a few other spots where his supporters wished to make an effort in his behalf. There were also limited write-in efforts in his interest in New Hampshire, Massachusetts, and Nebraska, without personal involvement on his part. The New Jersey organization slate of delegates, under the control of Governor Meyner, was understood to be pro-Stevenson, and he was advised to remain out of that situation. In eight elections he or his supporters put forth a maximum effort. His home state of Illinois was an obvious necessity. Alaska and the District of Columbia were in the hands of his backers, with little or no attention from him. In Minnesota, California, and Pennsylvania the Democratic state leaders preferred him to Kefauver and had urged him to enter; each of these states had a

[2] Only 86 of the 98 went to elected delegates. The remaining 12 votes were for delegates-at-large, selected by the Democratic state committee.

sizable number of convention votes, and each was in a different section of the country. Florida was in the fourth great section, the South, where he had to show his strength. The eighth primary —Oregon—was decided on only after Stevenson's unexpected loss in Minnesota made it advisable to attempt an additional show of support.

Kefauver lacked the kind of party organization assistance that Stevenson enjoyed in many states; therefore the Senator had to demonstrate his grass-roots appeal by entering more elections and accumulating as many delegates as he could. He and his advisers selected fourteen primaries. In six of them he was pitted against Stevenson: Minnesota, Oregon, Florida, California, Alaska, and the District of Columbia. New Hampshire was considered to be pretty much his domain, as it had been in 1952. He chose also to enter New Jersey, where in 1952 he had won the advisory presidential preference vote, although the delegation had eventually been nearly unanimous for Stevenson; in 1956 the state Democratic organization was in a stronger position, but Kefauver entered a full slate of delegates as well as placing his name in the preference poll. In six other primaries he was the only candidate on the ballot: Wisconsin, Maryland, Indiana, Nebraska, Montana, and South Dakota. Some write-ins were attempted in his behalf in Illinois, Massachusetts, and Pennsylvania.

There were five states where neither Stevenson nor Kefauver wished to make a vigorous attempt. New York was obviously Harriman's territory. Ohio had been staked out by Governor Lausche as a favorite son. Representative John W. McCormack was put forward by the Massachusetts party organization as a favorite son. Alabama appeared to favor an unpledged delegation. West Virginia presented difficulties, including an intense factional contest and a $1,000 filing fee.

Governor Harriman, maintaining the fiction of an "inactive" candidacy, was not entered in any of the presidential primaries. It was clear, however, that in his own state a large majority of the politicians of his party would support him for the nomination and that most of the delegates elected in the New York primary would be Harriman men.

Beside the primary states, there were twenty-nine others where delegates were selected by party conventions or party committees. Party processes were also used in the Canal Zone, Hawaii, Puerto Rico, and the Virgin Islands. The two active candidates for the nomination did not entirely neglect these other sources of delegates, but they did not campaign in them as vigorously or expend large amounts of time on them. In some cases it was better strategy to leave the situation in the hands of the local political leaders. Some of the state meetings were scheduled after all the primaries had been held, and others were conducted just at the time of necessary campaigning for crucial primaries. Several appeared to be predestined to declare for favorite sons: Kentucky for Governor Chandler; Michigan for Governor Williams; Missouri for Senator Symington; and possibly Texas for Senator Johnson.

In order to do an effective job, particularly in those primaries to which they gave top priority, Kefauver and Stevenson were busy campaigning most of the time from February through May 1956. Both men crisscrossed the United States from north to south and from east to west, making stays ranging from an hour to several days. They made short, impromptu talks at breakfast meetings, luncheons, and picnics. They gave prepared addresses at banquets and conventions. Radio and television carried many of them. They met with groups of politicians, shook thousands of hands, posed for countless pictures. The tempo increased as the months went by until in the last weeks they appeared more like automata than human beings.

PARTY MATTERS

The political party that these various candidates aspired to lead in the presidential campaign was far from a cohesive unit. Generally speaking, there were two main parts, divided from each other in three ways—along geographical lines, along ideological lines, and along organizational lines. One of the resulting portions was made up of states of the North and West, of liberal cast of thought, wielding influence through the Democratic National

Committee. The other was Southern, conservative, and through seniority ruling Congress. Both parts were necessary to win the White House, and both had to be relatively satisfied with the presidential nominee and the party platform. The biggest point of contention between them was the issue of civil rights.

In an effort to define the principal issues of the 1956 presidential campaign, the Democratic National Committee instituted a poll of party officials across the nation, including senators, congressmen, governors, state chairmen, county chairmen, national committee members, and such prominent figures as Truman and Stevenson. The results as given in the party publication were as follows:

1. Falling farm income
2. Tax favoritism for the rich
3. Public power giveaways
4. Favoritism in big business
5. Misconduct in government
6. Rising cost of living
7. Small business failures
8. GOP anti-labor policy
9. Inadequate schools
10. Growth of monopolies[3]

Two omissions were as notable as any of the inclusions: foreign policy and civil rights. All three chief contenders for the presidential nomination rated these along with the ten selected.

Kefauver Gains the Ascendancy

By the end of January 1956 the two active candidates for the nomination had their campaign organizations and schedules sufficiently completed so that they were ready to take to the road. Although the opinions of both men were presumably well known to a fairly wide audience, they were obliged to restate their positions on important issues—a process that was to continue right up

[3] *Democratic Digest,* Vol. 3 (December 1955), pp. 8-9.

to election day in November. Stevenson's preferred vehicle was the carefully prepared speech delivered from a platform, while Kefauver shone best in more informal surroundings talking in a casual way with a smaller group. This was to some extent the pattern for February and March, through the first two primaries, until Minnesota caused Stevenson to reconsider his tactics and techniques.

NEW HAMPSHIRE PRIMARY

Although it is a small state and had only eight votes for the coming Democratic convention, New Hampshire commanded a disproportionate prestige as the earliest presidential primary in the nation, falling on March 13 in 1956.

Kefauver was the only entry in the advisory preference poll, and he had a full slate of "pledged" delegates[4] on the other part of the ballot. He had scored an upset victory in the state in 1952 over President Truman, and his popularity there remained high. Therefore it was considered desirable for Stevenson to refrain from a head-on contest. He did not enter the preference poll, and his delegates filed as "favorable," thus sparing their candidate the formality of a written consent and the appearance of a personal commitment in the contest. Nevertheless, the names on the Stevenson slate included most of the leading Democrats of the state, and they worked diligently in his behalf. Stevenson did no personal campaigning, but obviously hoped that the "big names" on his side would net him some delegate votes.

Kefauver left nothing to chance. He campaigned assiduously, visiting the state several times, and bringing his attractive wife with him on one trip in early March. He covered the state thoroughly with the same kind of campaign he had waged so successfully four years earlier.

When the votes were counted, Kefauver had won both parts.

[4] "Pledged" delegates must have the written consent of their presidential candidate, and they sign a declaration that they will vote for that candidate "so long as he shall be a candidate before [the] convention." "Favorable" delegates do not need written consent, and they sign no pledge.

In the preferential poll he received 22,000 votes, compared with 20,000 in 1952, while Stevenson received about 4,000 write-ins, which were legal. All of the Kefauver "pledged" delegates were elected, giving him a clean sweep. The Senator said he had done "much better . . . than I thought I would." Stevenson said he was "surprised and pleased by the large vote" cast for him and "most grateful for this encouragement."[5]

MINNESOTA PRIMARY

The Minnesota primary was held on March 20, just a week after that of New Hampshire. This time thirty convention votes were at stake instead of a mere eight. Stevenson had announced his intention to enter simultaneously with his formal candidacy announcement in November; he was encouraged to compete in the primary by most of the leading Democrats of Minnesota, headed by Governor Orville Freeman and Senator Hubert H. Humphrey. Kefauver's decision to take part was not announced until near the end of January, making this the first contest in which the two aspirants faced each other directly.

The Minnesota primary had no separate presidential preference poll. Instead, the ballot contained slates of pledged delegates, each preceded by the name of its presidential candidate; one mark on the ballot would cast a vote for both candidate and delegates.

As in New Hampshire, Stevenson had the benefit of well-known political names at the head of his delegate slate, and a sample poll published on March 4 by the *Minneapolis Star and Tribune* showed him with a comfortable 59 per cent of the Democratic vote while Kefauver had only 24 per cent. The poll, however, had been taken in February while Kefauver was making his first campaign swing in the state, and he had created such a favorable impression that a second tour was planned for him.

Stevenson was accompanied part of the time on his campaign trips in the state by Senator Humphrey or Governor Freeman,

[5] *New York Times*, Mar. 15, 1956.

and at the end of the first trip pronounced his reception "very encouraging" but declined to assess his chances in the election.

However, there was still a second round of campaigning during the week preceding the election. Kefauver drew noticeably larger crowds this time, and he had added a new theme that he harped on advantageously: a charge that the state party organization (especially Governor Freeman and Senator Humphrey), by giving party endorsement to Stevenson and refusing to help Kefauver, was attempting to dictate to the people of Minnesota instead of allowing them the right to pick their candidates freely. The Tennesseean claimed they had thrown "obstacles" in his way, but asserted that he was an "expert in obstacles," having in his early political life beaten the Memphis organization of the late Edward H. (Boss) Crump.[6]

The charge of "bossism" and the implied resemblance between the Minnesota party organization and the Crump machine angered Stevenson, and the state leaders even more. Governor Freeman, touring with Stevenson, described Kefauver's allegation of "bossism" as "pure political demagoguery" and exhorted Minnesota Democrats to show their displeasure by their votes. Stevenson castigated Kefauver for serving the "great unrelenting purpose of the Republican party . . . to divide the Democrats and set us to fighting among ourselves."[7]

But another poll of the *Minneapolis Star and Tribune*, published almost on the eve of the primary, showed a sharp rise in Kefauver's percentage of the vote, from 24 to 39 per cent, while Stevenson had dropped from 59 to 52 per cent.[8]

The outcome was almost a disaster for Stevenson. Kefauver won all of the delegates-at-large and seven of the congressional districts, leaving only two for Stevenson. Final result: twenty-six delegate votes for Kefauver, four for Stevenson. Even worse was the psychological impact. Stevenson had gone into Minnesota at the invitation of the state's Democratic leaders and had expected a comparatively easy victory, to show his strength in the Middle

[6] *Ibid.*, Mar. 14, 17, 1956.
[7] *Ibid.*, Mar. 16, 1956.
[8] *Ibid.*, Mar. 18, 1956.

West farm section and to win a block of committed delegates. Not only had he lost this, but there might be an adverse effect on voters in primaries still to come. It was possible for the loss of a single primary election to destroy a presidential candidacy; it had happened to Wendell Willkie when he lost in Wisconsin in 1944, and to Harold E. Stassen with his failure in Oregon in 1948.

The commentators had a number of explanations for the Minnesota outcome. The state has a long history of nonpartisan politics; most state and local candidates, with a few exceptions, run without party identification. There is no party registration of voters, and primary elections are open. Thus it seemed likely that many independents and Republicans, with Eisenhower's victory on the Republican side certain, had found the Democratic contest more interesting and exciting and had chosen to vote in it. Such crossovers might also have taken place as a protest against falling farm income and the administration's agricultural policy. Kefauver was believed to have scored with the voters on the charge of "bossism" and with his generous farm promises and his informal style of campaigning.

Stevenson refused, however, to be counted out of the presidential race. Offering congratulations to the Senator on winning "the first round," he asserted:

"As for myself, I will work harder than ever. . . . My plans are not changed, and neither are my ideas. I have tried to tell the people the truth as I saw it. I always will. I have not promised them the moon. And I never will. This may not win elections but it is, in my opinion, the way to conduct a political campaign in a democracy."[9]

Stevenson's loss was not necessarily Kefauver's gain. The Tennessee Senator might have strong grass roots support, as he had demonstrated in the presidential primaries in 1952 and was trying to show again in 1956; but to win a nomination he also needed the backing of state party organizations and of high-ranking Democrats on the national scene. This backing in large measure he did not have and apparently could not obtain. According to one newspaper:

[9] *Ibid.*, Mar. 22, 1956.

The opposition to Senator Kefauver among his Democratic colleagues in the Senate and in many of the state organizations is massive and apparently immovable. This opposition has a common basis in a feeling that he does not pull his oar in the galley-work of regular committees, but goes sailing off on investigations that make the headlines. More particularly, the Southerners will not forgive his "un-Southern" stand on civil rights (he refused to sign the manifesto two weeks ago against the Supreme Court's desegregation ruling), and many Northern Democrats will not forget his crime-and-politics investigation which damaged some innocent Democrats as well as some guilty ones.[10]

The possibility that these two outstanding candidates might check each other caused elation in other Democratic quarters. Governor Harriman and his entourage felt that Stevenson's loss would be their gain in the long run, while the supporters of would-be dark horses—Senator Symington, Governors Williams, Lausche, Meyner, and Leader—began to meditate strategy.

Stevenson Fights Back

The Minnesota primary represented a turning point for many Democrats. Adlai Stevenson, hitherto the front runner, found himself in the rear and under the necessity of changing his tactics. Senator Kefauver, the perennial underdog, was thrust forward, but found himself in many quarters no more acceptable than before. Governor Harriman, the "inactive" candidate, stirred slightly but clung to his inactivity. Southern Democrats, erstwhile reluctant followers of Stevenson, confronted with more radical possibilities, wished they had worked harder for Stevenson, scanned Lyndon Johnson hopefully, but prepared to settle for Senator Symington if necessary. The liberal Northern wing was convinced that Minnesota had demonstrated that only a candidate of definitely liberal, even radical, stamp, and an aggressive campaigner, could defeat President Eisenhower; Kefauver, disliked by organization Democrats, was out of the question, therefore their choice

[10] *Ibid.*, Mar. 25, 1956.

would have to be someone like Harriman or Governor Williams. So great was the concern over the situation that Northern Democrats in particular, but also some Southerners, were said to be seriously considering the possibility of an eventual draft of former President Truman.[11]

But the presidential primary season was still young; only two out of twenty-one primaries had been held. Most state conventions for the selection of national convention delegates were yet to meet. The situation was fluid, and none of the principals had any intention of being counted out of the running. All proposed to exert themselves to the utmost. Ten weeks would elapse before the Florida primary, and eleven weeks before the one in California, both admittedly crucial for the hopes of Kefauver and Stevenson, and important for all the others who had a stake in the rise or fall of one or both of these men. At the end of those eleven weeks a new stocktaking would be in order for candidates and kingmakers alike.

THE "NEW" STEVENSON

While Stevenson's immediate reaction to the Minnesota primary results had been that neither his plans, nor his ideas were changed, developments over the next few weeks showed more flexibility than his words seemed to convey. Although his over-all strategy was not changed, new tactics shortly became evident. His California supporters, annoyed that Kefauver was now tagging them also as "bosses" because they had refused him their backing and had preferred Stevenson instead, immediately urged their candidate to "personalize" his campaign. It was not their idea that he should comb the streets and shake hands in the Kefauver manner—they considered this psychologically impossible for Stevenson—but rather that he should sharpen his definition of the issues and speak for himself instead of in the name of the Democratic party. In fact, it appeared in the long run that they did not know their man.

[11] *Ibid.*, Mar. 27, 1956.

Stevenson himself was also studying the reasons for his defeat and planning some modifications, but felt that there could not be a "new Stevenson" such as his supporters were pleading with him to create. He also proved to be incorrect in his estimate of himself. At the same time he resolved that in his campaigning in Florida and California he would try to meet more people. But he asserted: "I shall continue to speak my mind. I shall try to answer questions and perhaps learn where I am not 'getting through,' but I will not seek votes through the expediency of abandoning principle."[12]

Nevertheless, Stevenson canceled plans for a week's vacation in Florida with his son and hastened to California for a hurriedly organized two-day visit. Senator Kefauver had rushed out to California immediately after his Minnesota victory, in order to press his newly won advantage. Stevenson had to mount a counteroffensive at once, to show both the voters and his campaign workers that Minnesota was, as he had said, just "the first round" and that he was far from taking the count. In a televised speech in Los Angeles he attacked Kefauver's contention that support from party leaders constituted "bossism"; he pointed out that the Senator had endeavored to obtain the backing of these same people, and remarked tartly that their endorsement apparently "becomes reprehensible only when the Senator doesn't get it." He declared it made him "disgusted and just plain mad" to be charged with preoccupation with issues and not spending sufficient time shaking hands. Nevertheless, it was noted that a considerable amount of his time in California had been set aside for informal campaigning and handshaking.[13]

If there was not to be a new Stevenson, certainly an extensively remodeled one appeared when he spent a day in Jacksonville, Florida, on April 6. His first activity was to take a handshaking tour, saluting people on the sidewalk, the courthouse steps, and in a variety of stores, smiling broadly and saying: "I'm Adlai Stevenson and I need your support." Later he told reporters: "I really believe a candidate can find a balance between these personal

[12] *Ibid.*, Mar. 27, 1956.
[13] *Ibid.*, Mar. 29, 1956,

conversations and the presentation of important issues. I think a candidate owes both approaches to the people and I'm trying to do it."[14]

The smiling, handshaking routine became an established part of Stevenson's repertoire. He continued to combine the new technique with his discussion of the issues until he appeared quite different from the "egghead" who had appealed so strongly to the intellectuals in 1952. In mid-May one reporter described him as changed from a predominantly "detached platform orator" to an "earnestly gregarious" individual. The report continued: "Two months ago street strolling expeditions of only a block or two were intricately planned affairs. Now he automatically walks into drug stores and shoe shine parlors, and consumes frightening combinations of comestibles . . . for the sake of mingling in eating places." Instead of the sophisticated wit he was famous for, he had adopted "a repertoire of tried and true grass-roots wheezes that are dependable laugh getters but avoid any suggestion of flippancy."[15]

The change in campaign style did not portend a lack of interest in ideas and issues. One of the most controversial of the whole campaign was first enunciated by Stevenson in a foreign policy address on April 21 to the American Society of Newspaper Editors. Among suggestions for improvement in our conduct of foreign relations, he included the following:

> . . . I believe we should give prompt and earnest consideration to stopping further tests of the hydrogen bomb, as Commissioner Murray of the Atomic Energy Commission recently proposed. . . . Of course, I would call upon other nations to follow our lead, and if they don't and persist in further tests we will know about it and we can reconsider our policy.

He expressed the opinion that any progress toward armament reduction and control would come a step at a time: "And this is a step which, it seems to me, we might now take, a step which would reflect our determination never to plunge the world into nuclear holocaust, a step which would reaffirm our purpose to act

[14] *Ibid.*, Apr. 7, 1956.
[15] *Ibid.*, May 20, 1956.

with humility and a decent concern for world opinion."[16]

Meanwhile Stevenson and his advisers were planning to wage a strenuous campaign in the Oregon, Florida, and California primaries. For a period of nearly six weeks he spent all of his time in these three states, in an effort to reach every possible large city, small town, and country hamlet, and to meet every possible voter.

THE UNCHANGED KEFAUVER

Victory in Minnesota brought no lull in Senator Kefauver's campaign activities. He headed immediately for California for a hastily organized six-day tour. He continued with the same style and tactics that had just brought triumph in the Midwest: he likened the California campaign to that in Minnesota, with Stevenson having support from most organization Democrats in both states, but the "bossism" issue failed to attain the same potency again. He continued his low-pressure manner of speaking, his simplification of foreign and domestic issues, his "folksy" approach, and his endless handshaking. The trip proved rewarding both in publicity and in increased popularity and more adherents.

After an Easter week-end at home in Tennessee, Kefauver took off again for an almost unbroken two months of campaigning. With one or two exceptions, he made at least a token appearance everywhere he was entered in a primary. In addition he visited at least seven of the nonprimary states at one time or another in the months preceding the California election. However, he gave his chief attention to Florida and California, where he was meeting Stevenson head on.

One asset of Kefauver's 1952 campaign had been the presence of his wife Nancy on many of his tours. In 1956 she cut such appearances drastically, in order to spend more time with her chil-

---

[16] *Washington Post and Times Herald,* Apr. 22, 1956. Commissioner Thomas E. Murray, testifying before a Senate Foreign Relations subcommittee on disarmament, had proposed the cessation, not on the grounds of danger to health and safety, but because he knew of "no reason why we should develop bombs more powerful than those we now have." He also favored limiting the size and number of thermonuclear weapons, and restricting any further tests to smaller weapons. *New York Times,* Apr. 13, 1956.

dren. During May, however, she toured with her husband in the southern part of California, and later appeared in Florida at a crucial stage of that campaign. Her presence thus tacitly emphasized Stevenson's divorced status and pointed to the Senator as a "family" man.

THE STILL "INACTIVE" HARRIMAN

During April and May Governor Harriman maintained his profession of inactivity. After Stevenson was knocked from his front-running position by defeat in Minnesota, the role was tailor-made for Harriman's needs. Let Kefauver destroy Stevenson's hopes; Kefauver himself would be unable to win the majority necessary for nomination; a deadlocked convention would turn to the dark horses; Harriman, with the backing of the largest state and of some additional delegates, plus second-choice ballots, could well emerge as the Democratic candidate. Contending in any of the primaries against such well-known figures as Stevenson and Kefauver would be far too risky; any defeat there would spoil Harriman's chances. Besides, primaries were time-consuming, and neglect of his own state's concerns would do him no good at home.

Harriman had available for political advisers such men as ex-President Truman; ex-Secretary of State Dean Acheson; ex-Secretary of Agriculture Charles F. Brannan; former Democratic National Chairman Frank McKinney; Samuel I. Rosenman, former adviser to both President Franklin D. Roosevelt and President Truman.

Harriman had also a political intelligence office, set up about the turn of the year to collect information on convention delegates, to watch reaction to the Kefauver-Stevenson rivalry, and to note topics of special concern in states that Harriman might visit when he was able to leave Albany. This office was under the direction of George Backer, millionaire real estate operator, former editor of the *New York Post* and personal friend of the Governor. Associated with Backer in the Harriman drive was Robert W. Dowling, New York business man and civic leader.

The New York Governor received from former President Truman what was nearly an outright endorsement at the annual award dinner of the Four Freedoms Foundation in May. Presenting the award to Harriman, Truman praised him highly: "We miss his wisdom and energy and sure touch in our foreign policy today. . . . I don't think there is any man in the United States I think more highly of."[17]

Harriman momentarily forgot his inactive role once or twice during a western tour later in May. At the request of the Democratic National Committee, he visited Colorado, Wyoming, Montana, Washington, Idaho, Utah, and Nevada, to stimulate party enthusiasm. The trip incidentally offered a good opportunity to tour a section where he was popular with a number of party leaders, review his contacts, and meet groups of national convention delegates already chosen. At a breakfast meeting in Cody, Wyoming, in reply to an expression of good wishes for his campaign, Harriman asserted that his name would be presented to the convention "not as a native son but as a candidate"; and he added, "If any of the good people of Wyoming want to support the candidate from New York I'd be mighty proud." Later, at Pullman, Washington, answering a question as to his status, Harriman replied: "If you are interested in supporting me, I welcome that question very much."[18]

Most of the formal events of the tour drew so light an attendance as to disappoint Harriman's supporters, who would have liked to see him shed the pretense of an "inactive" candidacy. He did, however, collect some convention support—two Nevada delegates, at least six from Utah, twelve in Wyoming, eight in Idaho,[19] each with a half vote.

At the conclusion of the tour Governor Harriman declared that following the primaries, there would be a review of the situation as to likely Democratic candidates for the presidential nomina-

[17] *Evening Star* (Washington, D.C.), May 10, 1956.

[18] *New York Times*, May 20, 1956.

[19] The Idaho eight were contingent on his gaining others of the state's twenty-four delegates, because the unit rule would be in effect, giving the total vote to the candidate favored by a majority of the delegation.

tion, and reiterated that he would be placed in nomination by New York State.

Some ten days later, as the June primaries came near, Harriman and his various supporters could easily persuade themselves that their strategy, if not wholly sound, was not wholly hopeless. Stevenson had recovered somewhat from his position after the Minnesota election, winning all of the primaries he was associated with, but he looked far from unbeatable. The close result in the admittedly important Florida contest[20] appeared to leave the whole situation in a fluid state, exactly what Harriman needed. The Florida outcome was thought to have labeled Stevenson as "the symbol of compromise on the civil rights issue, especially the integration of Negroes and whites in public schools." This could cause difficulty in picking up uncommitted delegates from northern states where the Negro vote might provide the winning margin in the election. Thus the Harriman managers counted on Stevenson's drive to fizzle out, leaving Harriman "to forge ahead on the basis that he stands for unequivocation on civil rights."[21] This was the basis on which they planned further moves for the months of June and July, to be climaxed by the national convention.

PRIMARIES BETWEEN MINNESOTA AND OREGON

Although the Oregon, Florida, and California primaries were vital to the two candidates taking part in them and to others who hoped to profit indirectly by them, there were thirteen other primaries between March 20 and May 18 where the results might have some impact on the various candidacies. Kefauver won three of these and scored partial victories in two others; four of them went to Stevenson; two were taken by favorite sons; and two involved neither presidential candidates nor commitment of delegates.

The Kefauver victories were won in states where he was un-

[20] See below, pp. 52-56.
[21] New York Times, May 31, 1956.

opposed by any other presidential candidate. In Wisconsin on April 3 his slate of pledged delegates was elected, to give him 28 convention votes. In Maryland (May 7) his only opposition was the "uninstructed delegation" required by law to be on the ballot; his gain there was 18 votes. He won the Indiana (May 8) preference poll, thereby gaining the 26 votes of delegates to be selected later at a state convention. He also won the preference poll in Nebraska (May 15), although there were write-in votes for Stevenson and Harriman; but there was a separate election of unpledged delegates with 12 votes, only 5 of them favorable to Kefauver. He fared least well in New Jersey (April 17): as the only entry in the preference poll, he was the winner, but it was advisory only; the state Democratic organization, headed by Governor Meyner, had a full slate of delegates entered in opposition to the Kefauver slate; one Kefauver delegate, with one half vote, was elected, and the remaining 35½ votes remained under Meyner's control.

Stevenson's victories in these thirteen primaries did not net him any legally pledged delegates. He won advisory preference polls in Illinois (April 10), Alaska (April 24), and Pennsylvania (April 24); his was the only name on the ballot in Illinois and Pennsylvania, but Kefauver received write-in votes in both states, while both men were entered in Alaska. In Illinois and Pennsylvania district delegates were also elected in the primary; in Alaska they were to be selected later in a territorial convention. Stevenson was expected to have a majority of favorable delegates out of those chosen, but there were no reliable figures. The election in the District of Columbia was a different kind of affair. Under a newly enacted law for election of delegates only, there was no provision for formal slates identified with the name of a presidential candidate; but both the Kefauver and Stevenson local organizations endorsed full quotas of delegates, and their preferences were widely publicized, so that the result was essentially slate voting. The Stevenson delegates won a sweeping victory, although the Kefauver delegates were headed by his campaign manager, F. Joseph Donohue, a former District commissioner and well-known local Democrat.

The primaries carried by favorite sons were those of Massachusetts (April 24) and Ohio (May 8). In the latter Governor Frank Lausche won fifty-four out of fifty-eight delegate votes, with the other four uncommitted. Massachusetts had a preference poll, with all votes required to be written in, and an election of uncommitted delegates. Representative John McCormack received 26,000 votes, Stevenson 19,000, and Kefauver 4,500, with scattered votes for others.

The Alabama primary (May 1), for Democratic convention delegates, had no organized slates or officially pledged delegates, though it was understood that a substantial number favored Stevenson. West Virginia (May 8) had an advisory preference poll, but there were no entries; and the election of delegates was apparently only incidental to a spirited contest for the gubernatorial nomination.

OREGON PRIMARY

When Stevenson and his staff began to take stock after the reverse in Minnesota to see if he could advantageously go into any primaries not previously contemplated, last filing dates for many of those remaining either had already passed or were so close at hand as to present great difficulties. Elections in Montana and South Dakota would not be held until June 5, the same day as in California, and would therefore be of no help in retrieving lost ground. Some others were not worth a gamble: Kefauver had already entered or had announced future entry into some where that fact alone would give him an edge.

The only spot that seemed to offer an even break was Oregon, where the filing deadline had passed on March 9 without any Democratic entry. Write-in votes were legal, and the delegates elected would be committed to the winner of the presidential preference poll, even if only a few hundred votes were cast. The date of the primary, May 18, was before those in Florida and California so that a win in Oregon could help psychologically in those later ones. Of course a loss would have a correspondingly adverse effect, but primaries were speculative in any case. Oregon had been a turning point for Dewey in 1948 after Stassen had won a series of victories, and perhaps it could help Stevenson now.

Originally both Stevenson and Kefauver had apparently intended to remain out of Oregon, where Senator Wayne Morse was coming up for re-election, presumably against Douglas McKay, popular ex-governor of the state, who had resigned as Secretary of the Interior in order to run for the Republican senatorial nomination. Any division in the state Democratic party could be harmful to Morse's chances. Notwithstanding this concern, after the Minnesota election the Oregon supporters of both Kefauver and Stevenson saw good reason to reconsider the decision not to enter. For Kefauver the Oregon primary would present an opportunity to show a continuation of his capability for winning these elections, and would incidentally add another sixteen votes to his total. For Stevenson it would be a chance to demonstrate a dramatic reversal of form, more so than the primaries preceding Oregon in which he was entered. For either of them to put forth no effort might be the equivalent of letting sixteen pledged delegate votes go by default to his rival.

Therefore in early April the two candidates approved the organization of write-in campaigns by their supporters and made plans to spend at least a few days in Oregon before the election, though still giving the highest priority in both time and effort to the Florida and California campaigns. Stevenson managed to spend more time in Oregon than Kefauver did, and made appearances in the important and more populous sections. In addition to the usual topics of aid for farmers, labor policy, foreign policy, and social security, both candidates put much emphasis on conservation of natural resources and on power development, issues of particular interest in the Pacific Northwest.

Despite expectation of a rather small Democratic vote because of the write-ins, the final total was nearly double what had been anticipated. Stevenson received 60 per cent of the 163,000 Democratic votes cast. Thus he won the victory he had to have, heartening to himself and his managers, creating again a winning psychology among all his supporters, particularly in the two states where the final important primaries were about to be held.

FLORIDA PRIMARY

Scheduled for May 29, the Florida primary was important because of its twenty-eight delegate votes, its position immediately
preceding the California primary, and its location in the South.
Under the newly revised law, the delegates were grouped in
slates headed by the name of their preferred presidential candidate. Stevenson's slate, as in several other states, contained names
of well-known state political figures.

Although the outcome of the presidential primary was of great
importance to the two candidates, the residents of the state were
much more keenly interested in their May 8 gubernatorial primary, where six candidates were fighting bitterly, chiefly over
the issue of school integration. Normally, with so many candidates, no one of them would have won the majority of votes necessary for nomination, and a runoff would have been held on May
29 in conjunction with the presidential primary, ensuring a large
turnout. But for the first time in Florida history the gubernatorial
nomination was decided in the first primary: Governor LeRoy
Collins won renomination by a landslide, and the voters' main
reason for interest in the second primary was gone.

Another reason for lack of voter interest in a Democratic primary was the popularity of President Eisenhower. He had won
Florida in 1952, and many voters apparently anticipated that he
would repeat in 1956. The state contained a large number of retired Northerners who were Republicans but had registered as
Democrats in order to have a voice in choosing state and local
officers. Such people would have little interest in voting in a
Democratic presidential primary. And even some full-fledged
Democrats felt that no candidate of their party had a chance
against the popular President.

This monumental apathy failed to deter either Stevenson or
Kefauver. Winning the Florida primary was a necessary step
toward winning the Democratic presidential nomination, worthy
of any and every exertion.

And how they exerted themselves! They mingled with people on the streets, went into stores and barbershops, greeted workmen, shook every hand within reach. The process became so mechanical that Stevenson shook hands with a mannequin in a department store, while Kefauver, dozing in the seat of a car halted for doing eighty miles an hour, emerged half asleep to proffer his hand to the policeman who had stopped the car. There were few formal speeches, many brief impromptu ones from courthouse steps or some other handy vantage point; there were speeches to breakfast meetings, luncheons, and dinners. Each candidate utilized the services of the same hillbilly band on at least one trek across the state.

But these men were in deadly earnest about their ultimate objective. Each of them visited the state four times in two months, including an intensive week immediately preceding the primary. Both visited all sections of Florida, some more than once: the northwestern "panhandle," where the population was as "Southern" in its attitude as that in neighboring Georgia and Alabama; the populous area dominated by St. Petersburg, with its retired pensioners, and industrial Tampa; Jacksonville, where Kefauver was supported by the popular and politically powerful mayor; the fabulous "gold coast" of Miami and its metropolitan area, with the state's largest concentration of inhabitants; and the central portion of the state, with smaller towns, orange groves, and a middle-of-the-road outlook.

Despite trivia and occasional absurdities, the candidates made an earnest effort to discuss the important issues as they saw them, both in addressing audiences and in comments at press conferences. Both attacked the Eisenhower administration, as they had done previously, for its failures—in farm and labor policy, in not producing more aid to education, in favoring big business and neglecting small business. They dealt with facets of foreign policy of particular interest at the moment: the Middle East, where the Arab nations and Israel were far from a peace settlement and growing restive; NATO, which they felt needed strengthening in contrast to an Eisenhower claim that it was in good shape. Both gave serious attention to the Supreme Court decision on school integration, declaring that the decision must be complied with as the law of the land.

A joint radio-television appearance in Miami on May 21 only emphasized the similarity of their attitudes. The program was broadcast nationwide and was billed in advance as a "debate"; but there were no "fireworks." They disagreed mildly on the cessation of H-bomb testing and on Kefauver's alleged "absenteeism" from the Senate, but otherwise they demonstrated similar points of view as they discussed the Republican administration.

The last week of the Florida campaign brought a change of atmosphere, possibly due to the results in Oregon and to publication of a Gallup poll decidedly favorable to Stevenson. Kefauver launched a full-scale offensive against Stevenson, resorting to repeated personal attacks. He resurrected the charge of "bossism," picturing himself as a Senator dominated by no clique but responsible to the people, while he was opposed by political machine influences—a reference to the endorsement given Stevenson by six of the seven Florida Democratic members of the United States House of Representatives.

Another Kefauver accusation, labeled a "gross distortion" by Stevenson, was that Stevenson in 1951, during his governorship of Illinois, had vetoed a bill that would have increased by 10 per cent the pensions for the aged and blind. The Kefauver campaign aides passed out pamphlets to the same effect prepared by the California Institute of Social Welfare, an organization of "senior citizens" that had endorsed Kefauver two weeks earlier at its annual convention. Stevenson laid the veto to the refusal of the Republican legislature to provide the necessary funds, thus making a "fraud" of the bill.

Although in their joint television appearance the two men had unanimously regretted the "trend toward bigness" in industry and criticized the Eisenhower administration for giving too little help to small businessmen, three days later Kefauver asserted that Stevenson was "strangely silent" on the "growing monopoly" threatened by big business mergers. He attributed Stevenson's alleged silence to his employment by the Radio Corporation of

America to defend it "against an antitrust action brought by the United States," with an added critical comment on the role of the party's titular leader vis-a-vis the antitrust laws and their enforcement. Kefauver erred, however, by confusing two separate antitrust suits against RCA: one had been brought by the United States Government, and Stevenson had no part in that defense; the other, with which Stevenson was associated, had been brought by the Zenith Radio and Television Co.

Stevenson had a few sharp words to add when he corrected the Kefauver account of his work for RCA: "The Senator's continued false charges remind me that there is such a thing as wanting to be President too much. The Senator seems to be confronted with the dilemma of how to win without proving that he is unworthy of winning."[22]

For one phase of the Kefauver attack, however, there was provocation. At a meeting on May 22 in the largely segregationist "panhandle," ex-Governor Millard Caldwell introduced his candidate with a quotation calling Stevenson "the most moderate man the South can elect." He also read a contrasting statement characterizing Kefauver as "an integrationist . . . as a far left liberal . . . as a sycophant of the Negro vote."[23] Asked about this attack after the meeting, Stevenson said he had been unable to hear what was said. When he was given the information, he disclaimed responsibility both for the statements that had been read and for the reading of them, and added: "It is probable that I do not agree with all my delegates on all questions, including desegregation."[24]

Kefauver was incensed when he heard of the episode, and declared that Stevenson should have done more than disclaim—he should have denounced—and that a man should bear some responsibility for the acts and words of his managers and representatives. As the Senator elaborated on the affair over the next few days, he worked himself up to a high pitch, telling reporters:

There is a remarkable parallel in the attitude Mr. Stevenson takes

[22] *Washington Post and Times Herald,* May 25, 1956.
[23] *New York Times,* May 23, 1956.
[24] *Washington Post and Times Herald,* May 23, 1956.

toward his delegate, Caldwell, and President Eisenhower's attitude toward Nixon, when Nixon attacks Democrats. Nixon makes vicious attacks on the Democrats, and Mr. Eisenhower says he never read about them. Mr. Caldwell makes an attack on me, and Mr. Stevenson says he didn't hear it, even though he was sitting right behind Caldwell. . . . That's the same "smear and smile" technique the Republicans used in '52.[25]

When he was told of this attack, Stevenson said he would have "no further comment on these remarks by Senator Kefauver."[26]

For Kefauver's reaction in this instance, there was some justification. For some of the other accusations he made in the closing days of the Florida campaign, it is harder to discover equally valid excuses. And the points he was making in Florida were equally useful in California.

The Senator played yet another card three days before the primary. Reminding his audience that in 1952 his rival had carried only nine of the forty-eight states, Kefauver told them: "What was not good enough to win in 1952 will not be good enough to win in 1956" and asserted that Stevenson lacked the will to win.[27]

Stevenson won a majority of the delegates, including all twelve of the delegate-at-large votes and ten district delegate votes; Kefauver had the remaining six district votes. The total vote cast, however, was light, and Stevenson's margin of victory was narrow —less than 14,000 votes out of a total of some 450,000. The inconclusive nature of the outcome left matters in very much the posture that had been anticipated from the beginning: the California primary would be crucial in determining the eventual Democratic nominee.

CALIFORNIA PRIMARY

The California primary was crucial for two reasons. Because of its winner-take-all character, either Kefauver or Stevenson would receive the entire sixty-eight delegate votes, which represented

[25] *Ibid.*, May 26, 1956.
[26] *New York Times,* May 26, 1956.
[27] *Ibid.*, and *Washington Post and Times Herald,* May 27, 1956.

one tenth of the total (686½) required for nomination in the convention. It could also have a psychological effect on the convention if it resulted in a victory for Stevenson by an impressive margin; in this respect his Florida win was of little assistance. Kefauver's claim that the Florida result was a "moral victory" for him hardly squared with the facts: he had needed a resounding victory both there and in California to make a show of such strong grass-roots support that the organization Democrats who opposed him could nevertheless not refuse to consider him. He could scarcely achieve that end now by a win in California unless it was of truly spectacular proportions, and there were wide expectations that the result would be similar to that in Florida, with no very decisive margin for either man. Even Stevenson would need a healthier margin than was anticipated to be able to stampede the convention; but if his steady string of primary victories ever since the Minnesota debacle were culminated by a victory in California, he would be in a reasonably good position at the beginning of the convention. For either Stevenson or Kefauver a loss would be serious, perhaps fatal.

Since the Florida and California primaries were only a week apart, the campaigning in the two states ran concurrently. The two campaigns had several items in common. The party leaders in California were almost solidly behind Stevenson; among them were the state attorney general, Edmund G. (Pat) Brown, the only elected Democratic official of high rank in the state, who was campaign manager; the Democratic national committeeman; the state chairman; and the president of the California Democratic Council. Only the national committeewoman was supporting Kefauver. This was still another situation that lent itself to the charge of "bossism," and Kefauver capitalized on it.

California, like Florida, had a large number of retired pensioners, who had come from other parts of the country; they constituted a sizable voting bloc, especially interested in issues of social security and public assistance. They were organized into the powerful California Institute of Social Welfare; at their annual convention on May 10 they were addressed by Senator Kefauver and gave him their endorsement for the Democratic nomination. In the closing days of the Florida campaign, as mentioned above,[28] Kefauver's supporters distributed a pamphlet prepared by the Institute as a special appeal to Florida's elders.

California has long been split politically between Northern and Southern sections; and within these sections there are other geographical differences of political significance. The two rivals for the nomination addressed themselves to the three metropolitan areas around San Francisco, Los Angeles, and San Diego, respectively, and to the agricultural area of the Central Valley. There was a large labor vote, especially around Los Angeles and San Diego. Almost everywhere the issues of water resources and flood control were vital, and power development and distribution were important to the north of San Francisco. Civil rights and school integration were potent issues because of the Negro vote, particularly in Los Angeles; the situation was reversed from that in Florida, so that instead of appealing to a white audience for peaceful acceptance of integration, the candidates were speaking to groups composed largely or wholly of Negroes who favored integration.

Both candidates campaigned in California several times between the Minnesota primary in March and the June 5 California election, each of them spending a total of about four weeks of time. In California as in Florida both men on their early trips directed their criticisms at the Eisenhower administration and discussed their own proposals for a presidential program. They ran the gamut of campaign issues: school integration, social security and pensions for the elderly, foreign policy, federal aid to education, farm policy, big business versus small business, labor policy, and special emphasis on the role played by Vice President Nixon since they were in his home state.

When the contestants returned to the West for a last week of campaigning before the primary, the situation was different. This was immediately after the final week in Florida in which Kefauver had concentrated his fire not on the Eisenhower administration but on his opponent for the Democratic nomination. Stevenson, who arrived in California first, told the press that he de-

[28] See p. 54.

plored "the way the primary campaign deteriorated in Florida after the election in Oregon," with specific mention of Kefauver's "personal charges and accusations," and the hope that there would be no repetition in California.[29] Kefauver dashed such hope as soon as he arrived, telling newsmen he had stated nothing but the facts in Florida and would do the same thing in California, and regretting the "personal attacks" Stevenson had made on him.[30]

Stevenson struck back by calling Kefauver a "poor loser," adding: "As to personal attacks on me and continued distortion of the facts, he has apparently decided after five defeats in contested primaries that if he cannot win he will destroy." He also pointed out that Kefauver had waited until the closing days of the Florida campaign to hurl charges that he apparently had not wished to use in their television debate in Miami.[31]

Throughout the final days of campaigning in California, Kefauver was busy repeating the charges against his opponent, either outright or by implication. Furthermore, he by suggestion and his campaign manager by bald statement were saying that Stevenson supporters had a secret understanding with the more rabid segregationists. Donohue had voiced it first in these words: "The fact is that a vote for Stevenson is a vote for Eastland, Talmadge, Ellender and other white supremacy boys because the Stevenson bosses from Chicago have agreed to let them continue to control their political machines in their home states, while their hand-picked boy, Paul Butler, stays in power."[32] Kefauver was somewhat more careful in the words he used, but he chose a setting where they would be most damaging—a civil rights rally with a largely Negro audience. He conveyed his meaning in the form of questions.

> Since his, Adlai's, statements are not unlike my own, why then is it that the Talmadges, the Ellenders, the Caldwells flock to his support?
>
> Has anything been said in private to these segregationists that makes him more acceptable than I?
>
> What representations have been made by spokesmen from my opponent's camp?

[29] New York Times, May 30, 1956.
[30] Washington Post and Times Herald, May 31, 1956.
[31] Ibid., June 1, 1956.
[32] Ibid., June 2, 1956.

Have they been assured that the words of his supporters rather than his own personal words represent the correct position of his candidacy?

I think these questions are important. There comes a time when campaign promises—those made in public as well as those made in private—those made by the candidate himself as well as those made by spokesmen for him—must be dealt with.[33]

Stevenson refused to make any more direct answers. And it appeared unnecessary for him to do so. Public opinion polls showed that he had a sizable lead over his opponent, and newsmen were saying that Stevenson was drawing larger crowds. For additional assistance in the final campaigning he had former California Representative Helen Gahagan Douglas and Mrs. Franklin D. Roosevelt. Both of them backed Stevenson on the crucial issues of social security, pensions, and civil rights for Negroes.

The primary results, according to Stevenson's manager Pat Brown, "exceeded our wildest dreams." Stevenson won by a landslide in a much larger turnout of voters than was anticipated. He captured 63 per cent of the Democratic votes cast, and showed strength in critical sectors—Negro precincts by at least 2 to 1 and those in Los Angeles by 4 to 1; the farm counties, which Kefauver had counted on; the metropolitan areas; and, as one report suggested, if Kefauver won the votes of a majority of pensioners, "the size of the Stevenson victory overwhelmed such evidence."[34]

This single victory put Stevenson in the forefront for the Democratic presidential nomination. He had shown an ability to work hard for votes, to obtain a big turnout, and to win in a large pivotal state with a varied voting population. Southern politicians, though not enthusiastic about him, preferred him to Kefauver or Harriman and were reconciled to him as the least offensive of the strong possibilities. He was still short of a majority of convention votes, but he was ahead of his rivals, and his emphatic win in California would swing in his direction delegates who had hitherto been uncommitted.[35]

[33] *Ibid.*, June 4, 1956.
[34] *Ibid.*, June 6 and 7; *New York Times*, June 7, 1956.
[35] One year later Stevenson, speaking on television, declared that the presidential primary "is almost a useless institution." His objections were that most candidates

Kefauver had not only lost the primary. He had practically lost any chance he had ever had for the nomination. He had damaged his party as well as Adlai Stevenson. Also, in the event Stevenson won the nomination, Kefauver had furnished the Republicans with valuable ammunition.

OTHER JUNE 5 PRIMARIES

In addition to California, presidential primaries were held on June 5 in Montana, New York, and South Dakota. Kefauver was unopposed in both Montana and South Dakota and won twenty-four pledged delegate votes in those states. The New York primary was for election of district delegates only, with no preference poll. Delegate candidates for the most part had the backing of their local party organizations, and most were prepared to back Harriman. Ten candidates were pro-Stevenson; six of them won delegation places. Later in the month two more Stevenson supporters, Senator Herbert H. Lehman and Mayor Robert F. Wagner of New York City, were selected by the Democratic state committee among the delegates-at-large.

Enter Harriman, Exit Kefauver

With the primaries out of the way, other aspects of the nominating process claimed attention. President Eisenhower's operation for ileitis led to speculation that he might yet withdraw from the presidential race; with him either eliminated or obviously in poor health, Republican chances would be much worse, and the Democratic nomination accordingly more valuable. As had been anticipated, Governor Harriman at last became an avowed candidate. Stevenson, Kefauver, and Harriman all began canvassing

cannot afford the time away from their jobs; relatively few voters take part; there is no uniformity among the various primaries; and the expense is too great, both in monetary terms and in physical expenditure. *Washington Post and Times Herald,* June 2, 1958.

uncommitted primary delegations and nonprimary states for delegate support; and all aimed for second-choice backing from delegates whose first-ballot votes were committed to others. Claims
and counterclaims of delegate votes were made by the candidates
and their staffs, and calculations were made by the press. Ex-
President Truman's statement of preference was awaited, and
was sought by newsmen at every available opportunity. There
was animated speculation on the possibility of a Southern revolt.
There was talk about likely vice-presidential candidates. Senator
Kefauver's announcement of withdrawal in late July led to hasty
recalculations and renewed efforts to pick up delegates before
the opening of the convention.

On June 22, while President Eisenhower was still in Walter
Reed Hospital, Democratic National Chairman Paul Butler took
an important step toward fixing the tone and tactics of the election campaign. He held an all-day meeting in Washington with
representatives of the three avowed candidates for the nomination: Carmine DeSapio for Harriman; F. Joseph Donohue for
Kefauver; and James Finnegan for Stevenson. All agreed to plans
for a "vigorous" whistlestop campaign in addition to the use of
radio and television. Since the President had told the country on
February 29 that he would not travel extensively in the campaign, the Republicans would have to rely on radio-TV appearances; and the Democratic candidate could make a display of
physical energy in contrast. Furthermore, the Democratic treasury was low and would not permit heavy expenditures for broadcasting time. Fortunately, the idea of whistlestopping was congenial to all three potential nominees, not to mention former
President Truman. Because of this it was possible to attempt a
solution of a perennial problem of the party out of power: how to
make campaign plans before selecting a nominee.

DELEGATE POLLS

Immediately after the final primary elections, with 686½ votes
needed to nominate, a United Press poll of delegates showed:

Stevenson 377; Kefauver 164; Harriman 124½; Lausche 54½; Symington 46; Williams 45; others scattered or unknown.[36] Ten days later Stevenson's managers estimated that their candidate was reasonably certain of 510 votes on the first ballot.[37] This figure, however, was much higher than any of the Associated Press tabulations showed until the eve of the convention, and was probably based on private assurances about delegates not yet publicly committed. A series of polls from late June to mid-August yielded the following results.[38]

	June 25	July 17	July 29	Aug. 3	Aug. 13
Stevenson	301½	346	404½	457	509½
Kefauver	165	163	200		
Harriman	111½	115	141	163½	201
Johnson	57	58	56		
Lausche	54½	54½	54		
Symington	46½	48	38½		
Williams	44	44	44		

These showed Stevenson making steady gains. Although far behind, Harriman gained faster after Kefauver's withdrawal, and the favorite sons held about the same numbers of votes from one poll to another.

KEFAUVER BOWS OUT

Until the moment when Kefauver announced his withdrawal from the contest for the nomination, he continued to insist that he would carry on a vigorous campaign right up to convention time, with the expectation of collecting added delegate strength. However, he lost the backing of his own Tennessee when the state convention, held in late June, followed the wishes of Governor Frank G. Clement and left the delegates uninstructed rather

---

[36] *New York Times,* June 7, 1956.

[37] *Ibid.,* June 17, 1956.

[38] Dates given are publication dates; poll of Aug. 3 from *Washington Post and Times Herald;* all others from *New York Times.* The poll dated July 29 was based on reports from *New York Times* correspondents; all others from the Associated Press.

than pledged to Kefauver. The Senator nevertheless persisted, visiting Iowa, Utah, and Colorado on a delegate search, and attending a dinner of the New Jersey delegates. Speaking to the National Press Club in Washington, D.C., on July 17, he claimed that his first ballot total would be 250 to 275 votes.

Kefauver made a gesture of conciliation toward Stevenson on a television interview some two weeks after the California primary, when he suggested that both of them "got somewhat out of character" during the Florida and California primary campaigns. The Tennesseean asserted that Stevenson's charge that Kefauver was often absent from the Senate had been out of character, and the speech by former Governor Caldwell of Florida was an "unbearable provocation," following which "I got mad and lost my head." In California, the Senator said, he had "made many mistakes" in continuing the attacks on Stevenson. He declared he considered Stevenson "a fine man" and would support him wholeheartedly if he were nominated.[39]

Toward the end of July there was some indication that Kefauver was receiving suggestions of the vice-presidential nomination in return for support from his delegates on the second ballot and later, if he could control them.[40] But Kefauver said firmly that he was not considering a second-place nomination; although Stevenson was gaining faster than he in number of pledged delegates, he felt that his position as "underdog" would win sympathy and that his strength would increase as the balloting proceeded.[41]

Two days later (July 31) the Senator announced that he was withdrawing from the race and was asking his supporters to back Stevenson, the only other candidate to go into the presidential primaries. He observed that the public opinion polls showed that most of the Democratic and independent voters preferred Stevenson for the party's nominee and that the Democratic party leaders also gave him their support. Stevenson's delegate lead placed him in a position, Kefauver said, where "he could be stopped only by throwing the convention into a deadlock. I would not want to

[39] New York Times, June 18, 1956.
[40] Arthur Krock, "Southern Revolt Now Considered Unlikely," ibid., July 22, 1956.
[41] Ibid., July 30, 1956.

be a party to this." Paying tribute to his devoted followers, he expressed confidence in their understanding of his move and their wish for a party victory in the November elections. To them he sent word that:

> I do believe Mr. Stevenson has a good chance to lead the party to victory this fall. . . . He is a much more formidable campaigner today than he was four years ago. . . . Since the Minnesota primary, he has greatly improved his campaign methods, he has put much more personality and drive into his efforts. . . .

His own intention, he said, was to go to the convention to try to persuade his supporters "that the course I have taken, and advise them to take, is in the best interest of the Democratic Party at this moment in our history."[42]

HARRIMAN MAKES HIS BID

Governor Harriman did not enter until the last of the presidential primaries had been held, but the Stevenson landslide in California created a difficult situation for the governor. It was not made easier for him when David Dubinsky, president of the International Ladies Garment Workers Union and a vice chairman of the New York State Liberal party, told a union convention that it was clear that Stevenson would be chosen on an early ballot; Dubinsky added that Stevenson was the strongest candidate, and that Harriman's inactive candidacy was undermining Stevenson and harming the Democratic party and liberalism because of its divisive nature.[43]

Harriman waited no longer. He made an unscheduled appearance to address the closing session of the union convention the following day, June 9, and announced that "this hat is in the ring." He told the union members:

> I believe in the unity of the Democratic party . . . but I believe in the unity of the Democratic party as a liberal Democratic party. . . . I want to tell you I am going to Chicago as a candidate fighting for

[42] *Ibid.*, Aug. 1, 1956; *Washington Post and Times Herald*, Aug. 1, 1956.
[43] *New York Times*, June 9, 1956.

the . . . liberal principles of the Democratic party, fighting for the principles of Franklin Roosevelt and Harry Truman.[44]

The timing of this announcement was unfortunate. Because of President Eisenhower's operation in the early hours of the same day, Harriman appeared to have become a candidate for the nomination because the Democratic nominee now seemed to have a real chance to win the election. Apparently the challenge from Dubinsky and the attractiveness of the union convention as a forum, coupled with the necessity for getting into the race without delay, overshadowed any seeming indelicacy.

From this time on to the convention Harriman and his supporters were in the thick of the fray. Almost immediately a Harriman-for-President organization made its debut, with an ostentatious nucleus of western states to counterbalance the Tammany image conveyed by DeSapio. Two Oklahomans were prominent in the organization: Governor Raymond Gary was chairman of the organizing meeting at Denver, and Loyd Benefield, the state chairman, became national chairman of the Harriman outfit. When a national headquarters was opened in Chicago two weeks later, two newly resigned National Committee figures were conspicuous: co-director with Mr. Benefield was Mrs. India Edwards, erstwhile vice chairman of the National Committee; and Neale Roach, who had left his position as convention manager, was Harriman's assistant national director.

An obvious effort to render Harriman more palatable to the South was made at the Denver meeting on June 16. Before Harriman's arrival, Governor Gary told those gathered:

> Governor Harriman believes in the policy of the golden rule on civil rights. He believes that we can work these problems out on a local basis, just as we have done in Oklahoma. . . . I'll admit this is moderation. But Governor Harriman believes, like I do, that if you leave people alone to work out this problem on a local level they will do it.

When the Governor arrived later in the day, he said he would select a different word from "moderate" for his attitude, then added: "But I'm using different terms, that's all. Governor Gary's statement stands and mine does, too. I'd say with zeal. But then

[44] *Ibid.*, June 10, 1956.

I don't want to argue over the meaning of words."[45] Only the preceding day Harriman had described himself as a zealot against discrimination, and back in November 1955 he had pointed the finger of scorn at Adlai Stevenson for advocating moderation.[46]

The Governor found himself in the same difficulties that Kefauver and Stevenson had already encountered, in any attempt to woo support from both Negroes and Southern Democrats. The next month, answering a question from a Negro newspaper in Pittsburgh on using the power of the Presidency to "induce the leadership in so-called recalcitrant states to support a steady and progressive program of compliance [with the Supreme Court decision] rather than defiance," he asserted that the "leadership in all our states should take action to comply . . . as soon as practical (taking into account local conditions), and give some affirmative indication of intention to work for compliance." He added that President Eisenhower "has not lived up to his obligations, or seized the great opportunities . . . to inspire a universal desire for an advance toward new political morality and social justice."[47] When Harriman addressed the National Press Club in Washington on July 12, he was asked how he would use the presidential power to induce integration and whether he would "use Federal troops as a last resort." He insisted he would not use troops but that "men of good-will could work out the differences and relieve the tensions," if the President would call a conference of such men.[48]

In the latter part of July the New York Governor betook himself on a widespread search for delegates, first in the Midwest, then in New England. In six states—Kansas, Colorado, New Mexico, Nebraska, South Dakota, and Illinois—he addressed rallies, luncheons, barbecues, state conventions, and private gatherings of Democrats. The issues he discussed were those his rivals for the nomination had worked over frequently: the Republican record on farm problems, favoritism for big business, failure to encourage full development of the national economy, natural

[45] Ibid., June 17, 1956.
[46] New York Times, Nov. 27, 1955.
[47] Ibid., July 12, 1956.
[48] Arthur Krock, "Harriman Challenged on Integration Issue," ibid., July 15, 1956.

resources, and so on. At a luncheon in Kansas City, Kansas, he was introduced by ex-President Truman as "a man who knows where he is going and why he is going there."[49]

While Harriman was in New England, he learned of Kefauver's withdrawal, which, the Governor said, "clears the air—the issues are now clear and we're ready for the fight." He expressed assurance that he would receive more than half of Kefauver's two hundred delegate votes, which, added to those already committed to Harriman and some three hundred committed to favorite sons, would block Stevenson's nomination for at least two ballots, after which Stevenson's chances would deteriorate and Harriman's fortunes would improve.[50]

On the following day it was revealed that Harriman's representative, George Backer, had been holding a series of meetings with Kefauver's campaign manager, Donohue, in an effort to prepare an agreed statement condemning "strong forces of moderation" in the party and taking a determined position on half a dozen issues. Backer had had the impression that Kefauver would favor the idea until he had been informed, half an hour before the announcement, that the Senator was about to withdraw.[51]

Kefauver's expressed partiality for Stevenson failed to deter Harriman or his supporters. The Governor, looking for delegates in West Virginia, laid claim to an "overwhelming majority" of erstwhile Kefauver delegates, including a majority in Montana; all in North Dakota; three fourths in Minnesota; a "heavy majority" in Wisconsin; and all eight in South Dakota. At the same time his Chicago headquarters claimed he would receive 341 votes on the first ballot.[52] None of these claims held good.

STEVENSON CONTINUES HIS EFFORTS

Adlai Stevenson, having staged a good comeback from his defeat in Minnesota, pursued his quest with an air of quiet confidence.

[49] *Ibid.*, July 21, 1956.
[50] *Ibid.*, Aug. 1, 1956.
[51] *Ibid.*, Aug. 2, 1956.
[52] *Ibid.*, Aug. 5, 1956.

Like the other candidates, Stevenson sought uncommitted delegates and also second-ballot promises from committed ones. He
spent several days in the Midwest in early July, then moved to
New England. Later he appeared in Boulder, Colorado, to deliver
the keynote address to the Democratic state convention, which
also heard both of his chief rivals. From there he proceeded to
Nevada to confer with the delegates of that state.

While Stevenson was thus occupied, Governor Leader of Pennsylvania and Governor Meyner of New Jersey were endeavoring
to further his cause in their respective states, where the delegates
were not formally committed.

Word of Senator Kefauver's withdrawal on July 31, which was
not a complete surprise to him, reached Stevenson at his Liberty-
ville home, near Chicago. He immediately hurried to his Chicago
headquarters and gave out this formal statement:

> I have been trying to reach Senator Kefauver by phone. I want to
> express to him my gratitude for his gracious and spontaneous expres-
> sion of his support. He has often expressed his approval of the Presi-
> dential primaries and he has been as good as his word.
>
> I respect Senator Kefauver as a thoughtful, liberal Democrat. We
> share a grave anxiety about drift at home and deterioration abroad
> under a faltering leadership and a divided party.
>
> Senator Kefauver has expressed the hope—which I share—that we
> Democrats, united by a common purpose, can soon close ranks and
> get on with this fateful campaign.

Though obviously pleased at the development, Stevenson ceased
to smile when asked if he had made any "understanding, arrangement or deal" with Kefauver before his withdrawal. He replied
sharply, "No, sir. I did not."[53]

Both Stevenson and Mrs. Franklin D. Roosevelt spoke out
against Harriman's continuing efforts to depict Stevenson as too
"moderate" and not a true liberal in the New Deal-Fair Deal tradition. Mrs. Roosevelt, emphasizing her support of Stevenson in
both 1952 and 1956, pointed out that different conditions from
one era to another demanded new answers; but she asserted that
"Mr. Stevenson supports the basic principles underlying the general attitude of the Democratic party, and they are the general

[53] *Ibid.*, Aug. 1, 1956.

approach of my husband and Mr. Truman."[54] Stevenson himself, on a New York trip, declared that Harriman had no "exclusive rights to those principles" built into the New Deal and the Fair Deal by President Roosevelt and President Truman, and noted that he had in his camp such stalwarts of Democratic liberalism as Mrs. Roosevelt and Senator Lehman. Two days later he remarked sharply: "I think there is enough to criticize in the Eisenhower administration without Democrats criticizing one another. I presume Governor Harriman is doing what he thinks is best for our common purpose—the success of the Democratic party."[55]

However, as the preconvention committees began their work in Chicago, there appeared to be no necessity for Stevenson to worry much about his chances. His backers were claiming sufficient delegate votes to win him the nomination on the first ballot, though his official headquarters more modestly claimed victory only on the second or third ballot. With 686½ votes needed for nomination, his backers insisted he had 696½; in the event he received 905½, some 200 more than were claimed at this time.

OTHER DEVELOPMENTS

In addition to the main performances, there were others of lesser note.

One interesting actor was ex-President Harry Truman, as he maneuvered his way from a position of no preference between Harriman and Stevenson—though happy to see Kefauver defeated in California—to a wish for a "free and open convention" that would nominate a "fighting Democrat" who could beat the Republicans and win the Presidency.[56] This kind of neutrality apparently did not meet the expectations of Harriman and his staff, who wanted an outright declaration of preference. But the Truman utterances were no boon to Stevenson; as the front runner, he would find a "free and open convention" adverse to his

[54] *Ibid.*, Aug. 3, 1956.
[55] *Ibid.*
[56] *Ibid.*, June 19, July 6, July 7, July 11, 1956.

interests, and Harriman's self-estimate sounded like a "fighting Democrat." Thus the groundwork was laid for Truman's dramatic statement as the convention opened.

A group of performers from Southern states took the stage twice with the perennial threat to bolt unless the Democratic presidential candidate and platform were acceptable—referring, of course, to civil rights and particularly school integration. Governor Timmerman of South Carolina appeared as the guiding spirit in arranging a preconvention caucus; the purpose was to agree on a uniform attitude toward nominee and platform and to adopt the strategy of recessing their state conventions rather than adjourning them, so that they could be reconvened after the national convention if they were dissatisfied with the actions taken there.

The first public steps were taken after the Harriman candidacy became overt and active. Then came a preliminary meeting in Atlanta on July 13 and 14 of Democratic state chairmen, followed some two weeks later by the previously mentioned caucus of party notables, including three senators, four governors, and two former governors. By the second meeting Senator Kefauver had made his withdrawal, the Stevenson tide was running stronger, and Southern Democrats with a bent toward party loyalty had shown their strength. A strategy on civil rights procedure at the national convention was adopted but not divulged. The published declaration adopted by the caucus asserted that a platform acceptable both to the South and to the rest of the nation could be written, and stressed the need for mutual recognition of the "problems and political necessities" of the states. One reporter of the meeting concluded that "the moderate faction in the South . . . clearly were in control of most of the decisions."[57]

A third show was concerned with a subject that would normally have drawn no attention—the Vice Presidency. But in 1956 a dozen or more Democrats were mentioned more or less seriously for the number two spot, and there was even one formally announced candidate, plus a number of others who would admit

[57] *Ibid.*, Aug. 2 and 3, 1956.

willingness. The formal announcement was made on July 30 by Senator Humphrey of Minnesota, but his availability had been discussed for some time before. Also available, and with campaigns being waged for them by intimates, were Mayor Wagner of New York City and Senator Kennedy of Massachusetts. Talk of Senator Kefauver cropped up after his loss in the California primary had convinced others, if not himself, that he could not win the top place. After his withdrawal from the presidential race, some of his supporters immediately switched to promotion of his vice-presidential prospects; and the Senator himself ceased to say, as he had during July, that he was giving no thought to such a possibility.

Some of the other names that were discussed from time to time were those of: Senator Albert Gore of Tennessee; Governor Frank G. Clement of Tennessee, eventually chosen as keynoter for the convention; Senator Stuart Symington of Missouri; Senator Lyndon Johnson of Texas; and Senator John J. Sparkman of Alabama, Stevenson's 1952 running mate. The assets and liabilities of each possible candidate were explored: Some were too conservative for the North; some were too liberal for the South; some would appeal to urban populations, others to the farm vote; some were more favored by labor; some were Catholics and perhaps vulnerable on that account; some were too young; and one had suffered a heart attack. This discussion was coupled with full consideration of what kind of man could help the ticket most, with special attention to the fact that in the election campaign to come he would almost certainly be matched against Richard Nixon.

3

Republican Preconvention Activities

NORMALLY THE PARTY IN POWER, with an incumbent President eligible for renomination, has little drama in the preconvention period, as compared with the party out of power. There is some interest in whether the President will accept or decline another nomination; but no overt candidates in opposition appear unless he declines, and such refusals have been relatively rare. If he accepts, all that remains is to hold the convention; even the writing of the platform is unlikely to stir dissension.

Thus the Republican situation in 1955-56 was exceptional. Not only was there the uncertainty arising out of President Eisenhower's heart attack; after his decision to run was announced on February 29, there were still other unusual episodes to engage public attention. First there was a period of indecision from February to late April during which Eisenhower refused to make wholly clear his attitude toward Richard M. Nixon as vicepresidential candidate. This was incompletely resolved but terminated by Nixon's announcement in late April that he would be "honored" to be chosen again. Then followed some six weeks of quiescence. After the President was stricken with ileitis in June, there was a month of new uncertainty until he reconfirmed his intention. Paralleling these later phases ran the abortive effort of Harold E. Stassen to "dump" Nixon, which continued up to the convention itself. The whole period was dominated by the dogged determination of National Chairman Leonard Hall, with assistance to be sure, that the eventual nominees of the Republican National Convention in August 1956 would be Dwight D. Eisenhower and Richard M. Nixon.

With this determination fixed, it was only logical to plan for a convention in which the party rally function would overshadow the choice of candidates and the regulation of party organization and rules. Choice of city, length of convention, divisions of program into speeches, business, parades, and entertainment—these emerged as unusually important.

As to choice of city, it seemed obvious that a pleasant place, offering amenities sufficient to outweigh delegate boredom, was needed. Some counsel suggested Atlantic City, but early probings indicated that the East Coast spot, offering convention halls seating up to 40,000 as well as sea breezes, would be available only in June or in September. This ruled it out on grounds of party strategy. Other cities were brought forward—Chicago prominently on the ground of its central location, its ample facilities, and the conveniences it offered to mass media; San Francisco for its climate and comforts.

There was opposition from both political and media managers to the selection of San Francisco. Some political managers objected on the grounds of distance and expense, suggesting that delegates might not be able to afford a long trip. The media managers argued against a decision that imposed a heavy logistical burden on them, with additional financial outlays as well. But the issue had been in effect settled early in 1955 when the President acceded to a proposal by Harry Collier, a California oil executive, to come to San Francisco. After that, specific arrangements were worked out by Robert Humphreys of the Republican National Committee.

With little business to perform, the Republican managers wanted a convention as short as possible, but one that would satisfy the business men and hotel operators of the host city, and that would provide adequate spacing of the important speeches and events. The business men wanted five days if they could get it. Media requirements almost dictated a convention of at least four days, one each for the keynote speech, for the permanent chairman's speech, for the nomination speeches and the balloting, and for the acceptance speeches and party rituals. Since a major objective was Class A television and radio time, a plausible answer emerged early: a four-day convention running for a limited number of hours per day. Once this broad point had been settled, the Republicans brought on advertising agencies and co-partisans in the world of show business to marshal the talent and to arrange the details for supporting ceremony.

Assumption by the party managers that the Vice President would be renominated did not abolish uncertainty. Two key uncertainties remained: What was the attitude of the President, who wished not to foreclose the democratic procedures of the party as he conceived them? What was the attitude of Nixon, troubled by the President's unwillingness to give him full blessing?

Nixon Decides to Run

Nixon's possible candidacy had been a subject of inquiry by reporters even before Eisenhower came to a decision. But once the President had given his affirmative answer, the secondary question was of even more interest than before.

The very fact that there was interest in the vice-presidential choice was extraordinary. Two factors were involved: the nature of Richard Nixon, and the unusual circumstances of Eisenhower's candidacy. The President's age and state of health and his frankness about his physical condition caused exceptional attention to the possibility of a vice-presidential succession to the top office. Nixon himself had made enemies in both parties: Liberal Republicans regarded him as a right-winger chosen originally to appease the Taft wing of the party; some Taft Republicans felt he had gone too far toward embracing Eisenhower's Modern Republicanism; Democrats were outraged by his attacks on their party, particularly his charges of softness on communism. Thus many were alarmed by the prospect of his accession to the Presidency, as they had been during the fall of 1955 by the prospect of his being the leading candidate for the Republican presidential nomination.

Indeed, well before the President's heart attack, strong sentiment had developed against a second term for Nixon as Vice

President. Suggestions were heard that in 1956 he ought to be replaced by someone like Governor Christian A. Herter of Massachusetts who could better preserve the President's liberal coalition. Some Republicans and independent commentators felt that if in the 1956 campaign Nixon repeated the role he had played in 1954, he would alienate independent voters and pro-Eisenhower Democrats, losing votes for his party. Even if Eisenhower could again carry his original winning coalition, one had to think of 1960 when the twenty-second amendment, operative for the first time, would make him ineligible.

In the period of uncertainty following the President's heart attack, the thought that Nixon had the inside track for the Republican presidential nomination shook many Republicans and horrified or gratified many Democrats and independents. Alternative candidates were diligently sought—or volunteered themselves—and their availability demonstrated. As the weeks wore on and the possibility of an Eisenhower candidacy regained real substance, Nixon was still opposed, but once again as a vice-presidential candidate—the more now because the state of Eisenhower's health would center attention on the second office, where the wrong name would hurt the ticket. The search for other candidates continued, and there was discussion whether Nixon could be transferred to a Cabinet position for a second Eisenhower administration or even before the party convention in August.

However, the Vice President also had influential supporters in his party, chiefly among the conservatives and the organization men; to drop him would threaten party unity, weakening the ticket in a different way. It might also cause the public to question the likelihood of Eisenhower's completing a second term. There were, in short, political risks in either course.

President Eisenhower's visible role during the whole affair was extremely equivocal. Correspondents attempted at several press conferences to elicit a statement regarding whether he would like to have Nixon as his running mate again. The President voiced his "admiration, respect, and deep appreciation" for the Vice President, called him a "loyal and dedicated associate," and said there had never been "a Vice President so well-versed in the activities of government." But he took refuge in the technicality that he would have to see whom the Republican convention nominated for President before it would be appropriate to talk of vice-presidential possibilities. After the "dump Nixon" movement came into the open, the President on March 7 told his press conference:

> . . . I will promise you this much: if anyone ever has the effrontery to come in and urge me to dump somebody that I respect as I do Vice President Nixon, there will be more commotion around my office than you have noticed yet.
>
> . . . I have not presumed to tell the Vice President what he should do with his own future.
>
> I have told him this: I believe he should be one of the comers in the Republican party. He is young, vigorous, healthy and certainly deeply informed on the processes of our Government. And so far as I know, he is deeply dedicated to the same principles of Government that I am.
>
> The only thing I have asked him to do is to chart out his own course and tell me what he would like to do. I have never gone beyond that.

Asked if the suggestion to chart his own course implied that Eisenhower would be content to have Nixon as his running mate, the President responded:

> Well, I am not going to be pushed into corners here and say—and right now, at this moment—say what I would do in a hypothetical question involving about five ifs. And I don't think you should expect me to.
>
> I do say this: I have no criticism of Vice President Nixon to make, either as a man, associate or as my running mate on the ticket.[1]

It looked as if a typical decision was in the making—to persuade Nixon to take Cabinet office and to improve his chances of advancement, and at the same time to accede to those around the President who were pressing hard to have Nixon removed from the line of succession, the sooner the better. Mazo reports that this period was an especially difficult one for Nixon, who nearly elected to leave public life after the President suggested he "chart his own course."[2]

From this situation the Vice President was rescued on March 13 by the New Hampshire presidential primary—the first of 1956. This was the state where four years earlier Eisenhower's victory

---

[1] *New York Times*, Mar. 8, 1956.
[2] Earl Mazo, *Richard Nixon: A Political and Personal Portrait* (1959), pp. 163-66.

over Senator Taft had started the General on the road to the Presidency. This time only Eisenhower's name was printed on the Republican ballot as a presidential candidate; he received 56,000 votes, with a few scattered write-ins for others. No names were printed for vice-presidential candidates, but Nixon received 22,000 write-in votes—to the astonishment of nearly everyone, except perhaps Senator Styles Bridges. At the presidential press conference on the day after the primary, President Eisenhower was prepared; he told his listeners that apparently there were

> . . . a lot of people in New Hampshire who agree with what I have told you about Dick Nixon. . . . I am going to say one thing more about it and then . . . I will never answer another question on the subject until after August. . . . I am very happy that Dick Nixon is my friend. I am very happy to have him as an associate in Government. I would be very happy to be on any political ticket in which I was a candidate with him.[3]

Although none of this constituted a definite commitment, as of mid-March Nixon seemed to hold a lead for the vice-presidential nomination that would be difficult for anyone else to overcome. While some Taft followers had talked of Senator Knowland for the nomination, the only real effort at a boom had been for Governor Herter, and this had made no particular headway except in his own state.

Nixon himself was obviously encouraged by the turn of events. For the time being, he made no overt moves. However, his office was busily checking offers of support made by state Republican leaders in person, by phone, or by letter during this time of ordeal; and reportedly his staff concluded that Nixon "will win the second-term nomination with ease . . . unless President Eisenhower indicates a preference for another running mate."[4] Despite the President's reluctance to endorse Nixon outright, Eisenhower's repeated expressions of admiration for his Vice President made it less and less likely that he would be replaced on the ticket.

On April 25 a reporter asked the President if the Vice President

[3] *New York Times*, Mar. 15, 1956.

[4] Earl Mazo, "Nixon Sees Demand for His Return," New York Herald Tribune News Service, *Washington Post and Times Herald*, Apr. 26, 1956.

had charted his course and reported back. Eisenhower responded that Nixon had not reported back "in the terms in which I used the expression that morning." Pressed as to whether Nixon "had replied in any manner which gives to you an impression as to whether he would like to be renominated," the President refused to be drawn into talking about impressions "for the simple reason that a fellow can get those rather erroneously at times. . . . I would say this: He hasn't given me any authority to quote him, any answer that I would consider final and definitive."[5]

The next day after lunch the Vice President visited the White House. After talking with the President for half an hour, he spoke to newsmen who had been summoned by Press Secretary Hagerty. "I informed the President that in the event the President and the delegates to the convention reach the decision that it is in the best interest of the Republican party and his Administration for me to continue in my present office that I would be honored to accept that nomination again as I was and as I did in 1952."[6] Here Hagerty interjected: "The President has asked me to tell you gentlemen that he was delighted to hear of the Vice President's decision."

Uncertainty Again

With this announcement, the question of the Republican nominees appeared to have been settled as foreordained by Leonard Hall; and if any discontent remained with the man for second place, it had gone underground. Six weeks of comparative quiet on the Republican front ensued. President Eisenhower, speaking to a conference of the National Citizens for Eisenhower, told them that "the only way I know [I have been ill] is because the doctors keep reminding me of it."[7] But a week later he was stricken

[5] *New York Times,* Apr. 26, 1956.
[6] *Ibid.,* Apr. 27, 1956. This text is quoted as "in a statement filmed for later television broadcasts."
[7] *Ibid.,* June 1, 1956.

for the second time in less than a year. This time it was ileitis, necessitating a two-hour operation in the early morning of June 9.

Naturally there was speculation whether such a major operation might induce the President to reconsider his decision to run again. But his associates and managers refused to permit such thoughts to gain credence. Almost before the patient had regained consciousness, the operating surgeon, Major General Leonard D. Heaton, speaking for himself and for the whole operating team, was telling a press conference that there was no reason why this occurrence should affect the President's intentions; he should be able to return to his full White House duties in four to six weeks, with his life expectancy actually improved. And with this authoritative medical opinion as a basis, the Republican strategists refused to concede any need for second thoughts. Chairman Hall, in Chicago for a meeting of the Republican committee on convention arrangements two weeks after the President's operation, told newsmen: "You can paste the names of Eisenhower and Nixon in your hats. That will be the ticket. . . . Len Hall is speaking."[8] And Press Secretary Hagerty asserted, "I haven't seen anything rescinded."[9]

It was not surprising that the politicians preferred to foreclose any talk of reconsidering their presidential candidate at so late a date. The last presidential primaries had been held on June 5, and most of the convention delegates chosen by other procedures had also been selected. Of the twenty Republican primaries Eisenhower or an Eisenhower slate of delegates had won fourteen; delegates favorable to the President had won three in which no candidate names had appeared on the ballot; a "stand-in" for Eisenhower had captured one. In West Virginia there were no entries and no delegate contest based on presidential preferences. Senator John W. Bricker, unopposed, had won the Ohio primary— the only race captured by any Republican not wholeheartedly in the President's camp.

Again there was a carefully staged drama of convalescence at

[8] *Ibid.*, June 24, 1956.
[9] *Washington Post and Times Herald*, July 4, 1956.

Gettysburg and revelation of the President's plans. But this time the script called for underemphasis and, as one paper put it, "calculated nonchalance."[10] The impression was conveyed that Eisenhower had never needed to reconsider his decision; he had only to go through a normal period of postoperative recuperation and resume life as before. This was no testing period. On July 6 James Hagerty with a wide grin let reporters know that the President had "talked politics" both with him in person and with Sherman Adams back at the White House by telephone. Hagerty continued to grin at his meetings with the press for the next several days. Then, on the tenth, Eisenhower met Republican congressional leaders to discuss end-of-the-session legislative matters, and during the meeting casually remarked, "Well, I intend to take up these issues in our campaign this fall." When Senator Knowland took notice of the "our," the President replied matter-of-factly: "Why shouldn't I run? Last February 29 I reviewed all the reasons pro and con. . . . I am in better condition today than I was then. I have had a condition that has bothered me from time to time for years and my doctors say that I am better than I have ever been." After the President had left the gathering, the legislative leaders talked with the press, Senator Knowland serving as spokesman. Eventually a reporter asked, "Was there any discussion of the President running again?" The Senator answered: "Yes, there was. . . . He and we are looking forward to a vigorous active campaign under his leadership."

"Are you telling us," rejoined the reporter, "that the President told you he would keep his hat in the ring?"

"I'm telling you precisely that," replied Knowland.[11]

Stassen Rocks the Boat

While the President was recuperating, his disarmament adviser, Harold E. Stassen, was preparing a bombshell: nothing less than

[10] *New York Times*, July 11, 1956.
[11] *Ibid.*, July 11; July 15.

a proposal to replace Nixon as vice-presidential nominee with Governor Christian A. Herter of Massachusetts, announced by Stassen at a press conference on July 23.[12] Action had been precipitated by a call to Herter on July 13 from Hagerty, Hall, and Nixon, inviting the Governor to nominate Nixon for the vice-presidential candidacy. Herter had asked for time to think things over. Stassen learned of the call on the same day, and made his own proposal to Herter on the fifteenth; Herter promised not to answer the other three until Stassen had had a chance to talk to the President. This Stassen was able to do on the twentieth, as Eisenhower was preparing to leave for a meeting of Inter-American Chiefs of State at Panama.

Eisenhower gave Stassen to understand that he liked Nixon, but that he had closed no doors on the vice-presidential nomination and that he could not dictate to a convention that had not yet renominated him for President. Stassen took this as a green light, and told his associates that the President was for an open convention—managing to convey an added impression that Eisenhower wished to be something more than politically correct. Stassen called Herter, telling him the President had appeared interested in his analysis of the electoral situation and had interposed no objection to his communicating the results to Nixon and Hall.

Stassen tried to reach Nixon on the twentieth but was put off until the twenty-third—when Nixon suggested a further postponement, only to receive by messenger a note informing him of Stassen's now-or-never decision to do what he could to nominate Herter at the forthcoming convention.

Stassen took his first public steps in the affair with his press conference on July 23. He assigned two reasons for his advocacy

[12] Mazo, on whom the following account is based in part, says that Stassen himself does not know when he finally decided to undertake this enterprise. Returning on May 6 from a mission to London, he was dismayed to find the somewhat promising anti-Nixon movement, growing when he left, dwindling on his return for lack of leadership. Fearing to confront the President directly with suggestions to drop Nixon, Stassen conferred with a diminishing group of advisers and laid the groundwork of poll-taking for his case against Nixon. Mazo, *Richard Nixon*, pp. 169 ff.

of Herter, though only the first figured prominently from that time forward.

1. An Eisenhower-Herter ticket will run at least 6 per cent stronger than an Eisenhower-Nixon ticket. This difference is certain to reflect decisively in a number of senatorial and House seats, and may well be the margin of majority or minority in the Congress. Under some circumstances this difference may even be very important in the Presidential election itself. . . .

2. The independent people at home, important portions of the population abroad, and the uncommitted nations in the world, would have greater confidence in an Eisenhower-Herter ticket. . . .[13]

He expressed confidence that President Eisenhower would be pleased to have Herter with him on the ticket and suggested that "in a matter of this importance and this nature, it is tremendously important that the precise position of the President should be communicated only by the President. That is . . . it should not be interpreted from statements that Leonard Hall makes or that I make or that others may make." He said he had arrived at the 6 per cent figure "primarily from a Gallup poll and then cross-checked by some private polls I have made in order to verify it"; these had been taken over the last four weeks and had been financed by "a small group," none of whom he could identify "at the present time."[14]

At least two eminent newspapermen appeared to find some substance in the Stassen effort. James Reston, chief Washington correspondent of the *New York Times*, wrote:

It was generally believed by well-informed Republican politicians in the capital that while Mr. Stassen was not acting at the instigation of the President, he at least had the President's acquiescence in the move for Mr. Herter.

This reporter has personal knowledge that if the President had told Mr. Stassen that he was determined to have Mr. Nixon on the ticket, or even that a public move on behalf of Governor Herter would embarrass the President, today's announcement would not have been made.[15]

[13] *New York Times,* July 24, 1956.
[14] *Ibid.*
[15] *Ibid.*

Arthur Krock of the same paper expressed a still more definite conclusion:

> ... There was something in Stassen's words and manner today that fostered the impression he expects the President to make some comment on the Herter movement that will put it in high gear ... in effect he could encourage it merely by repeating his former statement ... that the choice of a Vice Presidential nominee was up to the convention.[16]

Naturally the Stassen announcement evoked immediate public reaction from the various principals involved.

James Hagerty issued a statement at Panama. The press secretary confirmed that Stassen had consulted with the President in advance, and that the President had told his disarmament adviser he could make any statement he desired as an individual but that it was "obvious that he could not make such a statement as a member of the President's official family."[17]

Vice President Nixon expressed himself as "happy to abide by any decision the President and the delegates to the national convention make," and said he would give a Herter candidacy "my full support" if the convention selected the Governor as "the man who could contribute the most to the re-election of President Eisenhower and the continued success of the Eisenhower Administration."[18]

Governor Herter declared himself completely astounded by Stassen's move. He took the position that "the decisive factor to be considered in nominating a vice-presidential candidate is the wish of the President." Asked what he would do if the President indicated approval of a contest, the Governor replied: "I'd do anything the President asked me to. I've said that before."[19]

---

[16] *Ibid.* As a matter of fact, the President did make such a statement at his press conference on August 1, but by that time the steam had already gone out of the anti-Nixon movement.

[17] *Ibid.*

[18] *Ibid.*

[19] *Washington Post and Times Herald*, July 24, 1956; *Evening Star* (Washington, D.C.), July 24. Mazo, quoting a Herter memorandum, says that Herter had no direct communication with Stassen between July 20 and August 22, when Eisenhower announced Stassen's capitulation; *Richard Nixon*, p. 172. He also reports earlier efforts by a New Yorker, Arthur J. Goldsmith, to promote Herter as a political

Leonard Hall also issued an immediate statement, concluding: "My own prediction is that the ticket will again be Eisenhower and Nixon."[20] These were no idle words, since Hall had Herter's promise to answer on the following day his invitation to nominate Nixon. And when Hall produced his card, it was a high trump: Herter had told him, the National Chairman announced triumphantly, that it would be "a privilege to nominate Dick Nixon at the Republican National Convention."[21]

This appeared to end the Herter boom. James Reston wrote that "the general feeling here [Washington] was that Mr. Stassen's campaign, instead of rallying support for Governor Herter, had helped Mr. Nixon, and opened up an even wider breach between Mr. Stassen and powerful members of the Republican political organization."[22]

Stassen explained, however, that Herter had been obliged to accept Hall's invitation because he was not actually a candidate, and that the incident had confirmed Herter's ability to unite the party as a vice-presidential nominee. Nevertheless, the next day Stassen offered to abandon his campaign if President Eisenhower personally expressed a preference for having Nixon on the ticket.

In order to devote himself to his project, Stassen finally requested the President to grant him a four-week leave of absence without pay. This was granted, emphasizing the private, unofficial nature of the campaign. Stassen immediately opened a formal headquarters and set about promoting his candidate. But a strong tide was running against him. His backers failed to come forward as he had apparently expected; instead, many Republicans of all factions expressed either staunch support for Nixon or sentiments adverse to Stassen's campaign.

With this support for Nixon, Chairman Hall by July 31 could safely issue a statement advocating "an open convention" and

candidate in the fall of 1955, with Herter's tacit consent, but without certainty regarding whether it was the Presidency or Vice Presidency he had in view. *Ibid.*, p. 162.

[20] *Evening Star* (Washington, D.C.), July 24, 1956.

[21] *New York Times*, July 25, 1956.

[22] *Ibid.*

supporting "the right of any delegate to nominate whomever he wishes." He closed with an expression of assurance that the convention would "come to a wise decision so that we can proceed with the fundamental business of electing a Republican Administration and a Republican Congress, which is what I am interested in."[23]

This was undoubtedly true. As National Chairman, Hall was confronted with the task of winning an election. Eisenhower and Nixon had formed a victorious combination in 1952; why break up a winning team? They had carried a Republican Congress into office with them, even though by a narrow margin in each house. To be sure, the Democrats had won the 1954 congressional elections, but again the margins were narrow, and the magical Eisenhower name had not been on the ballot. In 1956 the Republicans would have the advantage of that name again, plus prosperity and if not peace, at least no active hostilities involving American soldiers in their many widespread posts. To dump Nixon would sow dissension in the party, jeopardizing its chances. And perhaps Hall thought that Nixon would make the best possible successor in the event of presidential disability.

Not until August 1, when these events had already taken place, did Eisenhower meet the press for the first time since his operation. His comments on Nixon seemed equivocal and lukewarm. He thought "there should be no doubt about my satisfaction with him as a running mate," but he insisted that he upheld "the right of the delegates to the convention to nominate whom they choose." Asked if he thought Nixon would detract from the strength of the Republican ticket, he replied: "Well, I don't know. . . . He certainly didn't seem to in 1952." When a correspondent pointed out that the President's failure to comment on other vice-presidential candidates made it "inevitable that we should conclude that Mr. Nixon is your preference," Eisenhower responded: "Well, you have a right to conclude what you please. But I have said that I would not express a preference. . . . He is perfectly acceptable to me, as he was in 1952. But I am not going beyond that because in 1952 I also put down a few others that

[23] *Ibid.*, Aug. 1, 1956.

were equally acceptable to me." To a query whether he would be equally pleased with "some other well-qualified Republican," he replied, "I am not going into comparisons at all," and steadfastly refused to comment on any other possibilities. Thus, although the President declined to give an unqualified endorsement to his Vice President, he would not comment on any other individual than the incumbent.[24] Since it appeared that only an Eisenhower preference for another candidate, openly stated, would prevent the nomination of Nixon by the convention, the kind of endorsement he did give the Vice President was sufficient.

The anti-Nixon campaign for all practical purposes collapsed at this moment, although Stassen carried on for nearly three weeks longer, down to the opening of the convention. Leonard Hall had attained his objective.

[24] *Ibid.*, Aug. 2, 1956.

4

The Democratic Platform Hearings

QUADRENNIAL CONVENTIONS of the political parties traditionally serve four functions. They nominate the party's candidates for President and for Vice President. They adopt a platform, setting forth the party's position on most of the relevant and on some of the irrelevant political issues of the day. They adopt rules for the governance of the party during the next four years and provide for its organization and staffing. Finally, the conventions create the setting for an enormous rally. Thus they offer the major occasion on which the party shows itself to itself and to the world. In today's world of mass communications, this public view of the party is more prevalent, if not more important, than ever before. In these later years when conventions have come close to the final frenetic stages of campaigning, the rally function is of especial importance in creating confidence in victory and thus motivating strenuous efforts culminating on election day.

Conventions do more. They provide for an intermeshing of the forces of issue, candidate, and faction that not only largely determine the stance of the party during the immediate campaign, but also do much to shape the structure of the party in the years to follow. Fights and their outcomes in the national committee, in the credentials committee, or in the convention itself provide testing grounds for factional vitality and candidate strength. These struggles have consequences for the power structure of state parties. Changes in rules similarly affect the prospects and influence of state organizations and factions. They may alter the balance of regional power within the convention and thus within the party itself. Seemingly innocuous semantics in the platform process may be of great significance in the interplay between regional elements as well as in activating support from particular political groups.

Weaving their way throughout these decisional processes work the candidates, who conduct interpersonal and organizational struggles by attempts to shape decisions about seating, rules, and issues.

Conventions vary in their tone, temper, and specific operations depending on whether they are held by an out-party or an in-party. The out-party usually has greater freedom of action, and enjoys the opportunity to attack. It is usually more open to factionalism. The in-party is restricted by the need to defend its record in office, and its choice of candidate is small or nonexistent if an incumbent wishes to run again, or elects to play an influential role in determining his successor. Even the twenty-second amendment does not wholly alter this situation.

Recently observers have predicted a declining importance for conventions, on the ground that their nominating function is increasingly restricted to the ratification of a choice already made by nationwide agencies of public communication operating on the organs of public opinion.[1] Both the ground for this conclusion and the conclusion itself are arguable on present evidence. Even if it is true in some cases, conventions will remain important for choosing among national favorites where no one has achieved a commanding position at the time of the convention. The remaining functions relating to organization, issues, and campaigning remain as vital as ever. Even a party running an odds-on, routinely ratified candidate needs a convention as an instrument for projecting issue orientation and perfecting party organization and morale. A convention is necessarily much of the life of a national party.

In 1956 both conventions furnished innovations. The Democrats staged a free-for-all in choosing their vice-presidential candidate.

---

[1] See, for example, William G. Carleton, "The Revolution in the Presidential Nominating Convention," *Political Science Quarterly*, Vol. 72 (June 1957), pp. 224-40.

The Republicans produced a convention in which the choice for Vice President was as powerfully sanctioned as that of the incumbent President himself.

The Democrats had to choose among competing candidates, and decide how to deal with civil rights. The Republicans, ratifying a preordained choice of nominees, also had to make a choice on civil rights that might profoundly affect the future of the party. Both parties maximized—each in its own fashion—the rally functions of their conclaves. Both took pains to project a presumably attractive image to the electorate through the mass media, although the specifications for attractiveness varied from lusty infighting in the one convention to smooth decorum and pleasant entertainment in the other.

Setting on the Eve

As the Democrats started to assemble in early August, Stevenson had a solid advantage in committed delegates; his strength had been growing, but he was short of a majority. There was doubt in many minds about what the Kefauver delegates would do. The Stevenson forces strove to hold them to Kefauver's instructions, while the other candidates sought their favor. Mr. Harriman was well behind in his belated overt drive for the nomination. Several Southern and Midwestern politicians entertained hopes of being nominated after a deadlock. Uncommitted and favorite-son delegations held the balance of power. Therefore a major order of business was to woo them and win them if possible before the opening ballot.

Commentators noted that at no time since the adoption of the twelfth amendment to the Constitution had there been such a concerted drive in both parties for the vice-presidential nomination,[2] although there was only one avowed and active candidate for the Democratic vice-presidential nomination—Senator Hubert

[2] *Washington Post and Times Herald*, Aug. 2, 1956; *New York Times*, Aug. 2, 1956.

Humphrey of Minnesota. Others were "available," with Senators John F. Kennedy and Albert Gore, and Mayor Robert F. Wagner of New York prominent among them. Kefauver was not revealing his vice-presidential intentions, whatever his private expectations or arrangements with the Stevenson camp. Nevertheless, some of his supporters had come out openly for a Stevenson-Kefauver ticket.

Among controversial issues, civil rights was at the forefront of attention. Southern leaders caucused on August 1 in Atlanta and set their plans to gain an "acceptable" civil rights plank and to provide for interdelegation liaison during the platform hearings and the convention. At the same time, Governor Marvin Griffin of Georgia made it clear that although the Southern leadership planned no bolt, it would exercise maximum leverage on the platform from within the party. In his view the platform came before the candidate.

In the North, Harriman forces continued their drive toward an uncompromising statement of principles and position on issues, despite the failure of an attempt to get Senator Kefauver to make a statement jointly with Governor Harriman that would help prevent the party from being "drowned in a conservative platform."[3]

The Democratic National Committee, speaking through its Chairman Paul Butler, strove for party unity, especially on the rights plank. Butler forecast quick decisions both on the platform and on the national nominee for President, looking for a decision on the candidate in five ballots or less. He predicted there would be no fight on the civil rights issue on the convention floor. And he concluded that the party would emerge from the convention stronger than at its beginning.[4]

On August 5 Roy Wilkins of the National Association for the Advancement of Colored People and chairman of the Leadership

---

[3] Richard P. Hunt, "Anti-Moderates Fail in Coalition," *New York Times,* Aug. 2, 1956. Hunt says George Backer released the text of the proposed joint statement, and the accompanying story, to counter suggestions that Harriman had offered Kefauver "almost everything" to gain his support. Backer said that Kefauver's withdrawal did not relieve his delegates of their "obligation" to support liberal principles.

[4] *New York Times,* Aug. 6, 1956.

Conference on Civil Rights, released a proposed six-point plank on civil rights sponsored by thirty organizations, to be urged on delegates at both party conventions. This program called for the use of federal powers to secure the quickest possible elimination of all forms of state-imposed segregation, the ending of interference with the right to register and vote in state primaries, the abolition of the poll tax, and the creation of a Federal Fair Employment Practices Commission. It also drove at Senate Rule XXII governing the filibuster, and urged that Congress choose committee chairmen on the basis of "merit and party responsibility" rather than seniority.[5]

The Stevenson forces were displaying a hands-off attitude toward the platform, and it was reported that Stevenson might, if nominated, leave the choice of the vice-presidential candidate open.

In the week before the convention, the candidate of moderation seemed to be pulling out in front, as an AP check of pledged votes and first-ballot preferences reported on August 3 that Stevenson had gained 22½ votes since the Kefauver withdrawal, while Harriman had gained only 3½.[6]

Scheduled to open officially on August 13, the convention really swung into action a full week earlier. Preparations at the International Amphitheatre moved ahead as advance elements of the Democratic National Committee and of the various candidate and delegation headquarters moved into their Loop hotels. Main downtown activity centered, as in 1952, on the Conrad Hilton and Sheraton-Blackstone hotels. Radio and television and the printed press set up communications facilities of unprecedented dimensions.

On August 6 the 108-member Committee on Platform and Resolutions commenced a full week of hearings in preparation for

[5] *New York Herald Tribune,* Aug. 6, 1956.

[6] *Washington Post and Times Herald,* Aug. 3, 1956. The full AP tally there reported was: Stevenson, 457; Harriman, 163½; Others, 347; Unknown, 404½. Stevenson's gains came in Illinois (10½) and in Indiana (12); Harriman's in Indiana (3) and Iowa (½). Two days later, Loyd Benefield claimed 341 first-ballot votes for Harriman, while Stevenson backers claimed 600 for their man.

its final drafting and report to the convention, planned for Wednesday, August 15.[7]

This innovation in convention management offered several opportunities for political gain. It provided a forum for the highlighting of Democratic positions on major issues; it allowed representatives of national organizations, pressure groups, nationalities, and minorities to express themselves before a large conclave of Democrats with some hope of notice in the nation's mass media; it provided a stage on which Democratic notables could parade personality as well as issue. The hearings as well as the deliberations of the platform committee offered an arena in which the competing emphasis of contending candidates and factions could be tested. Within this arena the Democratic National Committee's advisory committees on labor, agriculture, natural resources, and foreign affairs could also undergo public and press inspection.

The general design of procedure was for the platform committee to devote each day to one or more major topics; to hear a major Democratic spokesman on each topic, who would outline main elements desirable in a party position, and who would present the findings of the pertinent Democratic advisory committee

[7] Strictly speaking, the platform committee was meeting by sufferance, on invitation of the National Committee. Normal procedure called for the committee to be formed by a special roll call on the first day of the convention. (See *Democratic Manual* for the Democratic National Convention, by Clarence Cannon, 1956, pp. 23, 25.) At this time, each state delegation, after caucus, was to announce the names of two delegates to serve as its representatives on the Committee on Platform and Resolutions. The procedure followed in 1956 took place under recommendation from the Democratic National Committee, and that body also recommended to the convention a change in the rules that would authorize the Democratic National Committee to call on state delegations to make their nominations for membership on the committees on permanent organization, rules, credentials, and platform at least seven days before the start of the convention; such committees to meet on call of the chairman of the National Committee. (The rule was adopted, as noted below, p. 144.)

Several members of the platform committee were serving on an interim basis, because they had not been formally nominated by their state caucuses. (In no case was there any repudiation of the work of any such representative who formally served.) Such interim participants represented Kansas, Massachusetts, Minnesota, Missouri, New York, Texas, and West Virginia. Democratic National Convention, Committee on Resolutions and Platform, Press Release, Aug. 9, 1956, 4 pp. mimeo.

if there was one; to hear witnesses presenting the positions or views of special groups; to interrogate witnesses, so as to highlight the position toward which the committee was trending; and to present the appearance of a body willing to listen and to take testimony before setting forth a draft of the platform to be presented to the convention.

Most witnesses played to known powerful general tendencies expressing consensus within the Democratic party—with the exception of civil rights, in which the great preponderance of testimony and argument supported the Northern liberal integrationist view. Here there was no real possibility of bridging divergence. Representatives of such organizations as the Chamber of Commerce of the United States and the National Association of Manufacturers· received a cold and critical hearing. But only two witnesses were roughly handled—one who brought religion too sharply into controversy, and another, a Jew who spoke against Zionism and for rapprochement with the Arab world.

Party notables—especially Mr. Truman—were given full honors. Party aspirants for lesser national and state office were spotlighted. Candidates for presidential nomination were conspicuously absent. Some vice-presidential hopefuls ventured appearances. Witnesses for Americans for Democratic Action got prominence on every day except Monday and Saturday. Witnesses representing labor unions also got red-carpet treatment, although their appearances were deliberately scaled low.

Most witnesses read or spoke from a prepared statement. As each witness testified, copies of his statement were distributed to members of the committee and to the press. A stenographic record was made of the entire proceedings.

Spokesmen on Agriculture

The full committee met in executive session on Monday morning, August 6, and emerged into public view that afternoon with a session on agriculture. First and most important witness was

Claude Wickard, former Secretary of Agriculture, chairman of the Democratic Advisory Committee on Agriculture, and candidate for the Senate from Indiana. Wickard put the extreme liberal position, both in its indictment of the administration's record and in its demands for 100 per cent parity for the farmer based on mandatory 90 per cent parity support prices. No committee member spoke out against this position, although a few of the more rabid among them attacked it as too weak. Following Wickard came a more controversial witness, the president of the Farm Bureau; committee members promptly attacked not only his views but also his position as a representative of all farmers. Words from the master of the National Grange proved more palatable, but most committee members relished even more the testimony of witnesses for the National Farmers Union. One of these, however, warned the committee that the farmer was neither a Democrat nor a Republican. "He will cast his vote in the interest of his economic survival and he will be difficult to fool."

During its first evening session, the committee turned to problems of cooperatives in agriculture, heard from a Harriman witness, listened to a representative of Democrats from abroad, accepted for the record a statement from Americans for Democratic Action, and paraded the party's treasurer, Matthew Mc-Closkey. The only controversy arose over a recommendation from the American Bar Association for nonpartisan choice of Federal judges. This prompted the unabashed partisans present to ask what was wrong with the appointment by Democrats of men who would support a Democratic philosophy in judicial office. The daily ADA statement deplored gerrymandering, and the daily Harriman witness deplored a me-too platform.

Foreign Policy

On Tuesday morning, the agenda called for foreign policy, but first the committee finished with agriculture, and listened to some complaints over tax favoritism for farm cooperatives. The committee also gave short, gruff hearing to a spokesman for the second Hoover Commission. Afterward, the bulk of its time went to problems of immigration, Israeli versus Arabs, recognition of Red China, liberation of Communist-oppressed nationalities, and the United States overseas information and educational exchange programs.

Press reports pointed out that the real discussion of the foreign policy plank was going on outside of the committee. An authoritative "draft plank" had been leaked out; and only one Democrat of any prominence came before the platform committee to deal specifically with foreign policy at this stage. The immediate function of the platform committee was to give hospitable hearing to friendly nationality groups, and to take testimony with equal courtesy from spokesmen for organizations devoted to world government, to the United Nations, to the nonrecognition of Red China, and to Fortress America.[8]

The most notable testimony was that of Senator William Benton of Connecticut. Fresh from a trip to the Soviet Union, he proposed a more liberal immigration policy, a more vigorous program of overseas information and cultural exchange, and above all a far more vigorous role for the Federal government in the field of education in the face of the Soviet challenge. The problem posed for the platform committee was how to deal with this last proposal without irritating entrenched educationists. They did so by asserting that the needed scholarships or other assistance were justified as "solely in the interest of necessary and adequate national defense."[9]

A brief flurry arose over candidate relationship to the platform process as a Harriman supporter on the committee questioned the chairman about the truth of allegations in the morning papers that Stevenson had let the committee know what he wanted them

---

[8] Foreign policy offered opportunity for a skirmish between North and South on Civil Rights, as Alabama's Judge Wallace wanted to know why we had to alter our long-established institutions to please foreign opinion, and the District of Columbia's Belford Lawson complained of the evil effects abroad of our racial practices at home.

[9] Kirk H. Porter and Donald Bruce Johnson, *National Party Platforms, 1840-1956* (1956), pp. 525-26.

to produce on several key topics. Chairman McCormack denied the existence of any such communication. (There apparently had been one, but Chairman Butler had held it in his own office.) McCormack said he could not say whether Stevenson would testify. The committee, he said, had no power to call witnesses before it, and there had been no request by Stevenson or any of his representatives to testify.[10]

During the afternoon, the committee demonstrated patience as the representative of the Women's International League of Peace and Freedom exercised her "right of petition" in calling for recognition of Red China; the committee gave a congressional flavor to proceedings by its reception of Representative Barratt O'Hara's proposal to send our classics abroad the better to fight the cold war; and it dealt roughly with the Counsel for the National Committee for Security and Justice in the Middle East. This witness demanded (and took) more time than the committee was willing to allot him; and a reference to his Jewish faith provoked the chairman to rule that religion had no place in the hearings. McCormack tried to save appearances by pointing out that the committee had listened to the witness "in the old American way" despite his "obviously provocative intent." Most of the witnesses who followed were pro-Israel; they took occasion to extemporize their feelings about the renegade, as they put the case for more military and economic support for Israel and attacked the argument that a pro-Zionist plank would only drive Arab states behind the Iron Curtain.

Main scheduled Democratic political figure witness for the afternoon was to be Governor G. Mennen Williams, appearing as chairman of the Democratic National Committee's Nationalities Division. But Williams was detained by primaries in Michigan, and his prepared statement—notable chiefly for its judgment that ethnic groups would be more influenced than others by the content of the platform—was read by Michel Cieplinski, Executive Director of the division. The division demanded more aid (eco-

---

[10] Observation of the senior author. See also *New York Times*, Aug. 8, 1956. The article said Stevenson was calling for unequivocal endorsement of the Supreme Court decisions.

nomic as well as military) for countries abroad and more vigorous pursuit of "liberation." It charged Republicans with failure to push foreign aid and denounced alleged GOP discrimination against persons with "foreign-sounding" names—especially in the loyalty-security program. Finally it called for attention to the problems of Indians and of migratory workers. Carried away by partisan spirit, Chairman McCormack even charged Eisenhower with "extreme fraternization with the Kremlin," as Cieplinski thundered that "we have complete proof that Ukrainians, Poles, Lithuanians, and others who voted for Ike in 1952 will no more vote for him!"

Most of the evening went to further discussion of foreign policy, with emphasis on Zionism, anti-Zionism, and "liberation." The rest of it touched on freedom of government information, much to the pleasure of Representative Moss of California, then engaged in a running battle with the administration on the right of Congress and the public to know. The final fillip was a battle of small business versus cooperatives on tax exemption.

Problems of Social Welfare and Veterans

On Wednesday the platform committee of the self-styled Party with a Heart turned to the problems of social welfare and of veterans. Under the surface, however, the civil rights issue simmered threateningly. The Stevenson statement of the night before had stirred Southern delegates to frustration, anger, or worse. There was puzzlement over the apparent softening of the Harriman position. Immediately after the invocation, however, the chairman named a preliminary drafting subcommittee composed chiefly of southerners or of persons from other sections regarded by southerners as "reasonable." Only one staunch Harriman representative was on the drafting group: Representative Emanuel Celler of New York.[11]

[11] This committee consisted of the Hon. John W. McCormack, Massachusetts, Chairman; Miss Grace Hudlin, Oklahoma; Mrs. Emma Guffey Miller, Pennsylvania;

The morning's session was uneventful, although witnesses managed to link their demands for better social security measures with trepidation over the certain continuation of Republican prosperity. Spokesmen for the associations of veterans sought more adequate or more equitable benefits for their special charges. Interspersed were resolutions for the record or testimony calling for import quotas against foreign textiles (without violating the principles of reciprocal trade) and support for tax deferment for payments by self-employed persons into pension plans.

After luncheon interest picked up markedly with a major ADA-Democratic Party showpiece: the testimony of Leon Keyserling, former Chairman of the Council of Economic Advisers. Keyserling's objective was to explode the "ridiculous myth" of Eisenhower prosperity. Beside this effort, Oscar Chapman's recommendations for a national resources plank paled despite evocation of the Republican giveaways symbolized by Dixon-Yates, Al Sarena, and Hell's Canyon.[12]

Keyserling moved toward his major objective—and his equally important side objective of putting some heart into the Democratic campaign as a whole—by a sophisticated argument. Admitting the fact of prosperity, he charged the Republicans not only with failure to maintain the proper rate of national growth, but with deliberate intent in contriving restrictions of production and excesses of unemployment. Compared to the period 1947-1953, he said, per-capita farm income had gone down 3 per cent, and "avoidable unemployment" had grown 28 per cent under the Republicans. Republicans welcomed lower production and unemployment since such small recessions would promote "healthy readjustments," would eliminate the inefficient farmer

Hon. Gracie Pfost, Idaho; Hon. John S. Battle, Virginia; Hon. Emanuel Celler, New York; Governor J. P. Coleman, Mississippi; Hon. William L. Dawson, Illinois; Governor Paul Dever, Massachusetts; Hon. Sam Ervin, Jr., North Carolina; Hon. Theodore F. Green, Rhode Island; Hon. Brooks Hays, Arkansas; Vann M. Kennedy, Texas; Hon. John Moss, California; Hon. Joseph C. O'Mahoney, Wyoming; and Hon. Jennings Randolph, West Virginia.

[12] Al Sarena referred to permissions granted by the Department of Interior to private operators for the exploitation of mineral rights in national forest lands near Al Sarena in Oregon. Hell's Canyon referred to the decision sanctioned by law and long a matter of heated debate in Congress, to allow the Idaho Power Company to build a series of low dams in Hell's Canyon on the Idaho-Oregon border.

and small businessman, and would "keep labor in its place." Keyserling concluded that there *were* issues in the election, and sounded a loud clarion to the party faithful to show the differences between themselves and their opposition. He called on them to "concretize in our platform and in our campaign the almost indescribable prosperity and plenty which are within the reach of the American people, if only the policies and programs of their Government can be brought into line with the people's bountiful abilities and endless aspirations."

The Republicans, said Keyserling, had dealt the farmer "a calamitous blow." Small business was being "pounded, squeezed, and anesthetized." The progress of poor families up towards an "American standard of living had been practically stopped." And the resulting fiscal effects were being used by Republicans as excuses to neglect needs at home and abroad, while we were losing out in the economic race with Russia. Excoriating Federal budget and monetary management, Keyserling wound up with an *ad hominem* attack on the Secretary of the Treasury.

The immediate morale effects were palpable. Members of the Platform and Resolutions Committee warmed to his suggestion that they speak in concrete terms, and not in generalities, and were visibly heartened by the demonstration that a facts-and-figures case might be made against the virtual omnipresence of Republican prosperity outside of the agricultural sector. Democratic spectators, who had filled the room, shared the lift in mood. Quickened, the committee listened to the proposal of Mrs. India Edwards, Harriman supporter, for a consumer's counsel in the Federal government; and slashed away at witnesses for the National Association of Real Estate Boards for their opposition to public housing.

Wednesday evening's highlight was an impromptu performance by Senator O'Mahoney, hailing the victory won for small business by the passage of the automobile dealers' "day in court" bill. The Senator spoke as if he were on the floor of the Senate; other congressmen present played to his cue. For the rest of the evening, there was a mélange of witnesses speaking up for the Townsend Plan, for disarmament, for aid to students in higher education, for the Utilities Users League, the Lithuanian American Council, and the Papago tribe of Arizona. Their testimony was punctuated by Congressman Moss's attack on the security "numbers racket" and by the first bit of audience participation, in which a spectator from the lobby cheered the Lithuanian witness on.

Appearance of Harry Truman

Proceedings on Thursday, August 9, centered on Harry Truman. His appearance as the most salient member of the party present, and probably one of the most influential, was well heralded. Southerners were apprehensive of what he would say on civil rights. They and others too were hoping for clues to whom he would support for the presidential candidacy. Suspense built up as the committee devoted its morning to issues of small business and public power, with appearances by Senator John Sparkman, Representative Wright Patman of Texas and Governor Harriman's counsel, Judge Daniel Gutman. A protectionist textile group, formed of a congressman, a lobbyist, a textile worker, and a farmer provided the first presentation by a team of witnesses. A spokesman for Keep America Beautiful and one for organized education rounded out the morning.

Speaking to a packed room with fullest coverage by television and the press, Truman dealt with four topics: foreign policy, domestic financial policies, resources and conservation, and civil rights. He disposed of foreign policy quickly, with characteristic personal recollections of his role at Potsdam and his proposal for internationalizing the Kiel Canal. He praised the United Nations, bespoke better consideration for our friends in Southeast Asia and in Latin America, and reported both great interest and great confusion abroad regarding what our foreign policy really was.

On civil rights he dwelt on the origin and work of his Civil Rights Commission of 1947, and the historical origins of the fourteenth amendment. Most important, however, he indicated that in his view the party need do no more than to reaffirm in the 1956 platform the planks of 1952 and 1948. Thus it was clear that Truman was for unity; he was unwilling to go to the lengths demanded by the all-out Northern liberals—explicit recognition of and support for the Supreme Court decisions of 1954. Yet they could easily live with Truman's advice to reread the Civil Rights Commission's report and remember that even though the actions following that report were controversial, "they have been right, and whenever anything is right, it makes no difference how controversial it is, we ought to make an effort to put it through."[13]

Truman's strictures on government financial policy and actions, including some sharp attacks on Republican officials, occasioned some later resentment among Republicans (notably by the President), but raised no explosive issues for Democrats. His stance on natural resources was equally unnewsworthy.

During the question period following, the former President gave the expected answers to questions about the farmers' plight, special privilege in the atoms-for-peace program, Democrats and prosperity and progress, and Hell's Canyon. Television followed the questioners, highlighting those who were candidates for a variety of national and state offices (other than the Presidency or the Vice Presidency). Women, farmers, Negroes, and other symbolically significant members of the platform committee asked questions to which the answers were known, and that pricked out key points in Democratic issue strategy.

In concluding, Truman told the chairman that slogans would not win the election.

"The man that can put over the fact that the welfare of this country is wrapped up in the welfare of the Democratic party rather than in General Motors, will be the guy that will put this thing over. It won't be slogans."[14] He fended off several attempts to get him to say whether he would be available as a candidate himself; he never had been a candidate for 1956, and didn't intend to be one—not even a favorite son.

[13] *New York Times*, Aug. 10, 1956.
[14] *Ibid.*

After forty-five minutes on the stand, the former President finished, the Southerners relaxed, and the committee went into short recess. Anticlimactically came a former Secretary of the Air Force under Truman, now firmly in the Stevenson camp, testifying temperately but somewhat inconsistently on planks for foreign policy. Although he deplored partisanship in foreign policy, he busily added up successes for the Democrats and failures for the Republicans during recent years. He called for an issue-by-issue effort to resolve all outstanding problems with all countries; he plumped for an air-atomic capability so absolute that no opponent would dare start a war or allow one to start; and he demanded initiatives toward foolproof disarmament. He was followed by Representative John E. Moss, speaking on government information.

During the remainder of the afternoon and evening, the committee demonstrated the attractiveness of its forum for spokesmen for a widely varying spectrum of demands, many quite technical. Here came spokesmen for scheduled and for nonscheduled airlines dealing with right of entry into the air transportation field; spokesmen speaking for tax equality between banks and savings and loan associations; spokesmen for a culturally permissive approach to the government's relations with Indians. Throughout, the committee kept sharp watch over small business, labor, and the disadvantaged minorities; proponents of right-to-work and of private power development got short shrift.

Civil Rights Day

Friday was civil rights day, the day of trial for the Southern strategy. Carefully prepared beforehand and regulated by daily hotel room caucuses, the Southern representatives on the platform committee combined patience in public with reiteration of the demand that there be no mention of the Supreme Court decisions in the platform. With this bargaining stance, they sought an ultimate solution that would be tolerable in their home districts.

They kept their public statements to a minimum, and blew off steam in private. By Friday, the absence of any Stevenson follow-up of his Tuesday statement, and the relative Truman moderation, augured a satisfactory outcome for their strategy.

The Northern liberals had their strategy too; they would use both the platform committee and the convention sessions to show a great drive for a clear civil rights plank; but they would not insist on it to the point of a split. Arrangements for appearances before the platform committee gave them the lion's share of time, and permitted them to bring forward a carefully selected array of witnesses. They could make a record and provide symbolic representation for these groups and the causes for which they spoke.

Intermixed with civil rights was labor's appearance—held to a discreet minimum. Labor shared with the other civil rights advocates a concern with the impact of Senate Rule XXII and of committee chairmanships on modification or repeal of the Taft-Hartley Act, and on other labor-liberal legislative demands.

Labor made its formal appearance late in the morning. George Meany, President of the AFL-CIO, read out a twenty-minute press release, presented fifty pages of platform recommendations, and answered questions about the evils of Taft-Hartley and the failures of Republicans to fulfill their promises to amend it. Meany pointed out that labor had decided to live with the Taft-Hartley Act while its representatives tried to get the law changed, while the southerners were trying to evade and break down the law as authoritatively interpreted. But Meany studiously avoided any temptation to praise Democrats and criticize Republicans, even though several committee members gave him openings to do so.

Other labor leaders were less reticent. George Harrison, President of the Brotherhood of Railway Clerks and Chairman of the Advisory Committee on Labor of the Democratic National Committee, appeared in his latter capacity—and showed no compunction for taking a more partisan stand, supported by leaders of seventeen unions. He attacked the GOP's "big business policy," uneven distribution of economic gains, increased unemployment, difficulties on farms and in small business, and the "trickle-down theory of economic gains." He called for reaffirmation of New Deal-Fair Deal policies in taxation, full employment, labor legislation, social security and welfare, education, and civil rights.

After introduction of several labor leaders who had been members of the advisory committee, and friendly questioning by committee members, Harrison stepped down to light handclaps. Chairman McCormack called for order, reminding the committee that they were "operating under the rules of the House," and asking them not to applaud since they formed "a deliberative body of a great convention." McCormack had to warn them again as they insisted on clapping for the testimony of Richard Stengel, Democratic candidate for Senate from Illinois.

Next came spokesmen for statehood for Alaska and Hawaii—the last such spokesmen to come before a platform committee. Then came those still persisting perennials—Home Rule for the District of Columbia, and ceremonial presentations by the Puerto Rican and Virgin Islands delegates. (Puerto Rico was satisfied with its Commonwealth status; the Virgin Islands wanted neither statehood nor territorial status, but only a little more self-government: local home rule, the right to vote for President and Vice President, and representation in Congress by a commissioner.)

With the afternoon came a set-piece presentation led by Roy Wilkins of the NAACP, offering a six-point program backed by some thirty organizations—labor, religious, ethnic, veterans, fraternal, and the ADA.[15]

Wilkins wanted a civil rights plank, however described, to be "incorporated into the party platform at this convention and faithfully followed during the next four years." The planks of 1948 or of 1952 would not do. At the end of twenty minutes, Wilkins concluded his testimony to sustained applause. McCormack made no effort to cut it off.

Following Wilkins, other witnesses dealt with the remaining points of the agreed-upon program: Joseph Rauh, Jr., National Chairman, ADA, brought up the guarantee of civil rights; James B. Carey, union leader, spoke of the need for changing the seniority rule; Max A. Kopstein of the American Jewish Congress de-

[15] See above, pp. 91-92.

manded support for legislation authorizing federal actions to guarantee civil rights; Senator Lehman made a moving plea for specific mention of the Supreme Court decisions.

During this testimony and questioning, the committee's leadership fought for moderation. McCormack ruled out Carey's attack on congressional procedure on grounds that the Democratic party should not deal with that subject. Negro Representative Charles C. Diggs of Detroit asked Carey whether the problem should not be met by electing progressives and liberals to Congress. Congressman Celler also strongly defended the congressional institutions, pointing to the position of Negro Representative William L. Dawson of Illinois, noting how he had been able to rise within the existing system.

The pro-civil rights witnesses insisted, however, on striking divisive notes. Leonard Woodcock, Vice President of the UAW, pointed out that the South was not the only region worth placating. No party could win the Presidency without carrying the North, that amassed 239 electoral votes, and where civil rights was a burning issue. And the right stand on civil rights would build favor with voters in other states where there were vital senatorial races: California, Colorado, Connecticut, and others. Committeemen Short of Minnesota and Lawson of the District of Columbia threw questions at Senator Lehman further designed to bring out the political value in the North of a clear mention of the Supreme Court decisions. Lehman responded: "We should speak of the Supreme Court, and say it is a moral and righteous decision." (McCormack did try to gavel down the ensuing ovation.) Lehman did his bit for moderation by refusing to attack the party policy committees as chief source of the civil rights trouble. Instead, the Senator insisted that such committees were needed for orderly legislation, and "usually, we have not suffered from them."

In mid-afternoon, the Southerners had their first inning, as Governor Timmerman took twenty minutes to "tell the client what he needs to know." He attacked the argument that the Democratic party, in order to win the Presidency, had to capture the Negro vote in key states with strong civil rights and pro-integration planks. He rehearsed the votes and the party platforms of 1952, concluding that civil rights and promises of integration were not the keys to success then—and that they had persuaded four Democratic Southern states to vote Republican. He defended segregation as best for white and Negro; deplored the effect on our foreign relations of racial mixing in the armed forces; quoted the Southern Governors' Manifesto, the Richmond Pledge and state legislation as evidence of the "true sentiment" of the South. He threatened that the South's 128 electoral votes might go astray if the platform were unacceptable. He charged that the Republicans, with their stand on civil rights, had created a mess in the public schools of Washington, D.C. Finally, he called for a strong platform and a strong candidate—but with the platform's strength shown in a strong stand for State's Rights.

The liberals demanded that Timmerman be questioned. But time had virtually run out; the session had to close at 4:00 P.M.—so that those present could go to the All-Star football game. The committee leadership scheduled a final public session for the next day—and then found time to hear a pro-civil rights witness, A. Philip Randolph of the International Brotherhood of Sleeping Car Porters, who presented the findings of the State of the Race Conference, a meeting of seventy-three Negro leaders that had taken place the preceding April in Washington.

During the day, the committee had run well behind schedule. Some twenty-eight witnesses had yet to be heard. The allocation of time had favored the presentations of the views of the Northern liberals, with a good deal of reinforcement and repetition. At times the Southern delegates were restive, but they kept their tempers and held to their planned course.

While most of the platform committee was hearing witnesses, some of its more moderate members were seeking compromise and putting a middle-of-the-road position in the form of a draft plank. Although not acceptable to the "more advanced liberals," this draft reputedly had the backing of Mrs. Franklin D. Roosevelt. It pledged Federal legislation for equal opportunity in employment, for protection of security of the person, for stronger civil rights, and for effective administrative machinery to enforce them. But it did not mention the Supreme Court.[16]

Miscellaneous Subjects

By Saturday morning, most of the tension had gone out of the atmosphere as the platform hearings went into their last day. Final passages-at-arms occurred between the Southern forces and the liberals. The labor spokesmen entered material for the record, but stayed out of sight. There were a few echoes of testimony on subjects raised earlier in the week, noncontroversial among Democrats then or now. Testimony on women's rights and the competitive freedom of the ladies handbag industry provided human interest and humor.

Attention to the afternoon proceedings trailed off as many committeemen and spectators joined the press in the room above to learn whom Truman would support. In proceedings throughout the day, the committee carefully buffered testimony on civil rights with testimony on less divisive points. The only one to break ranks was Congressman Celler, who fell on the Southern witnesses in a sharp ten-minute speech. The chairman was obviously annoyed, but could do nothing. Finally Celler gave up the floor, and the committee turned to the ancient topic of a women's rights amendment to the Constitution. The committee devoted the afternoon to women in politics, youth in politics, and religion in politics.

At 5:26 P.M. the last witness asked to put his recommendations for radio-television freedom into the record. Then in a wave of congratulations and thanks, the chairman and the co-chairman brought public proceedings to a close. Governor John Battle of Virginia added to harmony and unity, expressing his appreciation to the chairman, to the co-chairman, and to others for the "fair,

[16] William S. White, "Proposed Plank on Rights Avoids Citing Court Ruling," *New York Times,* Aug. 11, 1956.

open and complete hearing," despite discussion of matters of very deep concern. Senator O'Mahoney did not forget the Democratic party, "a national party speaking for no special interest," and supporting the "plain principles" on which free government can be won. Mrs. Bernice Kingsbury, spokesman for the Harriman forces, added her word for harmony, seconding the motion of praise for McCormack proposed by Governor James N. McCord of Tennessee.

The committee then went into executive session. Emerging at 6:25 P.M., McCormack announced that the drafting committee would meet the next day at 2:30. He said that civil rights had not been discussed during the executive session. He hoped to have a draft completed by late Tuesday. He did not expect there would be a meeting of the full committee until that time, as individual planks would be dealt with by the drafting committee.

It soon became apparent that the drafting committee had had little difficulty with the bulk of the document. A working draft was produced for all planks except for civil rights by Saturday night.[17] Whatever changes the drafters made took little time and occasioned little controversy on all matters except civil rights.

As for civil rights, more was needed than agreeable wording. Protagonists of the extreme positions wanted more opportunities to fight openly for their positions.

Effect of Public Hearings

To the range of content or to the tone of the platform document itself, the hearings contributed nothing. No information was adduced, nor were any points of view expressed that were not well known to the platform drafters (on or off the committee) before the week's start. The main points of consonance between

[17] Frederick Kuh, "Storm Abates Over Platform on Civil Rights," *Chicago Sun-Times*, Aug. 12, 1956. Kuh reports the skeleton planks were the work of a shirt-sleeved team directed by Joseph Duggan, city solicitor of New Bedford, Massachusetts. This team prepared alternative planks for every issue and a composite proposal for each title, as a basis for committee decisions.

testimony and final document occurred in the cases of testimony by official or known favorable witnesses, already influential in the formation of publicly stated Democratic party policy. The major exception to this general outcome was the agriculture plank, in which the forces of relative moderation (with subtly communicated approval from the Stevenson camp) rejected the proposals of the Wickard Advisory Committee, and came out with a more conservative position.[18] A few interpolations came about in response to immediate events—such as the passage of the auto-dealers' "day in court" bill that gave O'Mahoney the chance to put his interpretation of this event's significance for small business and economic freedom almost verbatim into the platform.

On most of the issues, the preponderance of testimony had gone along pre-established lines of New Deal-Fair Deal positions. Favorable witnesses got leading questions, as committee members echoed, reinforced, embroidered their favorite points. Unfavorable witnesses were ignored, wrangled with, or treated as "petitioners" being granted a democratic right to speak out.

Major candidates for the Presidency had the chance to put their particular slant on issues of importance to intraparty adjustment, but they made little use of it. Candidate communication to the platform process was *sub rosa*, and subtle. The Harriman forces made daily appearances, insisting on correct procedure and opportunity for discussion of the liberal point of view. But Stevenson forces provided them with no opportunity for a direct confrontation. The other hopeful candidates saw little opportunity to foster a deadlock by exacerbating issue politics via the platform.

Candidates for other offices had taken the opportunity to present themselves to their constituents and to the nation via the mass media. The committee's leaders had given them special prominence as interrogators or as witnesses whenever possible. Such appearances had as much or more to do with local campaigning as they did with the shaping of national party issues.

Primarily party-oriented professionals seeking influence or preferment within the party councils also found opportunity to play

[18] Kenneth Davis reports Stevenson's earlier reluctance to agree to a clear call for high, rigid price supports. See *Prophet In His Own Country* (1957), pp. 450-451.

roles as interrogators, henchmen, hatchetmen, and conciliators where the matters at issue concerned effective defense of party principles against hostile witnesses, or possible position-taking or compromises between conservatives and liberals, Southern and Northern factions within the party.

Although antithetical, the functions of factionalism and of party unity were both served by the presentation of divergent views on civil rights. Ostensibly the protagonists were talking to a committee about to draft a delicate compromise, or, in short, to themselves; in fact they were talking to their home constituencies, and for regional and national consumption. Factionalists at home could be gratified by unequivocal statements—and thus brought to accept with better grace the inevitable compromise of the final document.[19]

What of the effort? Over one hundred committee members had listened or questioned in sessions of some fifty hours.[20] The chairman, co-chairman, and eight or ten of the most diligent and involved committee members spent the greater part of this time in attendance and active participation. When not attending the hearing of the moment, they were occupied with the private business of the committee: its scheduling, its control of witnesses, its formation of a record.

Chairman McCormack announced that over two hundred witnesses had participated. Of these, some one hundred sixty were scheduled and had actually appeared. The others submitted material for the record and for distribution at the hearings. Further testimony and expression of opinion came in by telegram, much of which was accepted into the record in public, and some briefly described in the process.

[19] The question of the impact of unfavorable extremism needs examination in detail, beyond the scope of the present data. Differential perception often screens out the undesirable. It is likely that the factionalist sees what he wants to see, and is able to respond favorably to the total situation because he does not notice the elements in it that he disapproves.

[20] Total time spent in public session approximated 47 hours and 30 minutes: 6 hours on Monday; 10 hours and 35 minutes on Tuesday; 8 hours and 30 minutes on Wednesday; 9 hours and 20 minutes on Thursday; 5 hours and 25 minutes on Friday; and 7 hours and 40 minutes on the unplanned-for Saturday. This, plus some 3 hours spent in executive session on Monday and Saturday, totaled over 50 hours.

Most of the benefits to the party flowed from communications concerning issues and a successful contribution to the rally function. These communications not only went to the general public through the press; they served an educational function for many members of the platform committee. Partisans of varying interests and preferences could select arguments from the points made to reinforce their previous views or to demolish probable opposition. Party organizations derived lesser benefits. Lesser candidates got more attention than they could have gained from more concentrated hearings.

It was a gruelling week for anyone who watched the whole proceedings—let alone for those who took the most active parts in it. For the drafting committee and the major antagonists on civil rights, much remained to be done.

5

The Democratic Convention Committees
and Candidate Maneuvers

MAJOR ACTION FOR THE future governance of a political
party is taken each four years by its national committee and by
the rules and credentials committees both of the national committee and of the convention. In 1956 the meeting of the Democratic
National Committee did its preliminary work on arrangements
and made preparations for its own continuance on order of the
convention in the four years to follow, without setting any vital
precedents. But the rules and credentials committees of the convention, as well as the platform committee, did break new ground
by operating under new procedures approved by the National
Committee that brought them into play well before the official
opening of the convention itself. The main moves and contributions of each of these bodies are set forth below.

The sometimes confusing and concurrent timetables of the
committee and convention proceedings ran as follows. The Platform and Resolutions Committee of the convention started its
hearings on Monday, August 6. On Friday morning, August 10,
the Subcommittee on Credentials of the National Committee met.
On Saturday morning, August 11, the National Committee met,
and in the afternoon the Platform Committee concluded its open
hearings and went into executive session.

On Monday, August 13, the convention Committees on Rules
and Order of Business, and on Credentials, met in the morning.
At noon, the convention itself was officially opened.

While the party's machinery got up momentum, the candidates
and their organizations made their final preparations as the delegates gathered.

Committees of the National Committee

In the words of Clarence Cannon, *doyen* of Democratic party parliamentarians:

> The Democratic National Committee is the permanent agency authorized to act in behalf of the Party during intervals between Conventions. It is the creature of the National Convention and therefore subordinate to its control and direction. Between Conventions the Committee exercises such powers and authority as have been delegated specifically to it and is subject to the directions and instructions imposed by the Convention which created it.[1]

The National Committee ordinarily meets twice at convention time; first on the convention eve, when it completes its tasks of hearing contests on credentials, makes up the temporary roll, decides on changes in rules and other matters to be recommended to the convention for action, and perfects organizational and administrative arrangements for the convention about to take place. Second, it meets after the convention, with powers and directions given to it by the convention just adjourned. At this time, it elects a chairman, reconstitutes its committees and takes needed actions to launch the campaign.

Pursuant to this procedure, the Democratic National Committee met in open session on August 11, 1956 at 10 A.M. After Chairman Paul Butler read the call, introduced new members, and located proxies, the committee heard Treasurer McCloskey report that the committee was some $40,000 in the red, with $25,000 in cash and debts of $65,000. McCloskey reported on state quotas not yet met, and promised fund-raising meetings during the next two months.

SUBCOMMITTEE ON CREDENTIALS

Potentially the most interesting and important business had to do with credentials. The situation was not nearly so electric as

[1] *Democratic Manual* (1956), p. 3.

that preceding the convention of 1952,[2] but echoes of the loyalty fight and the fair-play procedures were faintly heard. Two delegations were contested, that from Mississippi headed by Governor J. P. Coleman and that from South Carolina headed by Governor George B. Timmerman, Jr. Northern liberal objectives of the contest were twofold: to punish for disloyalty, if possible; and to produce alternative sets of delegates who might be counted on both to support a stronger civil rights plank and to make a stronger fight for the nominees of the convention.

Monroe Sweetland and Gene Conklin of Oregon led the attack on these regular delegations before the credentials subcommittee[3] of the National Committee, and in the National Committee itself. Leader of the contesting Mississippi delegation was the Reverend Charles G. Hamilton, an Episcopal clergyman, college professor, and chairman of the True Democratic Party of Mississippi. In a prepared statement, he harked back to the Mississippi defection of 1948, and charged that the Coleman delegation had been pro-Eisenhower in 1952, and contained at least one man who was still actively working for the President.[4] How-

[2] See Paul T. David, Malcolm Moos, Ralph M. Goldman, *Presidential Nominating Politics in 1952*, Vol. I (1954), pp. 103-17.

[3] As for credentials, the National Committee's subcommittee dealing with this subject had met on August 10 to hear testimony from the contesting Mississippi and South Carolina delegations. The committee might have had more to do under the new procedure adopted by the National Committee as proposed rules 11 and 12, but the very procedure itself seemed to discourage trivial or hopeless contests. (Observations of Paul T. David. Judge Sellars of Texas later testified before the full Rules Committee that at least in one instance of which he knew, such a contest was fended off.) This procedure called for the certification of names of delegates and alternates to the convention thirty days prior to its opening, and empowered the National Committee to require "any contending group to file its brief, setting forth its position on the facts and laws, with the National Committee in Washington. . . ." Rule 12 authorized the National Committee "to deputize commissions to hear interested parties in Credentials Contests and make inquiry in the field, and to report to the National Committee." (*Interim Report of Special Advisory Committee on Rules of the 1956 Democratic National Convention*, 1955, p. 12. Hereinafter cited as *Interim Report*.) Thus the National Committee, in preparing the temporary roll, would be acting in a manner comparable to a court of first instance, with the function of clarifying issues and facts, while the convention Committee on Credentials and the convention itself could entertain appeals from the decision of the National Committee. This reasonable procedure was not put to any real test in 1956.

[4] *New York Times*, Aug. 12, 1956.

ever, the Hamilton group, in testimony before the credentials subcommittee, admitted that it had not fully complied with state law, but argued that neither had the Coleman delegation.[5] John H. McCray, leader of a group of ten Negroes, from South Carolina, challenged the Timmerman delegation, again on the basis of "disloyalty."

Mayor David Lawrence of Pittsburgh, playing a card for unity, defended Coleman on the basis of his performance in 1952 and expressed hope that nothing would be done to prevent seating his delegation. Sweetland replied that one could not judge a whole delegation on the performance of an individual within it.

But the nub of the report by Calvin W. Rawlings was that nothing in the record prevented seating of the Coleman and Timmerman delegations. The National Committee accepted this recommendation by voice vote. Sweetland promised action leading toward a floor fight on the issue; he said that several delegations were interested. He foreshadowed a strategy of attack on individuals rather than delegations.[6] But in the event, nothing was at stake; Sweetland was replaying a record from 1952 that did not match the concerns of 1956; only one or two of the non-State delegations were interested enough to back a floor fight on contested delegations, so the Oregon delegation acquiesced in the general mood of the convention for organization unity.

ADVISORY COMMITTEE ON RULES

The National Committee had discharged its major task with respect to revision of the rules on November 17, 1955, when it adopted as a guide to action for transmission to the 1956 convention the report of its Special Advisory Committee on Rules. That committee was empowered "to study, review and make appropriate recommendations concerning all rules governing the Democratic National Convention, including specifically, but not exclusively, the subject of the so-called or mis-called Loyalty Pledge

---

[5] Personal observation by Paul T. David, citing report of Calvin W. Rawlings, national committeeman from Utah and chairman of the subcommittee on credentials, to National Committee, Aug. 11, 1956.

[6] *Ibid.*

Resolution adopted at the 1952 convention and rules for the more expeditious handling of convention business."[7] It proposed three rules that would help forestall a "loyalty oath" fight; a fourth rule that would reduce the probability that a "fair play" resolution might be offered from the floor of the convention by providing that "Delegates on the temporary roll of the Convention may not vote on their own credentials";[8] a fifth to regulate the polling of delegations; a sixth changing the voting weights of delegations in filling vacancies on the national ticket; and a seventh governing the procedure for getting roll calls.

The advisory committee also recommended procedures (proposed rules 8, 9, and 10) for calling the main committees of the convention into action in the week prior to the convention itself. Finally, the advisory committee recommended revised procedures for the hearing of credentials contests by the National Committee during the month preceding the convention (proposed rules 11 and 12).[9]

Committees of the Convention

On Monday morning, August 13, the Committee on Rules and Order of Business and the Committee on Credentials met. The Platform and Resolutions Committee continued in executive session. All three meetings ran over into the first session of the convention proper.

COMMITTEE ON RULES AND ORDER OF BUSINESS

The Committee on Rules of the National Convention got off to a fumbling start, but finished strongly to make a contribution to the better governance of their party. By 10:30 an official quorum was announced, and the roll was called, revealing the presence of thirty-seven committee members and fifteen to twenty spectators and press men.

[7] *Interim Report*, p. 3.
[8] *Ibid.*, p. 9.
[9] *Ibid.*, pp. 10-13.

In the Committee on Rules as in the Platform and Resolutions Committee, the Democratic order of the day was to start with something other than the main business. The first witness (Mrs. Clara Shirpser of California, a Kefauver supporter) introduced a resolution intended to cut down on delegate demonstrations (mainly for favorite sons) and to eliminate parades on the floor of the convention, by bringing before the convention all candidates who polled 15 per cent or more of the total on the first ballot. This proposal was reportedly supported by members of delegations from 22 states but the committee took no action on it at the moment.

Chairman John O. Pastore of the Committee on Rules then introduced Stephen Mitchell, former National Committee Chairman and chairman of the Special Advisory Committee on Rules, who gave the background and led discussion on each of the rules proposed in his *Interim Report.* The committee spent some time in an inconclusive discussion of National Committee procedure and probable action in filling vacancies on the national ticket if the delegates of a state were divided. Most of the time went, however, to a rule-by-rule exposition and discussion, most of it amicable.

Two other members of the advisory committee—Governor John S. Battle and Senator Hubert Humphrey—spoke briefly in behalf of the committee's proposals. Battle especially favored the new procedure for getting a roll call. Humphrey explained that the Interim Committee had representation from every state and was not "loaded." He urged any persons having evidence of disloyalty to the party to present it to the Committee on Credentials.

Rules 1, 2, and 3 were of prime importance to the immediate convention, if they could be used to head off floor fights on loyalty and fair play, and ensure diligent support of the convention ticket by each national committeeman.

As presented in the *Interim Report,* these rules read thus:

RESOLVED, That it is the understanding that a State Democratic Party, in selecting and certifying delegates to the Democratic National Convention, thereby undertakes to assure that voters in the State will have the opportunity to cast their election ballots for the Presidential and Vice-Presidential nominees selected by said Convention, and for electors pledged formally or in good conscience to

·the election of these Presidential and Vice-Presidential nominees, under the Democratic Party label and designation.

RESOLVED, That it is understood that the delegates to the Democratic National Convention, when certified by the State Democratic Party, are bona fide Democrats who have the interests, welfare and success of the Democratic Party at heart, and will participate in the Convention in good faith, and therefore no additional assurances shall be required of delegates to the Democratic National Convention in the absence of credentials contest or challenge.

RESOLVED, That it is the duty of every Member of the Democratic National Committee to declare affirmatively for the nominees of the Convention, and that his or her failure to do so shall be cause for the Democratic National Committee or its duly authorized subcommittee to declare his or her seat vacant after notice and opportunity for hearing.[10]

Chairman Mitchell quickly dealt with one or two queries of drafting interpretation, explaining that the third proposed rule had its origin in Democratic support for Eisenhower in 1952—when at times it had been impossible, he said, for Democratic campaigners even to get certain of their national committeemen on the telephone.

Proposed Rule 4 read:

"Delegates on the temporary roll of the Convention may not vote on their own credentials." This leaf from the Republican book provoked no queries at all, despite the heated controversy over the matter in earlier conventions.

Proposed Rule 5 dealt with changes in the rules relating to the polling of delegations during roll calls. The established practice in 1952 and before provided that: "On roll call by States, a delegation shall be polled on challenge by any member of the delegation."[11] The advisory committee, noting difficulties created in 1952 by delegates eager to appear on television, sought to provide for polling for legitimate purposes without holding up the proceedings of the convention, by redrafting the procedure as follows:

Rule 5. (a) On roll call by States, a delegation shall be polled on challenge by any member of the delegation; and

[10] *Ibid.*, pp. 8-9.
[11] *Ibid.*, p. 38, citing Cannon's *Democratic Manual* (1952).

(b) The Convention Chairman may send a representative to the delegation to conduct the poll; and in the discretion of the Convention Chairman, the roll call may continue instead of awaiting the result of the polling; and

(c) The determination of the Chairman's representative of the results of the poll so challenged, shall be spread upon the records of the Convention, and shall be conclusive unless an open poll in the hearing of the entire Convention is demanded by one-third of the delegates of the State involved; and

(d) A demand for poll may be withdrawn at any time. In the event a demand for poll is withdrawn, the vote announced by the Chairman of the delegation will stand unchallenged, but the Convention Chairman's representative shall offer other members of the delegation opportunity to request continuance of the poll.[12]

Mr. Mitchell explained to the Committee on Rules that his advisory committee had considered and rejected a suggestion that a delegation requesting a poll should leave the convention floor for the purpose. Grounds for the rejection were two: first, that it was improper for the convention to proceed with official business during the enforced absence of an accredited delegation; and second, that the noise and confusion attendant on the exit and return of a large delegation would defeat the purpose of the amendment. Finally, Mr. Mitchell pointed out, Mr. Cannon was very strongly in favor of this rule.

The committee adopted these five proposed rules by voice vote. Mr. Mitchell dealt next with proposed Rule 7. This provided that "Roll calls should be taken upon the demand of eight delegations." The change altered the 1952 rule that roll calls of the convention could be had on demand of one fifth of all of the delegates present on the convention floor. This proposal promised to provoke some discussion, since it had been authoritatively bruited about that Speaker Rayburn and Parliamentarian Cannon were opposed to it; and certainly the proposed amendment curtailed the Chairman's discretion in deciding when conditions necessitated a roll call. Mr. Mitchell announced that Mr. Cannon had asked to testify in opposition to it, on grounds that it would slow down the convention and would not work well. But Mr. Cannon, who had

[12] *Interim Report*, p. 9.

looked in briefly on the committee's session and had noted its large and attentive audience, was not present to state his views.

In the event, however, the controversy was brief. After discussion of how to determine majorities in delegations (answered by Committee Counsel Harold Leventhal), Tom P. McDermott of Oklahoma moved to reject the proposed rule, and Ken Rinke of Oregon spoke in favor of rejection as support for Mr. Rayburn. On a standing vote, however, the motion to reject failed, and the rule was adopted, 19 to 11.

The committee next turned to proposed Rule 6, governing filling of ticket vacancies. Although no nominee of a major party for the two top offices had died after nomination but before election day since James S. Sherman, the Republican vice-presidential nominee in 1912, this possibility had special relevance in 1956. As proposed by the advisory committee, this draft rule read:

> In the event of the death, resignation, or disability of a nominee of the party for President or Vice President, the Democratic National Committee is authorized to fill the vacancy or vacancies, by a majority vote of a total number of votes possessed by the States and Territories at the preceding National Convention; the full vote of each state and territory shall be cast by its duly qualified member, or members, of the National Committee.[13]

Discussed but rejected (7-20) was a proposal that the National Committee in the event of a vacancy should issue a call to the national committeemen and committeewomen in the several states to poll the delegations in each state.

A second amendment proposed that in the event of a disagreement between the two committeemen, each should have the power to cast one half of the state's quota of votes. This was adopted, 29-3. Immediately the question was raised regarding who should determine "disability," and it was proposed from the floor that this should be a task for the National Committee.

Then Mitchell explained the four remaining rules, that provided for certain new procedures to be followed by the National Committee in advance of the 1956 convention and that as a mat-

[13] *Ibid.*, p. 10.

ter of fact were already being followed. Rule 8 provided for the certification by state delegations at least seven days in advance of the convention, of members to serve on the four major convention committees—Permanent Organization, Rules and Order of Business, Credentials, and Platform and Resolutions. Rule 9 authorized the Chairman of the National Committee to call these committees into session at any time in that preceding week as *de facto* bodies, to be confirmed *de jure* by later action of the convention. Rule 10 provided for payment of a per diem allowance for such members attending meetings in advance of the convention. Rules 11 and 12 dealt with new procedure for hearing credentials contests by the National Committee.

The proposals were adopted by voice vote, unanimously.

Some further amendments to rules, plus the main operational resolution providing that the convention should be governed by the rules of the 1952 convention including the rules of the House of Representatives as applicable, came up next. The committee voted down (2-24) a proposal to amend these rules so that the territories would be called after the states. (Puerto Rico argued for a place after Pennsylvania because it was a commonwealth, not a territory. Alaska and Hawaii, hoping soon to be states, saw no reason for demotion.)

The committee then considered and adopted three staff resolutions designed to speed up convention procedure. First they reaffirmed by a vote of 19 to 8 the 1952 rule limiting nominating speeches for candidates for President and Vice President to fifteen minutes each, with seconding speeches not to exceed five minutes each and not more than ten minutes for seconding speeches for any one candidate. They then restricted participation in all floor demonstrations to duly elected delegates and alternates, providing that demonstrations for candidates nominated be limited to twenty minutes. The third resolution restricted delegates to ten minutes' time in debate without unanimous consent of the convention, except in cases where total time for debate on an issue had been formally allocated to the two sides by the Chairman of the convention.

A further staff proposal recommended an order of business for the convention as a whole, for the Committee on Rules to recommend in turn to the convention. This laid out procedure for the convention in seven steps. The first four were reports in order from the committees on Permanent Organization, Rules and Order of Business, Credentials, and Platform and Resolutions. Then came nomination and selection of candidate for President, confirmation and selection of members of the Democratic National Committee, nomination of the vice-presidential candidate, and finally miscellaneous business and adjournment. After adopting this recommendation, the committee tabled Mrs. Shirpser's proposed amendment that had been presented at the beginning of the session, as the meeting considered that adequate action had been taken to speed up proceedings (insofar as this could be done by rules alone) by the proposals already adopted.

Before concluding, the committee heard from Paul T. David, serving as a spokesman for an informal caucus of political scientists.[14] Mr. David presented for the committee's information a proposed major reform in party committee voting, that would weight voting in committees with the relative strengths possessed by each delegation on the floor of the convention. He also presented three minor proposals for convention procedural reform, recommending that the names of delegation chairmen be printed in the final roll; that steps be taken to duplicate and distribute transcripts of each day's proceedings to delegates during the convention for immediate correction; and that better provision be made for scholarly research on the convention while the event was in progress.

Mr. David also reported that a caucus of political scientists had recommended approval of the Mitchell report, and disapproved continuance of the fractional vote system and changes in apportionment that led to larger delegations, more unwieldy procedures, and excessive pressure for tickets of admission to the convention hall. He suggested consideration of whether a committee on permanent organization was needed, and whether an executive committee of delegation chairmen might not be useful. He also

[14] Although a member of the staff of the Brookings Institution, Mr. David appeared in a personal capacity.

suggested another interim committee on rules changes to take advantage of experience gained in the 1956 campaign.

All these proposals and suggestions were received with interest, accepted for the record, and transmitted to the party chairman for consideration. (The proposal for change in voting composition of the convention committees had already been presented to the chairmen of both national committees the preceding February.)

The Committee on Rules made short work of the proposal to have another Mitchell committee. The District of Columbia delegate, Gerhard P. Van Arkel, proposed establishing one; but on suggestion of Chairman Pastore, the motion was voted down unanimously.

After contributing to the constitutional order of the Democratic Party, the Committee on Rules and Order of Business adjourned in the early afternoon. Its report was presented the following Wednesday, and accepted without dissent or debate. It dealt effectively with the problems of "loyalty," "fair play," and expedition of convention business.

COMMITTEE ON CREDENTIALS

The Committee on Credentials met concurrently with the Committee on Rules on Monday morning, August 13. In both Committees the watchword of the party leaders was unity. And just as in the Committee on Rules where the potential battle over loyalty, fair play, and the full power of the chairman to control roll-call voting failed to materialize, so in the Committee on Credentials the threats of attacks on conservative delegations from South Carolina and Mississippi were averted. The challenging factions, aided and abetted by liberals in the Oregon and District of Columbia delegations, threatened to continue their efforts to unseat the delegations headed by Governor Timmerman and Governor Coleman—if not as bodies, then on an individual basis. Yet when it came to a showdown, no delegation from a sovereign state was willing to vote to unseat the regular delegations from the two states. After four hours of testimony, in which Hamilton of the Mississippi "True Democratic Party" and McCray, of South Carolina, challenged afresh the loyalty and legitimacy of the credentials of the regular delegations, only two votes were cast in the Committee on Credentials in favor of a minority report. The opposition was unsuccessful in rounding up enough absentee or other ballots to sanction a minority report to the convention (six votes were required).[15]

Preconvention Candidate Maneuvers

While the party organs were carrying out their duties in the days preceding the convention, the main candidates continued their maneuvering.

On Saturday, August 4, Harriman was in West Virginia at a state convention of Young Democrats, trying to blast away at the Stevenson entrenchments. This was the twenty-fourth state he had visited since the previous May 5, when he announced active candidacy; it was his thirtieth state since the preceding November. But he found himself late in West Virginia as elsewhere, and the Stevenson supporters promptly released a list of names of influential political figures in the state who were firmly in their camp. In Chicago, Loyd Benefield told the press that when Kefauver joined Stevenson, Kefauver's delegates joined Harriman; and he claimed a Harriman total of 341—72 in the West, 118 in the Midwest, and 151 "elsewhere." Mrs. India Edwards said a Stevenson-Kefauver ticket would be weak. The delegate-rich Stevenson headquarters in reply claimed a "conservative" 600, and made ready for a $250 a plate dinner in Chicago on Monday.

On Sunday afternoon Governor "Happy" Chandler of Ken-

[15] See Philip Dodd, "2 Dixie Rump Groups Denied Parley Seats," the *Chicago Tribune*, Aug. 14, 1956. Dodd reported that Hamilton's position was weakened when he admitted his slate of delegates had been chosen in a secret convention. Secrecy, said Hamilton, was imposed by considerations of safety; but the admission destroyed Hamilton's claim that his was the only legally chosen delegation. This opened the way for the committee to seat the Southern leaders, including Eastland and Stennis of Mississippi, and Johnston, Wofford, and Thurmond of South Carolina.

tucky, appearing on the "Youth Wants to Know" television program, said he thought the Kefauver withdrawal had bettered his chances. Given a deadlock, and support from Harry Truman, he thought he had a good chance for the nomination. Once nominated, he had no doubt at all that he would triumph over Eisenhower. Describing himself as a "winning fellow," he emphasized that he was in no wise a candidate for the Vice Presidency. Senator Humphrey, avowed candidate for that office, said from Washington that it would be a good thing for the Democratic party if other candidates would announce for it too.

In Minnesota, Kefauver backers from six states (Illinois, Wisconsin, South Dakota, Nebraska, Iowa, and Minnesota), meeting under the leadership of Robert Short (a Minnesota delegate and prominent Kefauver supporter in that state) announced they unanimously favored Kefauver for Vice President. In Texas, the August 4 papers reported that the preceding day's Democratic county conventions had put the Lyndon Johnson "loyalists" far ahead of their ultra-conservative opposition.

Newspapers on August 6 published bad news for Harriman. Dr. George Gallup released poll figures showing that Northern Negroes favored Stevenson over Harriman by a wide margin—60 per cent to 14 per cent of those polled. Moreover, they favored Stevenson over Eisenhower 66 per cent to 34 per cent (a drop from the comparable 1952 figures of 79 to 21 per cent), while they favored Harriman over Eisenhower by the lesser margin of 59 per cent to 41 per cent. The Gallup interviewers reported that Northern Negroes put economic security first, well ahead of civil rights, and preferred Stevenson to Harriman chiefly on the ground that he would run better against the incumbent President. They predicted that the Negroes of the North would vote Democratic both for the Presidency and for Congress.[16] Stevenson supporters drew further comfort from the fact that one hundred and fifty people instead of the expected one hundred turned out for the Chicago fund-raising dinner.

Newspapers on August 7 announced Stevenson would come in from Libertyville on Friday. Hyman Raskin (executive director

[16] *New York Herald Tribune*, Aug. 6, 1956.

of the Stevenson campaign group) repeated the claim of 600 delegate votes, and pointed out that if any two of the large favorite-son states (Texas, Missouri, Michigan, Massachusetts, Ohio, or New Jersey) came in on the first ballot "it would be bingo." Raskin also said he had "definite word" from "Truman's friends" that the former President would not come out for Harriman. Another poll result favored Stevenson, as Elmo Roper reported a survey of New York Democrats, independents, and liberals, taken immediately before the Kefauver withdrawal. This showed Stevenson in the lead with 54 per cent, followed by Harriman with 19 per cent, and Kefauver 9 per cent.[17]

Meanwhile, the Harriman headquarters hummed with activity. The main hum came from telephone lines linking the headquarters with key (and presumably friendly) delegates in favorite-son states, as the Harriman men pleaded with the delegates to hold their delegations firm for the favorite sons, at least long enough to stop Stevenson. A secondary hum came from the liaison between the Harriman headquarters and their outposts in the platform committee. Third came from the mimeographs pouring out a barrage of campaign literature, chiefly devoted to a main theme: only "Ave" could win.

On Wednesday, August 8, the Stevenson headquarters moved from their La Salle Street offices to the center of activities at the Hilton-Blackstone area, as James Finnegan, Stevenson's campaign director, upped to 630 (from 600) his claim of delegates in the bag.

STEVENSON'S STATEMENT ON CIVIL RIGHTS

In the middle of the move, the Stevenson headquarters had to face its second biggest flurry of the week. The preceding evening, the film of a sidewalk interview by John Daly with Stevenson had been telecast. Its news that Stevenson had apparently moved to the left from his position of moderation on civil rights hit the Southern delegations at their most sensitive point. Coming out for a stronger civil rights plank, Stevenson added wry comment to his statement of position: "I have a very strong feeling that the

[17] *Chicago Sun-Times*, Aug. 7, 1956.

platform should express unequivocal approval of the court's decision, although it seems odd that you should have to express your approval of the Constitution and its institutions."[18]

The Southerners immediately went into a three-hour caucus. Leaders still striving for unity and moderation won out, as only John Sammons Bell, chairman of the Georgia Democrats, made an open break.[19] Governor Coleman pointed out that Stevenson had not gone all the way. "He didn't ask that it be done, and he didn't say he wanted the platform committee to do it. He just said he had that feeling."[20]

The Harriman forces pounced on the opportunity to drive a wedge between Stevenson and his Southern supporters.[21]

Paul Butler, dismayed by the rift within the party, chided both sides. He told the Stevenson group he saw no reason for having "platform positions on any law of the land," and he told the Harriman forces that "it's time for all Democrats to start talking constructively, and not critically, of each other."[22] Meanwhile, Stevenson stayed silent as his backers tried to smooth down ruffled feelings, revised their predictions of victory on the first ballot, and rechecked the number of Southerners in the claimed 630 supporters. They parried Governor Chandler's claim that the Stevenson statement had taken him out of the race, by pointing out Chandler's obvious interest in a deadlock. They announced support from Oscar L. Chapman, former Secretary of the Interior, a close Truman friend. G. Mennen Williams said the Stevenson statement was "very encouraging."[23] Roger Tubby, Stevenson's press secretary, issued a statement mollifying the tone but not

[18] *Ibid.*, Aug. 8, 1956.

[19] Said Bell of Stevenson: "Prior to this stupid blunder I had personally strongly leaned to him as the nominee of the Democratic party. This kindly feeling toward him on my part no longer exists. Whatever the remainder of my delegation may decide under the unit rule, I shall not cast my vote for him during this Democratic convention." *New York Times*, Aug. 8, 1956.

[20] *Chicago Sun-Times*, Aug. 8, 1956.

[21] Benefield accused the Stevenson camp of "packing" the platform committee, and threatened a floor fight if the resultant draft plank was not "satisfactory." (*Ibid.*) But other than to embarrass Stevenson, Benefield did nothing (and there was little he could do) to win dissident Southerners over to his candidate.

[22] *Ibid.*

[23] *Chicago Tribune*, Aug. 9, 1956.

modifying the substance of the Stevenson statement;[24] he stressed that Stevenson was not trying to "dictate" to the platform committee. And well he could not change the substance, because James Reston reported in the *New York Times* that Stevenson had made clear to reporters in a not-for-attribution press conference held just before his sidewalk television interview that he held firm views on all aspects of the controversy, not just those of school segregation in the South.[25]

Stevenson backers reported the loss of "only a few" Southern delegates. Harriman forces continued their attack on Stevenson as "vacillating," pointing out meanwhile that their man had never wavered in his clear stand on civil rights. The Associated Press delegate poll showed Stevenson with 462½ votes, Harriman with 165½, favorite sons with 305, and the rest of the votes uncommitted or unknown.[26]

Another Gallup poll showed Stuart Symington as the man to watch if Stevenson were to fade. In a final preconvention poll of Democratic county chairmen, it reported Stevenson leading with 38 per cent, followed by Symington with 17 per cent and Harriman with 16 per cent. Kefauver still had 7 per cent. In two-way trial heats, Stevenson out-distanced Symington by the relatively small margin of 5 to 4; he out-distanced Harriman by 2 to 1.[27]

Chandler, heartened by Stevenson's embroilment and unmindful of the Symington strength, still rated himself as an "almost certain" nominee if Stevenson and Harriman deadlocked. Humphrey, still the only avowed vice-presidential candidate, said he was "encouraged" as he left Washington for Chicago.

On Thursday, the civil rights controversy was still the big story. Former President Truman, in his platform committee appearance,

[24] *New York Times,* Aug. 9, 1956.

[25] *Ibid.* The main puzzle, thought Reston, was why Stevenson spoke out when he did—while the Southern delegations were still at home, and subject to the immediate political pressures of their local communities. He thought that Stevenson did so because "he is now so confident of the nomination that he is thinking about the campaign against the Republicans starting next month and is convinced that he must take limited chances with his support in the South to strengthen his party's appeal to the voters in the more populous areas of the North."

[26] *Chicago Tribune,* Aug. 9, 1956.

[27] *Chicago Sun-Times,* Aug. 8, 1956.

had called for a strong civil rights plank, but pointedly did not ask for specific mention of the Supreme Court decision. Governor Harriman, on his way to the convention, stopped off to address the annual conclave of Alpha Phi Alpha, Negro college fraternity, and not unexpectedly renewed attacks on "moderation" in civil rights, although he directed them more at President Eisenhower than at his Democratic rivals. The challenges and opportunities of the day are not moderate, he said; the counsel of moderation "is the counsel of timidity and stagnation—and defeat."[28] The Southerners replied to the slightly more conciliatory atmosphere in the Stevenson camp by sharpening their threat that an overstrong platform plank would split the party.

TRUMAN'S SUPPORT OF HARRIMAN

Suspense built up throughout Thursday regarding what Truman would do in supporting—or not supporting—either of the major candidates. Stevenson, already on the ground, made a point of being on hand to greet the former President on his arrival; Harriman supporters (notably Mrs. India Edwards) tried to keep the victor of 1948 and the loser of 1952 from appearing happily together in press or television.

The man from Missouri treated both sides in public with formal equality, and kept his counsel as both sides predicted and newsmen speculated. Truman, in his first press conference, refused to be tempted or trapped into a statement, but promised an announcement in time for the Sunday papers. Despite his obvious hint that he was "not a bandwagon fellow," the *New York Herald Tribune* headlined that Truman would come out for Stevenson within forty-eight hours, predicting chaos if he were to opt for Harriman. The Alsops reported that Truman had his coat halfway off for Harriman already, and the only question was whether he would take it all the way off.[29] On civil rights, Roscoe Drummond correctly predicted that the Southerners, after a show of recalcitrance, would accept the verdict of the platform com-

[28] *Ibid.*, Aug. 10, 1956.
[29] *New York Herald Tribune*, Aug. 10, 1956.

mittee; and he reported that the party leaders were favoring an "open" convention decision on the Vice Presidency, so long as it appeared that any possible nominee would be acceptable.[30]

On Saturday, August 11, the civil rights quadrille between South and North continued. Detroit's Representative Charles Diggs, Jr., and Minnesota's Robert Short told reporters that they were organizing blocs to file a plank specifically endorsing the Court decision and pledging Democratic action to enforce it—that is, if the platform committee did not come out with an acceptable version. Southern delegates countered with threats of a minority report and a floor fight of their own.[31]

In the afternoon, the news was dominated by the Truman announcement for Harriman. This put an end to the speculation about his choice only to provoke new speculation about the number of delegates who would move over into the Harriman column on the announcement. George Backer had predicted the day before that from two hundred to three hundred would come—a modest prediction in view of the psychological functions of such a claim.

President Truman, obviously enjoying himself enormously, read out to the crowd from his pencilled single-copy manuscript in the Sheraton-Blackstone:

> I have always believed in free and open political conventions, and I hope the delegates of this convention will have the fullest opportunity to express their free choice without undue haste.
>
> I have little faith in the value of the bandwagon operation or the reliability of political polls.
>
> I know that each delegate will exercise freely and independently the right of choice which is his under the law.
>
> Following the election of 1952, we all hoped that by the time the 1956 convention came around there would be developed a number of Democratic national leaders for consideration at this convention.
>
> Today I am happy to see that this convention has many qualified men to choose from—each of whom would make a good President. I have at all times encouraged worthy candidates to enter the race and campaign vigorously, and I did so without in any way seeking to influence the political fortunes of any one man.

[30] *Ibid.*
[31] *Ibid.*, Aug. 11, 1956.

I knew all along that eventually I would have to express my own choice. In making up my mind I have talked to many people in many parts of the country and in all walks of life. I have received and read thousands of letters from my fellow citizens. Since my arrival in Chicago, a steady procession of delegates, candidates, public officials, political leaders and representatives of workers, business and various minorities have called on me to express their views as to who would make the strongest candidate.

And now I have made up my mind.

I realize that my expression of a choice at this time will cause disappointment in some and may cause resentment in others.

But against the mounting crisis in the world, I know that this convention must name a man who has the experience and the ability to act as President immediately upon assuming office without risking a period of costly and dangerous trial and error.

In the light of my knowledge of the office of President I believe that the man best qualified to be the next President of the United States is Governor Harriman of New York.

He will make a fighting and successful candidate because he is dedicated to the principles of our party—the New Deal and the Fair Deal.

I know there are several other men who could wage successful campaigns with much credit to the party and the nation and they are men for whom I have great admiration.

But Governor Harriman has had long experience in top government positions at home. He has played an historic role in representing this country in Europe and Asia. He was a tower of strength all through the Roosevelt administration and all the years of my own.

I know him and you can depend on him.[32]

Whatever else this announcement did, it kept the convention alive. Support for Stevenson would have stampeded most of the delegates who were not already for him, into his camp. But Truman's choice sustained uncertainty and triggered off a desperate Harriman drive to cash the advantage to the full. Harriman himself, learning via television of the former President's choice, promptly issued a statement thanking Truman for his confidence, and pledging to "fight relentlessly for the liberal principles which have guided his career for the betterment of people everywhere."[33] Harriman aide Milton Stewart predicted that "this means we are

[32] *Chicago Sun-Times,* Aug. 12, 1956.
[33] *Ibid.*

going to break it wide open and make it on the second ballot."[34] Carmine DeSapio seconded the prediction. Loyd Benefield claimed five hundred votes on the first ballot and asserted that Truman's statement meant "a shift in the dominating spirit of this convention—from one of defeatism concerning the possibility of beating Eisenhower in November to one of conviction that we can and will win."[35] Harriman, more cautious, told reporters inquiring whether the announcement heralded his victory, "we will have to wait and see."

As the telephone wires hummed again from the Harriman headquarters to possible converts among delegates, the Stevenson organization stolidly demonstrated its organized and committed power. Stevenson keynoted his position with a formal statement soon issued over television:

> President Truman's announcement in no way alters my respect and regard for him. And I am grateful for the many kind things he has said about me in the past. I have based my candidacy on plain and forthright statements of what I believe.
> I expect to be the Democratic candidate.[36]

Leaders of delegations committed by primary or state convention action to Stevenson promptly asserted their continuing loyalty to their mandate; and others less clearly committed held their counsel. Attorney General Brown of California said the Truman announcement would cause no change in his delegation's vote. Other leaders spoke out clearly. Governor Meyner announced New Jersey would stand firm, although it was not clear for whom. Senator Humphrey of Minnesota reaffirmed his support for Stevenson (and of a Stevenson-Humphrey ticket).[37] Governor Ribicoff of Connecticut predicted that the only effect of the Truman announcement would be to delay Stevenson's victory by three ballots. Giving Harriman the lie direct, he said Connecticut would

[34] *New York Times,* Aug. 12, 1956.
[35] *Ibid.*
[36] *Chicago Sun-Times,* Aug. 12, 1956. Stevenson rested his case on the verdict of the electorate. His views, he said, had been "endorsed by millions of Americans in 1952, and more recently in a succession of primary contests in every section of the country. I think that is the best gauge of what the party wants." (*Ibid.*)
[37] *New York Times,* Aug. 12, 1956.

support Stevenson over Harriman because Stevenson was a moderate, and Connecticut was a moderate state, and moderation represented the thinking of Americans today. (Ribicoff also thought Truman had helped Senator John Kennedy's vice-presidential aspirations.)[38] Senator Kefauver came out with a three-part statement, recalling Stevenson's role as unifier, and calling on his delegates to close ranks behind Stevenson "and avert party-splitting disharmony."[39]

Other delegations were less positive. The Washington state delegation, said its chairman, was now split fifty-fifty. None of the favorite sons made any public predictions, but all their hopes soared. They could profit either by a deadlock (more likely now) or by making a high-payoff deal at the right time with the winner.[40]

The next morning, August 12, the *Chicago Sun-Times* forecast the first ballot as follows: Stevenson 470, Harriman 217, others 154½, and uncommitted 530½. The AP count published Monday, taking into account state caucuses held Sunday, was 509½ for Stevenson and 201 for Harriman, others 280, and uncommitted 381½.[41]

These caucuses were obviously giving weight to the Truman choice, but the outcome was not always to Harriman's advantage. Sensing deadlock, the New Jersey caucus unanimously urged its leader, Governor Meyner, to enter the race as a favorite son on his own. Governor Luther Hodges reported the North Carolina caucus stayed solidly behind Stevenson, as Stevenson had given a personal explanation to Hodges of his civil rights statement, and Hodges pointed out that Stevenson had to run in the whole nation.[42]

[38] *Ibid.*
[39] *Ibid.*
[40] The favorite sons at this point were these: Chandler of Kentucky, Johnson of Texas, Lausche of Ohio, Magnuson of Washington, McCormack of Massachusetts, Symington of Missouri, Timmerman of South Carolina, and Williams of Michigan. (On the critical first ballot, Kentucky went in the main for Chandler; Texas for Johnson; Ohio, Washington, Massachusetts and Michigan overwhelmingly for Stevenson. Missouri stayed with Symington and South Carolina with Timmerman. Harriman took none of them.)
[41] *New York Times,* Aug. 13, 1956.
[42] *Ibid.*

Most of the newsmen and commentators thought that the Truman announcement would not prevent Stevenson's ultimate victory, although they differed on whether this might affect a first-ballot win, and on the number of ballots to be required. A few noticed the weakness of a one-time loser if the balloting went beyond several ballots and judged that the chances of a deadlock and the ultimate victory of someone like Lyndon Johnson had been measurably increased by the Truman move. Johnson himself may have thought so—for about this time he arrived in Chicago, had a forty-line switchboard installed in his suite, and prepared to make and receive calls and callers.

The important immediate fact was this—no delegation or delegation leader started a parade to Harriman.

Speculation on who might be the vice-presidential candidate and the manner of his selection was damped down somewhat by the Truman statement, although it continued with the added complication of Harriman's views. Ticket-balancing figured less in this speculation than the symbolic position of the party against Richard Nixon.

ACTIONS OF OTHER PARTY LEADERS

Sunday, Mrs. Eleanor Roosevelt met the press in firm support of Stevenson.[43] She dealt with the main points advanced in criticism of him, presenting him as the right kind of fighter; strong in the right departments of foreign policy (stronger in Asia and Af-

---

[43] Mrs. Roosevelt gives some background on this in *On My Own* (Harper & Bros., 1958), pp. 162-63. On arriving in Chicago on the morning of August 12, she was met at the airport by a small group of Stevenson supporters who briefed her on the situation at the convention, and told her that she was going not to her hotel room but to hold a press conference. Although fearful of an ordeal, she writes "actually it turned out to be no ordeal at all. I said as simply and frankly as possible what I believed, and it was no more difficult than an ordinary press conference." Thus having got over the hurdle of a public disagreement with Truman and her dismay at "publicly pitting my political judgment against his," Mrs. Roosevelt kept a luncheon engagement with him and tantalized reporters expecting to overhear news of a deal by concentrating on generalities and culminating the luncheon conversation with a mutual assertion that each was doing the "right thing." She also reports that Truman said: "What I want to do is make this convention do some real thinking about issues."

rica than Harriman—in areas where the country most needed strength); ready to go forward in leadership of the youth of the party. Dodging a question whether Stevenson would appeal most to the women's vote, she praised his ability to put political issues in clear and simple language—as he had proved in California's primary. In dealing with Stevenson's "moderation," she pointed out that both Stevenson and Harriman were liberals, but redefined "moderation" as facing all the realities of a situation and dealing with them with wisdom and understanding. Moreover, she pointed out, Harriman's promise to carry out the policies of Roosevelt and Truman was "not enough."

Senator Lehman pointed out to friends that Truman's act had freed Stevenson; he would win the nomination, and he would do it clearly on his own. James Reston of the *New York Times* called it Stevenson's "consolation."

The only apparent defection brought out into the open, if not caused by the Truman choice, was that of a small group in the Illinois delegation. The dissidents, led by former Senator Scott Lucas and former Governor John Stelle, said that from 10½ to 17 votes would break away from Stevenson. Both had been at loggerheads with him, Lucas since 1954, Stelle for a much longer time. (On the first ballot, they delivered their 10½ votes for Harriman.) Stevenson did not attend the caucus.[44]

Meanwhile the remaining candidates came into town. Senator Symington arrived quietly, but held a press conference promptly, pointing out that he was an inactive candidate entirely in the hands of the Missouri delegation, but would obviously accept the high honor of the nomination were it offered. Governor A. B. Chandler led two hundred publicly noisy but privately dispirited supporters off their train down to the Conrad Hilton Hotel at the head of a queue of two thousand.[45]

As the various state delegations foregathered, caucused, dined, and attended receptions, the Leadership Conference on Civil Rights rallied Northern and Western liberals with speeches by Walter Reuther, California State Senator Richard Richards, Michigan State Chairman Neil Staebler, and others. The keynote was for strong planks on civil rights and the repeal or change of Senate Rule XXII—or a minority report and a floor fight.

As the week of strenuous preliminaries drew to a close, and the participants looked forward to the week of the convention proper, one outcome of the rally function was already apparent. Veteran observer William S. White concluded that the professionals dominating the scene had undergone a change of mood. They had lost the sense of futility and of defeat they had held two months before; they now believed there was a chance of victory. "A certain small optimism began to come on them; a small cheerfulness began to creep in."[46] They felt that the issue of Eisenhower's health was now being perceived around the country to the Democrats' advantage. The professionals were encouraged by the behavior of the Southern delegates, and a feeling of relative party unity suffused the delegations.[47] The Southerners, some of whom were under great pressure from home to be tough about civil rights, were not being stampeded. Surrounded by partisans of all hues assuming victory, the participants started to take the assumption seriously.

The fundamental conditions for party morale were palpably improving.

[46] *Ibid.* Aug. 12, 1956.
[47] A week later, Cabell Phillips reported that "the Chicago convention had, in a strange and human way, led toward a new degree of relative reconciliation and national understanding between the Negro politicians of the North and the white Southern politicians." *Ibid.*, Aug. 19, 1956.

6

The Democratic National Convention

THE HIGH POINT OF THE Democratic 1956 presidential electoral effort was the convention itself, and its strengthening of faith in victory among its participants.

In general intention and format, that convention followed the traditional pattern. On Monday, August 13, came two sessions, one to get the convention organized and another to hear the keynote speech. On Tuesday there were speeches and ceremonies featuring women, youth, veterans, and nationalities, plus adoption of reports of the rules and credentials committees. On Wednesday evening came convention action on the platform. On Thursday came nominations and balloting on the presidential nominee. On Friday afternoon came nominations and balloting for the vice-presidential candidate. On Friday evening came the acceptance speeches and final ceremonies. On Saturday, after the first meeting of the new National Committee, the delegates went home.

Formalities, Physical Arrangements and Preliminary Moves

Down at the amphitheatre,[1] protected by air conditioning against Chicago's heat and the noisome nearness of the stockyards, National Chairman Paul Butler surprised everyone, including

[1] The Democrats were benefited financially when the owners of the amphitheatre, with the approval of Paul Butler, rented one wing of the building, not needed for the convention, for an exhibition of consumer products. By this arrangement the Democrats saved about 60 per cent of the rental. The Republican decision to convene in San Francisco rather than in Chicago apparently prevented a similar offer to them. *Washington Post and Times Herald,* Aug. 7, 1956.

those few delegates present, by rapping his gavel for order at 12:06 P.M. August 13, and calling for the invocation a moment later. By the end of the Star Spangled Banner, about a quarter of the delegates were in their seats, and Butler told everyone: "We've begun on time and please tell the other delegates that starting times will be observed closely."

Physical arrangements had been carefully planned under the immediate direction of J. Leonard Reinsch, radio-television executive who was the over-all convention manager.[2] The main rostrum protruded well into the hall from the west, and the runway to the speakers' platform was flanked on both sides by the press. Back of the rostrum were boxes for party notables, and around the entire periphery of the hall were galleries for other spectators. The delegates were seated on the floor of the amphitheatre, with their alternates in the so-called "arena" around the sides. The main block of delegates was massed in the center around the principal television-newsreel platform. Thus there was no central aisle down which delegates or demonstrators might crowd in apparent confusion and disorder if television viewed the rostrum from directly in front. Demonstrations thus had to go in circles, following the aisles to right and left of the main block. Other television cameras were placed at sides of the hall and booths high on the west wall housed radio and additional television cameras. The decor was predominantly blue—a favorable television color, chosen in preference to the traditional red, white, and blue.

[2] There was an unprecedented pressure for tickets. The situation was as follows. The amphitheatre as remodeled seated about 11,000. Must requirements against this figure were:

4,327	for delegates and their alternates.
216	for national committeemen and women.
612	two each for Democratic Senators, Congressmen, and Governors.*
950	for daily newspaper correspondents.
200	for the weekly press.
400	for radio-television reporters.
160	reserved seats for VIPs.
6,865	

Thus some 4,135 seats were available for others. Tickets for most of these had been assigned to state leaders for them to distribute. The National Committee kept the small balance, with the list personally controlled by Chairman Butler. See *New York Times*, Aug. 14, 1956.

State delegations had been located on the floor more according to relative size than from reasons of political consanguinity. Each was identified by a standard. Each had a microphone that would be turned on only when the chairman of the delegation had been given recognition by the Permanent Chairman.

The first session was occupied with formalities. Mrs. Dorothy Vredenburgh, Secretary of the National Committee, read the official call for the convention. Marvin Griffin, Governor of Georgia, the only state that had always gone Democratic in presidential elections, presented the gavel. Mayor Richard J. Daley of Chicago welcomed all and sundry, drawing response from other Illinois notables. Chairmen of the senatorial and congressional campaign committees reported briefly. Chairman Butler announced appointments of chaplains and the chairmen of the major standing committees. He also appointed the ceremonial committees to notify the nominees and to escort the Temporary Chairman to the rostrum for his keynote address that evening.

By 1:50 P.M. the first session was history.

These proceedings, however uninteresting to delegates or others on the spot, were not unnoticed by the electronic media. During the average half hour of the session, more than 5 million homes watched the convention on television. The radio audience during the first half hour of the opening session was 3.4 million homes.[3]

In the evening the story was much more interesting both for those on the ground and those in front of receivers. The hall was jammed; by eight o'clock there were no seats or usable standing-room left, and many ticket holders had to content themselves with television coverage in the various courtesy lounges surrounding the convention hall. The average half hour of the convention was watched in whole or in part by more than 12 million homes, with the 9:30-10:00 half hour reaching 15 million homes.[4] Once past the formalities of opening [the presentation of colors, the national anthem, and the unnewsworthy report of Chairman Butler], the convention presented its first innovation: a double key-

[3] Nielsen Television-Radio Index.
[4] *Ibid.*

note. First was a keynote film depicting progress in America as viewed by Democrats, and narrated by Senator John F. Kennedy; second was the address of the Temporary Chairman, Governor Frank G. Clement of Tennessee.

Whatever impact the film and its narrator may have had on the morale of the assembled Democrats was punctuated by Chairman Butler's querulous resentment as he told them that one of the television networks had failed to carry it whole to the nation's viewers.[5]

After the hall settled down, Governor Clement, eager to propel himself into the ranks of politically available, gave an old-fashioned keynote speech. He attacked not only the Republican party and the Vice President, but even the President himself. Clement spoke too long. At the forty-five minute mark, the audience was still pleased with his Biblical oratory; a half hour later they were let down. Clement had put himself well beyond the range of serious consideration for higher office.

He was followed by audience participation in popular song— and then the quiet first lady of the party made a plea to produce fresh leadership and ideas adequate to the challenge of the day. The initiatives of the New Deal and the Fair Deal, however appropriate for earlier decades, were not enough in Mrs. Roosevelt's view.

As the preliminaries ground on, so did the politicking. On Monday, August 13, a top selection of labor leaders—including Walter Reuther of the United Auto Workers, George Harrison of the Railway Clerks, James B. Carey of the Electrical Workers, Emil Rieve of the Textile Workers, and Joseph A. Beirne of the Communications Workers—came out for Stevenson. These more than offset the announcement for Harriman made the day before by

[5] The Columbia Broadcasting System, considering the film to be poor television, substituted political interviews and commentary for most of the half hour, and then came back for the film's climax. Butler charged a breach of trust and demanded that CBS carry the entire film, with appropriate publicity, at a later date. CBS executives Frank Stanton and Sig Mickelson denied both the breach and the relief, asserting that the network had done no more than to exercise its properly free editorial judgment. ABC and NBC executives backed the CBS assertion of principle. As put by Frank Stanton: "Those who make the news cannot, in a free society, dictate to broadcasters, as part of the free press, to what extent, where and how they shall cover the news." *Chicago Sun-Times*, Aug. 15, 1956.

David J. McDonald of the Steelworkers. The *Chicago Daily News* reported that Reuther and his lieutenants were calling on as many of the two hundred unionists who were delegates as they could find. David Dubinsky, president of the International Ladies Garment Workers Union, an AFL-CIO official and vice-chairman of the New York Liberal party, said labor had friends in Stevenson, Harriman, and Kefauver, but "Stevenson is the strongest candidate and the man who can win the election. . . . It is nonsense for the liberal forces of the Democratic party not to be united around Stevenson."[6]

The Texas delegates solidified around Lyndon Johnson, as Senator Tom Connally promised they would stay with him until released "and we hope we aren't released."[7] Other delegations argued and wavered slightly, but in general the Stevenson lines held firm. Mayor David Lawrence, leader of the Pennsylvania delegation, reported small gains for him in their ranks, promising at least 65 on the first ballot. With 686½ convention votes needed to nominate, Tuesday morning's AP totals showed Stevenson with 548½, Harriman with 225½, others with 277, and 321 uncommitted. Of the favorite sons, Senator Lyndon Johnson, Governor Frank J. Lausche, Senator Stuart Symington, and Governor G. Mennen Williams had fractional support from states other than their own. Governor A. B. Chandler of Kentucky and Governor George B. Timmerman of South Carolina had none. Johnson led the group with 59.[8]

Harriman men kept the pressure on any and all delegates, despite warnings that excessive attempts to get support from weak Democratic organizations in rock-ribbed Republican territory might give Stevenson the same kind of moral issue that Eisenhower supporters had used so devastatingly against Taft in 1952.[9]

Seven states caucused on Tuesday morning, while the convention stood in recess. The platform drafting committee continued its closed sessions, putting preliminary drafts of planks on the

[6] *Chicago Daily News*, Aug. 14, 1956.
[7] *Chicago Sun-Times*, Aug. 14, 1956.
[8] *Chicago Daily Tribune*, Aug. 14, 1956.
[9] See Doris Fleeson, "Ave May Be Hurt By Steam Roller,'" *Chicago Daily News*, Aug. 14, 1956.

press table as they were completed. Extremists continued their undertone of a threat of floor action on civil rights.

Tuesday afternoon's convention session featured youth, women, and nationalities. The president of the Young Democrats delivered a routine address. Mrs. Katie Louchheim led seven Democratic congresswomen through a three-part skit entitled Political Fables of 1956, playing to a house one-third full and completely inattentive. The representative for Michigan's first district spoke for minorities. The real story, obviously, was developing off the convention floor.

The Tuesday evening session heard the report of its Committee on Permanent Organization and adopted it without discussion or debate.[10] Then Senator Wayne Morse of Oregon, the party's chief convert, linked the Republicans' waste of human resources with their waste of natural resources. The Permanent Chairman, Mr. Rayburn, heralded a mounting Democratic attack on President Eisenhower himself, and Wallace Carroll of the *New York Times* presciently deduced that his speech meant that the campaign would not only emphasize foreign policy but that it would go beyond moderation.[11] Also on the evening's program were California's State Senator Richard Richards, challenging Republican Thomas Kuchel for his United States Senate seat; and Harold Russell, armless former National Commander of American Veterans of World War II and Korea. Russell spoke out for union organization as well as for care for veterans.

[10] According to Cannon's *Manual*, p. 21, the convention "invariably elects as its temporary and permanent officers the officers and staff of the National Committee, with the exception of the temporary and permanent chairmen, who are selected primarily for the purpose of delivering the two principal addresses of the Convention.

"The Temporary Chairman, who delivers the keynote address, is nominated with the other temporary officers by the National Committee but other candidates may be nominated from the floor . . . and in such cases the vote on Temporary Chairman is a test of strength and usually indicates the control of the Convention.

"The Permanent Chairman is nominated with the other permanent officers by the Committee on Permanent Organization (1936-179), but any member of the Convention may offer an amendment to the report substituting another name or may move to recommit the report with instructions to report back forthwith with an amendment substituting the names of other candidates." A prominent example from fairly recent times was the replacement of Jouett Shouse by a Roosevelt man in the 1932 convention.

[11] *New York Times*, Aug. 15, 1956.

Almost completely lost in the evening proceedings were two actions of considerable constitutional importance to the party. First was the acceptance, by unanimous voice vote, of the report of the Committee on Credentials; second was acceptance of the report of the Committee on Rules and Order of Business.

Early Wednesday morning, James A. Finnegan heard that Michigan's 44 votes would go to Stevenson on the first ballot. This was the result, reported a Chicago paper,[12] of a decision by Governor Williams that the candidate came before the platform, approved by a delegation vote at the end of a three-hour caucus.

No daytime meeting of the convention was held on Wednesday, August 15. The platform drafters continued work on civil rights. Some twenty-one delegations caucused. The Stevenson tide flowed more strongly, as polls showed him now with 604 votes (a gain of 55½), while Harriman had picked up 18 for a total of 243½.[13]

The knowledgeable around the convention sites revised their estimates again. They were shaken briefly in their faith in an early Stevenson triumph by the Truman announcement, but the weakness of the Harriman drive now convinced them that Stevenson would win on an early ballot, possibly the first. The larger uncommitted delegations started to veer definitely to Stevenson, led by the majority of Michigan's 44 and New Jersey's 36 delegate votes.

Truman and Harriman, undaunted, promised a fight to the end. Truman told a press conference that he was not trying to split his party, but to get the convention to nominate a fighting candidate and to prevent the Democrats from becoming a caretaker party. On both counts Stevenson failed, and his "counsel of moderation," Truman snapped, "seems in reality a counsel of hesitation and is, in fact, a surrender of the basic principles of the Democratic Party." He remembered his political tactics in time to hedge, offering Stevenson his help, if nominated.

Governor Harriman was equally determined. Even as the New York delegation was preparing for a wholesale shift to Stevenson on the second ballot, he said:

[12] *Chicago Daily News,* Aug. 17, 1956.
[13] *Chicago Sun-Times,* Aug. 15, 1956. "Other" candidates had scarcely changed. The shift to Stevenson was coming out of the "uncommitted" column.

Somebody has been spreading a rumor that I'm withdrawing. If I'm the last man in the hall I'm going to stand for what I believe and, thank God, I won't be standing alone. I'm going to fight to preserve the Democratic party's principles and if I can't do it on a national basis, I will do it in New York State.[14]

John L. Lewis joined the man from Missouri—despite their historic feud—in supporting Harriman and predicting a sure Stevenson defeat. If the Democrats nominated him, "They might as well send Eisenhower a certificate of election."[15]

The Stevenson riposte was pure moderation, as he continued his no-deal strategy. The day before he had promised a fighting campaign and had recalled the need for party unity. Today, he pointed out that he had "said nothing unkind about any competitors. My fight is against the Republican Administration and not against my fellow Democrats."[16]

Well could he afford a soft reply, for the AP poll taken as of midnight and published in Thursday's papers credited him with another gain, this of 65 votes, to a total of 669 (still short of 686½), while Harriman dropped 5 votes to 239. The adjustment was from uncommitted votes. Although the favorite sons held, it was now clear there would be no deadlock, and their chances for nomination dropped even further. Their question now was: What price for their votes, and when?

The Platform

The big overt story on Wednesday was the platform. Having got by the possibility of a party split over loyalty or seating, the one remaining threat of a minority fight was civil rights.[17] The Northern liberals put pressure on various state delegations to get the required number of petitions from the floor for a roll call. They

[14] *New York Times,* Aug. 16, 1956.
[15] *Ibid.*
[16] *Ibid.* See also Douglass Cater in the *Reporter,* Vol. 15, No. 3, Sept. 6, 1956, p. 10.
[17] For an account and analysis of the whole civil rights performance, see Robert Bendiner, "The Compromise on Civil Rights—I" in the *Reporter,* Vol. 15, No. 3, Sept. 6, 1956, pp. 11-12.

needed a majority of delegates in eight delegations. They had failed in the drafting committee of the Committee on Platform and Resolutions, which had voted out a compromise plank.

The crucial moves in drafting took place at a closed night meeting that went on until the small hours of Wednesday morning. The Harriman draft proposal, that put the ultraliberal view, was voted down 16-1, with only Emanuel Celler voting for it. The decisive vote on the majority compromise draft was 12-5, with the Southern representatives voting en bloc against it: Governor John S. Battle, Governor J. P. Coleman, Senator Sam J. Ervin, Vann M. Kennedy (Texas delegate-at-large) and Brooks Hays (representative from Arkansas). This meant Grace Hudlin of Oklahoma and Representative William L. Dawson of Illinois had voted in favor of the draft. During its all-day meeting on Wednesday, the full 108-member committee adopted the whole platform as drafted. The Georgia delegation promptly caucused, and agreed to cast its 32 convention votes against the platform, and against "any amendment that would further challenge the Southern way of life and the principles of the Democratic Party."[18]

Early in the day the liberals seemed unable even to get the necessary eleven members of the 108-member platform committee to agree on a minority report.

By the time of the evening session, the dissident liberals had amassed fourteen members of the platform committee, more than enough to satisfy the rule, to propose a minority plank on civil rights. The majority and minority versions were very close. The majority plank pledged the party to continue to eliminate illegal discriminations against civil rights, while the minority plank called for federal legislation to secure them. The minority plank also pledged the party to carry out the Supreme Court decisions on desegregation.[19] For the first two hours of the evening session, the liberals negotiated with moderates and Southerners on exact wording, but these efforts collapsed.

[18] Frederick Kuh, "High Court Rulings Affirmed As Democrats OK Platform," *Chicago Sun-Times*, Aug. 16, 1956.
[19] Text of majority plank from *New York Times*, Aug. 16, 1956; of the minority plank from *Congressional Quarterly Almanac* (1956), p. 765.

Meanwhile platform committee chairman John McCormack superintended the presentation of draft planks on other subjects to the whole convention. Each plank was read aloud by a party figure prominently identified with its substance. As read, some of the planks showed minor changes from the versions previously distributed to the press. For example, specific mention of Cyprus as an area for self-determination was excised, pleasing Anglophiles and undoubtedly disappointing partisans of *enosis;* the paragraphs on farm policy were reversed so the objective of 100 per cent parity would be mentioned before the method of 90 per cent parity support prices. Eastern politicians got Niagara added to the Democrats' list of Republican crimes of Al Sarena, Hell's Canyon, and Dixon-Yates.

The reading took time—and time was what the convention leaders wanted. If there was going to be a squabble, let it come late when the television audiences would be small. By midnight, the readers had reached Natural Resources, with Washington's Senator Warren M. Magnuson the spokesman.

At 12:43 A.M. John McCormack read out the proposed majority version of the civil rights plank. A few minutes later he moved adoption of the entire platform by the convention.

At this point the presiding officer recognized Robert Short of Minnesota to submit a minority report. Assuring the chairman he had fourteen signatures, Short read the proposed changes, dealing first with the proposal of a pledge to carry out the Court decisions, and later with the recommendation for federal legislation.

Then the Chairman allotted to John McCormack thirty minutes of time, to be distributed by him among proponents and opponents of the two versions. First were the Northern liberals—Robert Short, Herbert H. Lehman, G. Mennen Williams, Richard Richards, and Paul Douglas; second the supporters of the majority draft, none of whom were Southerners—John Moss of California, Joseph C. O'Mahoney of Wyoming, Paul Dever of Massachusetts, John McCormack of Massachusetts. Then came the surprise witness, not even a delegate to the convention. Recognizing the courtesy of access to the floor being extended to him as a nondelegate, Truman struck out for harmony and the defeat of

Republicans. He cited his platform experience, recalling that he had "dictated" the platform of 1948, and asserted that "This is the best platform this convention has ever had put before it." This was due in part to the work of McCormack, the "best chairman since 1936," whose views on civil rights were as liberal as Harry S. Truman's, and Harry S. Truman "had done more for civil rights than any other President." Triggering an ovation with his advice to adopt the majority report, he moved the previous question.

First Rayburn put the question on the minority report to a voice vote. "In the opinion of the chair, the noes have it, and the minority report is rejected." Then he put the question on the platform as presented, and the ayes had it. He promptly moved to damp Southern enthusiasm by asking that flags offensive to anyone in the chamber not be displayed, and turned to Negro Congressman Dawson of Illinois for a middle-of-the-road wrap-up. (Dawson's most interesting point was that the platform committee had been struggling with the draft until 3:30 the preceding morning.) At 1:41 A.M., he concluded, and Rayburn terminated the session until twelve noon, when the roll would be called for nominations for the Presidential candidacy.

Television followed the delegates into their caucuses. Short of Minnesota admitted his disappointment, as he thought he had at least eight delegations in favor of a roll call. (He mentioned Minnesota, New York, California, Michigan, Colorado, South Dakota, Utah, Kansas, and Puerto Rico.) Governor Williams said he had gone to his delegation, but did not insist, since he had "done his bit" to make the liberal stand clear. Others suspected that the demands for recognition had gone unheeded. A correspondent in the Virginia caucus room averred that "Rayburn's gavel saved the South for Adlai Stevenson."[20] Senator Lehman charged that Rayburn had been arbitrary and unfair. "By the rules of the convention itself we were entitled to a roll call vote," he said, adding that the microphone for the New York delegation had "gone dead."[21] A television reporter tried to find out why the Georgia delegation had been trying so hard to be recognized even after

[20] Senior author's notes.
[21] *Chicago Sun-Times*, Aug. 16, 1956. In all probability, no one turned it on.

the minority report had been defeated. Georgia, he was told, was trying to get a clear negative vote firmly in the record against the platform, since neither version was satisfactory. Another reporter tried to find out from Senator Warren Magnuson why Truman supported the majority plank. "I am always amazed," said the Senator, "at Truman's faculty for bouncing back to lead."

The bounce had taken place sometime earlier, since Truman's acceptance of the compromise majority plank had told heavily in getting it accepted within the platform committee itself. HST was scrambling back toward unity. Harriman sought his tent.

The price of platform unity to the Harriman forces was loss of the last chance to deadlock the convention on any issue prior to the nominating ballot. The Stevenson forces of compromise and moderation had won. The clincher came at 2 A.M. Thursday morning, when NBC reported that Frank McKinney, Harriman's midwest manager, now conceded that his man had no chance to win.

Stevenson supporters turned attention to sorting out the most desirable vice-presidential candidates. Kefauver seemed to be overtaking Humphrey, despite persistent rumors that the primary battles still smarted sore and that Stevenson would much prefer another running mate. The proffered reasons: the hope that a Stevenson-Kefauver ticket would do much to promote Democratic unity in California; the support of Walter Reuther; Kefauver's own yeoman efforts to keep his delegates in line for Stevenson; and Kefauver's strength among farmers and small-town people, especially in the midwest.

Stevenson himself, however, withheld his preference of a running mate.

The Nominating Contest for President

Thursday, August 16, was the day for nominations and balloting for the presidential candidate. The issue was by now certain, despite the brave Harriman-Truman front. Before going to the amphitheatre for the nominating speeches, Harriman dispatched a telegram to chairmen of all state delegations, saying: "I have just talked with President Truman. We are determined to fight through to the nomination tonight regardless of any rumors you have heard or any you may yet hear. Frank McKinney flatly denies making the statement attributed to him." But at the hall itself, Harriman told a CBS reporter that he expected to be New York's governor for "many, many years," and quickly interpolated the qualification—"if I am not nominated tonight."[22]

Shortly after noon, the round of nominating speeches got going. Two states used their opportunity for special purposes. As Alabama yielded to Washington, Henry Jackson, junior senator of that state, put senior Senator Warren Magnuson in nomination. After a seconding speech by Don Magnuson (no relative) and an ovation, the convention's task was done: Magnuson withdrew with a television appearance to help him in his race with Governor Langlie. After the Stevenson nomination Georgia rose not only to nominate its favorite son, Representative James C. Davis —but also to clarify its position on civil rights. Governor Marvin Griffin told the convention his delegation had been unable to get recognition to vote "no" on the platform; but he also reminded the delegates of Georgia's consistent support of the party, and promised that Georgia would go down the line for party and candidate this year too.

The other states either nominated major candidates, favorite sons, or passed.

In order, after the Magnuson mention, the nominations were: Stevenson, Johnson, Davis, Harriman, Chandler, McCormack, Battle, Symington, Timmerman. Favorite sons Lausche and Clement had withdrawn, and the bulk of the delegates had moved into the Stevenson column.

The Stevenson nomination was made by Senator Kennedy of Massachusetts, and seconded by a carefully balanced group: Governor Hodges, a Southern leader (against school integration); Senator Lehman, a Northern liberal (especially on civil rights);

Governor Leader of Pennsylvania (rising Democratic youth); Representative William L. Dawson of Chicago (Negro old pro); and Representative Edith Green of Oregon (women, the West). Once the speeches were over, demonstrators paraded for twenty-two minutes: a few even stopped to shake the Truman hand.

The Harriman nomination was equally well planned, but showed somewhat thinner resources in national names. Governor Gary of Oklahoma made the nominating speech, stressing the standard Harriman themes of "fighting candidate" and "can win." Seconders included David J. McDonald (steelworkers), Representative Edna Kelly of Brooklyn (new national committeewoman, officeholder), and Arnold Olsen, Montana's Attorney General (the West). "Surprise" seconder was President Truman, who again was given the courtesy of the floor though a nondelegate. A further surprise was Truman's inclusion of a peace and unity theme along with the "Harriman can win" line: he told the delegates he was supporting the man he believed "best qualified," but he (Truman) was also a "Democrat with a Capital D" and he predicted the delegates would go home unified behind the convention's choice. This triggered an even more boisterous but no more convincing demonstration of twenty-seven minutes.

So much for the news of the afternoon. Its atmosphere was well captured by W. H. Lawrence who wrote: "For hour after hour, speakers extolled the virtues of the aspirants they were nominating or seconding. But the performance was essentially meaningless. The field had no chance against the favorite. The demonstrations were noisy but uninspiring."[23]

During the evening session, the expected happened. The bandwagon rolled on, flattening Harriman and Truman. Favorite sons staying in the race got their first-ballot recognition, as the Stevenson total piled up on the electronic totalizer that was flashing the running count from the tally clerks to the hall and to the country.

The key vote came as the Pennsylvania delegation held the floor. With Oregon's vote, the tally showed 674 for Stevenson and 191½ for Harriman. With Pennsylvania's vote of 7 for Harriman

[23] *Ibid.*

and 67 for Stevenson, the total rose to 741, well over the 686½ needed to nominate.

Governor Harriman, watching the television reports in a room adjoining the convention hall, promptly sent Loyd Benefield to Governor Gary asking him to move that the nomination be made unanimous at the conclusion of the first ballot. Meanwhile, the clerk continued his call of the roll, and at the end of the first ballot the count stood as noted in the table on page 153.

Chairman Rayburn put the question whether any state would like to change its vote. Ignoring Texas, he went ahead to announce: "Governor Stevenson, having received a majority of the votes, is declared the nominee of the convention."[24]

On Governor Gary's motion, Rayburn put the question of making the nomination unanimous. Hearing a chorus of "ayes," the chairman announced that there were no "noes"—without bothering to call for them. The dissident Southerners and disaffected liberals would have to express their recalcitrance on the vice-presidential vote, or later.

Meanwhile, Stevenson was engaging in a heated argument backstage. He was insisting on an open contest for the vice-presidential nomination. Against him stood Sam Rayburn, Lyndon Johnson, and Paul Butler—who insisted that any such move would deadlock the convention. Supporting him were Colonel Jacob Arvey, Mayor Richard Daley, Mayor David Lawrence, and Governor Abraham A. Ribicoff. Stevenson stood firm on his intention.[25] He told the delegates: "I have decided that the selection of a vice-presidential nominee should be made through the free processes of this convention, so that the Democratic party's candidate for this office may join me before the nation not as one man's selection but as one chosen by a great party, even as I have been chosen."[26]

The delegates roared their approval, mindful of the contrast they were going to make with the Republicans.

---

[24] *Chicago Daily News*, Aug. 17, 1956.
[25] Kenneth S. Davis, *Prophet In His Own Country* (1957), p. 478.
[26] *Chicago Daily News*, Aug. 17, 1956.

	Votes	Stevenson	Harriman	Johnson	Symington	Chandler	Davis	Battle	Timmerman	Lausche
Alabama	26	15½		½		3	1	½	5½	
Alaska	6	6								
Arizona	16	16								
Arkansas	26	26								
California	68	68								
Canal Zone	3	3								
Colorado	20	13½	6				½			
Connecticut	20	20								
Delaware	10	10								
District of Columbia	6	6								
Florida	28	25			3					
Georgia	32							32		
Hawaii	6	6								
Idaho	12	12								
Illinois	64	53½	8½		1	1				
Indiana	26	21½	3		½	1				
Iowa	24	16½	7			½				
Kansas	16	16								
Kentucky	30					30				
Louisiana	24	24								
Maine	14	10½	3½							
Maryland	18	18								
Massachusetts	40	32	7½	½						
Michigan	44	39	5							
Minnesota	30	19	11							
Mississippi	22			22						
Missouri	38				38					
Montana	16	10	6							
Nebraska	12	12								
Nevada	14	5½	7	1	½					
New Hampshire	8	5½	1½		1					
New Jersey	36	36								
New Mexico	16	12	3½		½					
New York	98	5½	92½							
North Carolina	36	34½	1		½					
North Dakota	8	8								
Ohio	58	52	½							5½
Oklahoma	28		28							
Oregon	16	16								
Pennsylvania	74	67	7							
Puerto Rico	6	6								
Rhode Island	16	16								
South Carolina	20	2							18	
South Dakota	8	8								
Tennessee	32	32								
Texas	56			56						
Utah	12	12								
Vermont	6	5½	½							
Virgin Islands	3	3								
Virginia	32								32	
Washington	26	19½	6		½					
West Virginia	24	24								
Wisconsin	28	22½	5			½				
Wyoming	14	14								
Total	1,372	905½	210	80	45½	36½	33	32½	23½	5½

[a] "Official Report of the Proceedings of the Democratic National Convention, 1956" (unpublished).

The Nominating Contest for Vice President

Back into caucus went the delegations and trooping into the Stevenson office for a possible hint of blessing went the several hopefuls. Estes Kefauver now said: "If the delegates and the nominee feel that I can make a contribution, I would be willing to accept." Within hours Kefauver said he'd "work like a beaver" for the nomination, and told the press that a professional polling organization showed he had more than 700 delegate votes already. He claimed support came not only from the Midwest, but also from Harriman delegates scattered elsewhere. But he was admittedly anathema to many Southern delegates for his stand on civil rights; the Southerners promptly indicated they would prefer either Humphrey or Kennedy to their own recreant.[27]

Of the other candidates, Humphrey was reported to have a good deal of support from some members of the Stevenson organization; he was properly liberal and had not created personal animus by open primary attacks. But he had little strength or appeal outside pro-liberal ranks, and for these votes there was plenty of competition.

Kennedy, who had been working diligently under cover for several days, now emerged as a formidable opponent.[28] He stood to gain support from the South as a man preferable to the other choices, Catholic though he was; and he could capitalize on his generally liberal record in the Northeast and in the West. He had had important opportunities to appear favorably before the convention, as narrator of the keynote film and nominator of the suc-

[27] *Ibid.*

[28] There was one attempt to win strength in a powerful quarter that did not pay off for Kennedy. An emissary called on Mrs. Roosevelt with a request for her support; she told him that she could not give it because the Senator had avoided taking a position on the McCarthy censure resolution. On getting the answer that was a long time ago, and of no current importance, Mrs. Roosevelt told him it did bear on the present situation. "I think McCarthyism is a question on which public officials must stand up and be counted. I still have not heard Senator Kennedy express his convictions. And I cannot be sure of the political future of anyone who does not willingly state where he stands on that issue." That brought a visit from the Senator himself; he took the same evasive position, and Mrs. Roosevelt did not support him. *On My Own* (Harper & Bros., 1958), pp. 163-64.

cessful nominee. He epitomized a favorite Democratic self-image as a party dedicated to youth.

Mayor Wagner had something of the same combination, but in lesser measure; he was young, he had the largest single bloc of delegates, and he enjoyed favorable perception among liberals. But he lacked widespread organization and the benefits of careful preparatory work.

Senator Albert Gore was also a most personable candidate, of proved legislative competence and acceptable to the South, but of somewhat less appeal to other sectors of the country.

These were the serious candidates—any one of whom would be acceptable to Stevenson, and thus compatible with a strategy of an open convention. The others, who might profit from a sudden turn of events, included Governor Luther H. Hodges of North Carolina, Senator Clinton Anderson of New Mexico, Tennessee's Frank Clement, and Pitt Tyson Maner of Alabama, A. B. Chandler's campaign manager.

The "Open Convention"

On the afternoon of August 17, the Democrats staged their first open contest for the vice-presidential nomination in many years. Dramatic and disorderly enough before it was finished, the afternoon session mustered hardly two hundred delegates when the Star Spangled Banner was played. The television commentators filled the air with rumors, speculation, and predictions while the delegates gradually assembled.

Rayburn cautioned the delegates about the urgency of getting their nomination done in the afternoon, so as not to interfere with the acceptance speeches scheduled for the concluding session in the evening. He announced "unanimous consent" agreements to limit nominating speeches to five minutes each, with only two seconding speeches of two minutes each. "Without objection," said Mr. Rayburn, ignoring the "noes" in the hall, "the procedure is agreed to." After more maneuvering, caucusing and candidate-interviewing on the floor, Mr. Rayburn said that "unanimous consent has been given that there be no demonstrations, and the chair will enforce it if he can." Archibald Alexander presented a resolution instructing the National Committee to decide on a time and place for the next national convention. The chair continued with other, similar routine housekeeping measures until 1:05 P.M. At this point, the clerk started to call the roll of states for nominations for the vice-presidential candidacy, as Mr. Rayburn again gaveled for order and asked members to take their seats.

First state on the list, Alabama, announced a caucus decision to yield to Tennessee for the nomination of Senator Gore. Lt. Governor Jared Maddux performed this function, stressing Gore's unearthing of Dixon-Yates, and his acceptability to Democrats of the North, the South, the East and the West. Senator A. S. Mike Monroney seconded the nomination, praising the fortunate Democratic party as not poverty-stricken in leadership or freedom, and highlighting the Gore legislative record. After the second from Alabama, a nascent demonstration started, and Mr. Rayburn called on the sergeant at arms to control it.

Arizona yielded to Ohio for the nomination of Estes Kefauver, expeditiously done by DiSalle. Connecticut sent Governor Ribicoff to the platform to nominate Senator Kennedy. Florida sent Congressman Robert Sikes up to nominate Governor LeRoy Collins.

There was a curious note as Kefauver-manager Robert Short yielded to Missouri for the nomination of Senator Humphrey, made by Senator Symington. New Jersey yielded to New York for the nomination of Mayor Wagner. Then North Carolina nominated Luther H. Hodges, and provided two seconds for him out of its own delegation.

At 2:30 P.M. the roll call was finished, and the first ballot started.

Alabama, caucusing, passed as the roll started. Alaska cast 6 votes for Kefauver. Arizona added 16, and Arkansas gave 26 votes to Gore. California gave 23½ to start Humphrey, and 10½ to start Kennedy. (Its remaining 34 votes went 33 to Kefauver, one to its Attorney General "Pat" Brown.) Delaware started Wagner with

10 votes. Florida initially gave its 28 votes to its governor, LeRoy Collins, only to switch at the end of the roll call. Kentucky gave its 30 votes to Maner. New Mexico gave its 16 to its Senator Anderson. North Carolina put its governor in the race with 36 votes. South Carolina honored the keynoter, Frank Clement, with 9 of its 20 votes.

And so the ballot went, with Kefauver forging strongly ahead, but by no means demonstrating the promised 700. After Wyoming's announcement, Alabama had made up its mind and recorded a well-scattered count: 12½ for Gore, 4½ for Clement, 3½ for Kefauver, 3 for Maner, 1½ for Kennedy, and ½ vote each for Collins of Florida and Johnson of Texas. Minnesota came in with 30 votes for Humphrey. At this point, Sikes of Florida asked for recognition, and announced that his group was changing its vote as follows: 17 for Kefauver, 9½ for Kennedy, 1 for Collins, and ½ vote for Humphrey.

As no other state sought recognition, the first ballot ended at 3:08 P.M. After struggles by the tally clerks to agree on a count, the chair announced totals at the conclusion of the first ballot:

Kefauver	483½
Kennedy	304
Gore	178
Wagner	162½
Humphrey	134½
Hodges	40
Maner	33
Anderson	16
Clement	13½
Collins	1½
Brown	1
Symington	1
Johnson	½

Three votes were missing—one from Illinois, two from Ohio.

The real story on the first ballot was the strength shown by Senator Kennedy. Although he moved ahead of the favorite, Kefauver, only twice during the balloting (when Illinois gave him 46 votes to put him in front, 114½ to 99, and later when Massachusetts gave him its 40 to put him ahead again, 190½ to 176½), and he did not hold the lead for more than the time it took the next state to put in its vote, he emerged as a serious contender, around whom Southern dissidents and others opposed to Kefauver might well cluster. His 304 votes came from 27 states, with heaviest support from Connecticut (20), Georgia (32), Illinois (46), Louisiana (24), Massachusetts (40) and Virginia (32). He also had votes from South Carolina (6½) in the South, California, Colorado and Nevada in the West, and from Rhode Island, Maine, and Vermont in New England.

The other hopefuls had demonstrated no comparable regional strength. Gore, with 178, had one vote from outside the South and was beholden to Arkansas (26), Mississippi (22), Oklahoma (28), Tennessee (32) and Texas (56) for his strong showing. Wagner's following was even more concentrated, as 98 of his total of 162½ came from New York and 31½ from New Jersey. Only 7½ of his votes came from off the Eastern seaboard, and 8 came from Puerto Rico, Hawaii, and the Virgin Islands. Humphrey had revealed wider regional appeal, but owed most of his 134½ votes to Minnesota (30), to California (23½), and to Missouri (34½). He had a small scattering from fifteen other states. It began to look as if overt campaigning for the Vice Presidency was a less sure means of getting that nomination than campaigning for the Presidency and failing.

While the convention waited for the official first-ballot tally, delegations caucused in their seats, as the television and radio reporters speculated on the changes in progress. Meanwhile Chairman Butler announced an organization meeting of the new Democratic National Committee for the following morning.

At 3:25 P.M., the second ballot started. At the outset, many states repeated their first ballot votes. But Arkansas, voting as a unit, shifted its 26 votes from Gore to Kennedy. Colorado shifted a half vote from Humphrey to Kefauver. Delaware shifted her 10 votes from Wagner to Kennedy. Florida shifted a vote from Collins to Kennedy, and Hawaii a half vote from Humphrey to Kefauver. Illinois, finding one of its missing half votes, gave 3½ more votes to Kennedy (49½) and dropped Kefauver down two votes to 10½. Iowa gave 3 more votes to Kefauver (18½), and 2 more to Kennedy (4), taking 4½ votes from Humphrey (1½) and a half vote from Wagner.

Kentucky, after a caucus, shifted its 30 unit votes from Maner to Gore, but this started no landslide. Maine gave 1½ more to Kennedy, taking ½ vote from Humphrey and 1 from Kefauver. Minnesota shifted 13½ votes from Humphrey to Kefauver. Mississippi did its bit for the Kennedy bandwagon by shifting its 22 votes from Gore. Missouri took 2½ votes from Humphrey, giving 2 to Kefauver and ½ to Gore. Montana consolidated 3½ Humphrey votes with 1 for Wagner and 1 for Kennedy, and gave the 5½ to Kefauver. Nevada took a vote from Wagner and 1½ votes from Kefauver and gave them to Kennedy. New Hampshire turned its previous ½ vote for Kennedy into a unit vote of 8 for Kefauver.

Up to this point, no serious shifting had taken place among the top leaders. Gore was clearly out, as he lost Mississippi's 22 votes (and all the South except Florida moved toward Kennedy). Humphrey was losing driblets from many delegations.

Now the Wagner forces made their bid, not for their own man, but for Kennedy. The New Jersey delegation took 31½ Wagner votes and gave 29½ of them to Kennedy. New Mexico made a counterbid, turning its 16 votes from favorite-son Anderson into 9½ for Kefauver, 4½ for Kennedy, and 2 for Gore. New York threw its tremendous weight into the Kennedy lists, giving him 96½ of the Wagner votes. This break sparked a demonstration, as North Carolina passed.

But the break was not enough. North Dakota (8) and Ohio stayed with Kefauver (Ohio's vote: 51½ Kefauver, 5½ Kennedy, 1 absent). Oklahoma kept its 28 votes with Gore, who had not yet given up hope for his own candidacy. Oregon was unmoved, 16 for Kefauver. Pennsylvania gave Kefauver 10 more votes—and in this case the 8½ Wagner votes did not go to Kennedy. (Kennedy lost 1, Humphrey ½). Puerto Rico, source of New York's newest ethnic minority, stayed with Mayor Wagner despite the New York delegation's example. Rhode Island with only a half Kefauver vote to shift, couldn't shift that to Kennedy. South Carolina did better, shifting 10½ of the Clement-Hodges vote to Kennedy, but also giving 2½ to Gore.

Tennessee, under instructions from its State Democratic Convention to vote for a candidate from Tennessee so long as one had reasonable chance of victory, held its 32 votes for Gore. Tension and uncertainty mounted on the floor, as the pressure toward a Kennedy victory seemed to be increasing, and Tennessee apparently was letting one of her sons down while keeping up the private hopes of the other.

The Gore hopes met their *coup de grace* a moment later, as Texas shifted its 56 votes from him to Kennedy, and hopes for the latter's upset victory soared. But there were no changes of any moment while the rest of the states down to Wyoming were polled. Alabama had pulled itself a little closer together, but cast another split ballot: 6 for Kefauver (up 2½); 12½ for Kennedy (up 11); and 7 for Gore (down 5½). (The losses were to Clement, Collins, and Johnson.) California then gave further impetus to Kennedy, adding 14½ to his total, while giving Kefauver only 4½ more than on the first ballot. (This cost Humphrey 18½ votes, and Brown ½ vote.)

At this point the TV tally showed Kennedy at 597, and Kefauver 522. An upset seemed certain as Kennedy surged toward the magic 686½.

Indiana reporting with 2½ of its votes absent, gave Kennedy another vote, as it took two away from Kefauver. North Carolina distributed its 36 votes for Hodges thus: 9½ to Kefauver, 17½ to Kennedy, 7½ to Gore, and ½ to Humphrey, with one vote not recorded.

At the conclusion (before switches) of the second ballot, 4:03 P.M. the TV tally showed Kennedy at 618 votes and Kefauver at 551½.

Several delegations shouted for recognition. Rayburn recognized Kentucky. The Blue Grass delegation, which had already called itself "unpredictable," switched again, this time going from Gore to Kennedy. Kennedy now had 648 votes, only 38½ short of victory, and with several probably friendly delegations clamoring for recognition. It was the tensest moment yet.

Rayburn recognized Tennessee. Gore spoke. He had given up. He released his delegates for Kefauver.

Oklahoma immediately got recognition, and shifted to Kefauver on Gore's release. Then Senator Humphrey released his delegates to Kefauver, and the issue was settled. But the tension did not diminish. Tennessee shifted its 32 votes to Kefauver. Missouri announced 37 votes for Kefauver, 1 for Humphrey. There was an immediate call for a poll of the delegation; meanwhile the chair asked if any other state wanted to be recognized.

Michigan consolidated its full vote behind Kefauver, pulling the previous 4 votes from Humphrey into the Kefauver column. South Carolina consolidated behind Kennedy (2½ from Gore, ½ from Hodges). Florida took a half-vote from Humphrey and gave it to Kefauver. Illinois gave Kennedy 5 more votes, bringing him to his peak total for the ballot of 656 votes. (At this point, Kefauver had 632.)

But then the Kennedy tide receded. The vote of the polled Missouri delegation showed 36 for Kefauver, a gain of 33; Kennedy 1½, a loss of 1; and Humphrey ½, a loss of 31½. This put Kefauver ahead, 675 to 655. Colorado gave him 4½ more votes, bringing him to 679½. Television reported that Iowa gave him its full 24 votes.[29]

It appears that gains from the District of Columbia (3), Montana (1½) and California (12½) gave Kefauver his victory. At this point the convention itself was too confused, and the official and television tally-indicators too various in their answers, for anyone to know for sure what the exact status of the balloting was. But the switches went on well beyond the point of victory, as delegations moved toward unanimity; Florida switched twice. Alabama gave Kennedy four additional votes, but the rest of the switches all favored Kefauver. At the conclusion of switching, the official count stood 755½ for Kefauver, 589 for Kennedy, 13½ for Gore, 6 for Wagner, 2 for Humphrey, Clement ½, and 5½ not voting.[30]

The state tally is given in the table on page 162.

[29] See *New York Times*, Aug. 18, 1956. The page one story credits Missouri with putting Kefauver over.
[30] *Ibid.*

State	Votes	Kefauver	Kennedy	Gore	Wagner	Humphrey	Others
Alabama	26	6	16½	3			½
Alaska	6	6					
Arizona	16	16					
Arkansas	26		26				
California	68	50	18				
Canal Zone	3		3				
Colorado	20	20					
Connecticut	20		20				
Delaware	10	10					
District of Columbia	6	6					
Florida	28	23½	3½				1
Georgia	32		32				
Hawaii	6	2	2	1		1	
Idaho	12	12					
Illinois	64	9½	54½				
Indiana	26	20	3½				2½
Iowa	24	24					
Kansas	16	16					
Kentucky	30		30				
Louisiana	24		24				
Maine	14	14					
Maryland	18	18					
Massachusetts	40		40				
Michigan	44	44					
Minnesota	30	30					
Mississippi	22		22				
Missouri	38	36	1½			½	
Montana	16	15	1				
Nebraska	12	12					
Nevada	14	½	13½				
New Hampshire	8	8					
New Jersey	36	6	30				
New Mexico	16	9½	4½	2			
New York	98	1½	96½				
North Carolina	36	9½	17½	7½		½	1
North Dakota	8	8					
Ohio	58	57					1
Oklahoma	28	28					
Oregon	16	16					
Pennsylvania	74	74					
Puerto Rico	6				6		
Rhode Island	16	½	15½				
South Carolina	20		20				
South Dakota	8	8					
Tennessee	32	32					
Texas	56		56				
Utah	12	12					
Vermont	6		6				
Virgin Islands	3	3					
Virginia	32		32				
Washington	26	26					
West Virginia	24	24					
Wisconsin	28	28					
Wyoming	14	14					
Total	1,372	755½	589	13½	6	2	6

[a] "Official Report of the Proceedings of the Democratic National Convention, 1956" (unpublished).

At 4:20 P.M., television brought Stevenson and Kefauver to the screen. Two minutes later Rayburn brought the convention to order, and recognized Senator Kennedy, who moved to suspend the rules and nominate the candidate by acclamation. Again there was a chorus of "ayes"; the chairman did not ask for the noes, and announced the favorable result.

Rayburn called Governor McFarland of Arizona to take over the chair, as the convention entertained a number of resolutions of thanks and praise while waiting for the arrival of Kefauver.

Kefauver entered the hall at 4:44, made his way slowly to the rostrum with his wife and his manager and, well in character, told the delegates: "I sure am tired."

The convention adjourned until eight in the evening.

Acceptance Speeches and Final Ceremonies

Other sessions, out of deference to radio-television requirements, had started on time. Not this last one. One network did not even start its coverage until 8:30; the others had to fill in the first half hour with summaries, interviews, impromptu panels, and commentary. A picture of both candidates had replaced the electronic scoreboard. Democratic notables populated the rostrum. They furnished welcome topics for commentators needing to fill up time.

At 8:42, Chairman Butler called for order and brought John McCormack to the chair for opening remarks. These were devoted to praise of his close friend, Sam Rayburn—and Rayburn got his ovation. The invocation made a none-too-subtle political point as the prayer inveighed against a pride that made some men believe that a political party is responsible for making the earth productive.

The business of the evening was twofold: first, to kick off the campaign, defining issues and trumpeting major themes and slogans; and second, to repair the breaches to party unity occasioned by the nominating brawls.

Harry S. Truman came to the rostrum to further both these aims. He led off:

> I am here tonight to give my full support to Adlai Stevenson and Estes Kefauver.
>
> Governor Stevenson is a real fighter, and I ought to know. Any man who can take this convention the way he did should be able to take the Republicans and Eisenhower this fall. He's given some of us here a pretty good licking. . . .
>
> The Democratic party is coming out of this convention stronger than it went in—stronger than it would be if we hadn't done a little scrapping among ourselves. A Democratic convention without a fight is not worth going to. . . .
>
> I say to all Democrats everywhere—no matter whom you supported before—get behind Adlai Stevenson and Estes Kefauver.

After a little advice about party contributions and campaigning, the former President told his co-partisans:

> We are fighting to save our resources.
>
> We are fighting to save our farmers.
>
> We are fighting to save the rights of labor.
>
> We are fighting to save small business.
>
> We are fighting to save our national defenses.
>
> We are fighting to save the unity of the free world.
>
> And, in short, my friends and my fellow Democrats, we are in the most important fight in all our history.
>
> We are fighting to save our country. And with God's help we shall win that fight.[31]

Kefauver followed, accompanied by his wife to the rostrum. He underlined the convention's "open choice," and pointed up the contrast with what was about to happen in the vice-presidential nomination at San Francisco. He saluted Stevenson and hailed Truman as the party's pride today and inspiration for tomorrow. He called for Democratic majorities in Congress, in state houses, and in court houses. He delineated a high moral obligation and

---

[31] *New York Times*, Aug. 18, 1956. Notably, Truman eliminated from his concluding list the fifth issue mentioned in his major address: the "fight to save the finances of all the people from control of the money changers and mortgage sharks." This was the one that drew most Republican counterfire, when the President resented Truman's warning that the people "are in danger right now from this bunch of racketeers."

rosy future for his party, calling it the party not of criticism but of inspiration. And he struck out at Nixon:

> The chief function of the Vice President should not be that of a political sharpshooter for his party.
> It should not be that of providing the smear under the protection of the President's smile. . . .
> As for Vice-Presidential candidate, I promise you, friends, that I will never demean that high office to traduce fellow Americans. I will never use it to sow the seeds of division and of distrust.
> In our party and in this campaign we're not going to have one low road and one high road. In this party and in this campaign we're going to have two high roads—both of them high roads to victory.[32]

Then came the high point of the evening—Stevenson. After a lush introduction by the chairman, Stevenson, his sons, his daughter-in-law and his sister, Mrs. Ives, waited out the ovation. The party management brought the major contenders of the previous sessions to the rostrum to show their unity. Rayburn, mindful of television's eye, shooed banners away from in front of the rostrum as the demonstration continued. Party officials came in for their share of recognition. Candidates in prominent state races showed up. After fifteen minutes of turbulence, the music died away, the candidate paid his compliments and began his vision of a "New America."

Announcing his major theme, Stevenson said that four years before, the country stood at the end of a Democratic era of unparalleled social reform and of glorious triumph over depression and tyranny. Tonight, however, it stood on the threshold of a new and decisive era.

> . . . History's headlong course has brought us, I devoutly believe, to the threshold of a New America—to the America of the great ideals and noble visions which are the stuff our future must be made of.
> I mean a New America where poverty is abolished and our abundance is used to enrich the lives of every family.
> I mean a New America where freedom is made real for all without regard to race or belief or economic condition.
> I mean a New America which everlastingly attacks the ancient idea that men can solve their differences by killing each other.

[32] *Ibid.*

These are the things I believe in and will work for. . . . These are the things I know you believe in and will work for with everything you have. These are the terms on which I accept your nomination.

He accepted the party's platform as a program that was

. . . more than a consensus of the strongly held convictions of strong men; it is a signpost toward that New America. It speaks of the issues of our time with passion for justice, with reverence for our history and character, with a long view of the American future, and with a sober, fervent dedication to the goal of peace on earth.

He grasped the thistle of civil rights:

. . . Of course there is disagreement in the Democratic party on desegregation. It could not be otherwise in the only party that must speak responsibly and responsively in both the North and the South. If all of us are not wholly satisfied with what we have said on this explosive subject, it is because we have spoken the only way a truly national party can.

In substituting realism and persuasion for the extremes of force or nullification, our party has preserved its effectiveness, it has avoided a sectional crisis, and it has contributed to our national unity as only a national party could.

He moved to take the Eisenhower illness out of the realm of campaign argument, saying that Eisenhower's "ability personally to fulfill the demands of his exacting office is a matter between him and the American people." He wished deeply for the President's health and well-being. But he also expressed concern for the sad condition of the Presidency, deploring Madison Avenue and money in politics—by implication a Republican monopoly. And he told Democrats they faced the fact that no administration had ever before enjoyed "such uncritical and enthusiastic support from so much of the press as this one."

Decrying Republican reassurance and complacency and allegedly wasted opportunities for leadership at home and abroad, he asserted: "What this country needs is not propaganda and a personality cult. What this country needs is leadership and truth. And that's what we mean to give it."

He launched into now-familiar criticism of the Republican administration: farmers without a "fair share" of the national in-

come, with no Republican help until an election year; small businessmen, teachers, workers, pensioners in trouble; many living
on substandard incomes; low governmental prestige abroad; military advantages slipping away; defeats in the cold war; wasted
opportunities.

He called for America "to be herself again" under a Democratic leadership that would do justice to children, repair the
ravages to schools, restore the vitality of the family farm, preserve small business, strengthen labor unions and collective bargaining, conserve resources of land and forest and water, and
rekindle the spirit of liberty. In the foreign field, he found the
challenge was as great but the opportunity less because timing
was not so clearly in our own hands. Nevertheless:

> . . . We must place our nation where it belongs in the eyes of the
> world—at the head of the struggle for peace.

In peroration he moved to moral matters:

> There is a spiritual hunger in the world today and it cannot be
> satisfied by material things alone. . . . We must not let our aspira-
> tions so diminish that our worship becomes rather of material achieve-
> ment and bigness.
>
> For a century and a half the Democratic party has been the party
> of respect for people, of reverence for life, of hope for each child's
> future, of belief that "the highest revelation is that God is in every
> man."
>
> Once we were not ashamed in this country to be idealists. Once
> we were proud to confess that an American is a man who wants
> peace and believes in a better future and loves his fellow man. We
> must reclaim these great Christian and humane ideas. We must dare
> to say again that the American cause is the cause of all mankind.
>
> If we are to make honest citizens of our hearts, we must unite them
> again to the ideals in which they have always believed and give
> those ideals the courage of our tongues.[33]

Any difficulty the Democrats present might have had in recognizing themselves in this picture did nothing to dampen their
enthusiasm for the candidate. As the candidate bade the delegates
goodbye and expressed his hope that they could "meet again in
every town and village of America," the delegates gave a final

---

[33] Adlai E. Stevenson, *The New America* (1957), pp. 4-9.

short, sharp roar; a Negro singer gave full tongue to an unrecognizable but deeply stirring version of the Lord's Prayer, and at 10:52 P.M. Chicago time, Mr. Sam Rayburn declared the Democratic National Convention adjourned *sine die*.

With the adjournment of the national committee the next day, the convention was history. Delegates and party officials retired to their home stations, mulling results, making final preparations for the campaign soon to be pressed.[34]

[34] They retired on a receding flood of words. The convention had set a new record. Western Union reported that it had transmitted 10,250,000 words from the convention site, topping 1952's previous high of 9,957,117. Peak volume for one day was the preceding Wednesday, when more than 1,700,000 words were carried (*Chicago Tribune,* Aug. 19, 1956). And these were only the written words of cables. Radio and television undoubtedly carried far more, and swelled the total finding its way into print. Oral utterance in hotel and amphitheatre was, of course, beyond count.

7

The Republican Convention Committees
and Candidate Maneuvers

UNITY, HARMONY, DISCIPLINE, dispatch, and decorum oddly intermixed with happiness, professional entertainment, and well-schooled mass demonstrations by the young, all under the aura of an apotheosized President—this was the amalgam aimed for by the managers of the Republican Convention of 1956.

Problems of issue and personality were already settled beyond serious doubt. The issues of organizational functioning and control were in no more serious question. All that remained was ratification of the decisions, performance of the rally, and launching of the campaign.

These steps called for action, if not decisions—action somehow to be spread over four days without triviality or boredom. Campaign functions called for iteration of the main lines of argument on issues, the parading of personages, and establishment of an image of contrast—contrast with the Democrats and their Chicago convention and with the Republican convention of 1952.

Despite elaborate preparations and precautions, the apprehensive organization men sensed two small but nagging threats to harmony: the Stassen revolt and the platform decisions. (Perennial intraparty squabbles in two Southern states needed no special attention.) The Stassen revolt, innocuous to date, might conceivably get somewhere if the President should curl a sentence around the idea that he would really welcome a genuine race among the latent vice-presidential aspirants. The platform process contained minuscule threats that extremists on civil rights or on foreign policy might get out of hand.

The result was tighter control than usual over all aspects of the convention, formal and informal. Ceremonial openings and closings; invocations; the appointment, functioning, and reports of committees; speeches by party greats and wheelhorses; nominations and voting—all were regulated in fine detail. Such informal manifestations as Stassen press conferences were kept in check by an immediate reply technique, in which dependables followed the semi-insurgent with correct doctrine. Critical points in the platform and credentials processes were met in executive sessions, while White House emissaries kept negotiators informed of the President's stated or imputed desires.

Preconvention Party Activities

Businesslike throughout, the party organization moved smoothly through the preliminary processes of committee hearings and reporting on platform, rules, credentials, and permanent organization. Meanwhile the Democrats were moving to the climax of their convention in Chicago, overshadowing the Republican preliminaries.

HEARINGS ON THE PLATFORM

Well before the convention assembled at San Francisco, preparations for the platform's verbiage were made in the offices of the National Committee and of Senator Prescott S. Bush, of Connecticut, already designated to head up the operation. The party had invited views and testimony from all interested persons, to be assembled by the Research Division of the committee for the perusal of the platform group. Staff men in the higher echelons of the federal government had prepared statements of the record and of the Republican position, for coordination by White House specialists and consideration by the platform committee. Senator Bush himself worked intensively on "the record" for five or six weeks prior to the San Francisco meeting, discussing matters with both President Eisenhower and former President Hoover. He reported they agreed on the desirability of a platform that was "brief, forthright and honest with the American people."[1] He also had discussed the treatment of foreign policy on two separate occasions with the Secretary of State.[2]

Operations in San Francisco commenced as Bush called together the 96-member Committee on Resolutions on Wednesday morning, August 15. The committee organized itself substantially as it had done in previous years, dividing itself into ten subcommittees, one each for agriculture; civil rights and immigration; government affairs; national defense; taxation and fiscal policy; business and economic policy; foreign policy; labor and welfare; natural resources and public works; and veterans affairs. Senator Bush told the committee members, the few visitors, and the handful of press men present that the platform would be "affirmative" and would fall into two parts: a Declaration of Faith; and a documentation of the record and an outline of Republican programs for "tomorrow."

The Committee on Resolutions then formally elected Bush as its chairman, and chose Mrs. Eva Bowring of Nebraska as its secretary. Bush then appointed the chairmen of the subcommittees, asked them to join him on the platform, and put a motion constituting them a drafting committee. The committee would, he hoped, conclude hearings by Thursday evening, complete drafting on Friday, and meet in plenary session on Saturday afternoon to agree on a draft to go to the full convention. Dr. Floyd McCaffree, Research Director of the National Committee, reminded committee members of the services available to them from his division, and the meeting adjourned.

The committee scheduled concurrent hearings by all the subcommittees, with twice-daily briefings for the press given by the subcommittee chairmen.

---

[1] Press release, Monday, Aug. 13, 1956 (mimeo.), p. 4.
[2] *Ibid.*, p. 6. In a press conference earlier in the summer, the Secretary told reporters that he would be delighted to work out a common position on foreign policy for the platforms of the two parties—provided the Democrats would accept his position; and he defended himself from the charge of occupying himself with platform matters instead of affairs of state.

The various subcommittee hearings varied in interest and content; the most noteworthy dealt with national defense, foreign affairs, and civil rights. Attendance at any one of these revealed significant differences from the Democratic procedure in Chicago. Witnesses could file their statements, if any, with committee secretaries at any time, before or after their testimony. (A press table offered distribution for statements reproduced in quantity.) Even the most controversial witnesses did not provoke the kind of mutual celebration or repartee practiced by the Democrats. Witnesses were expected to be far more drastic in summarizing their statements. Thruston Morton (former Assistant Secretary of State and chairman of the foreign policy subcommittee) told his witnesses to come promptly to the point. Similarly Senator Dirksen told witnesses appearing before his civil rights subcommittee that he did not want statements of position. These, he said, were well known to the public and need not be repeated. Instead, he wanted witnesses to bring out pertinent facts; but there would be no cross-examination by the subcommittee about their implications.

The practice of concurrent hearings made it impossible for the Republicans to stage a day-by-day show, with each performance devoted to a major aspect of party policy, and intended to capture major media attention for prominent party personalities, candidates, or officials of favorable pressure groups. Moreover, neither the press nor the pressure groups put on their top performers; regional representatives did the job in most cases. The Republicans made no stenographic record, depending on witnesses' statements and the notes of subcommittee members for documentation. (The major documentation, furnished by government sources, was not part of the public record.) Television and radio were absent from most of the hearings, but the working pen-and-pencil press covered the twice-daily briefings, and the electronic media gave some attention to the more colorful and potentially controversial sessions. This practice reflected judgments both by the Republican managers and by media officials that the Democratic nominations and acceptances were far more newsworthy than the Republican preliminaries.

Among the one hundred fifty or so witnesses scheduled (some

of whom appeared before more than one subcommittee), some turned up who had also appeared in Chicago, and most of the organizations were represented in both San Francisco and Chicago. Of course, no representatives of the Democratic party organizations came to testify, although the political liberals came to San Francisco just as the United States Chamber of Commerce had appeared in Chicago. Official Republican witnesses, representing national or state party organizations, were not publicized as their Democratic counterparts had been. Regional party representatives were more in evidence than national figures. For example, the main statement on foreign policy was made by an informal group of thirty-six California Republicans. It had been approved by the California State Republican Central Committee, and was based on policy documents and other assistance from the State Department. The statement, said spokesman Admiral Benton Weaver Decker, was "true to our own selves," as the drafters accepted only "what California Republicans could support."

Some of the San Francisco spokesmen proved to be more articulate and persuasive than their Chicago colleagues. Some, notably those for the Chamber of Commerce points of view, were more hospitably received in the West. The anti-Zionist Jews found a more tolerant atmosphere, although their pleas had little or nothing to do with the ultimate disposition of the platform statement on policy toward Israel and the Middle East. Some of the isolationists—notably the For America group—ran into counterargument and rebuttal on defense policy. Their spokesman, Thomas Werdel, former member of the House and shortly to be the Constitutional Party's vice-presidential candidate, encountered the firm opposition of Senator Duff of Pennsylvania. The Senator, fresh from the Symington subcommittee investigations on the role of air power in national defense, was armed with the latest data on the capabilities and requirements of our armed forces and was in no mood to accept arguments based on Werdel's outdated Washington experience or current outlook.

The Republican device of twice-daily press briefings put reporting of the platform process into a quite different framework from that of Chicago. There, the press had observed and reported colloquies between witness and platform committee. In San Francisco, the press heard reports by subcommittee chairmen, who presented witnesses' arguments at second hand, generally characterized the development of argument and opinion, and parried or answered questions about the probable shape of the ultimate planks in their appropriate fields. The press probed into specific contrasts with Democratic statements, since the Democratic platform was being issued in time for Republican response at the hearings stage. And the subcommittee chairmen contrasted position differences with the Republican record and probable platform. They recalled the Republican platform of 1952 where appropriate and underlined fulfillment or noted new emphases. In the more controversial fields, such as civil rights, the subcommittee chairmen of necessity dodged pointed questioning in the first day, before their groups had had a chance to complete hearings and firm up preliminary positions. Most of the others indicated they expected no difficulties in drafting their planks.

Questions about the appearance of administration officials as witnesses elicited the answer that none was expected. Chairmen also played down any communications from the Executive departments during the early stages, although newsmen evoked an early admission that each of the subgroups had received "white envelopes" containing some sort of platform recommendations.[3]

The minor mystery of who had furnished these communications,

---

[3] Comments of Thruston Morton to the press throw a little light on the details of platform committee procedure. He confirmed that State Department representatives would not testify unless requested, although appropriate officials were in town. He revealed he had learned only on August 14 that he was to chair the foreign policy group and speculated that his service as Assistant Secretary of State had had something to do with choosing him. He produced his "white envelope," admitted he had not read it carefully, scanned it briefly and pronounced it "background on the record." He quoted a sample dealing with the U.S. Information Agency, affirming the President's close personal attention to that agency. He pointed out that no screening of witnesses had been done by the subcommittee, noting that there would be testimony from witnesses favoring recognition of Red China, and in behalf of such organizations as the U. N. Educational, Scientific and Cultural Organization, the U. N. International Children's Emergency Fund, and the U. N. Food and Agriculture Organization. He expected, however, "no real trouble" except possibly on the tariff and reciprocal trade program. He gave a near-preview of one plank, asserting his "personal view" that the United States should guarantee the "physical integrity" of Israel as a nation, and say so in the platform.

and what they held, was solved forthrightly by Senator Bush. He told the press that he was the source. Each contained a brief of views submitted to him by "various sources," including federal departments and agencies. Bush promptly announced that neither these summaries nor the reports of subcommittees would be made available to the press.

There was little or no discussion of most of the platform issues outside of the platform committee, except for civil rights. That topic did get an airing in a clash of views between Maryland's Governor McKeldin and Virginia's former candidate for governor, Ted Dalton. McKeldin, taking the strong liberal position, called for a plank "so plain that we need nobody to interpret what it means." Dalton called for one mild enough so that it would not "pour salt into the wounds of the South." Delegate Thomas E. Stagg, Jr., of Louisiana, foreshadowed the position he would take next day in the hearings, supporting Dalton's moderate draft as needed if Republicans were to build a two-party system in the South. Another Virginia delegate recommended a similar states-rights approach.

Roy Wilkins, on arrival in San Francisco, repeated his six-point prescription given in Chicago for a satisfactory plank.[4]

The only subcommittee chairman to get himself even part way out on a limb during the preliminaries was Senator Dirksen. He made clear his preference for a strong civil rights plank. He called the Democratic version "the nicest nuthin' I ever did see," and said the Republican version would be "unequivocal"—and predicted further that the Republicans wouldn't have to fight about it, since they had a "unique capability for unity."

In the event, the nearest thing to a fight in the platform proceedings took place with respect to civil rights—and the real issue was strategy for the Republican party in making its way in the South, while making inroads via Negroes into Northern urban Democratic strongholds. The Republicans could either try for a party built on moderation, looking for white leadership that would not press on desegregation; or they could go all out for civil rights

[4] *Evening Star* (Washington, D.C.), Aug. 17, 1956. See above, Chap. 4, pp. 91-92.

and look for support among Negroes and liberals, not only in the South but in key districts of such populous Northern and Western states as New York, Michigan, Illinois, and California.

The Republican managers, even less desirous of a public fight on the issue than were the Democrats, insulated arguments about civil rights by interspersing statements about less controversial matters of immigration and naturalization.

Chief spokesman for the moderate Southerners was Thomas E. Stagg, Jr., Republican chairman of the 4th Congressional District of Louisiana. Speaking "from the bottom of a well-rounded Republican heart," he noted that the "Southland" had its problems, and called for a "moderate" plank. He recited the Louisiana vote for Eisenhower in 1952, emphasizing that 5 out of 7 parishes in his congressional district had returned a majority for the President in 1952, and Shreveport had gone for him two to one. He pointed out that after the 1954 court decisions, the "voluntary spirit" toward civil rights had evaporated. He noted the rise of citizens councils, and the fact that the States' Rights party had qualified for a place on the November ballot in his state. He recalled Republican efforts to get away from a "one-crop politics" in the South, in which the Republican party was coming forward as the party of states' rights. For Republican gains to continue, a moderate plank was essential. "We condemn bigots," he said, "and we want States' Rights. We can attract Democrats being pushed out of their party by Clements, Reuther and others. The South is the Golconda of the Republican party," he averred; "don't ignore it longer."

At this point an intervening witness, Aaron Sargeant, Chancellor-General of the National Society of the Sons of the American Revolution, spoke on immigration and naturalization. He pleaded for preservation of the basic principles of the McCarran-Walter Act—i.e., use of national origins as a basis for control—and called on the party "to follow principle" and deal with the problem without excessive vacillation in efforts to deal with individual cases of hardship.

Roy Wilkins and two supporting witnesses not only repeated the demands made at Chicago, but also pointed out the strength the Republicans could gain if they asserted and defended the rights of all citizens to vote. He tempted them with visions not only of Negro allegiance: he pointed to hundreds of thousands if not millions of white citizens in the South now silent on justice and civil rights because they were intimidated by "hoodlum thinking"—and only waiting for a chance to speak out with political effectiveness.

The next witness, William H. Oliver of the UAW, rehearsed special problems of labor and integration in the South. He was interrupted to allow Representative Keating of New York to make a speech. Keating dealt both with immigration and with civil rights; he came out wholeheartedly for the President's programs in both fields, pinned blame on the Democrats for torpedoing them in the last Congress, and left rough drafts of platform planks. Oliver then completed his statement, dealing with the special problems of Negroes and other minorities when unemployment struck. He was followed by another UAW representative, who argued against Rule XXII of the Senate, rounding out the liberal presentation.

The day's testimony was completed as Benjamin Peary of Los Angeles, representing the Republican State Central Committee of California, presented the text of a resolution adopted on August 5, favoring a pledge to enforce the letter and spirit of the fourteenth amendment.

At the conclusion of the *pro forma* Friday press briefings, the platform committee went into executive session, as newsmen speculated that the civil rights fight was so hot that the issue might go to the convention. They reported that platform committee members had met on Friday morning, and had agreed to file a minority report if the draft emerging from the committee were to endorse the Supreme Court decisions "too strongly." But winds of moderation started to blow. Senator Bush predicted that the plank would not be offensive to any fair-minded persons from the South.[5]

More important, the issue was taken to the White House. Sherman Adams heard the disputants and let it be known that a mod-

[5] *New York Times,* Aug. 19, 1956.

erate plank was wanted. White House aides superintended the drafting under tight security conditions. They left Dirksen and the other Republicans who had predicted a clear-cut stand to scramble back to the party line as best they could.[6]

Bush predicted that the executive session of the platform committee would undoubtedly be successful in summarizing the Eisenhower philosophy, but now admitted it would be impossible to keep the platform brief. He titillated hearers with promises of a "rather novel manner of presentation to the convention," foreshadowing the National Committee's well-laid plans to have the Cabinet do the job of talking about issues, after Bush himself had read out the Declaration of Faith.

Thus the public preliminaries ended, and the committee went underground. On Sunday, August 19, draft planks started to appear as the committee finished with them in preparation for the public unveiling of the full platform the following Tuesday.

CHANGES IN THE RULES

The Republicans had three items of business before them dealing with party rules. First was a rearrangement and terminological clarification of the rules approved in 1952. Second was a proposed change in the procedure for polling delegations when the division announced by the delegation chairman was challenged by a member. Third was a proposed change in the number of authorized delegates for the District of Columbia.

On Tuesday, August 14, the committee on rules met to consider these matters. None of them raised critical issues for the convention at hand. The proposed procedure for polling a delegation might affect future convention proceedings by reducing or eliminating a possible source of delay. To a convention eager to get on with a public show of efficiency in making decisions, this change would eliminate an obstacle. To one in which contending factions were seeking time-gaining (or losing) procedures to further private

[6] *The Reporter,* Vol. 15, No. 3 (Sept. 6, 1956), pp. 12-13.

group strategems, the loss of such freedom might not be altogether welcome to all contenders.

The rearrangement and terminological clarification was the work of a committee that had been headed by Governor McKeldin. The proposed rearrangement gave effect to a time perspective starting with the instant convention (Rules 1-18); proceeding to the election, composition, powers, and duties of the National Committee (Rules 19-29); establishing the membership in the next national convention (Rule 30); and concluding with rules for the election of delegates to the national convention (Rules 31-33). The terminological clarification was designed to eliminate possible confusions in the manner of electing delegates, and to make clear that the requirement (of old Rule 14, present Rule 16) of a call of the roll in voting on the nominations applied both to the roll call for the nominations and to the balloting thereon.

The redrafting committee eliminated old Rule 30, that empowered the National Chairman to create an advisory committee (and required him to do so if requested by a majority of the National Committee). This rule had been adopted in 1952 as one part of an effort of Midwest Republicans to gain a stronger voice for state party officials in the councils of the National Committee. The other part, and the more effective one, was old Rule 22b, that added to the National Committee the state or territorial chairman of any state or territory producing a Republican majority in the last presidential election, or which had sent a Republican majority to both houses of Congress, or where there was a Republican governor. This provision had resulted in the addition of some forty-two state chairmen to the National Committee, giving an adequate channel for expression of state organization views. No advisory committee had been appointed; there was little or no pressure to appoint one; and any pressure arising later could be dealt with under his existing authority, with the consent of the National Committee, to "appoint such other committees and assistants as he may deem necessary."[7]

[7] Interview with Mr. Fred C. Scribner, Jr., December 1958; see also Paul T. David, Malcolm Moos, and Ralph M. Goldman, *Presidential Nominating Politics in 1952*

The problem of the rule on roll call stemmed from possible difficulties and delays caused by delegates wanting recognition for themselves or their group on national television, when the delegate division was not really at issue. The proposal made to the National Committee to obviate this practice was very similar to that just adopted by the Democrats. It would have allowed the chairman of the convention, on challenge by a delegation member of an announced vote of his delegation, either to direct the roll of members of the delegation to be called forthwith in public; or to send an assistant secretary to the delegation to poll it in private. If the chairman took the latter course, he could direct the roll call of states to continue and record the results of the doubtful state after the conclusion of the regular roll call. But in any case, under the proposal, if one fourth of the delegation demanded an open poll of the delegation, they could have it.

The disposition made of the matter by the National Committee was short and to the point. Although the committee agreed the proposal could go to the Committee on Rules and Order of Business of the convention, it would go without blessing. Governor Mc-Keldin told the press of unanimous opposition to the proposal, "so we will do as we have in the past. If anybody wants to stand up and be counted, he can."[8] He did not elaborate; but it was more than plausible that at least three considerations underlay this attitude.

First was the almost certain prospect that there would be no delegation squabbles in the forthcoming convention and hence little immediate need for the rule. Second was a disposition to see to it that nothing would be done to make the convention even look closed. (The danger of disrupted television schedules due to the misbehavior of delegates seemed small to the well-disciplined

---

(1954), Vol. I, pp. 88-89. Scribner was General Counsel of the committee until September 21, 1955; he was a member of the McKeldin group up to that time, and subsequently served as a member of the Committee on Rules of the convention. Hugh A. Bone in his *Party Committees and National Politics* (1958), p. 15, suggests Rule 22 was adopted primarily by efforts of Eisenhower Republicans. Scribner attributed the rule to Taft supporters looking for a better voice in national policy. David, Moos, and Goldman support the latter view, adding that it had a natural appeal for Eisenhower forces.

[8] *Evening Star* (Washington, D.C.), Aug. 15, 1956.

Republican managers.) Third was recognition of the fact that convention delegates from many states had been elected to their posts only after considerable trouble and expense. Since the usual convention gave them little to do—and this one offered even less —there was no point in downgrading their office any further.

The problem of representation for the District of Columbia was more difficult. Although the committee on rules was favorably disposed to do something for the disfranchised District, it faced a near certain demand for more votes for other territories, if it raised the District's quota. As District representatives asked that their quota be raised from six to ten, Hawaii, with six regular and four bonus delegates already, asked for more too. And Puerto Rico, said McKeldin, "was getting ready." The immediate step was to create a subcommittee of five, chaired by Delegate George F. Etzell of Minnesota, to search for an equitable formula and to report to the Committee on Rules of the convention.[9]

The District of Columbia representatives, headed by George L. Hart, Jr., then appeared before the Etzell group, urging two main points: (1) that the District was larger in population than twelve states and Hawaii; and (2) that it had raised more money for the National Committee than any of thirty-six states and territories in the past six years.[10]

The Committee on Rules and Order of Business met on Monday afternoon, August 20, to dispose of these matters, and to prepare its report to the convention. Although the National Committee's committee on rules had had the matter under consideration for over a year, it was unable to find any appropriate and equitable formula to govern District of Columbia representation; and the spokesmen for the District and the chairman of the *ad hoc* committee were also unable to produce, in the public session or in the executive session that followed, a wholly acceptable basis. Neither money raised nor population in potential Republican votes seemed an adequate one.

Failing a general solution, the committee's immediate solution was to increase the District's representation from six to eight; to

[9] *Ibid.*
[10] *Ibid.*, Aug. 16, 1956.

adopt the *pro forma* changes in the drafting of the old rules; and to reject again the proposal for a change in procedure for a public poll of a delegation on the request of any member. The report as submitted was accepted by voice vote, without change, by the convention the next day.[11]

CREDENTIALS CONTESTS

The near-perennial contests in Mississippi and South Carolina did nothing in 1956 to strain the procedures for handling contests established by the 1952 convention. Under those arrangements,[12] a seven-member Committee on Contests was appointed by the Chairman of the National Committee to identify issues of fact and law and to make a report of a recommended settlement to the National Committee. This committee, under the chairmanship of Albert K. Mitchell of New Mexico, met on August 13 to consider the contests between the Messervy and Dows groups in South Carolina and the Black and Tan (Howard) versus Lily-White (Miller) groups in Mississippi.[13]

The South Carolina contest turned on an issue of law—as to which of the competing delegations had been selected by a legally called and convened convention. On examination of the legal merits, the Contest Committee unequivocally recommended to the National Committee the seating of the Dows group.[14]

[11] *Official Report of the Proceedings of the Twenty-sixth Republican National Convention, 1956,* p. 156. (Hereinafter cited as *Official Proceedings, 1956.*) For text of the rules as adopted see pp. 156-67.

[12] Rule 4, Rules adopted by the Republican National Convention Held at Chicago, Illinois, July 7, 1952. *Official Report of the Proceedings of the Twenty-fifth Republican National Convention, 1952,* pp. 292-94.

[13] *Evening Star* (Washington, D.C.), Aug. 14, 1956.

[14] See "Recommendation of Committee on Contests: South Carolina Contest" (no date, mimeo.), issued as a press release at the convention headquarters, by authority of the chairman of the Committee on Contests, Albert K. Mitchell, New Mexico. The report of the Committee on Contests summarized the issues of facts and law. The Dows group rested its claim on the fact that it was created pursuant to action taken at a legally constituted meeting of the State Executive Committee on December 31, 1955; the Messervy group on action taken at a meeting held on December 15, 1955, that was later adjudged by the South Carolina courts to be a nullity for lack of a quorum. The Committee on Contests rested its judgment on

The Mississippi case was less clear-cut. The Committee on Contests recommended a judgment of Solomon:

> The Committee is faced with the fact that neither group has presented a clear cut incontestable legal position. It is apparent from the briefs filed by both parties that neither group has been able to establish a continuing—or even existing—organization in a majority of the 82 counties of Mississippi. The Miller group admits that it held county conventions in only 28 counties and the Howard group appears to have held no more (and probably less) county conventions than the Miller group.
>
> Since the Republican National Convention is the judge of its own constituted membership and since each of these two contesting groups may succeed in establishing some, but not all of the equities in its favor, this Committee has concluded, after careful consideration, that a fair solution, under all the circumstances, lies in permitting a participation of both of these groups in the proceedings of the National Convention.
>
> The Committee therefore recommends:
>
> That both delegations be seated by the National Republican Convention;
>
> That the Howard delegation be allocated 8 delegates and 8 alternates;
>
> That the Miller delegation be allocated 7 delegates and 7 alternates;
>
> That each delegation advise the Secretary of the National Committee of the names of those delegates and alternates entitled to cast that portion of the Mississippi vote allocated to their respective group; and
>
> That all members of both delegations be entitled to the privileges of the floor of the Convention.[15]

The National Committee met on Wednesday morning, August 15, to consider these recommendations. In a session lasting until mid-afternoon, the committee decided that the Dows delegation was entitled to be seated by the convention, and it approved the

this latter decision and on the further requirement of South Carolina state law that the meetings of the state convention at which delegates to conventions should legally be chosen must take place in March. The convention at which the Messervy group had been elected had taken place in May. The Dows convention took place on March 28, 1956.

[15] "Recommendation of Committee on Contests: Mississippi Contest" (no date, mimeo.), pp. 2-3.

settlement of the Mississippi contest[16] outlined above.

The Messervy group made an insufficient and belated appeal to the Committee on Credentials, which decided that formally speaking there were no contests pending before it. That committee did entertain an appeal limited to the question whether adequate appeal had been taken in time (the convention rules required notice of an appeal from a decision of the National Committee within twenty-four hours). But hearing no new evidence of substance, and learning of evidence damaging to the Messervy case, the Committee on Credentials affirmed the action of the National Committee. It also approved certain noncontroversial changes in the delegations from Louisiana and Indiana; its report was accepted by voice vote and no dissent by the convention.[17]

Although the Mississippi Lily-Whites had circularized all delegates with copies of their briefs and a letter referring to uncited newspaper comment on the paramount interest of their cause, nothing of moment was at stake. The defeated Messervy group left the San Francisco meeting, protesting organizational revenge against them for having been Taft supporters in 1952. But they promised they would vote Republican in 1956; and nothing indicated that they would not have ridden the Eisenhower-Nixon bandwagon at the convention. No immediate Eisenhower-Nixon calculations rested on seating one or the other delegation, nor did the future of the Republican organization in either of these two Southern states seem to hang on one or the other choice.

THE PERMANENT ORGANIZATION

Ratification of the main decision of the Committee on Permanent Organization—the choice for permanent chairmen of the convention—offers a possible but rarely used opportunity for a test of factional strength. In the instant convention, nothing could have been less likely. The committee had done its *pro forma* job of selecting Joseph W. Martin of Massachusetts for his fifth term

[16] Reportedly the work of Hugh Scott, General Counsel, according to Wednesday (August 15) newspapers.

[17] *Official Proceedings, 1956*, p. 88.

of service as Permanent Chairman, and in recommending that the temporary officers of the convention become its permanent officers. (Martin's weakness in the party organization, revealed by the ease with which Representative Halleck of Indiana deprived him of the minority leadership in 1959, was in no wise heralded by the committee's choice.) They went even further; they dispensed with the reading of the names of the Honorary Vice Presidents of the convention (one each nominated by the states and territories represented at the conclave) proposed each year by the committee. This innovation in shortened procedures, along with the committee's report, was gratefully and promptly accepted by the convention.[18]

Preconvention Candidate Maneuvers

No casual visitor to the convention site at any time after August 15 could be in any doubt as to the choice of the management for President or Vice President. Great posters appeared everywhere, urging all and sundry not just to nominate Ike, or Ike and Dick— but to elect them. Leonard Hall, in dressing the set, had studiously overlooked Eisenhower's formal correctness in refusing to foreclose the last glimmer of appearance of freedom of delegate choice. His men gazed down everywhere.

Only the flickerings of an occasional brave Ike and Chris button in a dim corridor gave outward proof of wayward thought and freedom of choice. Stassen set up his headquarters on Market Street between offices of the Saints and Sinners Milk Fund drive and a regional committee for Eisenhower and Nixon. Few delegates bothered to come in to see what the latest Stassen poll data had to say about Nixon's probable drag on the ticket, or to meet the few youthful Stassenites willing to compromise their political futures by overt support of a cause so hateful to the dominant faction.

There were two other traces of independence. First was the rearguard action of Goodwin Knight in California, engaged with

[18] *Ibid.*, p. 154.

Nixon and Knowland in factional struggle for control of the state party. Second was the subdued but sustained drumming of Governor McKeldin for Vice President.

On August 14 Knight said he was "available" for the vice-presidential nomination, although he stressed he was not seeking it and that he would support anyone favored by the President.[19] Any remaining threat to Nixon from this quarter was quashed at the first meeting of the California delegation on August 19. This delegation was evenly divided among Nixon, Knowland, and Knight supporters, with Knight serving as chairman. Knight's election as chairman was balanced, however, with the delegation's decision to vote as a unit. Thus the Knowland-Nixon coalition won out, and Knight had to bide his organizational time.[20]

McKeldin made clear that he would be party to no such schemes as those apparently improvised to make the Republican vice-presidential contest look a little less rigged in comparison with the Democratic tactic at Chicago. The idea was for several delegations to put up nominees, all of whom would agree in advance to withdraw, while acknowledging the virtues of the organization's choice, and getting a little national notice. McKeldin announced he was a serious candidate (if the President wanted him to run) or no candidate at all. His delegation was certainly for him on this understanding.

McKeldin went further to say he would not "dissociate" himself from Stassen, because he had never been "associated" with him.[21] The Maryland Governor grumbled because he was not given a more prominent part in the convention—he who had nominated Eisenhower in 1952, and who alone among Southern governors was a Republican. But it did not seem prudent or worth while for him to trade the threat of a Maryland nomination for him for a

[19] *Washington Post and Times Herald*, Aug. 14, 1956.

[20] *New York Times*, Convention Edition, Aug. 21, 1956. This article reports that Donald Doyle, new Republican Senate Chairman, found sentiment for Nixon among delegates "by no means unanimous." He quoted a Southern delegate interested in Knowland as a strong states' rights man.

[21] *Evening Star* (Washington, D.C.), Aug. 15, 1956. McKeldin was quoted in the *New York Times*, Convention Edition, Aug. 21, 1956, as saying: "Nixon's got it, and that's it." He also conferred twice with Sherman Adams before deciding not to let his name go before the convention.

more glorious role than the chance to deliver a seconding speech for the Vice Presidency.

As for other possibles—Herter, Adams, Thornton, and others— any hopes were sacrificed to the demands of the team and its leaders. Stassen remained the recreant. Sole threat to the unspoiled panorama of Republican unity, discipline, and harmony, he stuck to his poll predictions and took full advantage of every opening offered by uncertainty and by the accepted formalities of convention and party procedure. Even though no major party figure spoke for his effort, and less than ten delegates of any sort were named as in favor of it, he pointed as long as he could to latent opinion that would express itself "at the right time." (At least one reporter agreed with him that such opinion existed, noting an undercurrent of anti-Nixon sentiment as well as an overcurrent against Stassen himself.)[22] Part of Stassen's stance was an avowed concern to play the good Republican—a role that caused him to defend Nixon stoutly against Democrats' attacks, and that compromised any image of independence.[23]

The former Minnesota Governor arrived in San Francisco on Friday, August 17, with results of his Advertest poll, but no new accessions of strength. San Francisco gave his planemates Secretary of Treasury Humphrey and Secretary of Commerce Weeks keys to the city, but had none for him. No happy group of young Republicans, let alone any party dignitary, was on hand to greet him. Despite his airport claim that his movement was growing stronger every day, Joseph W. Martin, Washington's Arthur Langlie, and Pennsylvania's Senator Edward Martin loudly agreed there would be "no trouble" in nominating Nixon.[24]

Saturday saw a battle of the polls. Stassen was allowed to hold a press conference, but the organization put Senator Styles Bridges and Representative Richard Simpson on him immediately afterwards.

Stassen's poll was professionally respectable but subtly constructed and hard to grasp. It was designed to show the difference

[22] See Crosby Noyes, *Evening Star* (Washington, D.C.), Aug. 15, 1956.
[23] *Ibid.*
[24] *San Francisco Chronicle*, Aug. 18, 1956.

in voter preference for the Republican ticket depending on whether Nixon or another vice-presidential candidate was listed. The poll showed that any vice-presidential candidate lowered the President's probable victory margin, but Herter did so less than Nixon. But it was also clear that the "don't knows" and the "refuseds" were sufficiently large to decide the election, and it was not shown how these two classifications might behave if Herter were substituted for Nixon.

A large press contingent listened carefully to Stassen's explanations and stayed for the organization's counterblast that followed at once.

The Bridges rebuttal was vigorous, tongue-in-cheek, and analytically suspect. He followed Stassen's half-hour of relatively complicated, sophisticated demonstration by releasing a poll of his own, which used an unstratified sample.

This poll asked four questions: (1) Do you know who Christian Herter is? (2) Are you a Republican, Democrat, or Independent? (3) If the election were today, would you vote for Eisenhower and Nixon? (4) Which would you prefer, an Eisenhower-Nixon ticket or an Eisenhower-Herter ticket?[25]

The answers revealed that 47.47 per cent of those questioned did not know who Christian Herter was; 57.7 per cent would vote for Eisenhower and Nixon (oddly enough, the final outcome was 57.8 per cent), 35.3 per cent would not, and 7 per cent had no opinion. The sample preferred Eisenhower-Nixon to Eisenhower-Herter 54.3 per cent to 25.7 per cent, with 20 per cent expressing no opinion.

[25] This poll, issued to the press in the form of a four-page flyer, was billed as "The-Truth-About-Nixon and the Voters. A *Non-Secret Poll* . . . Conducted in Each and Everyone of the 48 States, August 14, 15, 16, 1956, Made for and paid for solely by the Manchester New Hampshire *Union Leader* and the New Hampshire *Sunday News*, William Loeb, Publisher." (Loeb, long in Republican politics, was a well-known exponent of right-wing candidates and causes.) The poll was conducted by Robert Maheu Associates of Washington, D.C., "using only former FBI Agents in Each and Every State in the Nation. Questions asked at random of passersby in the streets of a large city in each state and a country town in each state of the nation. A Fair and Square Attempt to Attain the Facts. . . ." Neither the size of sample nor the procedure for choosing streetcorners was stated on the flyer. Conceivably financial-district street corners might have produced a different result from those in factory districts.

The fourth page of the flyer gave state-by-state results for each question. These revealed a tremendous scatter, raising serious doubts as to the nature and size of the sample. Some regional variations were both plausible and discernible: 100 per cent of those in Massachusetts knew who Herter was (although even this might be a little high for a Governor), and he was better known in New England than in the South. Other figures were less reasonable. The question on party preference showed that 98 per cent of Connecticut voters would go Republican, while 86 per cent of Vermonters, 83 per cent from Utah, and 78 per cent from Texas would do the same. The question on relative preference for an Eisenhower-Nixon or an Eisenhower-Herter ticket showed only five states in which Herter came out ahead (South Carolina, North Carolina, Louisiana, Maryland, and Georgia), two ties (Ohio and Alabama), and only five more states in which Herter was within 10 percentage points of his opponent. Herter lost his native Massachusetts, 46 to 50 per cent.

But the newly poll-conscious Stassen-doggers did not stop there. They also distributed another flyer, consisting of reprints of various Gallup and other polls showing that Nixon ran far ahead of Herter among both Republicans and Independents, and Eisenhower voters of either party.[26]

Stassen returned to the attack in a press conference held the next day (Sunday, August 19), attended by two hundred reporters. He still had to cover up, as he had no new evidence of strength to display. He dismissed the Bridges poll by pointing to its obviously unreasonable results in Pennsylvania, Connecticut, and New York, and what was more to the point, noted that evidence of Republican preference for Nixon did not detract from his find-

[26] These included the Gallup polls published on May 18 and August 15, 1956; a Trendex poll published July 25, 1956, a Minnesota poll published August 5, and a UP roundup story of April 18 stating that 58 out of 100 top magazine editors believed Nixon would be an "asset" to the 1956 Republican ticket. The polls also showed that Herter ran well behind other Republican figures, such as Dewey, Stassen, Lodge, Knowland, and Dulles. A roundup story headlined "Nixon Sweeps Polls; Independents for Dick," subheading that "3 out of 4 Republicans, 54 per cent of Independents Prefer Nixon's Re-nomination." A California survey authored by Kyle Palmer of the Los Angeles *Times* showed that Nixon was ahead of both Knowland and Knight as preferred presidential nominee among Republicans there if Eisenhower were unable to run.

ings that Nixon dragged most heavily on the President's popularity—so heavily that it put the ticket itself in danger. The press conference concluded with no real news to report.

In the following days, Stassen got a moment's comfort from Herter's urbane statement that he would accept a draft, although he did not expect it.[27] But still no major figure had come out for him, and even favorably disposed delegates found it prudent to go along with the obvious majority.

For the pro-Nixon forces, the task forced on them by their estimates of the public appeal of the Democratic open contest was to create as much of an impression as possible that the convention was "open," without going to the realistic lengths of letting Stassen have a free run. They canvassed a number of schemes, including search for some candidate willing to lend his name to a legitimate (although overwhelmingly unfavorable) vote by the delegates for whatever value it might have in furthering a state or national political career. Senator Bridges said that the convention would be as open as the Democratic convention "in theory," although he thought that the outcome would not be so close.[28]

On arrival in San Francisco, Richard Nixon carefully stated his official position:

> We are here for one purpose. All we Republicans are here to assure the United States and the world the leadership of the Man of the Century, President Eisenhower.
>
> Everything else and personal careers and considerations of anyone are insignificant in comparison. I include myself in that respect. I have constantly opposed any move to close the convention as far as the vice presidential nomination is concerned.
>
> I asked President Eisenhower and National Chairman Hall not to do or say anything that might seem to prevent the convention from being free and open.[29]

By such words Nixon risked nothing. With the organizational decision set by negotiations finished months before, why should there be anything to make the convention look rigged? Yet the organizational men found the prospect of a unanimous vote curi-

[27] *Sunday Star* (Washington, D.C.), Aug. 19, 1956.
[28] *Ibid.*
[29] *Ibid.*

ously disturbing. They disliked the contrast with the Stevenson maneuver, yet squirmed under the disquieting thought that any maneuvers made to bring even token candidacies before the convention might get out of hand. There is no evidence that Richard Nixon shared such lack of confidence; almost alone among his backers he maintained an air of personal security and good humor. Apparently he sensed that the Stassen maneuvers would not be harmful enough to warrant concern or counteraction visible to the public. Others, having little patience with Stassen's protestations of service to the President and his party, had difficulty in concealing their animosity toward him.

The one condition that would have given wings to the Stassen cause was withheld: any genuine indication by the President that he would welcome any of several persons as his running mate. Any delegates who privately had anti-Nixon feelings, or who might have been persuaded by Stassen's evidence, kept their attitudes to themselves, lest they be guilty of disloyalty toward the head of the team. The press kept driving away at the possibility that the President might issue, or might have prepared a "list," as he had done in 1952. Reporters pounced on White House people as they arrived in San Francisco, to see whether the President might have passed a "word" opening up the race. Neither Sherman Adams nor any of the others would go beyond the President's reticence.[30]

Meanwhile, Richard Nixon took nothing for granted; he made regular calls on delegations, and had breakfast by invitation with the Massachusetts and Minnesota delegations. He also received a visit from the Missouri delegation—that contained one of Stassen's few named supporters, Delegation Chairman Elroy W. Bromwich. But the Missouri delegation had hedged its bets, electing a pro-

---

[30] It is a moot point whether the President could have opened up the convention at this late date by asking for a free run. He might not have been able to do so even by a flat expression of preference for Herter or for some other candidate. The Nixon forces would undoubtedly have been embarrassed by having the weapon of loyalty to Ike, that they had so carefully sharpened, turned against them. But they possessed undoubted strength, and could have made a powerful fight for the nomination, based not only on the loyalties Nixon had earned by previous campaign support, but also on the President's earlier insistence on an open convention. See Paul T. David, Ralph M. Goldman, and Richard C. Bain, *The Politics of National Party Conventions* (1960), Chap. 4.

Nixon vice chairman. Even Mr. Bromwich hedged his position; refusing to come out for Nixon, he said he was for whomever Eisenhower wanted.[31]

Nixon himself took the occasion of these delegation sessions to outline the tone of the campaign and his role in it. He told the New York and Massachusetts groups that he would not reply to the Democrats "in kind." "We Republicans have something far better to offer than vilification of our political opponents. We are going to talk about the record. . . . The tone of this campaign is important. We must look to the future and let the people know we are the party of opportunity and progress."[32]

[31] *Washington Post and Times Herald*, Aug. 21, 1956.
[32] *Ibid.*

8

The Republican National Convention

SINCE THE REPUBLICANS were not on the attack and had decisions to ratify but not to make during the forthcoming four days of the convention proper, they left themselves one enemy—boredom. Their answer was short periods of party ritual and convention business, interrupted by big-name entertainment and by the planned cheers and card displays of a college football pep section. Their hope was for a successful rally in which party notables and candidates could parade before a national audience.

The day-to-day scheduling followed a normal pattern, although the length of the sessions was cut down to fit the amount of anticipated business, and to put major speeches and events on Class A television time for most of the country. Monday, August 20, went for organizational ceremonies and the keynote speech. Tuesday featured the party's patriarchs and its women and a novel presentation of the platform. Wednesday was for nominations. Thursday was for acceptance speeches and final ceremonies.

Physical Arrangements and Preliminaries

In February 1955, the Republicans had decided to hold their Centennial Convention in the huge Cow Palace just south of San Francisco.[1] This solved two problems that had plagued them and the Democrats in Chicago in 1952—air conditioning and space. The palace easily accommodated seats for 14,800, plus ample arrangements for television, radio, newsreels, the pen-and-pencil

[1] *Official Report of the Proceedings of the Twenty-sixth Republican National Convention, 1956*, p. 363. Hereinafter cited as *Official Proceedings, 1956*.

press, bands, VIP's and demonstrators, not to mention the 1,323 delegates and their 1,323 alternates. Provision was made for overflow space, too, in a large separate building to the north, where those not fortunate enough to gain tickets of admission to the main hall could watch proceedings on a giant television screen. Outside the arena itself, moreover, were courtesy lounges set up by transportation and communications companies, where those in attendance could refresh themselves, relax informally, and view matters on television at leisure. There were also caucus rooms, working space, and communications facilities for the press.

Space was achieved at the cost of acoustics. Even with yeoman efforts to equalize sound produced in the hall, the public address system muffled the voices of many speakers to the point where they could hardly be understood. The result, at times, was meaningless confusion—meaningless because the impact of speech was wholly irrelevant to decision.

Monday, August 20, was a busy day for the Republicans. There were two sessions. The first had two tasks: to get the organizational formalities and the geographical courtesies done with; and to parade Republican candidates for the Senate and the House in a series of short speeches designed to present "the case" for Republican majorities in Congress. The second session featured the keynote speech.

True to their instructions, most of the delegates and their alternates were in the aisles near their assigned areas at 11 A.M., occupied with informal caucusing and casual conversation. Meade Alcorn, Vice Chairman in charge of arrangements, pleaded with them to get in their seats. At 11:23, five massed color guards cleared the aisles as National Chairman Leonard Hall called the convention to order—for the photographers. After asking the assemblage whether everyone was happy, and getting a resounding affirmative, Hall called the convention to order officially at 11:26. For the next half hour, there were more preliminaries, as San Francisco's Mayor George Christopher demonstrated experimentally that the only thing that would get a rise out of the delegates was a mention of Eisenhower; and Governor Goodwin Knight removed all doubt on the subject.

At noon, Mrs. Gladys Knowles, Secretary of the Convention, read the first paragraph of the official call, leaving the rest for the printed record. A few minutes later, she presented the temporary roll. Hall nominated Senator Knowland as temporary chairman and named his escort committee; the convention ratified the roll of temporary officers of the convention.

Representative Richard M. Simpson of Pennsylvania, Chairman of the Congressional Campaign Committee, led off a series of speeches on "Why Ike Needs a Republican House." This may have been of interest to the radio and television audience, but those in the convention hall paid little attention.

While the delegates and alternates stood firm, the spectators thinned out in search of lunch or other entertainment. The session went on with Representative Hugh Scott of Pennsylvania (former National Chairman) dealing with Republican opposition to segregation and prejudice. Then came Representative Melvin R. Laird of Wisconsin, who praised the Republican farm policy as one for the generations, not merely for election years. Representative Katharine St. George of New York returned to the issue of peace from the mother's and woman's angle.

The representatives finished, Hall gaveled for quiet and asked for better attention for the senatorial half of the show. Senator Andrew Schoeppel of Kansas, chairman of the Senatorial Campaign Committee, led on his team, who underlined points already made by the congressional hopefuls.

Three operations occupied the rest of the morning session: appointment of the main convention committees; praises for Republican women and parades of their leaders; the same for Young Republicans. The lists sent to the chair of nominations from each of the convention delegations for the major convention committees (one delegate each for rules and for credentials; two each, one of each sex, for platform) were adopted by voice votes, made a part of the permanent record, and the nominees told of the time and place of their formal meetings.

With the committees formed and instructed, Chairman Hall called on Mrs. Carroll D. Kearns, President of the National Federation of Republican Women. Photographers clicked shutters busily while Mrs. Kearns told the women delegates that the Republican Party was now "on camera." Mrs. Herbert Brownell, wife of the Attorney General, presented the prize-winning campaign slogans culled from suggestions made by more than 6,000 people. The winners were these: "Peace, Prosperity and Progress, If You Want All Three, Vote G.O.P."; "A Bright Tomorrow with Eisenhower"; and "Not Trenches, but Work Benches."[2]

Now it was youth's turn, as Charles McWhorter, chief of the Young Republicans, came to the rostrum while young demonstrators marched and young bands played. After three minutes the chairman called for order and for McWhorter's speech. McWhorter introduced the young winner, David N. Krogsend of Minnesota, of the national essay contest on "Why I Am a Republican." His essay was not read, but was made part of the record. Hall declared a recess until 4:30, after congratulating the delegates on having the convention seats filled when the convention started. (The Democrats had failed to do so.)

The late afternoon session featured the keynote speech, but there was an hour and a half of preliminaries before Governor Arthur B. Langlie of Washington, candidate for the Senate, mounted the stand at 6 P.M.—in time to catch audiences in Chicago at 8 P.M. and New York at 9 P.M. For nationwide television, it was important to display Republican notables. Representative James P. S. Devereux of Maryland, a former Marine Corps general, led the salute to the flag; Chairman Hall previewed the campaign and keynote speeches; Senate candidate Thomas Kuchel of California introduced Temporary Chairman Knowland, who made his speech; Oregon senatorial candidate Douglas McKay introduced the keynote speaker, Governor Langlie. There was entertainment, too, and introduction of the campaign song.

As promised, the keynote speech was relatively short—pointedly in contrast with its Democratic counterpart of a week before and in partial rebuttal of it. It terminated, as did so many of the Republican speeches, on a religious note. While the keynote speech did not concentrate on vilification of Democrats, it pointed out inconsistencies between their charges and their behavior, such as

[2] *Ibid.*, p. 59.

their acceptance of service from John Foster Dulles prior to 1952, and their eagerness to have Eisenhower as their candidate in 1948; and it recalled "twenty demoralizing years of discord and defeatism in our public affairs, ending up in flagrant corruption."[3] In conclusion Langlie rehearsed the Republican record of four years of successful crusading.

Patriarchs, Petticoats, Platform, and The President

Tuesday featured four events: The advice of party patriarch Herbert Hoover; a placard pageant in which female Republican notables made little speeches on subjects, the initial titles of which spelled out "Republican Women"; an exposition of platform planks by the Cabinet; and the early arrival of the President.

After preliminaries the convention accepted the reports from its Committees on Credentials and on Permanent Organization and on Rules and Order of Business.

But the resolutions and platform report took longer and ran into production trouble. This presentation was in two parts. First came Resolutions Committee Chairman, the Honorable Prescott Bush, Senator from Connecticut. He was introduced by Senator James H. Duff of Pennsylvania, a co-worker on the platform, already engaged in a dog-fight for re-election to his Senate seat. Second came the Cabinet under the direction of Sherman Adams.

Bush took the opportunity to cement unity by calling for a minute's silent tribute "out of respect and in honor to 'Mr. Republican,' the late, great Senator from Ohio, Bob Taft."[4] Then he read the first part of the platform—the Declaration of Faith: "The preamble to our platform . . . a condensation of the principles for which we stand, the record of accomplishments of a great Administration and a great President and our program for the future."[5]

Bush moved to dispense with further reading of this platform,

[3] *Ibid.*, p. 77.
[4] *Ibid.*, p. 190.
[5] *Ibid.*, p. 191.

since it had received more publicity and was now better understood, he said, than any platform presented to any previous convention.

By this time, however, there was considerable milling about in the hall. Everyone knew that the President's airplane was due in at 6:30, but the Cabinet was about to take over. Most spectators, and many of the delegates, sought television sets in the lounges around the hall so as not to miss the historic arrival. Alternate delegates moved up to keep the delegate section filled. Meanwhile Sherman Adams brought on the Cabinet in protocol order. Only John Foster Dulles was absent. Under Secretary of State Herbert Hoover, Jr. read the statement on foreign policy. Each of the others read his five-minute summary of the platform planks appropriate to his department. Then came the Special Adviser to the President and United States representative at the United Nations, Henry Cabot Lodge. These high officials played to a dwindling audience in the amphitheatre. Television and radio switched their coverage away from the hall just before the Humphrey speech, and remained away until the Cabinet was through, and the President was safely ensconced in his San Francisco hotel.[6]

In doctrine, both the platform and the speeches of the cabinet members were pure Eisenhower.

To this doctrine the platform drafters systematically added their tribute to the President. The Declaration of Faith enshrined in the Republican catechism both Lincoln's formula for government action and Eisenhower's logical *tour de force* counseling humanity in dealing with people and conservatism in dealing with their money, their economy, and their government. It rehearsed Republican purposes of peace, prosperity, rights for all, unimpeachable ethical standards in government, care for human needs. It recalled Republican achievements, the greatest of which was the party's "part in bringing into a position of unique authority in the world

[6] *New York Times*, Aug. 22, 1956. Interviews with several high broadcasting officials revealed no repentance for this decision. The President's arrival *was* the news, and the jump in number of viewers or listeners tuned proved to them they had made the right decision. The incidental fact that nobody carried the Cabinet live, nor bothered to summarize it later, they dismissed as of secondary importance. Republicans prominent in convention management took the same view.

one who symbolizes, as can no other man, the hopes of all peoples for peace, liberty and justice. One leader in the world today towers above all others and inspires the trust, admiration, confidence and good will of all the peoples of every nation—Dwight D. Eisenhower."

Omitted from the declaration were both isolationism and sharp criticism of the Democrats. Replacing the former was a claim of achievement in the foreign sphere and the now unqualified statement: "We shall continue vigorously to support the United Nations." The only concession to the Midwest isolationist wing was this statement and promise repeated from 1952: "We maintain that no treaty or international agreement can deprive any of our citizens of Constitutional rights. We shall see to it that no treaty or agreement with other countries attempts to deprive our citizens of the rights guaranteed them by the Federal Constitution."[7]

Liberation of captive peoples also came in for approval, but without the unabashed opportunism of the 1952 platform or subsequent campaigning. The 1956 document was also more forthright and favorable on foreign aid and reciprocal trade, reflecting the decline in power of isolationist sentiment since 1952.

The platform held high once again the banner of human freedom, asserting "the major world issue today is whether Government shall be the servant or the master of men."[8] To keep government the servant, the platform not only invoked the Bill of Rights as the foundation of personal liberty, equality of opportunity, and civil rights under the law; it called for strengthened state and local governments and decried centralization of powers in the Federal government as leading to "expansion of the mastery of our lives." With characteristic fiscal emphasis, the platform further asserted that Republicans "hold that the protection of the freedom of men requires that budgets be balanced, waste in Government eliminated, and taxes reduced."[9]

The declaration came to its climax with a pledge of "best thought and whole energy to a continuation of our prized peace,

[7] *Official Proceedings, 1956*, p. 193.
[8] *Ibid.*, p. 194.
[9] *Ibid.*, p. 195.

prosperity and progress," and cited the six Eisenhower principles for guidance:

The individual is of supreme importance.
The spirit of our people is the strength of our nation.
America does not prosper unless all Americans prosper.
Government must have a heart as well as a head.
Courage in principle, cooperation in practice makes freedom positive.
To stay free, we must stay strong.[10]

Then came the 13,000-word Declaration of Determination: a rehearsal of the Republican record and a statement of Republican commitment or promise in fields titled Dynamic Economy—Free Labor; Human Welfare and Advancement; Rural America's Recovery; Federal Government Integrity; Governmental Affairs; Equal Opportunity and Justice; Human Freedom and Peace (*i.e.*, foreign policy); Bulwark for the Free World (national defense and veterans); Guarding and Improving Our Resources; and For a Brighter Tomorrow (oddly enough meaning atomic energy). The capstone was a Declaration of Dedication, not only to the President, but to the youth of America.[11]

This catalog, like the Democratic platform that preceded it, was an inclusive compendium of government actions designed to assure peace, prosperity, progress, welfare, liberty, and justice for all. Hardly a major segment of potential vote leverage was overlooked in this platform. Yet, mindful of their responsibilities as the party in power, the Republicans were less than wholly opportunistic. They promised to reduce taxes, balance the budget, and reduce the federal debt only so long as such action did not threaten maintenance of a superior national defense program and undepreciated quality of essential services of government to the people. Mindful of the claims of the "Party with a Heart," the Republicans called for "new wealth and new jobs for all the people." The platform expressed solicitude for the needs of small business, along with medium and large business. It pointed to "the largest highway, air and maritime programs in history, all soundly financed." No phase of labor relations was overlooked, as the plat-

[10] *Ibid.*
[11] *Ibid.*, p. 220.

form stressed the benefits of general prosperity and labor peace for the working man. It promised vigorous action in the fields of health, welfare, and social security.

The Platforms Compared

On many points, the platforms were in substantial agreement. On others there were real as well as synthetic differences.

For agriculture, the Republican platform offered a "many-sided, versatile and positive program to help all farmers and ranchers," setting the objective of "markets which return full parity to our farm and ranch people when they sell their products." It said that: "There is no simple, easy answer to farm problems." Here more than elsewhere the platform criticized the Democrats directly, saddling them with responsibility for the price-depressing surpluses accumulated as a result of earlier price-support schemes. It also charged Democrats with slowing down full Soil Bank benefits to farm families in 1956. The Republicans pledged an effective new research program, better marketing of agricultural products at home and abroad, and full freedom instead of more regimentation. Their platform gave qualified pledges of support to farmer-owned and operated cooperatives, for better rural communications, and for Rural Electrification Administration loans for generation and transmission of electricity. It was more forthright in promising improved rural mail delivery. And it bespoke a partnership between farmers and their government in achieving basic ends of soil conservation. In conclusion, the Republican party pledged itself to work in "bold new ways" for the family farm, improved farm prices and farm income, and for a prosperous, expanding, and free agriculture in a world at peace.

In respect to federal government integrity, while Democrats had assailed the security "numbers game" and Dixon-Yates, the Republican platform pledged a loyalty-security program heedful of the rights of the individual. It promised vigilance against corruption and waste and condemned "illegal lobbying." It pledged further efforts toward greater efficiency and economy, opposed growth of "unwarranted" centralized federal power, and promised to dispense with federal activities "wrongfully" competing with private enterprise. It pledged better postal service and support for the merit system. It plumped for unqualified immediate statehood for Hawaii and statehood for Alaska with adequate provision for "defense requirements." Puerto Rico and the Indians came in for proper attention, as did the voteless District of Columbia. Women found their usual platform endorsement of submission by Congress to the states of an equal rights amendment to the Constitution.

In the more delicate and controversial fields of civil rights, the Republicans went only a little farther toward the liberal position than had the Democrats, owing to an Eisenhower compromise. The plank rehearsed the Republican record—ending of segregation in the District of Columbia; Negroes appointed to "high public positions"; progress in eliminating employment discrimination on federal contracts; ending of segregation in the armed forces. Like the Democratic platform, the Republican platform recognized the Constitution as the supreme law of the land; but it insisted further on the constitutional grant of citizenship not only in states, but in the United States, as "an unqualified right, regardless of race, creed or color." It went beyond the Democratic platform in its cautious acceptance of the conclusion of the Supreme Court that desegregation should be accomplished "with all deliberate speed" through the federal district courts. It went beyond the Democrats also in its claim that true progress toward integration, attainable, "through intelligent study, understanding, education and good will" and without the use of force or violence, should be "encouraged and the work of the courts supported in every legal manner by all branches of the Federal Government."

On immigration, the party platform ventured no step beyond the President's program submitted to the Eighty-fourth Congress, although it favored extension of the Refugee Relief Act of 1953.

As for foreign policy, the Republican platform differed from the Democrats' chiefly in its rehearsal of "the record." With respect to goals there was no significant difference either as to the catalog or the values, down the list from support for the United Nations, the Organization of American States, collective security, foreign aid, economic aid both for Israel and for Arab countries, to flat rejection of the seating of Red China in the United Nations. With respect to methods there were some expectable differences. On presidential performance, the Democrats' version of part-time slothfulness and irresponsibility became wise and dynamic leadership in the Republican platform. The Republicans promised to uphold the integrity of an independent Jewish state, and to support Israel against any armed aggression, without specifying particular methods; the Democrats were willing to send arms. The Republicans strove for a little more fantastic combination of goals in protesting "impartial friendship" for Israel and for the Arab states. As for liberation of oppressed peoples under Communist domination, the Republicans expected that to come in time as a result of the vigorous prosecution of our "peaceful policies"; the Democrats hoped to achieve it through vigorous protestations in the United Nations. The Republicans said they wanted to continue bipartisan development of foreign policies in the interest of continuity; the Democrats recognized only bipartisan help on the part of individual Republican congressmen and assumed something less than full official partnership to have been the case.

In the foreign policy plank as in many others, the Republicans finished with an evocation of Eisenhower's vast experience, vital to the success of our foreign relations in a world where peace could be won only by vigilance and inspired leadership.

The comparison was similar in the area of national defense. The Republicans claimed to found their policies on more-than-adequate strength in being. The Democrats charged them with being satisfied with the position of a second-best power. The Republicans promised to spend all that was necessary to maintain superiority; the Democrats charged the sacrifice of fighting strength to budgetary considerations. The Republicans, naturally, cited the authority of the Commander in Chief for their position. Both platforms recognized science, education, and civil defense as sources of strength. The Republicans promised to keep the FBI and all other government intelligence agencies strong, so as to keep the nation safe and secure. (The Democrats omitted any such promise.) Again, the Republicans ended their plank with an evocation of the President, in whom the American people could place confidence, and from whom the peoples of the world abroad could draw a greater sense of security and of an opportunity for peace.

Promises to veterans yielded no comparisons of interest.

In the field of natural resources, there was a clear-cut contrast between the Republican espousal of the "partnership" policy and the Democratic plumping for public power. Here the Republicans made no concessions to the political expediencies of campaigning in the Pacific Northwest; they came out flatly for "partnership"— i.e., a major role for private power, working along with governmental authority (federal or state) in the development of power potentials. The design of this section of their platform was a rehearsal of achievements, praise for the record, and a few promises under each main head: recreation, parks, and wildlife; public lands and forest resources; fisheries; water resource development.

On atomic energy, the Republican plank was much the more general, stressing gains through partnership and government intent to continue progress. The Democrats had lashed out against Dixon-Yates and partisan administration of the Atomic Energy Commission, while professing the same ultimate goals of peace, progress, and technical development.

The Republican platform concluded with a Declaration of Dedication:

> With utmost confidence in the future and with justifiable pride in our achievements, the Republican Party warmly greets the dawn of our second century of service in the cause of unity and progress in the Nation.
>
> As the Party of the Young and in glowing appreciation of his dynamic leadership and inspiration, we respectfully dedicate this Platform of the Party of the Future to our distinguished President Dwight D. Eisenhower and to the Youth of America.[12]

By adjournment time at eight o'clock, the President was settled in the St. Francis hotel and the platform that so completely mirrored his views was tucked into the Republican record.

[12] *Ibid.*, p. 220.

President's Press Conference: Stassen Capitulates

The big news on Wednesday was neither the nomination nor the selection of the candidates for President and Vice President. Neither was it the slightly more newsworthy appearance of Emmet J. Hughes, self-styled nonpartisan independent (who had been a key Eisenhower speechwriter in 1952 and was going to be again in 1956), saying why he was for Eisenhower. Better candidates for the lead story were two: the Joe Smith episode as the one example of poor discipline and unplanned humor; and the President's press conference. At the latter event, the first to be televised live, two points came clear. One, the President was vigorous and healthy. Two, the Stassen revolt had collapsed.

Immediately before the press conference scheduled for 11:00 A.M., the President met privately with Stassen at the St. Francis hotel.[13] The President announced the results a short time later in his press conference, but first came a human touch, with the announcement that Nixon had gone to La Habra to be at the bedside of his dying father.

Then the President closed the open convention:

> Mr. Stassen called to see me a few minutes ago. . . . He said this morning that after several days here, he had become absolutely convinced that the majority of the delegates want Nixon, and in these circumstances he no longer—and particularly since his own candidate had withdrawn so decisively, he saw no reason for going further with his effort, and he thought in order to get his own position clear before the convention and the American public, he was going to ask the nation—the convention chairman for permission this afternoon to second—is it today?—Yes—this afternoon to second the nomination of the Vice President, Mr. Nixon, for renomination.[14]

Later in the interview, the President made clear that Stassen did not even mention his major stated reason for opposing Nixon —that he would detract from the popularity of the ticket.

[13] *New York Times*, Aug. 23, 1956. Mazo gives a fuller account, pointing out that Hall and Adams would not even let Stassen see the President for any other purpose than to announce his capitulation and to ask to be allowed to second Nixon. Earl Mazo, *Richard Nixon: A Political and Personal Portrait* (1959), pp. 101-21.

[14] *New York Times*, Aug. 23, 1956.

The reporters wanted more. They asked whether with Stassen in the fold, there would be 100 per cent harmony in Republican ranks—and got a cautious response that someone else might be nominated. They asked whether the President had prepared a list of acceptable candidates, as he did in 1952. Eisenhower confessed that during the period when he did not know that Mr. Nixon was going to run again, he "thought of a whole group." But he refused to name them for fear of embarrassing some hopeful that he might not approve.

As to health, the President reminded one reporter that even in Panama he said he was getting stronger every day, and at the moment except for a tendency to drag the head of his golf club a bit after hitting a few balls, he felt as good as ever. (Far more eloquent that his own testimony was his appearance and his obvious relish for the fray.)

As to Nixon, the President still refused to come out unequivocally for his colleague. Nixon, he thought, had done his job in "extraordinarily fine fashion"; he had been brought into central affairs more than any other Vice President. And "he has done everything I asked him beautifully. So that from my viewpoint, as far as efficiency, dedication to his job, loyalty to his country is concerned, I think he is as good a man as you can get."[15] And he added that Nixon had told him that "by no manner of means did he want to be a candidate where there was—it just looked like it had been a steamroller affair." But the President refused to say that he would vote for Dick Nixon, if he were a delegate from Pennsylvania. (Stassen was more forthright on this point; he told his questioner that if he were a delegate he certainly would vote for Nixon.)

As to other potential candidates, the President said no other man had come to him saying he would like to run; only those came who said they would not. And these included Stassen himself, along with Colorado's Governor Dan Thornton. The name of Goodwin Knight, he said, had never been presented to him as a candidate.

Mr. Stassen, in his own conference held after watching the

[15] *Ibid.*

President on television, said the President had stated his position "exactly."[16]

Nominations and Joe Smith

During the afternoon session for selection of the candidates, came Emmet Hughes, intellectual for Eisenhower; Governor Thomas E. Dewey, political organizer for Eisenhower and key man in assuring the Nixon decision; the nomination speeches and the seconding speeches for the Presidency and the Vice Presidency; the balloting—and Joe Smith.

Sandwiched between the invocation and musical numbers was the election of the new National Committee, by voice vote.

True to its show-business format, the Republican party presented Hughes as "another first"—the first "independent" to speak on a convention program. He spoke for the independent intellectual, disenchanted with the "stale promises and outworn programs" of the Democrats, looking for fresh leadership and solutions progressive in their relation to the problems of today, not of twenty years ago.

The delegates greeted Dewey with an ovation, containing no hint of the savage Dirksen attack of four years before. Nor did the Dewey speech recall earlier splits. First, Dewey said that here "nobody is mad at anybody else." Then he moved into his set text and produced the most skillful oratorical effort of the convention; drawing response from the delegates with every line. And every line epitomized an aspect of the Republican case.

With Dewey done and the delegates in a glowing mood, Chairman Martin put the motion needed to accommodate the rigid and austere Republican rules governing seconding speeches to the plans of the convention, thus allowing not more than nine seconding speeches of not more than two minutes each and permitting certain nondelegates to address the gathering.[17]

[16] *Ibid.*
[17] *Official Proceedings, 1956*, p. 259. Rule 14 permitted no more than four seconding speeches for nominations for President or Vice President, of not more than five minutes each. So the Republican plan still kept within the twenty minute total possible under the rule.

So freed, the show went on to the call of the roll of states for the purpose of nominating the candidate for President. Each state either passed or yielded in turn to Indiana for the purpose of nominating President Eisenhower; some with comment (Ohio noted that it was passing for the first time in twenty years), others with an appropriately disciplined economy of words: ". . . passes." When the roll call came to Indiana, the delegation's leader, Governor George N. Craig, asked that the Chair recognize Representative Charles Halleck. "That," said the Permanent Chairman, "will be done a little later." The roll call proceeded without incident through the pass of the Virgin Islands.

Then came Halleck, his ovation and his speech, followed by seconding speeches paying tribute from various sectors of the body politic to the President: a housewife from Texas, grateful for what Ike had done for children; a football coach expressing his gratitude "that our gifted leader will again give his badly needed, his desperately needed leadership to Americans and freedom-loving people the world over . . ."; a Republican from the deep South, a pre-1952 Democrat, the first Republican elected from his parish in eighty years, a states rights man eager to turn from government spending, government meddling, government messing; a Farmers Union farmer, voicing a cry for peace, defense, a good living, government economy, and "farm programs that help keep bureaucrats off our farms and new markets instead of wars to keep prices up"; a Negro woman educator expressing the yearning of her race to be first-class citizens; a card-carrying union man saying "Ike is good for America, and what's good for America is good enough for me"; a Jewish woman from Massachusetts recalling the President's deep concern for peace, education, public welfare, medical care; finally, Maryland's Governor McKeldin, the only one to speak anything like his own language, recalling the Republican record of fulfilled promises, and expressing "special gratitude for all that has been done in these years to revive the waning strength of our Republican form of government by reversing the treacherous tides sweeping away the proud sovereignty of our States and Commonwealths."

The convention then proceeded to the call of the roll for the selection of a nominee for President. Soon thereafter, the Permanent Chairman intoned: "The roll call shows that 1,323 delegates have voted. The score sheet shows President Eisenhower has received 1,323 and therefore, I declare him unanimously the nominee of the Republican Party for the Office of President of the United States."[18]

The convention turned at 7:05 in the evening to the nomination of their vice-presidential candidate. Chairman Martin reminded all that the rules of procedure would be the same and told the delegates that "We will first call the roll to see which of the various States have a candidate for Vice President."[19]

This exploration started with Alabama's announcement that it yielded to Massachusetts for the nomination of an unnamed person: "The name of a great American, a man whom President Eisenhower has repeatedly praised, a man at whom the Democrats always thunder because they dread him most."[20] Arizona made a brief speech and the Permanent Chairman asked "that the delegates . . . not make speeches on this call of the roll. This is simply to ascertain whether they want to nominate a candidate for Vice President or not, and it could be better answered if you just say 'pass' if you do not intend to make a nomination."

Heedful, succeeding delegation chairmen passed without elaboration until the call came to Nebraska. Then:

The Secretary of the Convention.—Nebraska.

Mrs. George P. Abel of Nebraska.—Mr. Chairman, one of our delegates, without concurrence with any of the others, desires to have the floor to make a nomination for Vice President.

The Permanent Chairman.—Will the lady tell—

Mrs. George P. Abel of Nebraska.—This name has not been revealed to me, the chairman of the delegation.

The Permanent Chairman.—Who does he desire to nominate?

Mrs. George P. Abel of Nebraska.—His name has not been told to me.

The Permanent Chairman.—I would say for the benefit of the Nebraska delegation, the reason I am making this inquiry is that I have a letter from a distinguished son of Nebraska in which he states he

[18] *Ibid.*, pp. 280, 287-88.
[19] *Ibid.*, p. 290.
[20] *Ibid.*

does not want his name to be presented. That being the case, I could not receive the nomination of that individual; and I make an inquiry for information.

Mrs. George P. Abel of Nebraska.—Shall I ask?

The Permanent Chairman.—Yes, that is what I am asking.

Mr. Terry Carpenter, delegate from Nebraska.—We are going to nominate Joe Smith.

The Permanent Chairman.—Joe—who?

Mr. Terry Carpenter of Nebraska.—Joe Smith.

The Permanent Chairman.—Nebraska reserves the right to nominate Joe Smith, whoever he is.[21]

So much from the official record. Reporters swarmed past sergeants at arms who sought to prevent the treasonable one from being interviewed. Carpenter, former Democratic congressman from Nebraska from 1933 to 1935 and a bona fide delegate to the convention, told reporters that Smith was a "real person, a symbol of an open convention," and "basically, it's been a dull convention."[22]

Carpenter's example found no followers. All other delegation chairmen passed promptly, in turn. Martin declared the nominations closed as the Virgin Islands failed to name a favorite son. After introducing Governor Herter to nominate Nixon, Martin closed the nominations again.

It took the genteel Governor Herter nineteen minutes to accomplish the expected. He pleaded with the willing delegates:

> If we support Ike, if we take pride in the record of his Administration, if we have faith in his crusade, we also take pride, we also have faith in the Vice President who has helped to create that record and direct that crusade. In him we have a unique combination of experience and maturity with youth and energy. It's a winning combination—part of a winning team.
>
> Let's not break up that winning team.
>
> Let's renominate the man whom Ike, himself, has called its most valuable member.[23]

[21] *Ibid.*, pp. 292-93.

[22] *New York Times,* Aug. 23, 1956. Carpenter, millionaire gas station operator and political candidate with a shrewd eye for publicity, had told the press on his arrival in San Francisco of his intention to make a nomination other than Nixon. He was forestalled from nominating Nebraska's Governor Fred Seaton, by the management's prompt extraction of a letter from Seaton refusing to have his name before the convention. But Joe Smith was not so easily reached.

[23] *Official Proceedings, 1956,* pp. 297-300.

There was a good ten minutes of demonstration. Martin called for order as demonstrators with "Win with Dick" placards departed from in front of the stand. The demonstrators subsided, and the seconders came on. The arrangement was similar to the routine for Eisenhower, a series of short speeches, each with a major theme, each working in the standard array of Republican, subthemes, each given by a symbolically representative figure.

In the midst of the two-minute speeches came an eleven-minute one drafted only the day before—by Governor Stassen. The delegates were not all sure what his role would be at the convention, despite the President's intercession and explanation earlier in the day; some of them greeted Stassen with incredulous oh's and other evidence of apprehension.[24] But there were no boos; and there was some welcome for the prodigal returned home.[25]

Stassen neither withdrew nor did he mention his argument that Nixon would detract from the ticket; but he did report his conviction that Nixon was the overwhelming considered choice of the delegates. He urged men and women of the country in and out of the party—especially independents, labor people, minority groups, and new younger voters—to join in accepting the selections of Ike's party. He insisted that it was important for the party, from its smallest units to the national convention, to realize that the freedom to differ is important to the success of the party and to the vitality of the nation. It should be made "easy to dissent and respected to differ."[26]

Stassen took care to praise Nixon, but he also reminded the delegates that his action did not foreclose the right of any one to vote for any man or woman he might wish to support. He ended with his personal declaration of loyalty to the team and to the party, no matter whether in future he were to win or lose any "preliminary test."

With no further nominations, the Chairman directed the clerk

---

[24] Senior author's notes. Mazo reports that Nixon agreed to have Stassen as seconder only if he were restricted to two minutes, and did not replace any of the seconders already scheduled. Stassen went on as an added attraction—but had his small show of independence by ignoring demands by Sherman Adams and Robert Humphreys that he cut his speech to the agreed-on two minutes. See Mazo, *Richard Nixon*, pp. 184-85.

[25] *New York Times*, Aug. 23, 1956.

[26] *Official Proceedings, 1956*, p. 306.

to call the roll for voting. With the seconding speeches out of the way, Martin was a little more generous in allowing elaboration on the announcements of states in casting their votes. Some carried mild political overtones. California's Governor Goodwin Knight signaled to all and sundry that he too was voting for his political rival as California's 70 went for her favorite son (under a delegation decision to vote as a unit). The party management used the roll call to underline a few noteworthy points: Florida's vote of 26 for Nixon was cast by the first Republican congressman elected from that state since 1876; Louisiana's vote was cast by the only Republican mayor in the deep south, Donald Fiske of Oak Grove. Elroy W. Bromwich of Missouri did not avail himself of the formal freedom outlined by Stassen to vote for his choice.

A few of the delegations signaled the dates on which they had decided unanimously to vote for the chosen candidate. Virginia voted first for Pat Nixon—and then for her husband.

Nebraska and Terry Carpenter got one more laugh. The original tally showed 17 for Nixon, one delegate passing. At the end of the roll call, however, pressure prevailed. To convention applause, Nebraska changed her vote to 18 for Nixon and the ultimate vote was thus without mar.[27]

With the appointment of the honorary committees to notify the candidates of the results of the convention's ballots, the convention recessed.

Acceptances

On the morning of Thursday, August 23, 1956, the new Republican National Committee held its organizational meeting. The steamroller, that had effectively guaranteed possession of weapons to the Hall-Nixon faction, rolled on during the open meeting. At the President's request, the committee renamed Hall its chairman, by unanimous vote. New Vice Chairmen were Clarence J. Brown of Ohio, a former Taft supporter; H. Meade Alcorn, Jr. of Connecticut; Eleanor S. Todd of New Jersey; and Kathryn K. Meloney of Wyoming. Miss Bertha S. Adkins was reappointed as Assistant to the Chairman. Representative Hugh Scott, Jr. of Pennsylvania was re-elected to the post of General Counsel. Mrs. Wesley M. Dixon of Illinois replaced Mrs. Gladys E. Knowles of Montana as Secretary, and W. Harold Brenton of Iowa was re-elected Treasurer.

A special subcommittee of the new National Committee had waited on the President for his recommendation for their action. They not only brought back the word for the renomination of Leonard Hall; they reported that all of them were "inspired" by the way the President looked.

The fifth and final session of the Centennial Convention came to order at 4 P.M., heard a thoroughly political invocation, and proceeded to pass some routine but important resolutions. First among these was authority for the National Committee to fill vacancies on the ticket, or to call a national convention for the purpose of filling such vacancy.[28] The convention authorized publication of its proceedings and gave thanks to convention officers, and other individuals and organizations.

The Permanent Chairman introduced Senate candidate Dan Thornton of Colorado, who read his hearers a sharp lesson on the difference between truth in San Francisco and something else in Chicago. This speech furnished truth-squad notes for the campaign to follow. Against the Democrats' charges made the week before—about labor, taxes, government spending, small business, prosperity, foreign policy, farm prices, farm freedom, Thornton interposed: "The motto and creed of the Eisenhower Administration has always been and will always be truth—truth—truth. The motto of the Republican campaign is and will be truth—truth—truth."[29]

---

[28] *Ibid.*, p. 325. This resolution, the same in form as had been passed by the previous convention, was of special potential importance in 1956 in view of the President's medical history. The only change was a clear specification that committeemen, when voting for this purpose, would cast a vote equal to that cast by their state delegation in the 1956 convention.

[29] *Ibid.*, p. 335.

Then came an introduction to the convention (and to the nation) of twelve candidates for governorships, and forty-six candidates for Congress. Each got a cheer from his own state delegation and a polite acknowledgment from a few others. The Nixons were introduced by "California Here I Come." The audience stood, cheered, paraded with the first genuine outburst of enthusiasm of the day, despite the artificialities imposed by formal staging. After five minutes, Martin gaveled for silence, but the band and organ kept on until George Murphy gave the approved direction for a fadeout. The Vice President rose as the Young Republicans precipitated themselves into a frenzy while onlookers and delegates watched quietly.

Nixon, taking over, got the standard-bearers to lower their cards so the delegates could see and hear. At 5:40 he got into his stride; and presently showed that this speech was pure New Nixon, designed to strike a note of positive accomplishment for the future, while maintaining and increasing the degree of tribute to the President. He did not mention the Democrats. He spoke of the greatness and nobility of America, and of its roots in freedom, courage, and faith. Praising the American vision of the past, he called for progress toward broader sharing in the common prosperity and education for every American. Noting the Soviet challenge in the field of scientific and technical education, he promised that "We shall not—we will not—allow them to outstrip us in this vital race."[30] Somewhat anticlimactically he called for a healthy climate for small business.

He called for fresh efforts in the struggle for world peace. He demanded not only military strength, but also a bold and imaginative program to win the minds and hearts of men to the ideals of freedom and democracy.[31]

This struggle justified, he said, any sacrifices necessary to maintain our military strength at the point of adequate deterrence; to keep vigorous our programs of economic aid and to maintain our political alliances; and to take steps (through the Voice of America and international exchanges) to see to it that the leaders and

[30] *Ibid.*, p. 343.
[31] *Ibid.*, pp. 344-45.

thinkers of the world had a full chance to compare the accomplishments of democracy with those of communism.

Then he evoked the great symbol:

> I say to you that we face this task that I have outlined inspired by the vigor and the vision of the man of the century—President Eisenhower.

Linking leader and party, the Vice President went on:

> The Republican Party is a hundred years old, but under his leadership it is again young and imaginative. It has captured the idealism and faith that is the greatness of America.

Further defining the party, he continued:

> Our party . . . is not a party of drift and self-satisfaction. The greatest moments of the Republican Party have been the many years in which it was progressive and forward-looking. We are conservative only in the sense that we keep what is sound and proven from the past. . . . But we use this true conservatism as a springboard for progress in the future.
>
> I need not tell you how great the stakes are. . . . America cannot settle for less than the best leadership it can get in the next four years because—make no mistake about it—the quality of America's leadership will determine the difference between life and death, slavery and freedom, plenty and poverty, happiness and sorrow for millions of people on this earth.
>
> Let us recognize, then, that our party is more than a machine designed to perpetuate its adherents in power. Under President Eisenhower it has been welded into a mighty instrument, a mighty instrument for good, which will lead America into that new age in which the dreams and hopes of our fathers will be realized not only for ourselves, but for peoples throughout the world.[32]

Nixon left the rostrum amid a great ovation. The Permanent Chairman announced the arrival of the President, at 6:04.

At 6:14 the last balloons popped, and the demonstrators resumed their seats. This outpouring of action and emotion had really spontaneous elements, as many in the galleries were caught up in the delegates' enthusiasm.

The President came forward to the speaker's rostrum to meet a fresh ovation, given special impetus as the President turned to

[32] *Ibid.*, pp. 345-46.

remember the VIP's at his back. He departed from his prepared text to emphasize his gratitude to the delegates for keeping intact the "team" of 1952, and for the warmth of their welcome. He added his own encomium to the already-described qualifications of the Vice President. "Whatever dedication to country, loyalty and patriotism and great ability can do for America, he will do, and that I know."[33] Then he addressed himself to what had been so carefully put together in advance.

Invoking the authority of Henrik Ibsen, the President read:

I hold that man is in the right who is most clearly in league with the future.

Repeating his leading motif:

The Republican Party is the Party of the Future.

Joining the themes:

I hold that the Republican Party and platform are right in 1956, because they "are most closely in league with the future."

Drawing the conclusion:

And for this reason the Republican Party and program are and will be decisively approved by the American people in 1956!

Departing again from the prepared speech:

My friends, I have just made a very flat statement for victory for the Republican Party in November, and I believe it from the bottom of my heart. But what I say is based upon certain assumptions. . . . And that is this: That every American who believes as we do—the Republicans, the independents, the straight-thinking Democrats— must carry the message of the record and the pledges that we have made and here make to all the people in the land.

Still outside the limits of the prepared speech:

Americans must register and vote. Here is a task not only for the Republican National Committee, for the women's organizations, for the citizens' organizations, for the so-called Youth for Eisenhower— everybody that bears this message in his heart must carry it to the country. In that way we will win.

Back to the prepared speech:

Now, of special relevance, and to me particularly gratifying, is

[33] *Ibid.*, p. 348.

the fact that the country's young people show a consistent preference for this Administration. After all, let us not forget these young people are America's future. Parenthetically, may I say I shall never cease to hope that the several states will give them the voting privilege at a somewhat earlier age than is now generally the case.

Into the body of the speech—five reasons why the Republican Party is the Party of the Future.

First: It is the party of "long-range principle, not short-term expediency."

Second: "It is the party which concentrates on the facts and issues of today and tomorrow, not the facts and issues of yesterday."

Third: The Republican Party draws people together instead of driving them apart.

Fourth: The Republican Party "is the party through which the many things that still need doing will soonest be done—and will be done by enlisting the fullest energies of free, creative, individual people."

Fifth: "A Party of the Future must be completely dedicated to peace, as indeed must all Americans, for without peace there is no future."[34]

The President outlined three imperatives of peace. First, the "elementary necessity of maintaining our own national strength —moral, economic and military." Second, collective security—not in the sense of the creation of a monolithic mass, but strength built on "the unity that comes of the voluntary association of nations which, however diverse, are developing their own capacities and asserting their own national destinies in a world of freedom and of mutual respect." And third, "Without for a moment relaxing our internal and collective defenses, we must actively try to bridge the great chasm that separates us from the peoples under Communist rule."[35] Given the glimmerings of a conciliatory policy by opposing governments, there was hope that "little by little, mistrust based on falsehoods will give way to international understanding based on truth."

[34] *Ibid.*, pp. 353, 354.
[35] *Ibid.*, p. 356.

As these hopes are realized, the President told his now-quiet listeners,

> It will not seem futile for young people to dream of a brave, and new, and shining world, or for older people to feel that they can, in fact, bequeath to their children a better inheritance than that which was their own. Science and technology, labor-saving methods, management, labor organization, education, medicine and—not least, politics and government—all these have brought within our grasp a world in which backbraking toil and long hours will not be necessary.
>
> Travel all over the world, to learn to know our brothers abroad, will be fast and cheap. The fear and pain of crippling disease will be greatly reduced. The material things that make life interesting and pleasant can be available to everyone. Leisure, together with educational and recreational facilities, will be abundant, so that all can develop the life of the spirit, or reflection, of religion, of the arts, of the full realization of the good things of the world. And political wisdom will ensure justice and harmony.[36]

This vision would not be realized by revolution or by the "sordid politics" of pitting group against group. It would be gained "by the ambitions, and judgment and inspirations, and daring of 169 million free Americans working together and with friends abroad toward a common ideal in a peaceful world."[37] In closing, he reminded the delegates that Lincoln had followed his prediction concerning the future of divided houses with the confident expectation that he did not expect the house to fall, but that it would cease to be divided. So with the world of today:

> We too must have the vision, the fighting spirit and the deep religious faith in our Creator's destiny for us to sound a similar note of promise for our divided world—that out of our time there can, with incessant work and with God's help, emerge a new era of good life, good will and good hope for all men. . . .
>
> My friends, in firm faith, and in the conviction that Republican purposes and principles are in league with this kind of future, the nomination that you have tendered me for the Presidency of the United States I now—humbly but confidently—accept.[38]

There was a rising ovation. The minister from the church in

[36] *Ibid.*
[37] *Ibid.*, p. 357.
[38] *Ibid.*

Chicago to which Adlai Stevenson had repaired for rest and strength the morning after Truman's announcement for Harriman, pronounced a short and thoroughly nonpartisan benediction. The gentleman from Maine, Mr. Fred C. Scribner, Jr., moved that the convention adjourn "without day." And at 7:03 P.M., the Centennial Convention of the Republican Party drifted off into the annals of politics and of show business.

Convention and Ceremony

What had happened? Contrast with Chicago had been achieved in more ways than one. In San Francisco, decisions made by the organization in advance had been ratified. Yet a sought-for prize eluded the victors: the believable appearance of an open convention. This was the triumph at Chicago, where the convention was in fact open—not so much because of the Kennedy-Kefauver race as because of the struggle between Truman and Stevenson for control of the party. The decisions in San Francisco were ratified by delegates whose nominal freedom of choice had long since been foreclosed.[39]

The decision in Chicago was made by delegates with feasible alternatives before them. Both Stassen and Harriman had made late overt starts in their efforts to turn delegates to their causes. But Stassen had to fight both the established decisions of the party hierarchy, and the aura of a President asserting the formal conditions of an open choice, but unwilling to create the practical conditions for one. Harriman had Truman's support, he offered a clear-cut ideological position, and the argument of victory. There

[39] This is not to say that the delegates were thwarted. No careful observer of the convention sensed any powerful undercurrent of sentiment against Nixon, or any powerful sentiment for another candidate. Such undercurrents were present but weak. Any uneasiness over the probable effects of Nixon as co-candidate on Eisenhower's chances of victory, or over Nixon's probable behavior as a successor President, was far outweighed by the fact that Eisenhower had praised him, had opted for no other—and their organizational chiefs were solidly in back of him. The President's obvious health pushed the contingencies into the background. Stassen undoubtedly spoke a hard-learned truth when he said that the majority of the delegates wanted Nixon. They had no viable choice.

was far less certainty in Chicago, despite Stevenson's commanding lead.[40]

As a result, Chicago provided a convention; San Francisco a ceremony.

But need the Republicans have sought the appearance of an open convention? A successful rally is an entirely acceptable objective for a convention—especially when the party has no matters of issue or candidate to settle. But to seek the appearance of an open convention when in fact it is not so, is only to risk a demonstration of hypocrisy and to weaken the party's reputation for sincerity and fair dealing. When a party is in a powerful and unified condition, the best tactic for a successful rally is to act naturally, and let the chips fall where they may. If there is a strong admixture of entertainment, it is sure to be prominent, because of the lack of genuine party business.

The Republicans in 1952—as the Democrats in 1956—did have a good amount of entertainment; but nobody thought it overshadowed the party fights. Possibly the Republicans would have looked less like the captives of professional opinion managers in 1956 if they had scheduled fewer paid entertainers and had allowed for a little more naturalness and careless timing on the part of the many speechmakers. There is question today whether the Republican convention managers would do things differently, given the same conditions they faced in 1956. Many Republicans praised the decorum and discipline, the smooth timing and the lack of haggling that the managers achieved in San Francisco. And if a rally or a ceremony is intended to edify partisans rather than to convert the wavering or the wayward, the taste of the partisans is important.

Two further aspects of the Republican ceremony should not be overlooked.

First was the public manifestation of the New Nixon—his clear response to Democratic attacks, and a response reinforced by Eisenhower's praise of him not as a campaigner but as a public servant. Second was the fact that the Eisenhower doctrines were

[40] See Walter Lippmann, "Chicago and San Francisco," *New York Herald Tribune,* Aug. 23, 1956.

supreme in the field of philosophy and speech, but less than dominant in the sphere of organization. Nixon's triumph gave many rightwingers hope that in the organizational decisions to come their preferences would quietly but effectively be taken into account.

The most telling effects from the convention as a whole arose from the renomination of Richard Milhous Nixon, the temper and tone in which he accepted the vote of confidence from the organized party, and the obvious health and vigor of the President.

9

Between Conventions and Campaign

CUSTOM IN AMERICAN political campaigning calls for a lull in traveling and speechmaking in the period immediately following the nominating conventions. Such a lull gives time: to repair breaches in party ranks torn by the nominating fights; to perfect organization, campaign propaganda and materials; and to make final adjustments in campaign tactics once the opponents are known and their probable strategies clarified.

During the days from late August up to the formal campaign launching at Gettysburg on September 12, there was much less of this than usual. The Democrats hardly slackened their public pace, although they were the party that had had an internal fight, and that faced difficult organizational questions. The Republican organization, acting all along in Leonard Hall's firm faith regarding who their candidates would be and what their major campaign arguments were, stood in no need of internal reshuffling. Only expansion was needed.

Campaign themes had long since been selected. Campaign materials—down to lapel buttons—had been prepared in advance, and the evocation of "Ike and Dick" could move ahead as soon as the campaign plan specified. So the Republicans eased off a good deal more than their opponents.

Nevertheless, both parties had to do certain things during this period—they had to tie their labor pleas to Labor Day, and appeal to veterans on the occasion of the American Legion convention in Los Angeles.

While the Republicans perfected organization, readied the Vice President and the truth squads, prepared speeches for the cabinet and the subcabinet, polished television shows and radio scripts, and marshaled party officials and dignitaries, they used the President's press conference as a main campaign vehicle.

The Democrats launched a "precampaign" trip that sent Stevenson and Kefauver careening across the country—chiefly to woo support from state and local organizations. They commenced work on a group of eighty-nine five-minute television spot-programs, to be placed after popular entertainment shows.

Political Estimates and Strategies

Much if not most of what went on during the campaigning immediately after the conventions comes clear if we recall the estimates apparently held by both parties of their strengths and weaknesses in electoral opinion. The Stevenson group had ordered studies of domestic opinion to guide them through the primary and convention periods. Summarized, these showed that the main strength of the Democratic party lay in its image as the party favoring the little fellow and willing to battle for popular interests against special interests. Its main weakness was its image as the party more prone to war.

The main strength of the Republicans was the conviction that the President was a man of peace, and that the Republicans would be less likely to land the country into another shooting war. The main Republican weakness was the widespread belief that the GOP favored big business and the rich.[1]

The Republicans apparently agreed with much of this estimate of their party's image. All factions placed unbounded faith in the personal popularity of the President, while some felt apprehension about the opinion of Nixon held by independents, Democrats, and first voters. Most Republicans also felt that the issues of communism and corruption were important to the electorate, and they were apprehensive over unrest in farming areas

[1] Adlai E. Stevenson, *The New America* (1957), p. xv.

and in pockets of depression. In the larger picture, they judged they had overwhelming assets in the undeniable and visible facts of national prosperity and the absence of shooting war.

What main conclusions did the parties draw from these estimates?

For the Democrats, it was clear that domestic issues should come before foreign policy. Here they could marshal available sources of discontent without making arguments that would recall to the electorate the unhappy association of Democratic regimes with periods of war.

It was also clear that they must attack. Somehow they would have to provoke enough discontent with the state of things under the Republicans, currently and for the future, to make a case for a change. Admitting progress, they could strive to show that the rate and direction and inclusiveness of the progress were not enough.

Hence, the "New America." Relying on their popularity among the little fellows, and their superiority in registration figures, they had to stir Democratic registrants—voters notoriously less prone to go to the polls than their outnumbered but more deeply involved Republican opponents. Admitting broad evidence of prosperity, the Democrats had to attack in areas of farm discontent and unemployment, and agitate among disgruntled small business men. Admitting peace, and desiring to soft-pedal discussion of foreign affairs, they nevertheless could do two things if the campaign forced much talk of the foreign policy issue: (1) point to increasing signs of unrest abroad; and (2) attack the President for complacency and part-time leadership.

Above all, faced with the towering prestige and personal popularity of the President, the Democrats had to find ways of cutting him down. They correctly sensed that he was far stronger than his party—therefore, they must identify him with the party and saddle him with its relative unpopularity. Believing that the voters considered him above both his party and his administration subordinates, they concluded they must saddle him with the responsibility for their shortcomings, which should be his by virtue of his office, but which the American people did not place on him. Better yet—they should raise directly or subtly the issue of the President's health, and point to Nixon as the odds-on heir apparent, and ask what were his qualifications for the Presidency.

One difficulty with this strategy of campaign argument was the temper and experience of the Democratic candidate. He recognized the wisdom of concentrating on domestic policy; but his personal concern and interest were in foreign policy. He had talked of domestic issues intensively (but far from exclusively) since the commencement of the primaries—and to a degree, well before that. He felt he had exhausted them, and they had exhausted him. Why not turn to foreign policy, where not only he would be fresh, but where the issues were burning?

The American people, he reasoned, would respond to his appeals if he told them forcefully and frankly why they were not really at peace, why the nation's foreign relations were deteriorating, and what should be done about them. He believed, correctly or not, that he could rouse the voters in time to see that the formal appearance of peace was not peace at all. Only reluctantly had he acceded to the desires of his managers that he concentrate on domestic matters. He took up the gage when progressive deterioration of the Western position and in the prospects for democratic principles in the Middle East and the visible unrest in the Soviet satellites demonstrated to him, if not to the electorate, that the real issues faced by the country were in the foreign field and in the governmental policies and leadership at work in that arena.[2]

For the Republicans, their conclusions counseled these tasks: to show the President, to dwell on a record in keeping with the deep desires of the electorate, and to offset the effects of farm discontent and scattered unemployment on electorally critical situations. Reasoning that they had the Presidency in their hands if the President did not physically falter, they nevertheless had to guard against apathy and complacency, and to translate the President's popularity into Republican majorities in the House and Senate.

[2] *Ibid.*, pp. xvi, xxvii.

Democratic Organization and Leadership

Meeting on Saturday morning, August 18, the Democratic National Committee organized itself for the campaign and for the ensuing four years. The main item for consideration was settlement of who was going to run the campaign: Butler or Finnegan. Butler had done yeoman service in keeping the Democratic national organization together and strengthening it; he had played a considerable diplomatic role in promoting party unity during the convention. But he had also created some resentment in the Stevenson camp. Finnegan had brought Stevenson through the rigors of the nominating campaign; he was closer to the Stevenson campaign group in being, and normally would have succeeded to the job as Chairman of the National Committee and director in charge. Stevenson was well aware of the weaknesses and difficulties of divided command in 1952. This time, he planned to centralize command under Finnegan.

But the event was not wholly within his hands. Congressman Kirwan, head not only of the Democratic Congressional Campaign Committee but also key subcommittee chairman of the House Appropriations Committee, thought that to jettison Butler would not only be an injustice, but would provoke public confusion. On the last day of the convention, he talked to Rayburn. Rayburn talked to Stevenson. The next day, at the meeting of the new Democratic National Committee, Stevenson surprised everyone (including Butler) by asking Butler to serve again as National Chairman. (Butler, in responding to tributes brought from many quarters, had told the committee that he was "sure you do not know you are writing my political epitaph.") Only one committeeman voted "No," on the motion instructing Butler not to submit his resignation.[3]

---

[3] The foregoing is based on accounts in contemporary newspapers and in John M. Redding, *Inside the Democratic Party* (1958). A more detailed and somewhat different story is recounted by Sidney Hyman in "The Collective Leadership of Paul M. Butler," in *The Reporter*, Vol. 21 (Dec. 24, 1959), p. 10. Hyman reports a "dump Butler" movement in the Stevenson entourage that nearly succeeded. But Stevenson, while making clear to Butler his desire that he resign, was unwilling to make it a

The committee heard that there had been no credentials contests on any of its members. It formalized the election of a new Executive Committee, consisting of regional representatives plus three members at large chosen by the National Chairman. It authorized new credentials committees and elected Mrs. Katie Loucheim its Vice Chairman. It heard a Treasurer's Report from Matthew McCloskey, who noted the absence of several states from important meetings and outlined regional organization and financial goals for the rest of the campaign.[4] He sketched a financial plan calling for outlays of $1 million per week for seven weeks of the campaign to follow.

Butler put main stress on a registration drive, but also reminded the members of the National Committee that they would have to fill out immediately the affirmations of intention to support the national ticket, required by the new rules.

In settling the question of chairmanship, Stevenson also announced his desire for Mr. Finnegan to serve as Campaign Director. The committee accepted by acclamation, thus repeating for 1956 the dual form of organization that had plagued the Democrats in 1952. Finnegan responded to Butler's assurance of full cooperation by pointing out that the foundation of a successful campaign rested on a good candidate, good issues, and good organization. There was room for improvement, he thought, in organization.

Both Stevenson and Kefauver, in addressing the committee, stressed their intention of appealing to the "stay-at-home and independent bloc" of voters. They promised an active campaign, country-wide, in contrast to the expected Republican strategy of a limited campaign featuring Eisenhower on television.

Kefauver stressed the need for cooperation in organization, asking the National Committee to welcome his people with open

---

blunt order in a meeting immediately before the Democratic National Committee met August 18. Hyman also says that during the entire campaign Butler conferred with Stevenson once and with Finnegan twice.

[4] He divided the country into eight regions with regional headquarters, and announced quotas for each state, ranging from $275,000 for New York and $175,000 for Pennsylvania down to $5,000 for Maine and $2,000 for the Virgin Islands. *New York Times*, Aug. 19, 1956.

arms, for they were ready to close ranks. "All my people want to cooperate, but in some of the states there has not been much cooperation with them."[5]

One of Stevenson's continuing problems was how to create confidence in the prospect of victory that would be at once believable and heartening. The convention itself had created the illusion of victory among partisans present as Stevenson's triumph in winning the nomination against vigorous opposition symbolized the possibility of a similar victory over the Republicans. How to keep that illusion fresh and compelling, when up against the opposition of the President as well as of the Republican Party, called for continuing imagination and effort. Stevenson returned to the victory theme at numerous times, probably more often in his talks to organization men than in public addresses early in his campaign,[6] but he always touched it lightly. The Eisenhower charisma and the periodic indications from the polls were consistently against him.

Basic to a Democratic formula for victory in 1956 was to get those Democrats who voted for Eisenhower in 1952 back into the fold. And more important than just any Democrats, would be Democrats in those states where the Republicans had won by small margins in 1952, and in those precincts where small shifts of votes would result in disproportionate Democratic gains. Analysis revealed that if the Democrats could hold their 1952 position in the nine states that went for Stevenson then, and add fourteen more close states, they could amass 270 electoral votes—with 266 needed to win. (The fourteen states are tabulated on page 229.) A shift of 851,000 votes in these states in 1952 would have brought Mr. Stevenson victory then. Finnegan used this as a prime argument among state and local politicians for strenuous efforts in these states in 1956, especially during the immediate post-convention meetings with them.

Finnegan's plans for Stevenson and Kefauver were equally di-

[5] *Chicago Tribune*, Aug. 19, 1956.
[6] *New York Times*, Sept. 5, 1956.

rect, simple, and relevant: meet the leaders in those areas where they can make the difference; fire them up, and then turn to campaign traveling and morale building elsewhere.[7]

In gearing their organization for an all-out effort, the Stevenson-Kefauver Democrats had to make special efforts in those areas of the South disaffected by the presence of Kefauver on the ticket and disgruntled by the national party stand on civil rights. They

State	Electoral Vote	Republican Percentage of Total Vote for President, 1952
Tennessee	11	50.0
Missouri	13	50.7
Rhode Island	4	50.9
Delaware	3	51.8
Pennsylvania	32	52.7
Texas	24	53.1
Massachusetts	16	54.2
Washington	9	54.3
Oklahoma	8	54.6
Illinois	27	54.8
Florida	10	55.0
Minnesota	11	55.3
Maryland	9	55.4
New Mexico	4	55.4
Total	181	

also had to do what could be done in Harriman territory—*i.e.* in New York; with secondary attention to Kennedy's home state of Massachusetts.

In the immediate aftermath of the two conventions, earlier threats of an organized Southern bolt were largely dissipated. South Carolina, which had committed itself to have a state Democratic convention after the national convention to take appropriate remedial measures, rejected party bolting and enthusiastically accepted interpretation of the Republican civil rights plank as

[7] *Ibid.*, Sept. 2, 1956.

"harsh" and of Eisenhower himself as a party-labeled Republican extremist on the issue. Mississippi, that had also threatened to hold a subsequent state convention, found no reason to do so. Georgia and Alabama stayed firmly behind the party loyalists.

Regional leaders thus saw their way clear, in these states as well as in Virginia, North Carolina, Alabama, and Louisiana, to a flexible and not wholly unpalatable political solution. They would be willing to condone a certain amount of flexibility of campaign talk on civil rights in the North, provided it was not too rough—*i.e.*, that it did not go beyond the Republican position, and thus make it impossible for them to keep their local organizations in line.[8] As for Democratic leaders in the North, they had a tactic that was compatible with the Southern line of action: quietly to point out to Negro voters in the North that a vote for the Republican candidate in Northern states was a vote for candidates who would probably go along with Eastland.

In New York and Massachusetts there had been no overt indications of disaffection or revolt; but there was continuing evidence that the machine politicians in both states had no stomach for a full-scale effort on Stevenson's behalf. The occasions for apathy were several—in some cases dislike of Stevenson personally, or of his entourage, who kept to themselves and seemed unable to grasp the style and tactics of local politics. In others it was diffidence born of a conviction that Stevenson could not win. Neither Harriman nor Kennedy, by their own efforts in their own states or elsewhere, was able to fire up the local organizations.

Campaigning Eisenhower-Nixon Style

If there were any doubts about the kind of campaign the President wanted to wage, he set them at rest early. At his press conference—his first since the convention—on August 31, Eisenhower refused to estimate the Democratic chances, or to give any comfort to Republican critics of a "too-high-level" campaign (such as lost in 1948).

[8] *Ibid.*

This Administration has a record. Now I am going to stand on that record. I am going to show what we are trying to do in the future, and to let the record and the way we have attempted to carry out every promise we have ever made be the earnest of what we intend to do.

Now there is going to be no lack of candor. That does not mean that I am going to indulge in petty name calling and attempt to making phrases to belittle someone. I don't believe in it.[9]

On the convention morrow, at a strategy conference in California, Nixon had outlined his expectations about the Republican campaign:

In 1952 we were confronted with an Administration that had to be thrown out if we were to move in. We had to give the reasons why there should be a change.

On this occasion we are confronted with the necessity of returning ourselves to office. So our campaign should be directed to talking about ourselves rather than about our opponents.

My own analysis is that the campaign for our ticket should emphasize the positive accomplishments made up to this time and should paint for the people the picture of what we believe in addition to what we can accomplish in the next four years.

In Chicago, the Democrats tried to find issues and couldn't. Our job is to inform the people of our record and draw the people a picture of what they can expect in the future. That's the general character of this campaign.[10]

Nixon also disclosed that the division of labor between himself and the President "always was the plan"—even before the President's illness—because it was most effective and sparing of the President's time for the duties of his office. For the Vice President, the campaign would be a full-time activity.[11]

Labor in the Campaign

With the conventions finished and party positions on issues taken, it was now open season for public endorsements by major

[9] *Ibid.*, Sept. 1, 1956.
[10] *Ibid.*, Aug. 26, 1956.
[11] *Ibid.*

political groups, especially labor organizations. On August 24 the New York State CIO came out for the Democrats' slate,[12] and on August 28, the Executive Council of the AFL-CIO came to its decision. Despite the fact that New York's Attorney General Jacob Javits, soon to be candidate for the Senate, warned labor not to ally itself irretrievably with one or the other of the parties, labor's Executive Council recommended to its General Board that it endorse Stevenson and Kefauver, and the Board acted accordingly.[13]

On the Vice President fell the burden of the official Republican response to the AFL-CIO Executive Council's decision, made public on August 29, to support the Democratic ticket. The result was a shrewd bit of fencing. Nixon recognized the personal rights of any laboring man to take a position on the political candidates and on issues; but he doubted whether labor's leaders had any right to try to bind union members or to dictate to them.

The Republicans would stand, he said, on their labor record, and on labor's prosperity during the preceding three and a half years. He balanced his thrust against potential dictation by labor leaders with praise for their fight against communism, and their efforts to present abroad a sound picture of American democracy. The Nixon version of "the speech" contained these salient points of appeal to the rank and file. Labor Secretary James Mitchell took on the chore of more detailed exposition of the Republican case, dwelling on the record of industrial peace and higher sustained take-home pay than in any comparable previous period.

As the Republicans rumbled along in low gear, the Democrats moved more swiftly, starting with their Labor Day speeches, going through the Legion convention appeals, and culminating with their victory in the Maine elections on September 10.

The Republicans had started quietly in their appeals to labor —the President ceremonialized the first labor commemorative stamp, called labor a bulwark of the nation and a terror to its enemies, and Secretary of Labor Mitchell dwelt on the comforts enjoyed by labor's rank and file.

---

[12] *Ibid.*

[13] *Ibid.*, Aug. 29, 1956. The decision was reached by two critical votes: one, whether to endorse at all, approved 14 to 8; the other, whom to endorse, the Democratic ticket by 17 to 5.

The Democrats, however, put matters much more sharply. Stevenson provided an intensely partisan, intensely pro-labor speech in Detroit on the afternoon of Labor Day—time and place of now expected Democratic tactics.[14] He went beyond strictly labor interests to mention civil rights—establishing more definitely than did his platform his position on the matter.

> The New America means to me an America in which every man and woman and child enjoys equally and without regard to race or religion the freedoms of conscience, belief, expression and opportunity.
> The Supreme Court decision on the desegregation of the public schools gave new emphasis to a traditional American principle. That decision is the law of the land.[15]

He launched another campaign technique by linking his attacks on the President for part-time, ineffective leadership with attacks on Republican claims of civil rights gains. He charged that it was the Chief Executive's responsibility to create the climate of opinion in which those decisions could be made effective; leaving the broad implication that the President had not acted forcefully. Finally he invoked the image of Republican heartlessness by saying: "We need a government which really cares about people—all people—cares about them, not as statistics in a poll, but as children of God."[16]

Stevenson on Draft and Bomb Tests

In an inclusive, characteristically Stevensonian speech to veterans, this time with a little pepper in it, the Democratic candidate

[14] There was nothing new in this effort to describe the New America in terms familiar and acceptable to labor's articulate spokesmen. Stevenson harped on unemployment in the midst of Republican prosperity and complacency; he called Republicans callous, and recalled Secretary of Defense Wilson's kennel dogs to the enjoyment of his partisan crowd. He did mention the necessity of wiping out labor racketeering, but kept the great balance of his speech on more welcome topics. He called for expanded unemployment insurance, worker retraining, guaranteed annual wages "and other programs aimed to share equitably between business, the consumer and the displaced worker the transitional cost of technological change." *New York Times*, Sept. 4, 1956.

[15] *Ibid.*

[16] *Ibid.*

made a fateful step. He introduced into the campaign the linked issue of the military draft and continuation of testing of hydrogen weapons. Launched at the Legion convention, fixed in the campaign dialogue by the immediate Nixon reply, unsuccessfully exorcised by Eisenhower at several points in the campaign, this issue grew into the sharpest point of controversy over issues by the end of the campaign.

Yet draft and bomb-testing were not major topics of his speech. Most of it was devoted to an analysis of the problems of peace, war and foreign policy—and was intended as a defense against the Republican charges and innuendoes that the Democrats were the war party. He tried to approach the broad issues neither in terms of partisan monopoly of the desire for peace, nor of personal recrimination. It was within this context that he spoke of the draft and the end of bomb-testing—a context promptly obscured or forgotten by those wishing to turn the Stevenson remarks to their partisan ends.

Moreover, Stevenson did not do himself or his topics the justice of a full exposition. He spoke in brief terms about the draft, and in even briefer terms about the prospects of a halt to testing H-bombs. Although he had long been interested in problems of adjusting the draft to the realistic requirements of developing military technology he had not said much if anything about them in public; and in his previous statements about the need for an end to bomb-testing, he had not gone into very much detail. For these reasons he had left himself wide open to partisan interpretation.

What did he actually say at the convention, and what was the immediate response?

Calling for fundamental rethinking of our military strategy and requirements, Stevenson pointed out:

> Many military thinkers believe that the armies of the future, a future now upon us, will employ mobile, technically trained and highly professional units, equipped with tactical atomic weapons. Already it has become apparent that our most urgent need is to encourage trained men to re-enlist rather than to multiply the number of partly trained men as we are currently doing.
>
> We can now anticipate the possibility—hopefully but responsibly—

that within the foreseeable future we can maintain the military forces we need without the draft.

I want to say two things about this prospect:

First, I trust that both parties will reject resolutely any thought of playing politics with this issue. . .

Second, I think it is the national will, shared equally by every American—candidate or voter, Democrat or Republican—that the draft be ended at the earliest possible moment consistent with the national safety. I subscribe with all my heart to this purpose.[17]

As to bomb-testing, Stevenson regretted the administration's casual dismissal of his April 1956 proposal to suspend tests provided other nations did likewise. He called attention to the expressed willingness of those nations to do so now. And he dropped the subject (for the moment) thus: "I deeply believe that it is the destiny of our generation to choose life or death, not only for ourselves but also for our progeny—that it is our destiny meanly to lose or nobly to gain peace for ourselves and all mankind."[18]

He called for full support of a balanced military establishment —however composed or however costly. And he called for stronger economic and moral bases of peace in our time, asking for more adequate foreign aid, for a better posture at home with respect to civil rights and schools, for stronger alliances based on other foundations than the brandishing of military might. He pleaded again to keep the great motives and objects of foreign policy out of debate, while soberly and without personal acrimony discussing the methods for achieving agreed great ends.

But the larger outlines of the speech were immediately lost in the furor created over the implications that the draft might end soon or that the military posture of the country could be relaxed or that bomb-testing could be ended safely.[19]

---

[17] *Ibid.*, Sept. 6, 1956.

[18] *Ibid.*

[19] As Stevenson's warm supporters Arthur Schlesinger, Jr. and Seymour E. Harris put it, "Where he was affirming the need for new ideas in foreign policy, it looked to some as if he had become involved in trick proposals to the exclusion of more basic foreign policy issues. Moreover, there was a widespread, though wrongheaded, feeling that the two policies were inconsistent and that together they represented a weakening of American defenses in the face of a continuing Communist threat. The Democrats seemed to be carrying water on both shoulders; and, though they weren't, they should not have got themselves into the position of seeming to do so." Stevenson, *The New America* (Harper & Bros., 1957), p. xviii.

The initial Republican response was shrewdly delivered within twenty-four hours, when Nixon addressed the final session of the Legion convention. Without mentioning his opponents by name, he told a convention that was more receptive than it had been to Stevenson:

> I realize that there are those in the United States who sincerely believe that we should have discontinued testing of the hydrogen bombs if other nations would have offered to follow a similar policy. I respectfully submit that for us to have followed this advice would have been not only naive but dangerous to our national security. To have taken such action would have been like telling police officials that they should discard their weapons provided the lawbreakers would offer to throw away the machine-guns. . .

And, as to the draft:

> I realize that in an election year it is always tempting to tell the voters that there is an easy way to meet difficult problems. I would like to tell you that we can safely cut our armed forces, get rid of the draft, cut our defense spending and thereby reduce our taxes. Unfortunately, however, in international affairs, particularly, the easy way is seldom the right way. This is no time to suggest to our friends or our possible opponents abroad that America is getting soft and tired and is looking for an easy way out of world responsibilities.[20]

Thus Nixon was able not only to interpret the Stevenson position in a manner favorable to the Republicans, but also to define the Republicans as the party of stern devotion to the hard way of public service and national security, unwilling for partisan advantage to compromise with world reality.[21] Admittedly he dealt with the plausible implications rather than the specific denotation of Stevenson's words; but he did no more than respond to a highly plausible political interpretation of a mention of the draft problem —for why should Stevenson mention it during a partisan political

---

[20] *New York Times*, Sept. 7, 1956. Reporter Gladwin Hill, who covered the convention, reported that Nixon was applauded forty times in a thirty-minute talk, and received no boos; Stevenson got twenty-four rounds of applause in a forty-minute talk, and received some boos for his sharply partisan speech. Both spokesmen got concluding ovations of some forty-five seconds each.

[21] Senator Knowland and the Republican National Committee were less delicate. They called the draft proposals "a blatant attempt to get votes." *Ibid.*, Sept. 6, 1956.

talk unless he expected to draw some political gain from it?[22]

Neither the immediate public response, nor that later in the campaign, was on balance favorable to Stevenson. The Stevenson cause had suffered a severe blow; how severe, was not immediately apparent. For the argument over the draft and bomb-testing —initially undertaken to demonstrate the need for new ideas and leadership in foreign policy—only proved that when the Democratic candidate moved from the realm of general demands to concrete issues he failed to capture the imagination and win the assent of any groups who were not already on his side.

Whatever Stevenson's immediate estimate of the effects of his Legion speech, he threw himself into a whirlwind of speaking and rallying. Flying East from California, Stevenson told a Sangamon County Court House audience in Illinois on September 8 that the issues were not peace and prosperity, but how we go about getting them. On the same day he rallied an Ohio State Democratic Convention on farm policy and small business, charging the Republicans with defeatism in both fields. The next day he spoke to an airfield crowd in New York, conferred with Democratic party notables, met with the Nationalities Division of the Democratic National Committee and held a rally session with the foreign language press. At a New Jersey rally hosted by Governor Meyner he struck at corruption in the GOP.

After a Monday meeting with regional party leaders in Con-

[22] The draft/bomb issue brought clearly into focus a central paradox in Stevenson's role as a public man and as a campaigner. As a public man, he felt under great obligation to contribute to the formation of serious opinion and policy on vital issues. This obligation must have outweighed any perception that to conduct such debate within the context of a political campaign was sure to prompt distortions. For as a campaigner he—and his opponents—were under political stress if not moral obligation so to conduct themselves as to put their arguments and their causes in the most favorable light.

There would be campaign advantages, to be sure, in adopting the role of "talking sense to the American people." But these were almost certain to be outweighed by the campaign advantages to be derived from denigrating the opposition and putting dramatically the issue of qualifications for leadership. The discussion was sure to suffer—and so would the Democratic prospects if the candidate insisted on spending his time and energy in politically unprofitable ways.

The Republicans were under no such handicaps. They could use the aura of Eisenhower leadership and military judgment to settle popular judgment of the issue—and would lose no time or energy from the central and strongest appeal of their campaign.

necticut, he and Kefauver flew to Albany for a session with the New York Democratic State Committee. There he accused Eisenhower of operating a government "with a false front"—a government manned by top officials who did not believe in the missions of their agencies; a government afraid to repeal the New Deal in public but eroding it in the "infighting." Kefauver, who had joined him, stressed Eisenhower's link with his party, as a man "right down there with the rest of the boys as an aggressive fighter for special interests." In Harriman territory, Stevenson took special pains to heal party rifts.

Back in New York City on September 11, Stevenson and Kefauver accepted the nomination of the Liberal Party of New York—a nomination that might swing several hundred thousand votes in a key state. Stevenson keynoted civil rights in his acceptance, repeating his charge that Eisenhower was not using his office or position to create a favorable climate for execution of the Supreme Court decisions. He ridiculed Eisenhower's neutrality between liberals and McCarthyites in his party, and slashed at the "New Nixon." He called on his audience to revive the old American mission—"the conception of our nation as the bearer of hope and freedom to oppressed peoples everywhere on earth."

Interim Republican Moves

As the President continued campaigning by press conferences and by ceremonies, the lesser Republican campaigners took up their stances on the various preselected issues. Between the convention's end and the campaign kick-off at Gettysburg, they kept up a subdued counterfire against the Democrats. Charles Halleck prepared the "case" for a Republican Congress by stressing figures showing that the Democrats did not really support the President in Congress. Other lower-ranking Republicans took on the chore of prompt answers to Stevenson attacks, downgrading him both by their replies and by the implication that he was not a worthy antagonist for top Republicans. Senator Karl Mundt of

South Dakota, recalling Truman's backing of Alger Hiss, sent Stevenson the first in a series of daily telegrams asking whether Stevenson still supported Truman on the Hiss affair. Senator George Bender of Ohio controverted Stevenson's allegations about the plight of labor under the GOP.

The Republican National Committee, adopting the immediate-reply strategy used in 1952, announced that Republican "Truth Squads," composed of senators and representatives, would follow Truman and other "Democrat" spokesmen around, "just to keep the record straight."

While Eisenhower golfed with business elite at Pebble Beach in California, the Republican National Committee sent out special detachments to clinch the hoped-for favorable response by Negroes to their civil rights declarations at the convention. Thalia D. Thomas, assistant chief of the Committee's Minorities Division, took a wide swing around the West, trumpeting the main calls in the Republican line for Negroes. She stressed at the outset Republican appointments of Negroes to high Federal office, as well as civil rights gains. She wove into her speech themes of women in Republican politics and counterpropaganda concerning how many wealthy persons were found among Democratic politicians and adherents. The full treatment for Negroes was to be added later by Val Washington, chief of the division. Together they sparked a continuing campaign, among Negroes, mostly in the North and West, but also in a few selected southern communities, where opportunity seemed to beckon.

The Republicans lost little time in launching their campaigns directed at women and nationalities. The National Federation of Republican Women met in Chicago on September 7, taking as their theme, "The Republican Party and the American Home." The gathering dealt not only with organizational matters—the election and installation of officers—but more importantly with the campaign themes of women and the party. They paid chief attention to the family life of the President and of the Vice President.

As for nationalities, Senator Homer Capehart of Indiana spoke to the nation's Poles on September 5, denouncing Democrats for Yalta deals and lashing out at Stevenson for his attacks on Republican "liberation" policy. He praised Eisenhower's efforts for subject nations, the spirit of Geneva, and the Secretary of State's uncompromising stand for liberation. He recounted the administration's help to the Poznan rioters in Poland.

As for the "ethnic" vote—the Republican euphemism for the Jewish vote—Leonard Hall sent greetings for Rosh Hashana, varying the usual Republican trilogy of peace, progress, and prosperity to speak of justice, equality, and the dignity of man, while recounting progress toward those ideals under the President—progress that would be continued and strengthened if a Republican majority were returned.

On September 10 the Republicans announced plans to play another card open only to a party occupying the Presidency: the dedication of Saturday, October 13, as Ike Day. The necessary nonpartisan theme was to be get-out-the-vote, wrapped up in tribute to the man and what he had done for all. Co-chairmen were to be actress Irene Dunne and top young business executive Charles Percy (also a top young Republican fund raiser in the state of Illinois).[23]

In an area where they could be matched by the opposition, the Republicans planned nationwide tours by the Vice President.

Maine Heartens the Democrats

On September 10, Maine went to the polls to elect its three congressmen, its governor, and other state officials. The voters gave incumbent Democratic Governor Edmund S. Muskie a clear-cut victory, elected one Democratic congressman and nearly elected

[23] The "Ike Day" was a shrewd but supererogatory device to get nationwide participation from both Democrats and Republicans alike in an event that would keep the President's above-politics personality well to the forefront. The celebration called for the proclamation of Ike Day by the governors of the several states; for the circulation and signing of a pledge of twenty-four hours of extra community service work, preferably in the field of registration and get-out-the-vote; for the presentation of birthday cakes to children's wards of hospitals; and for community celebrations featuring family, voting, and public service. While formally nonpartisan, every aspect of it served Republican campaigning purposes.

another, cutting sharply into previously safe Republican territory. The Democratic national politicians immediately hailed a trend.

Leonard Hall naturally said it was no such thing, charging the defeats to a "sleeper pulled by CIO-PAC" (ample funds plus a systematic effort to register voters and a last-minute drive to get out the vote). Hall insisted that Muskie had won on local issues and carried other Democratic candidates to their victory, but the GOP would win in November. Nevertheless, Hall used the results to warn local party workers against complacency. The President, at his news conference on September 11, underlined Hall's analysis and gave it far wider circulation.

The Democrats, meanwhile, were elated. Paul Butler said the Maine result "clearly debunks two political myths—one, the myth that President Eisenhower is so popular personally that he could carry his unpopular party to victory this fall and, two, the myth that the Democratic party faces an unconquerable obstacle in the limitless campaign funds available to the G.O.P."[24]

[24] *New York Times*, Sept. 12, 1956.

10

The Campaign: First Phase

THE CAMPAIGN PROPER, said one commentator, was one long shout. And shouting there was, but into it the candidates introduced variations. Gradually they shaped the campaign into three phases.

First came a period of some three weeks from the time of the Gettysburg and Harrisburg rallies (September 12 and 13) to early October, ending as the major candidates completed their first swings around the country. Second came a period of sharpening tone, as the issues were drawn closer about foreign policy, the draft, and testing of the H-bomb. This period lasted from October 5 almost to the end of the campaign, ending as Israel knifed into the Sinai Peninsula on October 29 and British-French troops occupied the Suez in the days following. The third period, consisting of the last seven days, commenced as both parties reacted to the overt outbreak of hostilities in the Middle East and ended with election day.

During the first period, both parties followed methodically their pre-arranged strategies. The Democrats, attacking, concentrated more on Nixon than on Eisenhower. While criticizing the Republican stance on peace, they devoted major attention to domestic issues. The Republicans evoked the Republican record; repeated "peace, prosperity and progress"; and rebutted the Democrats. During the second phase, the Democrats gained courage, strove to bring Eisenhower himself into the fray, and Stevenson in particular shifted the brunt of his attack to foreign policy. During the last phase, everything centered on efforts by both parties to interpret world events in a manner favorable to their causes. The top Democratic campaigners promptly claimed that events proved their charges about peace and foreign relations. Nevertheless, in the opinion of many Democratic leaders at state and local levels, the turn of events shattered any remaining prospects of a Stevenson victory. They dissociated their candidates and organizations from the national ticket, and concentrated on perpetuating and extending power at state and local levels. The Republicans responded to Suez by hoisting higher the banner of their leader as a standard of security in a time of crisis. Their cry for a Republican Congress was drowned out in the final clamor.

During these phases Stevenson and Nixon dashed across the country in seeming random movements, now in the same state or region, now separated by half a continent or all of it. Both were acutely aware of what the other was saying and doing, judging the best initiatives and the best responses to the apparent opportunities or dangers opened by events, setting up arguments that only occasionally came into direct counterplay. Above the Republicans was the amiable figure of the President; threading the byways for the Democrats rambled the indefatigable Kefauver.

The smoothly integrated national Republican organization moved along under the unrelenting drive of Leonard Hall, with counterpoints furnished by the senatorial and congressional campaign committees on occasion. The Democratic national organization, two-headed in 1956 as in 1952, moved forward with surprising unanimity and coordination, as talk issued chiefly from the Stevenson entourage, abetted by occasional outbursts from Paul Butler; and Finnegan dealt chiefly with campaign administration and liaison with local organizations. Both parties had special problems in regulating their relations with state and local organizations. The Republicans sought to drive their local cohorts to a maximum showing in the senatorial and congressional races. The Democrats tried to gear the more popular and powerful state and local organizations into the party machine working for the national ticket.

Both parties launched their formal campaigns in the critical state of Pennsylvania. The Republicans staged a party rally at Gettysburg on September 12. The Democrats staged their party rally, with a major radio-television effort, at Harrisburg on the 13th.

Launching the Republican Campaign

Ever with a penchant for original productions, the Republican campaign directors did not open the formal campaign with full-dress speeches. Instead they combined a party rally and a report to Ike with a picnic at the Eisenhower farm on September 12. The theme was "to talk over the campaign," with reports of the course of political events as seen from the main regions of the country, by Citizens for Eisenhower, by party figures, by youth. The climaxes, however, came from speeches by Nixon and the President.

Nixon told the party workers his conception of the campaign and of his role in it—and set up his justification for slashing attacks on Democrats who might make personal attacks on the President or distort the record.[1] He insisted that foreign policy should be debated in the campaign, since the nation needed the best thinking of the wisest men on the subject (but the Democratic thinking to date, on bomb testing or draft, hardly qualified as "best"). He was equally deft in dealing with domestic communism: Normally such a subject should not be debated, since it should not divide Americans on party lines. Moreover, some of the most eager and effective anti-Communists were Democrats. (By implication, what were the others?) But so long as Stevenson supported Truman in his loyalty to Alger Hiss, the Republicans, he said, had no alternative but to debate the issue, and let the people decide which party was best fitted to deal with domestic communism.

The Vice President lashed out at Democratic claims that prosperity was phony and the Republicans were a one-class party. He pinned Stevenson on civil rights, asking if he were so forthright about it now, why was he so quiet in Chicago? He welcomed Democratic challenges to debate corruption in government, and to match records as to who had thrown more rascals out faster. He

---

[1] This justification was not without interest. Nixon said he and his co-campaigners could either ignore personal attacks, or attack the other side in kind. It was wrong to reply in kind to personal attacks, but it was both right and necessary to set the record straight, lest error be taken for truth, wherever there was misrepresentation or distortion of the administration's record of accomplishments.

praised the vaunted Republican return of dignity to government, while telling the Democrats no party had a monopoly on morality. He ended with praise to the President and with exhortation to all party workers to leave no doorbell unrung in their efforts to bring the "magnificent story of this administration" to every precinct in America.

The President produced a long, rambling discourse, much of it in his own characteristic prose. But he dealt at the outset with the real issue: "Ladies and gentlemen, I feel fine."[2]

He praised Nixon and described the kind of government that Republicans could promise to every household in America. He outlined major objectives for the campaign—first, to awaken the nation to the issues at stake; second, to generate a conviction that the Republican party by reason of its platform, its record, and its candidates offered the best hope of progress; third, to ignite a zeal to make converts by logical conviction.[3] He called for a crusade like that of 1952.

The President went on to define his concept of leadership and his concept of the Republican party. Who is a leader? "Anybody that can influence any other single person in this world—that's leaders." What is the Republican party? The party devoted to Lincoln's concept of proper government, oft quoted, oft repeated: a government that would do what needed to be done but which the people could not do, nor do so well, for themselves; government of, by and for the people.

From these heights, the President descended to the practical issue of getting voters registered, and getting out the vote, with the help of the top officials of the radio, television, and the movie industries.

He compared the party's defeat in Maine to the Allied defeat at Kasserine Pass in 1942, demanding further efforts in the national campaign. He spurred the old hard-bitten professionals on with the example of enthusiastic twenty-year olds working for the party. He pleaded with them for maximum use of the ammunition

[2] *Washington Post and Times Herald*, Sept. 13, 1956.

[3] The President's recommended strategy was not to ask a voter whether he was Republican, Independent, or Democrat, but to say to him: "Do you believe this— do you believe this? These facts being so, you must vote Republican." *Ibid.*

furnished by party headquarters, in order to prove "that the Republican Party is dedicated to the welfare of all the people of America, and to an honorable and just peace abroad."[4]

With high principles in their ears, shrewd advice in their brains, and a Pennsylvania farm picnic in their stomachs, eighty busloads of party workers rolled back to the nation's capital. The nation's press told the country the Republicans were off to a resounding start.

THE CASE FOR A REPUBLICAN CONGRESS

The fundamentals of the Republican "case" for a Republican House and Senate were packaged in a letter from the President sent out to 4,000 state and local party leaders by the Republican National Committee on September 15. The letter said in part:

> I am sure you share my conviction that our American system of Government operates most effectively when the executive and legislative branches are operated by the same political party. I believe this accomplishes two important results: first, it fixes responsibility for the legislative program of the Administration. Second, it enables the Administration to enact into law those measures which it believes are right and necessary for the country.
>
> Consequently, those who believe in and intend to support the Republican Administration will wish to further assure the success of our cause by aggressively supporting Republican candidates for Congress and the Senate.[5]

The result was to set off a debate between lower-echelon Democratic and Republican partisans regarding who had really supported the President's program during the preceding two years in Congress—and over the partisan record of the Congress preceding it. Both sides accepted, at least for the purposes of the debate, support for Eisenhower as a gauge for judging the value of a Republican majority on Capitol Hill. The Democrats argued in effect that such a majority would not mean support for the President's program, because of the extent to which prominent Republicans had opposed the President. They came close to arguing that if the

[4] *Ibid.*
[5] *New York Times,* Sept. 16, 1956.

voters wanted support in Congress for Eisenhower's program, they had better elect Democrats to supply it. The Republicans cited the record of votes on administration proposals to show that they had done more to support the President than had the Democrats—but they had no excuse or explanation for the behavior of their party's extreme right wing on a few outstanding controversies.

GOP FIELD FORCE

The Republicans moved into a more active phase of their campaigning as Nixon, Seaton, and the "truth squads" moved out into the country from Washington, D.C., on September 18. The President told his campaigners to "tell the truth; tell it forcefully," and counseled against much counterpropaganda.

Nixon told the President he and the other campaigners regarded it as a high responsibility to follow out the President's charge. He also said they would explode the theory that "you can't get the American people as excited when they are for something as you can when they are against something."

Nixon took to the country what soon came to be known as "the speech." Its main theme was peace, prosperity, and progress under Eisenhower leadership. Then came four major developments: First: honesty and integrity in government—so good as to warrant a duty to set the record straight against any attacks or vilification. Second: Eisenhower got us out of war and is our best hope to keep peace without surrender. Third: the American people have had the best four years of their lives—with more jobs, higher wages, more take-home pay for 66.6 million American wage-earners. (Counterdevelopment: there are some who do not share fully, but Republicans will take care of them in good time.) Fourth: farm prices are up; and the Republicans, who inherited the farm problem, will do their best to solve it by striking at its sources.

At each stop,[6] Nixon improvised variations to take account of

[6] The itinerary for the first half of Nixon's nationwide speaking tour, billed as the greatest in political history, commenced on September 18, and covered more than 15,000 miles, penetrating 32 states, taking 14 working days, and ending on October 3 in Philadelphia. With Nixon went his wife, 12 staff men, and more than 30 members of the working press. The swing started in the District of Columbia, touched down

local opinions, candidates, and needs; and to weave in interpretations of the latest events. In concluding the first swing of his campaign, he played the political analyst, packaging political claims in the novel form of a public report to the President that the "most compelling" issues in the public's mind were these "facts": (1) peace-in-being; (2) prosperity; and (3) the elevated moral tone of the federal government.

As he moved from town to town, Nixon got best reception for references to the new "moral tone" in Washington. This, said one observer, "goes over with the impact of a tent revivalist's promises."[7] By contrast, his references to economic policies and his expressions of concern for farmers left his audiences cold. One result was a stream of suggestions to Washington for improving immediate conditions for pockets of discontent among farmers. Another was an exhortation to local organizations to get out into the precincts.

On September 19 the President started off with his above-the-fray contribution to the campaign: a series of television speeches

at Indianapolis, and made Whittier, California, on the first day. Then, visiting two and three cities and one or two states a day, the tour went to Nevada, Oregon, Idaho, Washington, South Dakota, North Dakota, Minnesota, Iowa, Colorado, Arizona, Utah, Oklahoma, Texas, Missouri, Kansas, Kentucky, Illinois, Tennessee, Ohio, West Virginia, Maryland, Florida, Michigan, Wisconsin, Connecticut, New Hampshire, New York, New Jersey, Massachusetts, and Pennsylvania, all in order.

Thus the tour covered every politically important part of the country, omitting only the safest or the near-hopeless states. No region was excluded, as Nixon invaded Florida, Texas, Oklahoma, Tennessee to bring the South within range. Nixon himself identified Oregon, Washington, California, New York, Ohio, Pennsylvania, Kentucky, and Illinois as the chief battle-grounds. (*New York Times*, Sept. 11, 1956.) It might be noted that these battlegrounds were all as important, if not more important, for their senatorial contests as they were for the presidential race.

The shape of the itinerary suggests that considerations of timing did not call for pinpointing forays, but that the convenience of the campaigner and the requests coming in for help from senatorial or congressional candidates did much to shape the order of appearances.

The presence of 30 members of the working press assured fullest nationwide coverage for anything important the Vice President might say—and this fact diminished the regional significance of matters. The press was not going to be caught short as to the exact text of anything the New Nixon might say in any possible accusations or innuendoes concerning his opposition. The fact that one member of the press party carried a wire recorder with him—not unnoticed by the Vice President or the Secret Service—was a further guarantee of probity in charge and characterization.

[7] William M. Blair, in *New York Times*, Sept. 25, 1956.

giving the people "some account of how my Republican associates and I have discharged the responsibilities you placed on us almost four years ago."

First was his "peace" speech, which stretched the concept of peace well beyond the customary assessment of the state of international politics. Those who wrote the speech made peace cover the President's health, the mood of the country, the farm problem, and civil rights as well. In it the President also sought peace from certain areas of political debate, attempting to put farm policy and civil rights above the search for voters. Here as elsewhere the President continued with a veiled partisanship—a calculated failure to name his partisan opponents as he attacked their positions on policies or deeds.

Launching the Democratic Campaign

Although more elaborate than the Republican, the Democratic ceremony officially opening the campaign at Harrisburg, Pennsylvania was hardly a kickoff. The Democrats had been busily at work since the close of their convention. Covering the local and state organizations, speaking to many different kinds of audiences, Stevenson alone had covered 12,000 miles in the preceding month; he had set up his position on the draft and on the bomb-testing programs; he had wooed labor and the farmer, and had spoken to those hungry for public power and public works. He had complained over the lot of the small businessman. He had rallied party organizations in New York and New Jersey, appealing publicly for healing of rifts torn in the party fabric at Chicago. He had signaled he would be less moderate in his 1956 campaign than in 1952, calling his opponents a "party with a false front."

How then could he raise the pitch of the campaign at the formal launching of it at Harrisburg on September 13? The Democrats, with an outlay of some $200,000, had arranged nationwide coverage by all three television networks, with a full complement of radio and press coverage too. There would be some 8,500 of the party faithful on hand who had paid $50 a plate to dine with their candidates.

First thing to do—and Stevenson did it—was to compare the Republican "elite" at Gettysburg with the Democratic common Pennsylvanians at Harrisburg, and at the same time to invite all Americans to vote Democratic, in the cause not of peace, progress and prosperity, but in the "cause of freedom, the cause of human welfare and . . . the cause of peace."[8]

Next thing to do was to claim victory, both for Democratic candidates from Pennsylvania and for the national ticket. Maine pointed the way, as evidence that voters there and everywhere were penetrating the "fog of half-truths and amiable complacency."

Third thing was to distinguish Democrats from Republicans, and dispel the notion that there were no issues between them. Admitting the truth that both parties agreed on most issues, Stevenson likened the parties' promises to checks signed by different people. "The question is which one can be cashed and which one will bounce." Rehearsing accomplishments of the New Deal, Stevenson then slashed at the Republican record, posing "facts" against the Republican slogan of the three p's. He charged losses in schools, public welfare, public health, farm prosperity, and bankruptcies for small businessmen—let alone lost ground in the race with the Russians—to a government "which neither fully understands nor wholly sympathizes with our human needs or the revolution that is sweeping our world." The Republicans provided businessman's government, effective in promoting the interests of business in the world of taxes and resources, but unable to lead in the world where human interests are concerned.

Fourth thing was to pin failure on Eisenhower and isolate Nixon as the real target, as the probable heir to an administration that the President could no longer rule because he could no longer succeed himself under the terms of the twenty-second amendment.

Fifth thing was to end on a note of positive gains under a new Democratic administration:

[8] *Ibid.*, Sept. 14, 1956.

So I say to you, my friends, let us be up and doing, probing cease-lessly for solutions of today's problems and the new ones tomorrow will leave upon our doorstep. And if you share my view, if you share the Democratic view, that this election is a summons to a sleeping giant, then I hope you will join us to make that summons clear and strong on Election Day and to help us march forward toward the new America.[9]

However well written, this speech failed to come off in delivery.

Said James Reston, "Stevenson made an undistinguished speech. His voice was high and thin. He was popeyed in his race with an erratic mechanical teleprompter and so nervous that he even mis-pronounced the name of his running mate."[10] Stevenson seemed out of character in his efforts to speak to the organization men in-stead of to the intellectuals, and he may have felt uncomfortable in this role, too.[11] Kefauver, on the contrary, was thoroughly in character during his short remarks: he was at ease, unpretentious, busy with his common-touch phrasemaking. But he was not the main performer. The call for a New America had yet to be voiced in a slow-paced, resonant, confidence-building baritone.

Nevertheless, political observers noted that there was more con-fidence among Democratic leaders than at any time since the con-vention. The Maine results had been unexpectedly favorable. The South seemed to be well in line. Polls showing a smart Eisenhower lead could be discounted by reference to 1948. James Finnegan reminded the politicos of Magnuson's lead of 136,500 votes over Langlie in the Washington primaries. More to the point, Treasurer McCloskey, in announcing October 16 as Dollars for Democrats day, said that money was easier to get.[12]

After the near-fiasco of Harrisburg, Stevenson flew to Washing-ton, D.C., officially to open his campaign headquarters, while Ke-fauver winged to Sarasota to appeal to youth and not-so-Southern Democrats. Stevenson quipped his way into the nation's capital, announcing that after victory he would go to Washington (not

[9] *Ibid.*
[10] *Ibid.*, Sept. 16, 1956.
[11] See Kenneth S. Davis, *A Prophet in His Own Country: Triumphs and Defeats of Adlai E. Stevenson* (1957), p. 455.
[12] *New York Times,* Sept. 14, 1956.

Korea), and playing Joe Smith against the Republican defeat in Maine. For the next week, he combined staff work at headquarters with organizational rallying at grassroots in Fairfax, Virginia, and at other nearby points. He started getting the first official CIA briefings on the world situation promised him by the administration, for his personal use only. In talking to potential voters in the immediate environs of Washington, Stevenson played hard on local dissatisfaction with government procedures for dealing with employees whose loyalty or discretion might offer undue risks to the nation's security, and pledged the new Democratic administration would restore dignity, honor, and self-esteem to the public service.[13]

On the 17th, Stevenson in a searching press conference settled his position on Alger Hiss and grabbed some other thistles too. Unlike Truman, he thought Hiss had properly been adjudged guilty of perjury. He coupled the admission with an effort to get the communism issue out of the 1956 campaign and asked Eisenhower to state whether he approved the efforts of Hall and Nixon to keep the issue alive. He said he still believed that "ultimately" the armed forces could be kept at a high state of efficiency without the draft and praised the efforts of Governor Frank Clement of Tennessee to use the police power promptly to protect "the processes of integration." He wrote off Truman's charge of Republican "racketeering" in the use of natural resources, to which the President had taken such personal and violent exception. He said Truman's help had been on balance effective in the campaign, but he did not conceal his coolness in references to his opponent at the Chicago convention.[14]

On the tension gathering over Suez, he took a very correct position—he wished to say or do nothing that might imperil the success of the continuing delicate negotiations concerning the canal. On the draft, he made clear that he wanted sober, detailed debate —and implied that this was an issue he intended to exploit further.[15]

[13] *Ibid.*, Sept. 16, 1956.
[14] *Ibid.*, Sept. 18, 1956. On Hiss, Stevenson said he had "never doubted the verdict of the jury which convicted [Hiss]. Nothing has happened since to change my views. If what I said four years ago places me in disagreement with what President Truman says now, that is where the record must rest."
[15] James Reston, "A Model of Deportment," *New York Times*, Sept. 18, 1956.

Kefauver's role in the campaign was to play the folksy hand-shaker, working the small towns and the rural areas, concentrating on farm discontent and its ramifications, with special emphasis on the Middle West. In the Far West he dwelt on public power and Republican skullduggery. He did not often travel with Stevenson, nor usually appear on the same platforms with him. He stressed personality more than argument. His was a complementary role, both geographically and ideologically.

Kefauver also played opposite the Republican "truth squads," conducting a truth-telling swing of his own through "the Main Streets of America." His itineraries were notable for their selection of friendly territory, in much of which the candidate's previous primary efforts had paid off well.

Kefauver more directly than Stevenson engaged in verbal battle with his opponents, searching for and scoring debaters' points. In his diligent efforts to work the highways and byways, by motor-cade and whistle-stop as well as by airplane, Kefauver symbolized the Democratic party's interest in the "little man." Although his crowds were small—rarely exceeding the 1,000 mark and far more frequently in the low hundreds—Kefauver spoke to them in words easy to understand, and created something of a midwest legend.

An innovation in campaigning introduced by the Democrats was the series of high-level reports on the New America. On September 19, Clayton Fritchey, the Democrats' press chief, announced that a series of reports on the subject would be released. This was done in part to show the electorate that the Democratic candidate did have some new ideas about the future as well as the past; and also in response to the intellectual needs of the candidate and his immediate entourage. Stevenson and his advisers had thoroughly canvassed the whole field of foreign and domestic policy for issues since the immediate aftermath of the 1952 campaign. It seemed vital that the campaign somehow should extend discussion of those issues in ways not wholly compatible with the normal procedures of modern campaigning—especially when in-

---

Stevenson was deliberate at this conference. He had anticipated the major questions, had prepared text in advance to deal with the most important of them, and refused to be drawn into extemporaneous statements.

dividual speeches were constricted by the real or presumed requirements of campaigning on television. The candidate wanted to make his views known on important points in some detail and with sufficient length to be fully grasped.[16]

The New America became the core of the campaign for Stevenson. The first of these reports dealt with problems of the aging; others dealt with schools and education, health, material resources, the rebuilding of cities, draft and H-bomb, and foreign aid. They varied in length from 3,000 to 10,000 words. They made no compromise with entertainment values and were sent to all and sundry Democratic campaigners as resource materials to use in campaign discussion. Much of Stevenson's time went into their preparation. Each got nationwide publicity on release in the mass media. The Republican response to each guaranteed further attention. But on balance it is doubtful that they swung many votes.[17]

Competition for the Farm Vote

Competition for the farm vote was brisk. Campaigners in both parties spoke to farmers not only about farm policy, but about linked issues they considered of special interest to farmers—the absence of shooting war for Republicans; GOP failures in conservation and natural resources for Democrats; and the conditions for national prosperity for both. The big farm speeches came at Newton, Iowa, for the Democrats, and at Peoria, Illinois, for the Republicans. The Republicans sent Ezra Taft Benson, Secretary of Agriculture, on extended trips with an extended speech. Nixon clamored for administration action to support agricultural prices—especially in the last days before election. The Democrats sent a host of campaigners to the field to complain of lowered farm prices

[16] Adlai E. Stevenson, *The New America* (1957), pp. xiv-xxiii.

[17] *New York Times*, Sept. 20, 1956. See also Stevenson, *The New America*, in which seven of the papers are identifiably reprinted. Distribution figures during the campaign are not conveniently available; but the timing and content of these essays undoubtedly restricted their impact to the intellectuals. The paper on foreign aid was not completed in time for distribution during the campaign, although its line of argument was undoubtedly important in shaping the candidate's utterances.

and threats to world peace. The peace argument seemed to be as vital to farming people as to any, and both parties tried to profit by it.

The President made his first foray into farm country low keyed, but politically positive. At the plowing contest in Newton on September 21, he addressed an enormous but apathetic crowd, dealing in humble personalities and generalities about the beauties of America's granary and of a straight furrow of fresh-turned black earth. He scarcely mentioned administration farm policy at all. Moving through Des Moines to the airport, he passed through huge, demonstrative crowds. At the airport itself, he said he could no longer restrain a political note to his speech—so he praised Iowa Republicans, candidates for senator, congressmen, and governor, as modern Republicans who would serve their people well. As the President took to the field, he demonstrated remarkable endurance for a man of 66 but recently recovered from serious illness.

Again Stevenson followed the Republicans with a full-scale effort rather than a show of personality. He gave his major farm speech the next day at the same plowing contest. Stevenson concentrated fire on twin concerns of the farm areas: farm ills and foreign policy. It was a speech of attack—from the initial charges that Eisenhower was responsible for what he had promised farmers at Kasson, Minnesota, in 1952 even if he didn't quite understand what he was saying, down to the overblown assertion that the Republicans were so preoccupied with big business that they were unable to understand, let alone tell the story of the position of the American farmer. In the last quarter of his speech, Stevenson raced over peace, schools, health, social security, roads, strengthening of small business, and natural resources—all wrapped up again in the concept of the New America.

The Republican rebuttal came from a lesser figure as Republican tactics specified. In this case Benson replied that the Stevenson combination of attack and promises was "weary and backward-looking . . . a rehash of old issues plus an endorsement of wartime programs which have proved unworkable in time of peace."[18]

[18] *New York Times*, Sept. 23, 1956.

As Stevenson started on a jaunt through the South, the Republicans fired their major salvo in the battle for the farm vote—Eisenhower's Peoria speech. This speech did two things—it added the President's full authority and attention-getting powers to the GOP position, and it presaged a shift to sharper speech by both sides.

Before a large and responsive crowd in Bradley University's field house, the President moved far below the benign and lofty mood of his first speech on peace.

He blamed as much of the farm problem on the Democrats as possible—for perpetuating a system of price supports appropriate to war but not to peace; for creating the problem of price-depressing surpluses that the Republicans now radically wished to attack; for delaying or complicating for political expediency such programs as the soil bank. He predicted "better times for every farmer," and promised to strive for a situation in which farmers would share equitably in the national prosperity, gaining parity in the only place where it could be effective—the market place. He proved unrepentant about what he had promised at Kasson in 1952, and what he had tried, against opposition blocking, to do since in fulfillment of the promise.

Immediately after his Newton speech, Stevenson flew to Denver for appearances with Governor Ed Johnson and Democratic candidates for the governorship Stephen McNichols and for the Senate, John Carroll. Carroll's presence cued Stevenson to attack Nixon for "the ugly campaign of vilification" waged in Colorado in 1954 (in which Republican Senator Gordon Allott defeated Democrat Carroll by a small margin after a hard-fought campaign). He stressed conservation policy and the Democratic line on natural resources, charging Republicans with give-away, and the administration with hypocrisy. He closed with an elaboration of Walter Lippmann's recently published generalization that the Republicans were the party of the passing generation and the Democrats that of the future.

In reply Nixon gave something of his own version of a New America. He told a Colorado Springs audience on September 22 that technological trends and a continuation of the administration's policies promised in the not too distant future a four-day work week for the average American.[19] The Democratic riposte was to interpret the promise to mean that the administration would shortly "order" a four-day work week—*i.e.*, a reduced opportunity for most of labor.

The Republicans simply continued to dwell on the prospects of unbelievable prosperity, with prompt measures to wipe out whatever occasional pockets of discontent might appear. Nixon spoke his mind on farm politics—not in a speech to farmers but in a communication to reporters, designed chiefly for organizational purposes. With commendable candor, he said he looked to recent improvements in farm prices to do more than anything else to help Republicans in farm areas. He did not think campaign talk could do much to help the GOP cause, "because in my experience with farmers I find that farmers are concerned far more about the market than what politicians say."[20]

Returning to the prosperity issue, Walter Reuther, for the Democrats, asked Nixon if he was intending to introduce legislation to bring the four-day work week into effect. Nixon replied that no "mere artificial legislation" could bring it about; it would have to be done by "joint efforts of labor, management, government and research." But he thanked Reuther for his implied opinion that the Republicans would win the Presidency and Congress in November.[21]

Flying down to Tulsa from Denver on September 24, Stevenson gave a sizable speech, and motorcaded to Oklahoma City for the second in the same busy day. At Tulsa he dealt with Nixon's Colorado statement by reminding his hearers of Herbert Hoover's predictions in 1928, doubting whether the Republicans were serious about prosperity for all.

Later in the day, at Oklahoma City, he gave his support to senatorial candidate A. S. Mike Monroney, mentioned other local political notables, praised farms and farmers, and launched into an attack on the Republican "curse of bigness." It was a hedged

[19] *Ibid.*
[20] *Ibid.*
[21] *Ibid.*, Sept. 26, 1956.

attack; Stevenson was not alienating any source of funds or votes—and the Democrats counted a few largish businessmen in their fold. Big business, he maintained, was not wholly bad—it had become more responsible, and had "a respected place in the national community." Yet big business, he charged, does not think of people; it thinks in prices, statistics, figures. When big business captures government, "government becomes indifferent to the interests of the people." The Republican administration, he implied, was indifferent to human concerns.

Stevenson on Civil Rights, Foreign Policy, and Education

At Little Rock, Arkansas, on September 25, Stevenson performed one of the more courageous feats of the campaign. He bluntly bearded segregationist sentiment as he challenged Democrats to rise above the division in their ranks. He declared his clear support for the Supreme Court civil rights decision and called on all law-abiding citizens to support it. He quoted with approval the Democratic platform declaration against any use of force to interfere with the orderly determination of such matters by the courts. And, he concluded, "the office of the Presidency should be used to bring together those of opposing views in this matter—to the end of creating a climate for peaceful acceptance of this decision."[22]

Stevenson did not tempt fate with a longer appearance or with other issues. He made his point and left for New Orleans and a routine effort to reunite his party and recall Eisenhower voters to its fold.

By the time Stevenson arrived in Miami he was in a fine fighting mood. Here his compulsion to stress foreign policy caught up with him. He told his audience that Republican foreign policy was going nowhere and getting nowhere; it was a policy of lost op-

[22] *Ibid.*

portunities. American policy had "too often placated America's enemies and advanced their intrigues and [had] disregarded our friends, treating them all too often like poor relations to be sent for when needed." In the Middle East, it seemed that those countries got the most in aid who had been ugly, threatening, and who had been flirting with communism. In the world at large, the candidate charged, it seemed as if the administration thought there was nothing in the sphere of foreign relations that could not be bought. Our foreign policy was "completely off the track—morally, politically, and economically."[23]

In the middle of this onslaught Stevenson interpolated an *ad hominem* attack. He alleged not only that American aid policy had resulted in personal gain for Peron, rather than help to the Argentine people; he also charged that the administration had kept an ambassador on in Buenos Aires because Peron liked him. He accused the President's brother, Dr. Milton Eisenhower, of appeasing Peron.

The Peron charge was a serious mistake, both of fact and of tactics. The Republicans immediately replied that part of the facts were true—that Peron had made off with a great deal of aid money—but they also pointed out that none of it had been granted by the Republicans. All had come from Truman-authorized credits. Moreover, the attack on Dr. Eisenhower looked like a low blow. The Democrats dropped the charge forthwith, although the Republicans kept it alive for counterpropaganda for the rest of the campaign.

Tactically, Stevenson's sortie into foreign affairs gave Nixon just what he was looking for—a chance to raise the issue of comparative qualities of leadership, while reiterating the undeniable superficial fact that no American boys were being shot at on battlefields abroad, so therefore there was peace. At Kansas City, Nixon stated that "When it comes to the qualifications for leading the United States internationally, Mr. Stevenson just isn't in the same league with the man who is recognized everywhere as the outstanding leader of the free world today." He went on, "the Democrats were

[23] *Ibid.*

attacking the Republicans at the very point where the Democrats themselves were weakest."[24]

While Nixon rebutted, Stevenson capped his Florida charges with a direct attack on Eisenhower's leadership, delivered on September 26 in Kansas City. In Truman's old territory, the new Stevenson produced a "give-em-hell" speech in the best Truman tradition, designed to cut the President's reputation down to size. He asked bluntly, "Who in this businessman's administration, keeps the store"?[25] He asked who was protecting the public interest from Cabinet officers eager to advance special interests.

The next day in St. Louis, Stevenson spoke in a more philosophic vein on expansion of the economy to halt the Soviet challenge in the economic race. He charged further that both the Republican campaign and the Republican administration were dominated by show business.[26]

On September 28 Stevenson delivered a nationwide television address on the subject of education. In a surprisingly non-partisan speech, he called for a national educational policy as important as defense policy or foreign policy, and one animated by vigorous national leadership. He dealt warily with the political power of entrenched educational organizations and attitudes, tempering his demands for Federal support for education with the qualifications that Federal funds should not be used to supplant local funds, and that Federal grants should never "be a means of transferring to the central government any degree of control over the content of the educational process."[27] He asked for a leadership going beyond the capability of any one man, and he trailed off his

[24] Press release, Republican National Committee, Sept. 26, 1956. In the same speech, however, Nixon dealt with the farm vote by insisting that: "The farmers of America are not as easy to fool as our opponents think they are. They vote the market, rather than the law; prices rather than politics." (And the Republicans were preoccupied with the probable prices of corn and hogs in the week preceding the election.)

[25] *New York Times,* Sept. 27, 1956.

[26] *Ibid.,* Sept. 28, 1956. Stevenson characterized the Republican campaign formula thus: "Don't think, just feel—feel it's all fine and the product is splendid. Pour out the money. Forget that mushroom cloud. Don't mention Suez. The world stops at the water front. And whatever the gales of change and upheaval and revolution roaring around the world, take it from us that this is no time for a change."

[27] *Ibid.,* Sept. 29, 1956.

speech with an anticlimactic appeal to all Americans to rise to the new challenge.

Winding up the first half of a 7,500 mile campaign tour, Stevenson arrived in Minneapolis and St. Paul, Minnesota, on September 29, buoyant and confident he was making gains. Again he restated his views on H-bomb and draft, and chided the President for evading debate on these points. He did his best to imply that the Republican refusal to debate the Democrats on peace was tantamount to admission that their charges were true.

Republican Demands for Coattail Help

As the campaign gathered momentum, Republicans in trouble redoubled their pressure on the White House for Eisenhower appearances to help them. On September 26 White House Press Secretary James Hagerty announced that the President would do more television speaking, announcing a fourth address for Pittsburgh on October 9. The campaign of Senator Duff against Philadelphia's former Democratic Mayor, Joseph Clark, seemed in need of more help than the President had been able to give at his Gettysburg kickoff. Help had already been scheduled for Senator Bender in Ohio, and the two Republican candidates for the two senatorial vacancies in Kentucky.[28] But Nixon, in view of his calculatedly less optimistic appraisal of Republican chances than was current in Washington, was pressuring the President to speak more and travel more.

At his news conference on the same day, the President readily admitted he was stepping up his campaign participation to please "his many good friends," although he still was not going to do a tenth of what he was being asked to do, and he still ruled out any barnstorming or whistle-stopping.[29] Three days later in an unusual Sunday afternoon press conference the White House announced a fresh addition to the President's itinerary—a trip to Washington, Oregon, and Minnesota.

[28] *Ibid.*, Sept. 27, 1956.
[29] *Ibid.*

For what it was worth to coattail riders, and as an anticomplacency document, the Republican National Committee announced availability on September 27 of a campaign film, jointly produced by the three national campaign committees. Eisenhower was the star; Nixon, Martin, Knowland, and Bridges appeared for Republicans in Congress; and all the Cabinet came in to round out the story of the Eisenhower record, and to package the party's campaign arguments in a single vehicle.

On October 1 the President flew out to the Middle West for a double purpose: to shore up the candidacies for the Senate of Ohio's George Bender, seeking a full term, and Kentucky's John Sherman Cooper and Thruston Morton; and to make a nationwide television speech countering the Stevenson New America pronouncements.

In Ohio he spoke to 40,000 people in Cleveland's Public Square, combining Hoover-type "facts" with references to "the record" reminiscent of Al Smith. The President drew distinctions between the parties—the "opposition" was the party of "Big Government," the Republicans the party of "all the people"; the opposition was made up of "orators"; the Republicans were "men of action."

For the first time in the campaign, the President gave public vent to his growing resentment of Democratic allegations about Nixon and his party.

> The opposition say that they alone truly care for the working men and women of America and that the Republican party is really a vague kind of political conspiracy by big business to destroy organized labor and to bring hunger and torment to every worker in America.
>
> This is more than political bunk. It is willful nonsense. It is wicked nonsense. And they know it.[30]

Later in the day, at Lexington, Kentucky, with the triple advantages of salable candidates, enthusiastic crowds, and a nationwide audience, the President had a better opportunity and his purpose was sharper. Here he made his official response to Stevenson's New America—a response at once less pretentious, less intellectualized, and more party political than the New America

[30] *Ibid.*, Oct. 2, 1956.

statements themselves.[31] Again the President repeated the theme of the Republicans as a party favoring everyone, while "the opposition" played section against section, interest against interest, class against class.

But the main concern of the speech was with the issue of public education, and the partisan responsibility (or lack of it) for progress (or lack of it) during the preceding years. The candidate's technique was to insist on his legislative proposals and to point to one vote in which Democrats opposed them 215 to 9 as being the critical vote. He went on to recall his proposals concerning unemployment, minimum wages, labor safety, promising to recommend "again" to the Congress that remedial legislation be enacted. He concluded with his own muted version of the New America:

> When I spoke to you from San Francisco, I said that there was within our reach a new world of good life, good will, and good hope. We have made real progress toward such a world. For we have found—and are following—the new direction of our nation.
> We still have a distance to go. It can be an exciting journey, a satisfying journey, a confident journey—for we know how to get there.
> Four years ago we set out to do a job together. When I think of the America that we would like to see by 1960, I say: Let us get on with the rest of the job.[32]

The First Phase Ends

As September drew to a close, so did the first phase of the campaign. Eisenhower's charge of "wicked nonsense" symbolized the new tone of the second phase, but it took several days—from late September until the Eisenhower press conference of October 5 on the H-bomb—for the definite turn to be made.

[31] At the same time, the Republican National Committee made specific rebuttal via the Cabinet. Statements by Marion Folsom, Secretary of Health, Education and Welfare, and by Sherman Adams took point-by-point issue with Stevenson on education and on small business. Press release, Republican National Committee, Oct. 1, 1956.

[32] *New York Times*, Oct. 2, 1956. The phrasing of this conclusion was probably the Republicans' best answer to the charge of dominance by Madison Avenue.

Meanwhile, Stevenson and Nixon completed their respective campaign tours, made their concluding reports for the first swings, rested momentarily, and sallied forth into new territory. Both sides reassessed their positions and their strategies.

Stevenson and his advisers believed they had opened up weak spots in the Republican front. Facing the Democrats was a Stevenson sally into more difficult territory—the industrial East and New England, possessors of 153 electoral votes of which only West Virginia's 8 had gone Democratic in 1952. Main efforts had yet to be made in Pennsylvania and Massachusetts, with secondary efforts in New York and New Jersey. Meanwhile Kefauver would swing into Texas, out to the Pacific Coast, back through the Mountain States, into the East and then finish in the Middle West.

To the Democrats the South seemed solid once more, with the exception of Florida. They looked for gains in the border states and in farm areas where they felt the advantage of the first round had gone to Stevenson on points. They assessed the major gains of the first Stevenson tour as exposure of serious Republican weakness in the farm belt and general activation of the cost-of-living issue. It seemed that Stevenson's vigor in attacking the peace issue might be a sufficient antidote to Republican efforts to whip the Democrats with the charge of "war party."

On October 2, the Republican "truth squads" completed their first swing with a list of twenty-one Democratic "falsifications"— each answered by a Republican "truth."[33] In reports to the party chiefs they reflected considerable self-satisfaction. Other public estimates were less glowing, reflecting enough pessimism to make sure that Republican workers and candidates would run scared. Private estimates seemed to be that the presidential election was safe, but that continuing efforts must be made to deal with weakness in the farm areas and in areas of economic slack, and to strengthen the campaigns in the senatorial and congressional races. Meanwhile they would take every opportunity offered by Democratic mistakes, and would defend the administration record.

[33] Example—charge: that Peron had profited from Republican foreign aid; rebuttal: Harry S. Truman gave Peron $130 million. Press Release, Republican National Committee, Oct. 2, 1956.

11

The Campaign: Second Phase

BY EARLY OCTOBER both major and minor figures were thoroughly embroiled in the argument of the campaign—each seeking for the advantage in public opinion, parrying, thrusting, bludgeoning, sidestepping. Visitors to the White House reported the President in a fighting mood over Democratic moves made, he thought, to divide the country into classes. Stevenson was criticizing the President for falling into patterns of "political looseness." Nixon was telling racial minorities that the Republicans weren't going to write off the enslaved nations abroad. Kefauver was saying the nation would have had a school-aid bill if the President had really worked for it in Congress. Senator Case of New Jersey was calling on Stevenson to repudiate the Democratic Southern Manifesto. Speaker Rayburn was calling the President wrong about who blocked the school-aid bill—he had cited the right figures but had picked the wrong vote. Democratic Negro Representative Dawson of Illinois was predicting no significant defection of Negroes from his party; Democratic Negro Representative Adam C. Powell of New York was calling on his race to vote Republican. Nixon, using government actions to dramatize GOP claims, ordered an investigation of alleged discrimination by employers against Negroes in the trades—carpenters, draftsmen, electrical workers.

As Stevenson strove to pull the President even further down into the political hurly-burly, most of the Republican campaign managers tried to keep the President above it. Nixon in a Philadelphia speech on October 3, took on the task of answering Stevenson's "appalling" and "catastrophic nonsense" on the H-bomb. Less highly placed Republicans replied to Stevenson's newfound aggressiveness by charging him with being a low-road candidate, as did Governor Dewey in a nationwide telecast in October 3.[1] Benson took on the main task of putting the Republican case on the farm issue; Kefauver countered for the Democrats.

During this near-chaotic second phase Stevenson moved into the Northeast with an increasing violence of attack. Nixon set off on his second swing, told Stevenson he would nail every distortion personally, and frequently couched campaign arguments in the language of the analyst.

Eisenhower traveled through the West and Northwest juxtaposing his pleasure over the obvious happiness of the people with an increasing sharpness of tone toward the Democrats. The Republicans, in an effort to hurt Stevenson where it would make the most difference, planned to send Eisenhower on one-day trips into key southern cities.

Stevenson to the Northeast

With Eisenhower's charge of "wicked nonsense" ringing in his ears, Stevenson started off on October 2 into New Jersey and the Northeast. He took the opportunity offered by the President's bitter words to express the hope that Nixon's penchant for the low road was not to prove unduly contagious. And he slashed out harder than ever at Republican foreign policy. Motorcading from Morristown through Paterson, Passaic, and Newark, he kept up a scathing attack on all aspects of the Eisenhower performance. He stopped off to discuss disarmament at Fairleigh Dickinson College, praising the institution for its World Arms Control Center, and damning the administration for its excessive emphasis on military elements in foreign policy.

At Jersey City, he lashed the Republicans for their opposition

---

[1] Dewey spoke in a fifteen-minute telecast timed for "after the fights"—from 10:50 to 11:05 P.M.—and achieved an audience of better than 2 million homes. The Republican National Committee on the 7th said that the speech had provoked "hundreds" of commendatory messages, over a thousand requests for Dewey to speak, and had resulted in a decision to push the Governor's projected Flint speech forward in order to get a bigger radio/television audience. Press release, Oct. 7, 1956.

to public housing, and charged that the President had put the housing program "in charge of an overt enemy." He threw back at Republicans the familiar charges of talk, not deeds, in the fields of education and immigration. He asked: "Why are there words without action wherever human interests are at stake?" He answered: because the Republicans by philosophy and by history have been the representatives of the privileged, the well-to-do, the big interests, protecting those who need protection the least. He promised that victory for the "party with a heart as well as with a head" would pave the way to action in behalf of all the disadvantaged.

Despite this dashing technique, Stevenson was getting something less than ecstatic attention. He was competing, to be sure, with the World Series; he was competing also with voter apathy. He may also have been competing with lethargy among machine politicians. Even in Newark—Democratic territory—only some 4,500 turned out to hear him in the center of the city at 4:30 in the afternoon. And when he arrived in Jersey City, things looked worse. He had been booked for a small hall; his motorcade was not routed through the main part of the city. Some of the Stevenson-Meyner entourage suspected sabotage.

Moving into Pennsylvania, Stevenson eschewed air transport for the well-tried whistle-stop. Now labeled the "Joe Smith Express," a railway car built for Woodrow Wilson carried the candidate across Pennsylvania for eight speeches.

On October 4 Stevenson delivered a routine speech on conservation at Elkins, West Virginia; and almost got caught by raw nature. Storm clouds grounded scheduled flights, and he was barely able to get to New York by chartered plane to fill his street corner engagements in Harlem that evening. His theme there was human dignity; his purpose was to make adequate counterattack in an area threatened by Republican gains in civil rights. His tactics were first to stress Republican opposition in Congress to public housing, slum renewal, minimum wage legislation, and extension of social security benefits; and second to deflate Republican gains in the civil rights area by stressing their partisan, Johnny-come-lately character.[2]

[2] *New York Times,* Oct. 5, 1956.

On October 5 Stevenson tried for an unusual triple play: party rally and fund raising functions in Brooklyn in the morning; a nonpartisan, sport-loving American's visit to the World Series in the afternoon; and an intellectual appeal to the undergraduates of Yale in the evening. It was in the latter effort that the candidate made his most ambitious pitch of the day. Stevenson called for fresh ideas and for action in building the future, instead of complacency. He decried the view that an election is a mere horse race. "Our purpose," he concluded, "is to show how a great nation rises to the responsibility of self-government—and how it emerges from the experience purified in purpose, strengthened in resolution and united in faith." He scored something of a personal victory, reported the press, reducing the pro-Ike cheers and the boos frequent early in his address to a preponderance of "We Want Stevenson."

The Republican Second Wave

The Republicans moved into the second wave of campaigning without much change of tone or pace at the outset. At the conclusion of the first phase of his campaign tours—after speaking in 32 states and traveling 15,000 miles—the Vice President reported privately to the President and publicly to the people on October 4 via television and radio. The public report came in the form of a "press conference" in which the Vice President responded to queries from reporters brought to him by television screen from all over the country.

The result was a hitherto untried form of capsuling the Republican campaign arguments, along with the Vice President's estimates of political response to his pleas. As with the other forms of novel packaging, the result was contrived if not awkward. Over 6 million homes were tuned in to the screen, as the Vice President gave unrehearsed but not unpremeditated answers to questions. These concerned: partnership power policy; what the soil bank would do for drought-stricken areas; reported Democratic gains in farm states; the Republican concern not just for the "little man" but for all Americans; the draft and H-bombs; school desegregation; relations with the Philippines and foreign aid; and inter-American relations.[3]

While Nixon reported, Secretary of Agriculture Benson was already on the road with an extended version of his farm speech. He preferred philosophy and technical detail to Nixon's realist insistence that the administration see to it that hog prices stay above $15 per hundredweight until after election. He dealt with farmers as Americans, talking not only farm problems but also labor, small business, and peace.

On October 5 the White House released a report of its position on H-bomb testing designed to deflate the Stevenson proposals and to state the administration's point of view. The President heartily wished that this statement would take the issue out of political controversy—a hope suggested by his somewhat testy response to a later press-conference question that he had said his "last word" on the subject. The President made full use of his position of experience and authority, and drew up the Atomic Energy Commission and the Joint Chiefs of Staff in support. Noting their responsibility "to weigh, at all times, the proper emphasis on various types and sizes of weapons, their testing and development," he insisted that: "Such emphasis is necessarily subject to constant review and re-examination. This specific matter is manifestly not a subject for detailed public discussion."[4]

The President exploited a major forensic weakness in the Stevenson position by quoting several differing ways in which Stevenson had expressed his recommendations on the bomb-testing issue, and by asking what Stevenson really meant. Eisenhower quoted Democratic Senator Clinton Anderson, chairman of the Joint Congressional Committee on Atomic Energy, to the effect that the Russians would not stop their testing, and so we could not "call off ours." He drew from this the conclusion that "the testimony of such a responsible Democrat makes clear that this is not—as it

---

[3] *Ibid.* Needless to say, all the reporters were from Republican-oriented papers; none laid any traps for the candidate.

[4] *New York Times*, Oct. 6, 1956.

should not be—a partisan political issue, but an issue raised by one individual."[5]

On the morning the H-bomb statement was issued, the President held a press conference in which he expressed himself on the course of the campaign and its tactics. He not only rehearsed at length the history of civil rights gains in the armed forces; he explained why he did not care to use makeup for television, and announced his willingness to shout hello to people lining roads along which his motorcades passed. He also made clear his preference for going out on political campaign forays about once a week to getting reports in his office.

Asked about the substance of Nixon's reports based on his recent campaign trip, the President said they were "encouraging," and that except for people with "specific ideas" on the farm problem or depressed areas, he had found people "quite happy." Beyond this, however, the President said he could not go.[6]

The correspondents asked what underlay the President's decision to shift to the attack. The President pointed to the importance of laying "the truth as I know it before the American public" and to the necessity of clearing away the "underbrush of misunderstanding" created by his political opponents. He said he was trying to "stick to the truth," and added that it was not true he did not know what was going on in his own organization. He parried Democratic attacks on his minimum wage position by insisting that it was more important to get new categories of employees covered under minimum wage legislation at existing levels, than to raise the minimum for those already covered and thereby complicate the process of including more workers.

He also denied rumors (reported by reliable newsmen) that Nixon had been urging him to do more in the campaign, by saying Nixon had advised him not to "let them work you to death. He just told me to go on and do as I have been doing." He spoke on "revitalized Republicans," explaining his support of Senators Bender and Dirksen. He tried to take the sting out of the charge that his earlier-reported look at a possible third party meant he was dis-

[5] *Ibid.*
[6] *Ibid.*

gusted with the Republicans by pointing out that he really had reference to disfranchised opinion in one-party states.

The President admitted that the campaign had become more argumentative than he had hoped it would: "I had hoped to be completely expository in my approach rather than, you might say, approaching it in a debating side."[7] In discussing his position on abolition of the twenty-second amendment, he praised the good sense of the American people, in expressing his doubt about the wisdom of that amendment and upholding the right of the people to have anyone they wanted for President so long as he met the other requirements specified in the Constitution. In closing, he reported that his doctors were placing no effective restrictions on the extent of his campaigning.

Two other events occurred on this politically significant day— the Census Bureau released its estimate that 102,743,000 Americans would be of voting age on November 6; and Estes Kefauver picked up the Republican Governor of Arizona's unhappy improvisation that the "right to suffer" was one of the "joys" of a free economy.

On October 6 the President issued a statement on the draft, repeating the official arguments for the draft and rehearsing administration efforts to apply the newest technology and to put the nation's strength at its highest peacetime level while the over-all level of forces was being reduced.

Meanwhile the Republicans sought to improve their standing with Jewish voters. Nixon spoke to the National Convention of the Zionist Organization of America on October 7. He stressed Republican interest in world peace, emphasized Zionist efforts to create international friendship and understanding, and recalled the Republican platform declaration favoring preservation of Israel's independence as a vital tenet of American policy. He noted that the Democrats had done about as well in their platform, and therefore this should not be a partisan issue. He also put the problem in a larger context, insisting that it was necessary to deal with refugees and economic development in seeking a just and lasting peace between Israel and its neighbors.[8]

[7] *Ibid.*
[8] *Ibid.*, Oct. 8, 1956.

The next day Nixon issued a press statement setting the tone for his next campaign swing. He served notice on Stevenson and the Democrats "that from this day forward to the extent my campaign schedule permits I shall personally nail on the spot every slander, every distortion, and every falsification of the Eisenhower Administration's record by Mr. Stevenson." And, after saying that those candidates who can't take criticism shouldn't run, he announced: "There is only one rule of the game as far as our tactics in this campaign are concerned, and that is to tell the truth. If the truth reflects unfavorably on our opponents, that is their fault and not ours."[9]

On October 7 Chairman Leonard Hall announced the appointment of an Executive Committee to work closely with Republican national headquarters during the remainder of the campaign. This was composed of ten ex-officio members, plus fifteen specially appointed ones from New England, the Midwest, the South and the Far West. The Republican headquarters organization was rapidly burgeoning. Shortly thereafter Hall announced that the staff had been doubled, with some 750 in Washington (250 regulars), an office in New York for the Ethnic Division and one in Chicago for the Agriculture Division.[10]

On October 8 Postmaster General Arthur Summerfield made one of the more notable efforts to assure participation of former Taft supporters in the 1956 campaign. He spoke before the Ohio Federation of Republican Women in Columbus; he eulogized not only "Bob" Taft but also Republican women, holding up a goal of 31 million women's votes for Eisenhower and a Republican Congress in 1956. (This could be achieved if all 54 million eligible women voted in the same proportion for the parties as they did in 1952.) To gain the female vote, he evoked the great man: "In this campaign, greatness is under attack by mediocrity; integrity is belittled by incapacity; a superb record is derided by Candidate Stevenson, a man who has yet to make an acceptable record of public service."[11]

---

[9] Press release, Republican National Committee, Oct. 8, 1956.
[10] Ibid., Oct. 11, 1956.
[11] Ibid., Oct. 8, 1956.

In Pittsburgh, October 9, Eisenhower delivered his "reluctant campaigner" speech, one he was forced to make, he said, to put the record straight. It dealt with the issue of what principles, policies, and programs would give Americans a continuation of peace, prosperity, and progress, all at the same time. It compared the record of the administration with the "verbal record" of its opponents, countering their "partisan" and "distorted" charges with "the facts."

Stevenson-Kefauver East to West

Coming out of his swing up into Massachusetts and Rhode Island on October 6, Stevenson stopped in New York long enough to record an address on Polish Liberation for Radio Free Europe and to review a Pulaski Day parade. Then he flew off to Libertyville for a day prior to his "flying-front-porch" campaign in California and the West. On the 8th he released his third policy statement, this one on the nation's health. He called for Federal grants and loans to subsidize a national health insurance program, while with equal fervor he abjured "socialized medicine." He also called for more funds for medical research, the training of more medical personnel, and the construction of more hospitals.

Also on October 8 he lent support to the Dollars for Democrats drive, speaking by telephone to Democratic chairmen in the various states, urging their full support for the efforts to get money on the 16th for television time for himself and Senator Kefauver. He issued a bulletin on the campaign to date, noting a rising tide of optimism. "We are winning the campaign, but we must not be allowed to run out of gas."[12] He pitched his appeal for cooperation specifically to county chairmen, telling them they could make or break the operation.

On his campaign plane, the "Joe Smith Express," Stevenson flew out to the West Coast on October 9. His first stop was Seattle. Here in the middle of public-power country he came out for experi-

[12] *New York Times,* Oct. 9, 1956.

mentation in the production of atomic power, and, surprisingly, for a full role for private enterprise in it. His formula sounded strangely like the Republican partnership policy.

> Before science can extract power from the atom as cheaply as from coal, oil, or falling water, years of costly experimentation still remain. . . . Clearly, this is not a job for private enterprise alone. Private concerns, responsible as they are to the stockholders . . . cannot be expected to gamble on bold new types of nuclear power plants. . . .
> This is not a question of excluding the private power industry from its full participation in the development of an atomic power reactor program, or even of competing with the power industry. Rather it is a question of helping private industry through the costly period of experimentation and of hastening the day when atomic power can be produced cheaply and safely—by private enterprise.[13]

Balancing his middle-of-the-road proposal, the candidate pitched a major political attack on the President's alleged abdication of leadership, his undue delegation of power, and his failure to meet fairly the Stevenson proposals on ending hydrogen-bomb testing.

Two days later Stevenson announced the formation of a fifty-member National Business Council supporting his candidacy. Honorary co-chairmen were William L. Clayton of Houston and Joseph P. Kennedy of Boston. Co-chairmen were James Bruce of New York and Prentiss Brown of Detroit. Others included well-known Democratic partisans, with no prominent converts among them.[14]

Meanwhile Kefauver moved into the Northeast. In a speech in Delaware, he went after the housewife's vote on the grounds of peak consumer prices, and "a rising tide of inflation."[15] He drove into GOP territory in New Hampshire, taking a one hundred mile automobile tour on a circuit of five small farming towns, honoring a primary campaign promise to come back and stump the state no matter how he fared in the primary itself.[16]

Kefauver wasted some time by moving into solidly Republican

[13] *Ibid.*, Oct. 10, 1956.
[14] For the full list, see *ibid.*, Oct. 11, 1956.
[15] *Ibid.*, Oct. 9, 1956.
[16] *Ibid.*, Oct. 10, 1956.

areas in upstate New York and elsewhere. On this foray, he got no support from New York State Democratic leaders. They told the Kefauver managers they could not meet the stumping candidate or travel with him "because of other commitments." To the Kefauver party, this looked like deliberate withdrawal of support from the national ticket—an opinion not mollified by a telegram from Governor Harriman praising Kefauver for the "great campaign for the principles and policies we New York Democrats believe in." F. Joseph Donohue smoothed things over, meeting with Carmine DeSapio and announcing previously unscheduled Kefauver appearances to take place in New York the following Monday and Tuesday (October 15 and 16).

The contrast with Republican organizational support for Nixon was sharp—not to mention that with other Democratic organizations, in which at least the state chairman or national committeemen would be on hand for a Kefauver arrival. Rural New York did not seem a good place for Kefauver to be—no matter what the national committee strategists had thought. The Tennessean scuttled back to the Middle West for more bouts with Ezra Benson and a stop at every schoolhouse.

Stevenson was getting a better reception in Oregon than Kefauver found in New York—and the returns from Alaska's elections on October 9 and 10 showed a marked preference for Democratic candidates. Stevenson said that this was the best news since Maine, and recalled Alaska's vote for its representative in the House had gone with the winning presidential party in every presidential election since 1916. This portended a "Democratic tide" that would sweep him to victory in 1956. Not so, said Leonard Hall, who averred that Alaska's concern over statehood made her a poor indicator of national trends.[17]

In Portland, Oregon, on October 10 Stevenson replied to the President's Pittsburgh speech. After the standard opening gambit of support for local candidates and praise for Kefauver, he remarked that Republican party managers didn't mind a part-time President but couldn't stand a part-time candidate. In Portland he had no part-time praise for private power development, but made

[17] *Washington Post and Times Herald,* Oct. 11, 1956.

a full-scale attack on former Secretary of the Interior McKay for his alleged efforts to integrate the public domain with the private economy. Stevenson, holding back some of his ammunition for his San Francisco speech the following night, finished off with similar attacks on Treasury Secretary Humphrey (tax cuts for big corporations and lower defense spending and higher interest rates); on Agriculture Secretary Benson (for lowered price supports); on Chairman Leonard Hall (for conservation posts put into the political realm), and on Senator McCarthy (campaigning on twenty years of treason).[18]

He picked up the President's implied charge that Democrats were trying to weaken the nation's defense by pointing out that it was a Democratic majority in Congress that voted an extra billion for an Air Force, while the President's "budget balancers" were cutting back outlays, and on occasion not even consulting such defense specialists as General Ridgway.

Still in full cry after the President for not telling the whole truth, and baying at Dulles for "deception," Stevenson delivered a nationwide television speech from San Francisco after a little motorcading and political rallying elsewhere in the Bay area. For the second time in two days he sought to lay personal responsibility on the President for shortcomings in office, and he hammered hard on failures of Republican leadership.[19] In this speech he allowed himself the luxury of a strong conclusion:

> These challenges, the challenges of justice, of equality, and of peace, can be met. They can be met with firm leadership. They can be met by a party with a heart as well as a head. A party that cares about people. They can be met by men and women who do not fear new ideas and new solutions.
>
> We have had enough of complacency and stagnation. The time has come to resume our onward march toward a new America.[20]

On the 11th and 12th, Stevenson led his team of top Democratic campaigners—Governors Leader of Pennsylvania, Meyner of New Jersey, and Clement of Tennessee, and Senators Humphrey of

[18] *New York Times,* Oct. 11, 1956.
[19] *Ibid.,* Oct. 12, 1956.
[20] *Ibid.*

Minnesota and Gore of Tennessee—to an assault on twenty California communities, culminating in a pungent speech in San Diego.

The President's "Last Word" on Bombs

At the President's press conference on October 11, the reporters quickly drove for a significant statement—or at least a highly publishable reaction—to Stevenson's charges on bomb and draft. Quoting Stevenson's Seattle speech of October 9, one reporter asked the President for his comment on the charge that "Republican politicians, including the President, have little understanding or sympathy with attempts to save man from the greatest horror his ingenuity has ever devised." The President noted that he had always had the advice of scientists in whom he had confidence on defense matters involving scientific aspects. Then he asserted that "the record is there that we have done everything that is humanly possible, consistent with our own concern for our own national safety, to get this thing under control and use it for peace."[21]

Another reporter immediately asked whether it was true that the Republicans had planned to announce an end to the draft and suspension of bomb testing, but had banned these policies because Mr. Stevenson had "beaten them to the punch." This needle went deeper. The President replied that he was hearing things about his administration he never knew, and added:

Now, I tell you frankly I have said my last words on these subjects. I think I have expressed all that is necessary to express on them for the purposes of any political campaign, and as far as the record of the Government to provide for our security in the fairest, best, most economical way we can, to make certain that we are doing our share in seeing that the free world is kept free from attack, it's right there in the records of three and a half years to read.[22]

The press conference yielded more of significance for the cam-

[21] *Ibid.*
[22] *Ibid.*

paign. The President explained his unwillingness to endorse the Supreme Court decision on school integration on the ground that he was sworn to uphold the entire Constitution; and any announcement that he would uphold a particular decision or part of the Constitution might imply that he was not equally willing to uphold all other parts of it.

Asked to appraise the 1956 campaign to date, he ingenuously noted that running the Presidency was harder to combine with political campaigning than it was with vacations in Denver; hence he was doing relatively little campaigning. But on his trips, he did have his heart warmed by his reception by crowds, and was willing, as in 1952, to abide by the decision of the American people. He felt that no one was against peace, prosperity, or progress, and that the real issues came down to "the management of America's affairs at home." And he rehearsed the now-familiar Lincolnian dictum coupled with a "Jeffersonian" prescription that the least government is the best. Then he attacked his opponents:

> Now, I believe that the opposing—the Democratic party, approaches it—I mean, the leaders that are now speaking for them, I don't know whether the party as a whole, I am not trying to speak for them—as I understand the speeches being made on the other side, they start from the other end. "We take a Government and we run things from Government. There is where we start."
>
> Instead of trying to release, to guide and to help the great and illimitable results you get from a free people doing these things, they want to guide and direct, and they are not concerned particularly with the sound dollar because they talk about raising, raising expenditures, cutting taxes, and that means, as I see it, deficit spending. And you cannot continue to spend on a deficit basis without hurting your dollar.
>
> So I think that in those things we are—you have got a real issue. How do we manage America's internal affairs?
>
> I really believe this: In the foreign affairs, no one has debated, so far as I know, on general broad policy. But the debate has been on, are we competent or are we not competent. Do we know the right people, I guess, or what don't we know.
>
> I don't know exactly what the argument is. But it's not there down to issues. It's the whole management, I believe it is.[23]

[23] *Ibid.*

Nixon's Second Campaign Swing

The second Nixon campaign swing—covering 10,000 miles and fourteen states—was designed chiefly to concentrate Republican forces in seven key states: California, Illinois, Michigan, Ohio, Pennsylvania, New York and Massachusetts. The Republicans looked on this block of 197 electoral votes as vital, and considered Texas's 24 as "insurance." With these 221, plus other states considered sure, the Republicans saw certain victory on November 6. Starting for the insurance votes, Nixon visited San Antonio on October 9, playing the tunes of peace and antisocialism, looking for Texas Democrats disenchanted with the New Deal wing of their own party as well as for others hoping to ensure a conservative White House for another four years.[24]

Flying on to California on the 10th for appearances in four cities and to celebrate in San Francisco's Chinatown the forty-fifth anniversary of the Chinese Republic, the Vice President still harped on peace, although he moderated his invective against Democrats. He gave a hostage or so to fortune when he praised his party's handling of foreign policy: "No greater compliment could be paid to our President and Secretary of State than the fact that they have avoided rash, impulsive, inexperienced decisions which could have resulted in war." And he held forth hope of ultimate liberation to Chinese and to other oppressed peoples by suggesting that "there is always the possibility that a dictatorship will run out its time."[25]

The Republicans on Television

On the occasion of a Citizens-for-Eisenhower-sponsored "Citizens Press Conference" on October 12, the President lent himself to a highly structured "spontaneous" televised press conference, based on the normal procedure of his weekly press conference

[24] *Ibid.*, Oct. 10, 1956.
[25] *Ibid.*, Oct. 11, 1956.

but without the possibility of surprise questions or press needling. These conferences begin with an announcement, if the President has one. For this occasion, he told the country of good news from Suez.

> Now before we start . . . I have an announcement. I've got the best announcement that I think I can possibly make to America tonight.
>
> The progress made in the settlement of the Suez dispute this afternoon at the United Nations is most gratifying. . . . I don't mean to say we're completely out of the woods, but I talked to the Secretary of State just before I came over here tonight and I'll tell you that in both his heart and mine at least, there's a very great prayer of thanksgiving.[26]

He then went on to answer the set-piece questions of a representative group personally selected by the Citizens for Eisenhower. In this carefully plotted line-up was found a "discerning Democrat," mayor of Alexandria, Virginia, and nominator of Eisenhower in 1948 at the State Democratic Convention. ("Will you tell the nation who is in charge, sir?") There was a TV money winner. ("I wonder if you could tell us what sort of a man Vice President Nixon is?") There was a member of the UAW. ("Some fellers feel that the Democratic party is on their side. I happen to know that you are on their side even more so . . . And I wish, Mr. President, that you would explain and enlighten my buddies back home as to your stand on labor unions and the things that they are inclined to do.") There was a dairy farmer from New York. ("What does the soil bank offer a farmer from the Northeast?") There was a mother from Dallas. ("Will you tell us the reasons for our need of the draft?") There was a Negro pastor from Chicago, often called on to patch up broken homes, admiring above all fine points in Eisenhower "the beauty of your home." ("Will you be an ambassador of good will to all the homes in America, so that we can be one nation indivisible?")

There was Lewis W. Douglas, former Ambassador to England, former Democratic Representative and Budget Director:

> I am deeply convinced that your re-election will best serve the interests of the American people . . . I have not agreed with you, sir,

[26] *Ibid.*, Oct. 13, 1956.

on every question, but you have brought to American politics an unusual integrity—a quality of tolerance which encourages harmony and not discord, unity and not division, trust and not distrust. And in the administration of your office, sir, you have risen above the pettiness of a partisan politician.

But more important, in the forum of international affairs you speak with an authority which no other American possesses. And in these uncertain times this voice of authority is needed to preserve the peace. [Could you comment on reports of British press skepticism about the reliance possible on the continuity of our publicly announced foreign policies?][27]

Just before closing, Eisenhower defended rich men in his cabinet by posing a false alternative. He asked whether the people would prefer "a successful businessman" or "some failure" to run big-spending government departments. Nothing in the President's answers was newsworthy—he restated settled points from campaign doctrine as each sector of interest came up. But the President enjoyed himself immensely. On being notified that the program was running out of time, he told his questioners: "I'm going to stay here as long as anyone wants to. If we go off the air, why all right. But I'll stay here because I'm thoroughly enjoying this."[28]

On October 15 the Republicans started their major series of five-minute television programs, with a brief talk by the President outlining the subject of the series—"Your Government and You"—and foreshadowing the points to be made by various administration spokesmen concerning their achievements in office and their outlook for the future. Secretary Dulles would show how the administration had kept the peace. Secretary Humphrey would tell how it had checked galloping inflation, had cut taxes, and reduced the debt while balancing the budget. Secretary Wilson would point out that billions of dollars had been saved in the armed forces, where fewer men were providing a more secure defense. Secretary Mitchell would talk about employment, wages, and income—all at higher levels. Others would show how the administration had fought monopoly, extended social security. The President invited the American public to listen, to talk things over; the administration would rest on the voters' "honest judgment."

[27] *Ibid.*
[28] *Ibid.*

These talks were scheduled over all the major networks, but not necessarily at the same time on each. Each talk was scheduled for the last five minutes of a top nationwide television show, to reap the advantage of a major audience already tuned in.[29]

This was neither a "first" nor a capturing of the media initiative for the Republicans. The five-minute speech had been pioneered in earlier campaigning, and the Democrats had launched their series of five-minute shows with Stevenson on October 8, speaking over ABC. The Democratic theme was "The Man from Liberty-ville." The series aimed to show the Governor's position on major issues—sometimes with the Governor himself, sometimes with a well-qualified Democratic spokesman talking on a particular topic.[30]

Stevenson-Kefauver on Bombs and Corruption

Whatever the private estimate of his advisers, Stevenson passed the point of no return on the bomb-testing issue with his Chicago television speech on October 15. He dealt with the matter as a prime test of leadership: "I say to you that leaders must lead; that where the issue is of such magnitude I have no right to stand silent; I owe it to you to express my views, whatever the consequences." And as for the President's insistence on silence on the subject, said Stevenson: "We cannot brush the hydrogen bomb under the rug. But we can discuss it seriously and soberly, with mutual respect for the desire we all have for progress toward peace. This is one subject on which there cannot be, there must not be, any last word."[31] He gave the voters his own version for 1956 of Eisenhower's 1952 promise to go to Korea. Stevenson said

[29] The President's telecast (over ABC and NBC on Oct. 15, CBS Oct. 16) reached 4.1, 6.1, and 5.3 million homes respectively, with perhaps a total unduplicated audience of about 10 million homes. Nielsen Television-Radio Index.

[30] Early plans for some 89 five-minute periods foundered on lack of money in advance—and on the requirements for flexibility in the late stages of the campaign, when Middle East events far overshadowed in importance such subjects as the party position on youth in government.

[31] New York Times, Oct. 16, 1956.

he would go any place, any time, and confer at any level to halt bomb tests if he were elected President. Although Stevenson invoked the authority of "many distinguished scientists,"[32] he left matters largely to a choice by the public between his authority and that of the President; a weighing in the scales that was hardly to his advantage. Stevenson's headquarters reported the biggest fan mail yet for his proposal. Dr. Henry DeWolf Smyth, former Atomic Energy Commissioner and top physicist, praised Stevenson for "transcending the partisanship of the current campaign." Five nuclear physicists from the Argonne Laboratory telegraphed the candidate that his proposals were "wise, workable, and in the best interests of the United States." A labor leader, a housewife, and a doctor were among those applauding his stand.[33]

By this time, the parties were fully engaged on the H-bomb issue. Eisenhower still stayed with his "last word," as Dulles said Stevenson was too ignorant of the facts to propose sound plans for ending H-bomb testing. Democratic Senator Mike Mansfield called on the President to debate the issue openly with Stevenson. The President emphasized atoms for peace, as a "constructive service to our civilization." Nixon charged Stevenson was "hedging." Dewey at Flint called Stevenson's proposal "an invitation to national suicide." Meyner disagreed with Eisenhower's estimate of contribution, and called for "full and frank discussion." Senator Gore joined Senator Mansfield in supporting Stevenson's proposals, as Governor Harriman praised his "statesmanlike" talk on the tests. Even the Republican "truth squads" got into the argu-

---

[32] Stevenson had had a small and publicly unnoticed assist from Professor Ralph Lapp (on October 7); he got further help from a group of ten other scientists at the California Institute of Technology. They expressed disagreement with Eisenhower's regret that the test issue had come under political discussion; they expressed their own regret that serious discussion of the issue had occupied so little of the political debate. They did not agree that acceptance of Stevenson's proposals would enable the Soviets to gain a lead in nuclear technology.

The scientists were these: Carl D. Anderson, Nobel laureate in physics in 1934; Harrison S. Brown, professor of geochemistry; Robert F. Christy, professor of theoretical physics; James W. M. Dumode, professor of physics; Robert V. Langmuir, associate professor of electrical engineering; Thomas Lauritsen, professor of physics; Charles R. McKinney, senior research fellow in geochemistry; Matthew Sands, associate professor of physics; John M. Teem, research fellow in physics; and Robert L. Walker, associate professor of physics. *Ibid.*, Oct. 15, 1956.

[33] *Ibid.*, Oct. 17, 1956.

ment, charging that Stevenson had retreated from his original proposals to agree with the President.

A nationwide Kefauver television show on October 16 featured Republican "corruption." The main purpose was to come as close to a "rogues gallery" technique as possible without using those very words for it—showing pictures of Republican officials from Adolphe Wenzell (Boston financier and former Bureau of the Budget consultant) to Sherman Adams in poses worthy of police files, and with commentary by Kefauver. These, he said, were faces of "friends Eisenhower would like to forget." They documented, he said, the charge that "more heads of Government agencies have been involved in corruption than . . . since the Republican Administration of Ulysses S. Grant." Proceeding to comment on "the Cadillac Cabinet," Kefauver also displayed pictures of each, underlining their big business affiliations, and concluding:

> They are not bad men. They are simply men with limited—very limited interests. But President Eisenhower says he represents all the American people. How can his Administration do that when nine out of twelve Cabinet members are big business men? I say this is class government. It doesn't represent Joe Smith.[34]

Kefauver's style usually brought him to more violent wrenchings of the truth than was usual with the head of his ticket. While Stevenson carefully suggested that the more powerful weapons yet to be created in pursuit of a policy of deterrence might be able to blow the earth off its axis, Kefauver left off the qualifications. On October 16, he told a press conference in New York (preceding his nationwide television appearance) that hydrogen bombs could "right now blow the earth off its axis by 16 degrees, which would affect the seasons."[35]

[34] Ibid.

[35] Ibid. This howler brought forth prompt denials from even such sympathetic specialists as Dr. Ralph Lapp. And the candidate, in reply, was forced to rely on implications from testimony given by unnamed but presumably authoritative witnesses before the Joint Committee on Atomic Energy. For the critical viewer, Kefauver had lost a round; for the mass audience, he may have picked up some slight advantage from the circulation of a charge, almost always more potent than its rebuttal.

Nixon at Cornell, Eisenhower in the West

At Cornell University on October 17 the Vice President ran into one of his most hostile audiences of the campaign: editors of student papers from colleges throughout the country. Most of them came primed with questions rooted in "liberal" opinion concerning Communists in government, security procedures, fifth amendment, Democrats as the party of treason, and so on. The atmosphere had been well fogged before the conference by a charge from the Harvard *Crimson* that Cornell, an institution partly supported by public funds, was allowing its facilities to be used as a platform for Republican propaganda. The local Democratic organization had taken up the cry, and Governor Harriman had sent a telegram of protest to the Cornell president.

The conference went on as scheduled—with the clear advantage to the Vice President of being obviously unrigged. Nixon fielded all questions skilfully, although many of the questioners came out with the same opinion of him they had taken into the affray. Some thought he was "shifty." Others felt he handled himself very well.[36]

While collegian editors were giving Nixon a hard time in the East, Eisenhower moved into the West, exuding confidence and optimism. Basking under a warm Minnesota autumn sun, he combined satire and serenity, belittling his opponents ("anguished politicians") while holding out peace and bright economic hopes before the farm vote. At St. Paul the President spoke of great heritages, of great enterprise, and great visions. He bespoke unity in diversity; he found the "miracle of America" in the demonstration "that human freedom works." He even found a high role for political campaigning:

> . . . A political campaign seems a futile exchange of argument unless it produces in those who participate:
> A rededication to the American heritage of spiritual values.

[36] For an account of the political dispute, see *ibid.*, Oct. 18, 1956.

A revitalization of the American mission of freedom for all men.

A renewal of the American vision that the good of all is the job of all; that the freedom of all is the concern of all; that government for all is government by all.[37]

In Minneapolis he took occasion to attack his opponents—still not by name—and to appeal to farmers.

He struck his real keynote of the day in speaking to 1,200 school children at the Minneapolis airport: "I haven't seen quite so much happiness in a long time, and you don't know how good that makes me feel."[38]

Sharper Campaign Talk

In Seattle, buttressing the hard-pressed Governor Langlie in his try for a seat in the Senate, Eisenhower delivered a short speech. He was enthusiastic about the prosperous, healthy America he had been traveling through during the preceding few weeks, but he spent most of his speech in a biting attack on his unnamed opponents. Contrasting his own reassuring view with the "angry hum of a locust swarm of partisan orators," he denounced the Democratic platform as a "dark and mournful document." He charged the opposition with uttering half-truths, following hit-and-run tactics, straddling incompatible positions, and using a "rubber yardstick." He ended with "ten clear facts" of his own and a staccato finish:

I have stated the record of facts.

I do not believe it needs any added ornament of oratory or exhortation.

I commend it to your scrutiny.

I am confident of your judgment.[39]

The President took his "happiness" theme into Portland, Oregon, on the 18th. There he was greeted by a crowd of party workers in the Civic Auditorium. He deviated from his concentra-

[37] *Ibid.*, Oct. 17, 1956.
[38] *Ibid.*
[39] *Evening Star* (Washington, D.C.), Oct. 18, 1956.

tion on happiness to mention again problems of bomb-testing and disarmament; his "last word" was not going to be the last—especially since the Secretaries of State and Defense and the Chairman of the Atomic Energy Commission were preparing a long report rebutting Stevenson's "extraordinary statements" on the issue.

As the President snapped at Democrats, Stevenson moved into Michigan where he continued his belittling of the President's leadership, took a few warm-up swings at Dewey, and spoke out more sharply than ever against Nixon. Encouraged by the response of his California crowds to the mention of Nixon, Stevenson dropped his deft sarcasm to say: "There is no man who can safely say he knows where the Vice President stands. This is a man of many masks. Who can say they have seen his real face?" He matched his summary of the Nixon "record" against the requirements of the Presidency as "the supreme post of leadership in the world search for peace" and concluded: "His record is short and dreary. It is not the record of a man who is likely to lead us into a New America." The final Stevenson thrust was against the Vice President's qualifications as a moral leader. "It is impossible to think in these terms of a man whose greatest political talent is a mastery of personal innuendo, who cries 'treason' and spreads fear and doubt, a man who uses language to conceal issues rather than explore them, a man whose trademark is slander."[40]

In Ohio Stevenson moved toward a crisis in his campaign tactics. At Youngstown, he dealt at length with the problems of the draft. He rebutted Republican charges that his proposal was to create military weakness; he called it a proposal for strengthening the armed forces. He dwelt on the costs of the draft, and the interference it caused in the "ordained careers" of all our youth. He talked of the steps that could ultimately be taken to turn our armed forces into a professional, long-term service. His immediate plea was for thorough discussion, so the proposals could be decided not by any one person, not by any one general or military man in the White House, but by the American people. Above all, he said, this decision could not be entrusted to a party that had "built up a four-year record of rigid refusal to consider new ideas

[40] Ibid.

or new ways of doing things—and a four-year record of appalling indifference to human concerns."[41]

And with that appalling campaign charge ringing in the ears of his listeners, Stevenson left for Lexington and Louisville, Kentucky, for a day of campaigning, returning that night to Cincinnati for an all-out smash at the administration's foreign policy.

At Cincinnati Stevenson wasted no time on local political preliminaries. He threw down a challenge to the President and his administration in his first sentence:

> I want to talk with you about the most serious failure of the Republican Administration. I mean its failure in conducting our foreign policy.
>
> I'm not going to spend much time on the Secretary of State, Mr. Dulles. Under our Constitution, the President conducts America's relations with the rest of the world, and he is responsible for them, and for his Secretary of State.

Crediting the Republicans with one new idea—the ability to describe defeats as victories—and castigating them for their failure to unify Korea, to keep Indochina together, and to keep an Ambassador in India, he hit his climax in charging the President with misleading the country about Suez.

> ... there is no good news about Suez. Why didn't the President tell us the truth? ...
>
> This reverse was not inevitable. I cannot remember any other series of diplomatic strokes so erratic, naive and clumsy as the events of the past few years through which Russia gained welcome to the Near and Middle East.
>
> The trouble is that neither there nor anywhere else has the Administration shown any real capacity to adjust its policies to new conditions.

Stevenson's partisan crowd responded heartily; but the candidate's momentum was rapidly taking him onto dangerous ground. He admitted that the Democrats should offer workable alternatives, and he admitted further that he had none. All he could do was to rehearse the familiar areas of difficulty, call for a fresh look, and demand that the government deal frankly with the peo-

[41] *New York Times,* Oct. 19, 1956.

ple. His final political demand was hardly tempting to the mass of voters desperate to believe that they were in a period of peace:

I ask your support not because I offer promises of peace and progress but because I do not. . . .

I ask your support not because I say that all is well, but because I say that we must work hard, with tireless dedication, to make the small gains out of which, we may hope, large gains will ultimately be fashioned.

I ask your support not in the name of complacency but in the name of anxiety.[42]

The next day, reactions to the Cincinnati speech apparently convinced Stevenson and his advisers that they were making progress and that they should continue and heighten their attack on the foreign policy salient as the campaign neared its climax. They planned to carry the attack directly to Eisenhower the following Tuesday night, October 23, in a nationwide address at Madison Square Garden. They had taken the immediate response of the partisan audiences as indicator of a widespread but diffused concern over foreign policy felt throughout the nation. They concluded that the campaign had risen to a new pitch; they wanted to build up even more momentum before election day.[43] Why change an apparently winning game?

The result was to fix attention on issues where the Democratic professionals had correctly judged that Stevenson was not at his strongest. Stevenson, in characteristic translation of American idiom, felt that at last he was "batting on his own wicket."

Nixon's Many Masks

As Stevenson opted for unrestrained attack, Nixon provided ironic contrast as he addressed the annual Al Smith Memorial Dinner in New York. This was in several ways the ideal setting for Nixon's effort to delineate his new image—but the event came late in the campaign and received comparatively little media notice.

[42] *Ibid.*, Oct. 20, 1956.
[43] *Ibid.*, Oct. 21, 1956.

The occasion was a great opportunity for Nixon—to memorialize a Democrat, a great supporter of the rights of minorities, a poor man who had risen to the top in fulfillment of "the American dream"; in so doing to make a powerful plea to men of good will everywhere, and to show himself as a man above partisan interest or rancor. He made all the important political points of the campaign in the highest level manner and showed how he could deal softly with some of the issues that he had used in earlier campaigns to earn a reputation as a political hatchet man.

Nixon found the true greatness of America in its assertion and striving toward the ideal of the equality of man; the search for dignity for man as a child of God. He dwelt on man's inalienable rights, and compared their practice in America to their denial in Russia. He noted how America had come through the prejudice practiced by Know Nothings and Ku Klux Klan to emerge stronger and more unified than ever; and he predicted that the evils of segregation would finally be overcome—not by law alone, but by changes in the hearts of men. But he insisted that "the sovereignty of Federal courts shall strike down any law, ordinance or action that tries to make any American a lesser person before the law."

In dealing with the domestic Communism issue, he did not lash out by direction or indirection against his partisan enemies; he took a positive line, pointing out:

> We grant full rights to Communists, for example, not because we are soft on Communism, but because we dare not be soft in regard to the great principles of law that have molded our nation. We will vigilantly protect our nation against treason and subversion, but we shall do this within the framework of due process and our proved concepts of justice.[44]

He dealt with the Democratic efforts to fondle the little man and to depict Republicans as sole lovers of big business by using favorite Democratic phrases, and then topping them with his own inclusive phrase: "[Alfred E. Smith] typifies the truth of the statement that in America there is no forgotten man, no common man, no little man, no average man. There is only our fellow-man."[45]

Again, without mentioning partisan targets, he concluded his

[44] *Ibid.*, Oct. 19, 1956.
[45] *Ibid.*

address by asserting that America could not afford the moral cost, the economic cost, nor the international cost of segregation and race prejudice. Our international struggle, he said, was even more vital in the realm of the spirit than in those of economics or war. In such a struggle,

> . . . The kind of people we are counts much more than what we say. To the diverse people of the world—different in race, religion and national origin, but one in the sight of our Creator—let us show forth the highest meaning of our democracy, a nation under God to seek welfare of all, rich and poor, learned and unlearned, powerful and weak.

He raised a banner that all could rally round: the completion of these ideals of our Revolution, until they become a full reality "not only for Americans but for people throughout the world."

By the next day, October 19, Nixon had *Noh* mask No. 2 back on—the scowler used for sharp attack. Recalling Stevenson's charge that he was unfit for high office, he referred to Stevenson as a "second string quarterback." He challenged Stevenson to let the reporters go after him in a free press conference, there to deal with "the questionable issues he has raised during this campaign." Assuming Stevenson would refuse the challenge, the Vice President drew the political conclusion: "If a man's views are so unsound and unsure that he is unable to defend and explain them in a free American press conference, he raises a grave question as to whether he is capable of being President of the United States."[46]

Ending his second swing, Nixon gave out a confident appraisal of Republican chances. He discerned "tremendous Republican momentum" and thought that Republican gains in the "industrial East, the big cities and the industrial West" would assure the seats needed for GOP control of Senate and House.

Foes, Friends, and the Bulganin Letter

The President took the occasion of his recently added Los Angeles speech to deal on October 19 with Democratic charges of "corruption." This he did at a Republican rally in the Holly-

[46] *Ibid.*, Oct. 20, 1956.

wood Bowl—and however unnecessary such a speech might have been in terms of the preoccupations of the electorate, it probably had some value in warming up the spirits of the Republican organization workers, and some cathartic value for the President himself.

The President had just drawn his first unfriendly audience of the campaign—at the Lockheed aircraft plant in Burbank. But that evening, the Hollywood audience was in the usual tradition, responsive as the President went over the familiar issues, appealed to the labor vote, and said that the "man who today dismisses our military draft as an 'incredible waste' is a man speaking incredible folly."[47]

Few Republican partisans noticed Truman's charge that Eisenhower was a "part-time President before he was sick"—or if they did, they had living disproof in front of them.

On October 20 the President flew back to Washington from the West Coast, stopping off at Denver for a half-hour's talk and a joint appearance with Senate candidate Dan Thornton. After the sharp partisanship of Portland and Los Angeles, the President settled down to his favorite theme. He told the Denver audience he had not found confirmation in his travels for the Democratic picture of America. Instead, ". . . we see a glow of happiness on people's faces. They are believing something. They are holding a faith."[48]

On October 21 the campaign took a novel twist. The White House released the text of a letter to the President from Soviet Premier Bulganin, together with a White House reply. The Bulganin letter both attacked Secretary Dulles and noted with approval that "responsible quarters" were once more suggesting the termination of H-bomb tests. The White House reply not only rejected the Bulganin suggestions out of hand, on the ground that they represented no new move in the long drawn out international negotiations on test-cessation; it read the Russians a stern lecture for their violation of the niceties of diplomatic correspondence and for their offensiveness in attacking the Secretary of State.

[47] *Ibid.*
[48] *Ibid.*, Oct. 21, 1956.

Both parties turned the incident to partisan advantage. The Republicans did everything they could to associate the Stevenson proposal—and Stevenson—in the public mind with Bulganin and the Communists. The Democrats, without arguing the merits of the *démarche,* castigated the administration for its summary dismissal of the Bulganin note without a deliberate attempt either to expose it as phoney propaganda or to explore it for any hopes it might harbor of leading toward test cessation or disarmament. The Democrats also argued that if Bulganin favored anybody in the electoral race, it was Eisenhower and had been so for some time. Governor Harriman added the fillip that the Bulganin proposal showed that Stevenson's proposals had "caught the imagination of the world."[49]

Nixon—Third Swing

On his third swing around the country, Nixon added campaign train to plane and motorcade as he moved through Michigan, Ohio, Indiana, and Illinois. He sounded special overtones of appeals to minority groups as he trotted out familiar football similes in the land of the Big Ten. More important, he now emphasized the functions of political prediction, used both to assure voters of the certainty of Republican victory and to get precinct workers out in full force. Underlying his tactics more clearly than before was his assumption of victory.

In Michigan, where pockets of unemployment were most frequently found, he drove hard on the prosperity issue, promising larger, more widely shared gains to come. In Indiana, he dealt with communism and the H-bomb. (Stevenson's plan would be no more effective in stemming an atomic war than was Acheson's write-off of Korea in avoiding war on that unhappy peninsula.) He urged voters not to put in an eager, inexperienced, jittery second-stringer and leave an All-American on the bench during the "last quarter" of this great international football game.

[49] *Ibid.,* Oct. 22, 1956.

In Illinois, he talked as if the presidential race was over, and the only problem was that of returning a Republican Congress. Assuming further that the argument over the H-bomb had been won by Eisenhower, he insisted that every candidate for a seat in the House or Senate should say whether he backed the President or Stevenson on this issue. Motorcading in and around Chicago, Nixon showed concern to avoid anything that might hurt the cause of resistance in Soviet satellites, but at the same time to use the uprisings to advance President Eisenhower's foreign policy.

Moving into the Far West, Nixon emphasized positive prediction as well as assumption of victory. He told audiences at Great Falls, Montana, that the President would win by a larger margin than he had previously thought. Forty per cent of Negroes would now vote for him, instead of 20 per cent as in 1952, because Negroes were better off as well as more pleased with the Republican version of civil rights. Labor would go more heartily for the President, too. But all these things would happen only if the Republicans worked hard—right down to the precinct level.

On October 26, in Oregon, Nixon went flat out against Wayne Morse for his vote against the Formosa Resolution in 1955. Since Morse had opposed Eisenhower on other issues as well, the challenge to Oregon Republicans, Nixon said, was to see that the President should have a full vote, not a half vote.

Confrontation in the West

On the 27th both Nixon and Stevenson toured California; Nixon worked the valley towns—Santa Rosa, Fresno, and Bakersfield; Stevenson worked metropolitan areas—San Francisco and Los Angeles. Nixon during these days peppered his speeches and press conferences with predictions of Republican triumph—Kuchel pulling away from Richards in the senatorial race in California; McKay's prospects improving for a Senate seat from Oregon—and again and again, Eisenhower to win by a larger margin than earlier predicted. The Vice President added concreteness and emphasis to this claim—seeing improved Eisenhower majorities in New York, Ohio, Illinois, California, Pennsylvania, Massachusetts, and Michigan. He drove the point home by giving reasons:

(1) The people realize that recent international developments underline the need for seasoned leadership;

(2) Democratic campaigns of distortion have backfired; and

(3) Stevenson is the captive of the ADA left wing of his party, and has deserted the principles of millions of Democrats.

The leitmotiv of Nixon's efforts to get a Republican Congress was the refrain: Eisenhower deserves it on his record. Nixon pressed the President to get into the political campaign as deeply as possible, in the hope that some of the Ike popularity might rub off on Republican hopefuls. Nixon also did everything he could to support individual candidacies and to make predictions of victory without unduly jeopardizing his reputation as a knowledgeable political professional and a man able to engineer victory. This latter aim called for careful execution, for there is good reason to believe that at no time in the campaign did Nixon privately regard the achievement of a Republican majority in the House of Representatives as probable.

Nixon's scheme of action was to support a limited number of local figures that seemed to have reasonable chances of victory; to go all out for key figures such as McKay even in the absence of assurance of triumph; to dissociate himself from candidates or other political figures who would remind voters of his earlier associations with Jenner and McCarthy (happily not candidates in 1956); and to make carefully qualified predictions of victory. He tried to weight Democratic senatorial and congressional candidates with the drag of Stevenson, as much as he tried to get help for Republicans from Eisenhower.

In Los Angeles on October 29, for example, Nixon said that the Stevenson stand on the H-bomb and the draft jeopardized the chances of Democratic candidates—and they would have to accept those risks or dissociate themselves from the head of the ticket. He discerned a reversal of the earlier trend toward a Democratic House of Representatives, since he thought it would be harder for Democratic candidates for Congress to resist the undoubted preference for the President than it would be for senatorial candidates. Again he used specificity to gain sharpness and strength: watch the races, he said, in Oregon, Ohio, Pennsylvania, Kentucky, and New York, where, if the trend continued, the GOP would win; and it might well pick up additional seats in West Virginia and Washington. He repeated his earlier prediction that probable Republican gains in industrial areas and cities would suffice to give them a majority in the House. He produced a plausible formula:

> I do not know of any House or Senate seats which will be lost by the Republicans in predominantly agricultural areas though their winning margins in some instances will be reduced. . . . I am basing my optimism on the fact that we will gain votes in those areas where there are close races and we will lose them in those areas where we can afford to because of the margin we have to begin with.[50]

And he qualified everything again—all these things would come to pass *if* campaigners would work hard right up to election day.

Bomb Testing and Draft: The Administration Reply

On October 23 the Stevenson forces won something of a Pyrrhic victory. They got a reply to their statements about bomb-testing— a ponderous reaffirmation of the administration position in every point; a recapitulation of the chronology of developments on the issue; memoranda from the chief government agencies concerning the United States program of testing atomic weapons, the fall-out from atomic tests, the possibilities of long-range detection of the detonation of nuclear weapons, and the international atoms-for-peace program.

The official papers clearly narrowed the differences between the fundamental positions of the administration and the challengers to one simple point—was it worth while to make a unilateral start in foregoing bomb tests, in the hope of moving negotiations a little closer to the trust that could lead to disarmament, normalization of relations, and relaxation of tensions? Or should there be no such start until there were ironclad safeguards?

---

[50] Press release, Republican National Committee, Oct. 29, 1956.

Stevenson was for taking the risk. The President would take no concrete initiatives unless he was completely sure that he was running no new risk of the security and integrity of the American people.

This was no argument for the general public. The issues were technical; the propositions and rebuttals hard to follow (for they did not always come to confrontation). The public apparently did as it could be expected to do: the people trusted the President and either did not notice what the opposition was doing or did not regard it as important. Among the technicians—including scientists—there was more disposition to attribute the greater merit to the Stevenson position. But it could not be said—and the Stevenson forces did not themselves think—that the Democratic cause at the polls in 1956 would be helped much by this argument.

Stevenson at Madison Square Garden and the Waldorf

Stevenson gathered his forces and his by now well-worn arguments at the Democratic State Rally in New York's Madison Square Garden on October 23. His speech trailed off without climax. Despite the appearances put in by New York state top politicos and officials, the rally lacked point and punch.

The next day Stevenson addressed a businessmen's luncheon at the Waldorf Astoria, under the sponsorship of the Volunteers for Stevenson. His object was to tell those assembled why the Democratic Party was the "best friend American business has." His argument was the phenomenal twenty-year growth between 1933 and 1953, a period in which the New Deal made America safe for capitalism, and vice versa, by establishing ground rules within which decent business could develop. Seven hundred convinced partisans from the business world responded with enthusiasm: $30,000 worth on the spot. And during the remaining rallies in the New York area that day—in Queens, the Bronx, Nassau, and Westchester counties—Stevenson got enthusiastic, responsive crowds. Few people lined his route between rallies, however.[51]

[51] *New York Times*, Oct. 25, 1956.

Republicans Consider a Tactical Shift

By October 24 the Republicans decided that Eisenhower must do something to shore up Republican chances in key border states and the South. Here was territory that Stevenson had to take; the prospects were close; and a couple of days of campaigning by the President might be useful insurance. But the foreign situation was looking less and less certain. Unrest in the Soviet satellites and the continued festering of Suez led to a decision to keep the President at the White House, and to arrange instead a series of trips, none lasting more than a day, from Washington to airports in the South. At each he could give a speech, and be able to fly back to Washington immediately without any motorcading. The loss of the downtown audiences would have to be taken to assure flexibility in the President's schedule. Hence a plan to send him to Miami, Jacksonville, and Richmond on the 29th; to Dallas and Oklahoma City on the 31st, with the later addition of a speech in Memphis.[52]

The ever-inventive Republican gimmick-designers came up with another television "innovation" for the afternoon of October 24— a program aimed chiefly at the women's votes, with seven carefully chosen ladies asking seven carefully chosen questions of the President. The answers were all tangled, authentic, spontaneous Eisenhower. They were far less important than the informal picture of the President and his wife, chatting easily with women from everyday pursuits, giving their questions as much respect and attention as he would those of the Washington press corps.

The Second Phase Ends

On October 25, the second phase of the campaign drew to a close with routine activities in both parties. The President took

[52] *Ibid.*, Oct. 25, 1956, and Oct. 27, 1956.

the train to New York for an appearance at a ten-hour political rally featuring conferences with local political leaders and a half-hour speech at a Citizens for Eisenhower fiesta at Madison Square Garden. The President's speech was by now routine; but New York crowds received him more warmly than they had greeted Mr. Stevenson two nights earlier.

Stevenson meanwhile moved back through the Midwest to the Far West on his last great swing. At Springfield on the 25th, he dwelt on the collapse of farm income. At Rock Island he talked about farm issues and Republican corruption, and intensified his attack on the bomb problem.

Moving out to Albuquerque, in the heart of bomb-testing territory, Stevenson charged the President with outright misrepresentation of his position on the testing issue. Stevenson pointed out that he had only suggested action that officials of the Eisenhower administration had also proposed—but a course that called forth epithets of "incredible folly" from the President and the Vice President when offered by Democrats.

Winding up his Western campaign, Stevenson delivered a highly partisan wrap-up of the campaign arguments and issues to an eager crowd in San Francisco's Union Square. In Los Angeles, he was even more partisan, straining the bounds of fairness in his efforts to support his charges that the administration was caught "off guard" by the uprisings in Poland and Hungary, and in juxtaposing the President's presence on the golf course with the outbreak of bad news for the free world in lands abroad.[53]

As described by Harrison Salisbury of the *New York Times*, the Los Angeles rally at Gilmore Park was the most successful of the Democratic campaign to date. Stevenson essayed a point-by-point attack on Eisenhower's leadership. By the time he was half finished, the partisan crowd of 25,000 was booing or hissing every mention of Eisenhower or of Nixon.

Meanwhile, in the East, James Finnegan appealed to Democrats to give money as well as votes, and Democratic farm leaders charged that the Secretary of Agriculture was withholding "very

---

[53] *Ibid.*, Oct. 28, 1956.

unfavorable" information about farm prices until after the election.

In Springfield, Stevenson's staff released the fourth in the series of program papers—this one dealing with a financial program for the New America. It was designed in part to answer the persistent question raised by the earlier programs—where is the money coming from? And, like the others, it was designed to put the contrast between a Republican administration "running on its record," allergic to ideas, and understandably ambiguous about the future on the one hand, and a Democratic set of proposals for the future on the other.

On October 26 the nation's newspapers published a Gallup Poll that probably measured the high point of the Stevenson-Kefauver effort during the campaign. Measuring sentiment tested immediately before the publication of the exchange of letters between Bulganin and Eisenhower on H-bomb testing, the poll showed that 51 per cent of the nation's voters favored Eisenhower and Nixon; 41 per cent Stevenson and Kefauver, with 8 per cent undecided. Assuming that the undecided voters would either not vote or vote in the same proportion as those who had made up their minds, the trial heat showed the Republicans leading, 55 per cent to 45 per cent of the popular vote. The regional percentage breakdowns were as follows:

	Eisenhower-Nixon	Stevenson-Kefauver
Eastern states	60	40
East Central states	58	42
West Central states	53	47
Far Western states	53	47
Southern states	55	45

These reflected opinions of voters who had made up their minds, and who expressed an intention to vote on election day.[54]

The Stevenson campaign was running into difficulties. Whatever achievements could be read into this poll (against Eisenhower's 64 per cent in June, just after his operation), cleavages

[54] *Washington Post and Times Herald,* Oct. 26, 1956. The article reported a survey in progress measuring sentiment on the States' Rights party, that had qualified for the ballot in 14 states—9 in the South, 5 in the North.

arose among the various supporting groups—the professionals and regular Democrats; the ADA; the Liberal Party; the supporters of Wagner—and more effort seemed to be going into recrimination than into conjoint work for the whole ticket.[55] State and local Democratic canvassers turning up pro-Ike people among their party cohorts let the issue of the Presidency go, and tried instead to get the voter to support the state or local Democratic ticket. If they tried to argue out the issue of Ike, they told the Stevenson men, they would lose the whole ticket.

The President Enters Walter Reed

On October 27 the President fulfilled a pledge to go to Walter Reed and have a two-day, head-to-toe physical checkup. The main point of uncertainty seemed to be whether the attendant doctors would be made available for press questions. The President's own health had been vouched for by his strenuous campaign and by his radiation of vigor from bubble-top car and campaign platform. Only columnist Drew Pearson tried to make capital of the examination by alleging presidential illness at Minneapolis and Seattle—drawing a virulent White House denial.

The next day Pearson and the nation had their answer—the President, said his doctors, "gives every appearance of being in excellent health."[56] The published report, signed by General Snyder, gave the curious public a part by part appraisal of the President's condition from ears to arches.

[55] *New York Times*, Oct. 26, 1956.
[56] *Ibid.*, Oct. 29, 1956.

12

The Campaign: Third Phase

WITH THE FAVORABLE REPORT from Walter Reed Hospital on the President's health, an Eisenhower-Nixon victory seemed almost certain, despite the fact that Stevenson and Kefauver campaigned ever more vigorously. Events were now in the making, however, that were to resolve any remaining uncertainty, and subject the campaign arguments to a dramatic inversion. Taking advantage of the weakness and uncertainty usually attributed to American governments during times of presidential elections, Israel, Great Britain, and France put actions in train that at once confirmed much of the Democrats' charges against Republican foreign policy, and ensured re-election for the President.

While the President was still in the hospital and Stevenson was firing things up in California, unmistakable evidence of war clouds appeared.

Israel mobilized. Its Ambassador in Washington, Abba Eban, promised "Israel would start no war" and explained her near-total mobilization (in classic fashion) as a move dictated by the need to be ready to meet an attack. The State Department, alarmed by the extent of the call-up, said Americans in the Middle East would be warned to leave "as a matter of prudence," and advised new visitors to the area to defer their travel. Israeli officials expressed private wonder at United States official alarm, pointing to recent Arab disorders and the "careful development" of Arab policy. The President told Israel's Premier Ben Gurion of his concern and asked for explanations. He further suggested talks with Britain and France on the subject, apparently unaware of their immediate intentions.[1]

[1] *New York Times,* Oct. 29, 1956.

Closing the Campaign

At Boston on October 29 Stevenson was in a high mood; he glowed over the successes of his rallies in New York, in Illinois, and in California during the preceding week.[2] On a platform with gubernatorial candidate Foster Furcolo, he spoke words about Senator Kennedy that must have grated on the ears of Mrs. Roosevelt—"And I am honored, indeed I am honored beyond my deserts, to have been introduced by a man whose personal friendship I value so highly and whose leadership America seeks so eagerly."[3] In polyglot Boston he took special pains to rejoice over the relative freedom recently granted by the Communists to Poland's Cardinal Wyszinski, and to praise the brave men and women of Poland and Hungary then risking their lives on the barricades.

But when he referred to the Middle East, he found the going admittedly harder. He used the outbreak not as an occasion to come out foursquare for arms for Israel—as he had done not a great many days before—but to stress the point that the Republican administration had not told the truth about the situation there. He dwelt further on his charge that the administration of America had been taken away from "the people" and turned over to a "board of directors"—"men selected not for their familiarity with ordinary people and their interests, but men selected for their ability to make money." He picked up Eisenhower's false distinction between a successful business man and anyone else—who had done nothing. "Abraham Lincoln wouldn't even rate a job in a Republican Cabinet." He followed up with a recapitulation of the times when Eisenhower "didn't know."

Here as in Los Angeles Stevenson made local headway with his attack on the President's leadership. As he insisted that the process before the voters was not a popularity contest, but an election, his hearers drowned him out with applause.[4] He pointed to in-

---

[2] *Ibid.,* Oct. 30, 1956. Stevenson called the rallies in Nassau and Westchester counties the largest and most enthusiastic ever held; he termed those in San Francisco and Los Angeles two of the biggest in California history. "The issue there, where they know him best, and everybody, and everyone knows in his heart that it is one of the central issues of this campaign, was Richard Nixon. Well, believe me nobody is going to be fooled about that issue either." *Ibid.*

[3] *Ibid.*

[4] Interpolation in text of speech, *ibid.*

creasing evidence he and Senator Kefauver had been turning up
that the Republicans believed the country could be governed
without the people's help; he complained that the Republicans
had responded to truth with sneers. He ridiculed the Republican
formula of "don't worry, just trust Ike." He ridiculed the notion
that the people should trust Ike's cabinet officers, or worst of all,
Nixon: ". . . the short of it is that President Eisenhower is the front
man for the Republican party, and the reason for the chorus of
just trust Ike is that they don't dare say trust us Republicans."[5]
He wound up—off the air because he had overrun his television
time—with a by-now-familiar evocation of the New America, and
a confident prediction of Democratic victory one week later.
Whatever marginal loss of impact he may have suffered because
of his television timing, Stevenson had had a good day. He had
delighted the 8,000 in Mechanics Hall, and during the day his
motorcade had built up street crowds of 100,000—the largest of
the campaign yet.[6] He gave no public inkling of any private judgment that the impact of events in Egypt would tell heavily against
him.

On the same day as his Boston rally, Stevenson made his detailed response to the President's written statement on the H-
bomb in a "White Paper." This summarized the President's argument, quoted pertinent parts and made point-by-point replies.
Stevenson used this verbal passage at arms to underline his campaign arguments of lack of Republican ideas and creativity; of
Republican distortion of argument and facts; of callousness to the
human needs of people at home and abroad; of inadequacy in the
fields of national defense, disarmament, and peace. But in the
end the memorandum was a lawyer's brief: a memorandum of
rebuttal and argument, recirculating the President's allegations,
and posing counterargument and objections. It left matters much
where they were before—the judgment of the President (and his
150 scientists) against that of his opponent (plus many other scientists).[7]

With the onset of Suez, the niceties of the hydrogen bomb argu-

[5] *Ibid.*
[6] *Ibid.*
[7] *Ibid.*

ment drifted out of the arena of main political concern.

Despite the rumblings from the Middle East, the President made a political sortie into the South on the 29th, flying 1,800 miles to airports serving Miami, Jacksonville, and Richmond. At Miami he spoke of the issue of civil rights, but he did not mention the matter in the other two cities. He affirmed his faith that the problem should best be handled on a state and local basis; he expressed his conviction that progress would have to be made in the hearts of men rather than in legislative halls; and he concluded with a note of fine disrespect for his opponents: "I believed then, as I believe now, that there must be intelligent understanding of the human factors and emotions involved, if we are to make steady progress in the matter rather than simply to make political promises never intended to be kept."[8] For the rest of his Miami speech he spoke again of peace, prosperity, and progress, attuned to the energy and accomplishment of people seeking their achievements without waiting for a government bureaucracy to do it for them, or suffering government interference. For the first time in the campaign, he went in for handshaking—and found it hard work. He got back into his plane in the eighty-degree humid heat in a full sweat.

At Jacksonville he departed from his prepared speech and lashed into some Democrats while praising others. Recalling the Kefauver-Stevenson donnybrook in the Florida primaries, he asked his audience whether they wanted "this pair" in Washington. At Richmond he praised Senator Harry F. Byrd as the "living symbol of the simple old fashioned virtue of not spending more than you make. To him I am proud to pay my respects. He is true to your heritage." The President also made a point of praising General George C. Marshall, placing him along with such Virginia greats as Washington, Robert E. Lee, and Woodrow Wilson.[9]

On his return to Washington, the President called an emergency meeting of his counsellors. Israeli armor and paratroops were thrusting deep into the Sinai peninsula, and the British Mediterranean Fleet was moving menacingly east from Malta to Cyprus. The next day the English and French sent their joint ultimatum

[8] *Ibid.*
[9] *Ibid.*

to Nasser, demanding withdrawal of troops from the Suez canal area and agreement for Anglo-French troops "temporarily" to occupy the area. Nasser rejected the ultimatum and promised a bitter battle from village to village. Eisenhower appealed to Paris and London to hold off and await action by the United Nations. In the Security Council the United States found itself in the unprecedented position of having its closest allies use the veto against a resolution sponsored by the United States, and of finding itself bedfellow with Khrushchev and Nasser.

The consequences for the political campaign were immediate. The perceptions of foreign policy and performance changed in the minds of many voters. The Republicans replaced their slogan of "the guns aren't firing anywhere" with "he kept us out of war." The Democrats sprang to the attack—finding in the outbreak confirmation of all their most serious charges against Eisenhower and Dulles. Stevenson made one of his strongest addresses of the campaign in Philadelphia, attacking Republican "phoneyness," asserting that Eisenhower had not told the people the truth about the situation in foreign policy, and citing the Middle East as one more proof of Eisenhower's inattention to his duties. Eisenhower immediately dropped plans for further speechmaking in the South, canceling scheduled appearances in Texas, Oklahoma, and Tennessee. He said that work in Washington was the order of the day: "The turn of events yesterday leaves me no option—in the interests of working for peace—but to remain at the White House Wednesday to deal with the situation developing in the Middle East."[10]

Sage observers immediately concluded that what the President would lose on the peace issue he would recoup as Commander in Chief.

Nixon instantly jumped to the new party position, telling a California audience after consultation with Sherman Adams in the White House: "This is not the moment to replace the greatest commander in chief America has ever had in war or peace with a jittery, inexperienced novice who is eager to have the job but who is utterly unqualified to make the great decisions demanded by the times."[11]

[10] Ibid., Oct. 31, 1956.
[11] Ibid., Oct. 30, 1956.

The Republican position among Jewish voters was immediately put in jeopardy; and the prospects of Jacob Javits in his New York senatorial race were discounted by the political wiseacres.

As the campaign moved into its last week, Stevenson raised the tone of his attack on the administration to a shrill pitch. His speech to 12,000 persons in a crowded hall in Philadelphia was carried over a statewide television network, on October 30. The issues now becoming clear and distinct, he said, turned on one underlying issue—"phoneyness." He charged the Republican advertising campaigners with cynical attempts to confuse issues—even the issue of life and death. He charged them with trying to get one man elected so another group of men could run the country.

> I call this phoneyness. Perhaps deceitfulness would be easier to find in the dictionary.
> And if this seems like blunt or angry talk then I better just admit that I'm fed up with eight weeks of this mealymouthed Republican campaign talk, this squeaky chorus—peace, prosperity and progress—a peace that is as unreliable as a Republican promise, a progress that is nonexistent, and a prosperity they inherited, except they have dropped the farmer, the small business man and all too many others.[12]

He sharpened his charges against Eisenhower's leadership, recapitulating all the major instances in which the President had been golfing when crises were breaking out abroad. He did not leave the question of the President's health to implication, insisting that the electorate must face up to the issue of his ability to meet the full responsibilities of the job. "This isn't a matter of one man's health. This is a matter of a nation's health." And it was also a matter of Republican truth telling, on foreign affairs, and on domestic affairs, in which Stevenson charged that the President did not know what was going on, or was deliberately misinforming his listeners in his recent speeches in the South. "These were the speeches of a man who either does not know what is going on in the country, or does not care, or does not want you to know—or to care."

He railed against the Republican tone of smugness and of moral superiority, the imputation of a crusade "loftier and more spiritual than the ordinary political campaigns of us ordinary politicians."

[12] *Ibid.*, Oct. 31, 1956.

He flailed at the "myth" that the President was in charge and that Nixon did not exist. He apologized for not discussing the New America with his hearers, but excused himself by asking a prior question—where will we find the leadership we need?

> I say we will not find it in a President who has already withdrawn from the obligations of leadership.
> I say we will not find it in a Vice President whose deportment and views are not the products of principle or conviction but of ambition and expediency.
> I say we will find this leadership only in ourselves—that we can seize the limitless promise of the New America only if we meet its challenge together—as a people—working through a government which takes its decisions and finds its power and its inspiration in the wisdom and the strength and the ideals of all the people.

He posed the alternatives for the electorate:

> Whether we move boldly ahead to fulfill our destiny, or whether we spend four more years in delay and defeat and deceit; this is the issue we decide a week from tomorrow.
> We know what that decision will be. It will be a victory for the Bill of Rights, a victory for peace, a victory for the truth, a victory for the servant of all the people—the Democratic party.[13]

With the world on fire in Poland and Hungary as well as in the Middle East, the Republicans were more than happy to take on Adlai Stevenson on the ground he preferred—foreign policy. As Soviet tanks rumbled into Hungary, Richard Nixon said the "butchers of Budapest" would make mincemeat out of Stevenson. Nixon then fired two direct shots at his foe, asking that he answer two questions in his next speech:

> What different policy would he have followed in the Near East which he thinks would have kept Israel's forces from moving into Egypt?
> What would he be doing now if he were President other than what President Eisenhower is doing?[14]

The Republicans had special advantages here, beyond the towering prestige and experience of the President. Among these was the clear Democratic platform call for arms for Israel, while the Republicans had adopted a policy better calculated to keep

[13] *Ibid.*
[14] *Ibid.*

the Israeli in check. Stevenson's position on the draft was vulnerable—and Senator Bridges drove into it, asking where we would be, with the world in turmoil, if we had followed Stevenson's advice on the draft? The chief of the Republican National Committee's Veterans Division released a statement signed by forty-four past commanders of veterans' organizations saying that the key to peace was to keep America strong.

Most important, the President and the administration enjoyed the advantages of their central position at the helm of events. They could act—and their actions would be the best propaganda. The President could also speak—and speak he did, not as partisan but as President of all the people. Stevenson could only speak. And speak he did, concentrating all his efforts on the gap torn in the Republican façade of peace, forgetting other aspects of the campaign, moving happily into that sector of the campaign in which he felt most competent, no matter what its discounted value in electoral choices. Had he discerned powerful, feasible alternatives to the Republican course in response to the crisis, he could have announced them. Lacking these he had to recall his earlier, near-diffident suggestions for a United Nations trigger force and his earlier Cassandra cries. He could call for a new beginning, but in response to the Republican question of what he would do that was different, he responded weakly. Stevenson thus heightened the public impression of the President as a man of action, a man of experience, to be trusted in time of crisis. All the Stevenson efforts to picture him as a man unwilling to shoulder his responsibilities, ignorant of vital developments, paled before the favorite American spectacle of an indignant President striving to hold back colonialist aggressors and to maintain peace in the world. (The overtones of attitudes toward Israel were lost in the larger, louder symphony.)

Stevenson's great chance came at Buffalo on November 1, in which he got free time over nationwide television and radio networks to reply to the President's speech to the nation made the day before. The President had spoken of the inescapable necessity of upholding one law in our relations with the nations—one law for the weak and the strong, one for the aggressor and the victim, for the ally and the neutral and the enemy. He had spoken of

America's intention to pursue the fight with Soviet Communism while preserving her moral integrity—"to practice the peace we preach." He told his audience that America would continue to build its military strength so as to be spared the necessity of using it.

Stevenson, in reply, took the negative. Our nation had lost control of events in the Middle East; our policy was at a "dead end." We had given the Communists two great victories—a foothold in the Middle East and a breakdown of the Western alliance. He made three points: our failures could have been averted; the administration had withheld the consequences of its mistakes from the American people; many things could have been done during the past year to reduce the Middle East crisis. He rehearsed administration errors, and asked what we should do about the situation now—and rehearsed administration errors again. Repeating his question, he agreed that the President was right in trying to check the use of force on both sides, but insisted that restoration of the *status quo ante* would not be enough.

With the ground now prepared for a clear and concrete call, Stevenson provided only broad and moral generalities:

> We now have an opportunity to use our great moral authority, our own statesmanship, the weight of our economic power, to bring about solutions to the whole range of complex problems confronting the Free World in the Middle East.
>
> The time has come to wipe the slate clean and begin anew. We must, for a change, be honest with ourselves and honest with the rest of the world. The search for peace demands the best that is in us. The time is now. We can no longer escape the challenge of history.[15]

With that flight of words, in the opinion of many observers, Stevenson irrevocably lost the campaign. His only chance to present himself as a better choice than Eisenhower to conduct the nation through its obvious complexities and perils depended on his ability to outline a believable and constructive alternative policy. He fitted only too closely the role Nixon and other Republicans had cast for him in their comparison between the man of phrases and the man of proved reliability in times of crisis. He had drawn the

[15] *Washington Post and Times Herald*, Nov. 2, 1956.

issue on leadership, and he was unable to prove himself the superior in leadership at the critical time of choice. It did no good to point out that the Republicans had based their campaign on being the party of peace, and now had to present themselves as the party capable of dealing with war. The majority in the country knew it; and was willing to trust the President in any case.[16]

Could Stevenson plead lack of time for these shortcomings? The Buffalo speech had been prepared under pressure, and was completed only a few minutes before air time at 7 P.M. But the candidate had had help from top aides, and by the evidence of his own speeches, he had long since anticipated the possibility of a break-out in the Middle East. He left himself completely open to the attack voiced by Nixon at Pittsburgh, that his "shocking action in criticizing the President and American foreign policy without offering a constructive alternative proved again that he completely lacks the great qualities of leadership which America needs in these four years."[17]

In the closing phases of campaigning, Stevenson went from Cleveland to Chicago on November 3; and then moved up to Minneapolis for a last word before going to Boston for a nation-wide election-eve telecast. In Chicago he issued a full-dress indictment of the President. Almost anticlimactically the Stevenson headquarters issued a final program paper on natural resources that was unnoticed in the national concern with Suez.

The strategy behind the last-minute foray into Minnesota—and the decision to say something that might be noticed in the North-west concerning natural resources—was in keeping with the Finnegan plan. If Stevenson could win all the South and the border states (187 electoral votes), pick up Pennsylvania and California (64 votes), he would be within 15 votes of victory—and that could be supplied by Minnesota's 11 and Rhode Island's 4. Although these last states had been classified as leaning toward Eisenhower, they represented an outside chance. The Democrats took it.

In Minneapolis Stevenson started in a reminiscent mood—after-

---

[16] This seemed to be another case in which the candidate's local response, as reported by the press, was out of line with larger responses. At the rally in Buffalo immediately following the television speech, 14,000 partisans cheered the candidate heartily when he made his point about the Republican switch in arguments. *Ibid.*

[17] *New York Herald Tribune*, Nov. 2, 1956.

thoughts on a campaign almost over in which he reflected on his efforts (and Kefauver's) to tell the truth and talk sense, while the Republicans dealt in deceit. . . He dwelt further on farmers' difficulties. He charged (for the only time in the course of his public speeches in the campaign) that in South Dakota the Republicans had been waging "an especially dirty smear campaign." He noted that Nixon "had put away his switchblade and now assumes the aspect of an Eagle Scout." He quoted a "certain Senator" from Wisconsin as saying (as Eisenhower had not said) that it was "important beyond words" to elect Wiley, for if the Republicans controlled the Senate, Wisconsin could get some more McCarthyism. Stevenson asked: "How do you reconcile the fact that the President holds forth in the pulpit while his choirboys sneak around back alleys with sandbags?" The answer—Eisenhower doesn't run the store. And that was bad enough for farmers, but in foreign policy it was disastrous. Golf in times of crisis. . . Caught off guard by critical events. . . Inability to act even when forewarned. . . Compare Truman in Greece, Iran, and Korea. . . Egypt in Russia's arms, and "our democratic friend, Israel, has lashed out in desperation."[18]

Stevenson did make and acknowledge Republican acceptance of one constructive suggestion with respect to Hungary: send help via the United Nations Peace Observation Commission if possible. But otherwise he used the rest of his time in a long harangue against Republican shortcomings, and managed a false note in wishing Mr. Dulles a speedy recovery—"as an old friend." He finished with a tribute to the ballot as an expression of freedom —and America's trust in the wisdom of all the people.

Election Eve

At Boston, in the concluding election-eve rally, Stevenson delivered another set speech, interrupted by messages from speakers in various other cities in a format patterned on the 1952 Republi-

[18] *New York Times*, Nov. 6, 1956.

can Report to Ike. Stevenson commenced on a high tone; he left off his ranting attacks of the preceding two weeks, and delivered an eloquent evocation of America, the American people, and the Democratic party. Democratic speakers in cities throughout the nation spoke to the select issues of the campaign, ending with a speech from Kefauver in Washington. Then Stevenson completed the oratory.

Kefauver's task was first to display his family, and then to show the Democrats as favoring social welfare, and the Republicans—including the President—as opposed to programs guaranteeing it. He asked his listeners, when voting, to choose the party best for family and children. He turned the microphone back to Stevenson with a jolly reference to Stevenson's new grandson, wishing the nation "good night from all the Kefauvers."[19]

In front of the television cameras again, Stevenson concluded his remarks. They stayed on a high level comparatively speaking, even at the point where he told the country that the real choice was not Eisenhower but Nixon.

> . . . Every piece of scientific evidence we have, every lesson of history and experience, indicates that a Republican victory tomorrow would mean that Richard Nixon would probably be President of this country within the next four years.
> I say frankly, as a citizen more than a candidate, that I recoil at the prospect of Mr. Nixon as custodian of this nation's future, as guardian of the hydrogen bomb, as representative of America in the world, as Commander in Chief of the United States armed forces.
> Distasteful as it is this is the truth, the simple truth, about the most fateful decision the American people have to make tomorrow.
> I have full confidence in that decision.[20]

A final flight into the perspectives of the New America; a quotation from church liturgy; and the candidate was done.

But not his running mate. For the next day saw Kefauver in Miami for a final three hours of campaigning—in anticipation of 1960?—before he went off to Chattanooga to vote and then to Washington, D.C., to await the voters' verdict.

The Republicans ended their campaign in Boston, too. They

[19] *Ibid.*
[20] *Ibid.*

had planned another full-scale, set-piece Report to Ike and Dick, but curtailed it sharply to permit the President to watch over the cables and wield the reins of power from Washington. Eisenhower did speak to the Boston rally over a closed-circuit television hookup, and a Boston station broadcast it; he missed no political tricks. He said the many recent crises had tested the nation's firm devotion to its principles; he hoped Hungary could accept $20 million worth of aid; he rejoiced over the release of Roman Catholic cardinals from captivity in Hungary and Poland; he underlined Republican determination to seek a peace "that all the world may participate in." On the domestic front, he asked for Republican victories so his party would have more time to build desperately needed schools, to aid distressed industrial areas, to build more highways and airports, and to revise immigration laws. He pleaded for a Massachusetts Republican victory in the governorship race, and finally urged all voters to use their franchise, whether to vote for his party or not.[21]

The rest of the Republican rally was confident but anticlimactic. Party workers cheered Nixon as Leonard Hall corrected himself after calling Nixon the "President." Nixon said the country in choosing a commander in chief couldn't risk a man who would play politics with the H-bomb and the draft. Dewey took the same line.[22] Meanwhile James Hagerty denounced rumors (called non-existent by Paul Butler) that the President had been ill during the past few days and went on to slash at Stevenson's unprecedented closing argument that voters should not vote for the Republican candidate since he was sure to die in office.[23]

Thus the campaign drew to a close on a curious juxtaposition—of Stevenson charges (made in the Chicago Stadium on the night of November 3) that President Eisenhower "lacks the energy for full-time work" in a critical period of national history, against the obvious activity of the President in mobilizing his government and free-world opinion to check-rein hostilities in the Middle East and

---

[21] *Washington Post and Times Herald,* Nov. 6, 1956.

[22] Kefauver, in a companion piece, dwelt on domestic matters, but nevertheless accepted the bomb-testing charge. *Ibid.*

[23] *Ibid.*

to find a formula for freedom in Eastern Europe. The Stevenson charges, although on page one of most metropolitan papers, had to compete in attention and weight with headlines announcing that the United States "Presents Plans for Palestine Peace and Suez Accord Through New U.N. Groups; Eisenhower Bids Bulganin Recall Troops." The President had correctly canceled his proposed trip to Boston for an election-eve television show. Stevenson and Kefauver—with nothing better to do—kept their radio-television date with their final political rendezvous.

During these last days Stevenson was getting better crowds and good immediate response from them—his Chicago motorcade audience was estimated at 250,000; but it was not apparent that this improvement in immediate attention was going to elect him. Even James Finnegan kept the usual victory predictions of a political manager at modest levels.[24] The Democratic high command said the results could hinge on the outcome in California, Massachusetts, and Pennsylvania—and a loss in any one would mean a national defeat.[25]

The Gallup Poll reported on November 5 findings based on interviews made between October 30 and November 2. The estimated division of the major party vote was 59.5 per cent for Eisenhower and Nixon, 40.5 per cent for Stevenson and Kefauver. Including third-party preferences and undecideds, the figures showed Republicans leading with 57 per cent, the Democrats trailing with 39 per cent, Andrews-Werdel and other splinter groups, 1 per cent, and the remaining 3 per cent undecided.[26]

As the campaign closed, key economic indicators showed that the Republicans were home safe with their prosperity issue. On November 1 the New York stock market snapped back from its

[24] As reported by Harrison Salisbury, practical Democratic politicians (including Finnegan) felt that the public was being swept by so many powerful forces that earlier poll data might be misleading, but they were unwilling to claim that the voters were now ready to elect Mr. Stevenson. Democratic political professionals had not given up hope of an upset victory to be achieved through victory in the solid South, in the border states and in a few critical states in North or West (Pennsylvania, California, and Minnesota plus one or two smaller ones such as Rhode Island). *New York Times*, Nov. 4, 1956.

[25] *Washington Post and Times Herald,* Nov. 6, 1956.

[26] *Ibid.,* Nov. 5, 1956.

losses following the Franco-British-Israeli invasion. Oils, steels, shipbuilding, metals, and defense issues led rises of one to four points, as an over-all gain of $3.2 billion offset the previous day's decline of some $2.8 billion.[27] In agricultural prices, both war-scare buying and a variety of other factors combined to shore up markets in the last few days before election. Unemployment was trending down in the nation as a whole.

Weather was good, and voter turnout was expected to be high. The chairmen of both parties welcomed a large vote, as each claimed victory for his own side. Leonard Hall predicted that if the voters got out to vote, the Republicans would have a land-slide "at least as great as in 1952."[28] Paul Butler predicted "an across-the-boards Democratic victory," in view of the probable political impact of political events abroad that had "shown the failures of the Eisenhower-Nixon dead-end diplomacy." He as-serted there had been a strong pro-Democratic trend during the last week that had been missed by the professional poll-takers.[29]

Both parties made muffled noises about dirty rumors and unfair practices. Party Chairman Leonard Hall uttered the traditional last-minute cry of "Foul" from party headquarters.[30] The Demo-crats pointed to scurrilous literature attacking their candidates in Oklahoma and North Dakota—but these were the only instances brought to the attention of Senator Gore's subcommittee.[31] The Fair Campaign Practices Committee Inc. later reported that nearly all smears were local or regional in origin and effect.[32]

Their work done, their arguments made, the candidates and their supporters rested. The event was now in the hands of the electorate.

[27] *New York Herald Tribune,* Nov. 2, 1956.

[28] *New York Times,* Nov. 6, 1956.

[29] *Ibid.*

[30] Hall released telegrams to forty-eight State headquarters, warning them that the Democrats were putting out "a flood of scurrilous last-minute opposition litera-ture across the nation plus an all-out opposition ward and precinct leader drive in an attempt to pull a blitz." *Ibid.,* Nov. 5, 1956.

[31] Senate Committee on Rules and Administration, *1956 General Election Cam-paigns,* 84 Cong. 1 sess., Committee Print, p. 19.

[32] Fair Campaign Practices Committee Inc., *The State-by-State Smear Study* (1958 mimeo.), p. 1.

Election Day

On Tuesday, November 6, the voters went to the polls. Television, radio, and the press kept a noisy watch through the night. Candidates, friends, and supporters figured both as viewers and as subjects as the electronic media totaled the incoming returns, peppering the swelling figures with political commentary and periodic interviews with available notables.

On Wednesday morning, shortly after 1 A.M., Eastern Standard Time, Adlai Stevenson conceded. At that time the President held a commanding lead in states totaling 367 electoral votes, with Stevenson ahead in states counting 104. Stevenson withheld comment at the moment, awaiting fuller returns from the Pacific Coast. In his suite at the Sheraton Blackstone Hotel in Chicago—scene of his smashing nomination victory not three months before—the defeated candidate relaxed with advisers who had already conceded the fact of election, and took heart from the victories over Republican stalwarts in Pennsylvania, Ohio, Oregon, and elsewhere in the senatorial, congressional, and governorship races.

The President, arriving mid-evening at Washington's Sheraton Park Hotel, came into a jubilant atmosphere, undamped by the apparent Republican failure to recapture Congress. Leonard Hall had claimed victory just after 10 P.M., although he still did not foresee a margin greater than 1952. Nixon, even more reticent after his gruelling 35,000 mile campaign trip, would say only that "there was a tide running."[33] Eisenhower, who had privately predicted a victory by more than 400 electoral votes, took the event with characteristic humility—and struck a blow for reshaping his party more nearly to his liking. In his victory statement, made on television at 1:50 A.M., the President said:

> This is a solemn moment. The only thing I should like to say about the campaign is this: It is a very heartwarming experience to know that your labors—your efforts—of four years have achieved that level where they are approved by the United States of America in a vote.

[33] *New York Times,* Nov. 7, 1956.

Such a vote as that cannot be merely for an individual. It is for principles and ideals for which that individual and his associates have stood and have tried to exemplify.

To all the people of the United States who have understood what the Administration—the Republican Party—has been trying to do in these past four years, and consequently have worked so hard for the re-election of the Administration, my most grateful thanks.

. . . .

And now let me say something that looks to the future: I think that modern Republicanism has now proved itself. And America has approved of modern Republicanism.

. . . Let us remember that a political party deserves the approbation of America only as it represents the ideals, the aspirations and the hopes of Americans. If that is anything less, it is merely a conspiracy to seize power. And the Republican Party is not that!

Modern Republicanism looks to the future. Which means it looks to that area—that time—in which our young are most interested. And this means that it will gain constantly new recruits from the youngest of our voters. And as such, as long as it remains true to the ideals and the aspirations of America, it will continue to increase in power and influence for decades to come. It will point the way to peace among nations, and to prosperity—advancing standards here at home in which everybody will share, regardless of any accident of power, of station, of race, religion, or color.

And if we cling to these ideals, if we uphold them, if we fight for them, then I say: Republicans deserve, then, the vote of confidence that Republicans, friendly Democrats, and Independents have given us this day.

He concluded with a pledge, for himself and his associates, to work unceasingly for the interests of 168 million Americans.[34]

Adlai Stevenson, to whom control of his party may have seemed less important on November 7 than in the months previous, told the President in his telegram conceding the race:

You have won not only the election but also an expression of the great confidence of the American people. I send you my warm congratulations.' Tonight we are not Republicans and Democrats, but Americans. We appreciate the grave difficulties your Administration faces, and, as Americans, join in wishing you all success in the years that lie ahead.[35]

[34] *Washington Post and Times Herald,* Nov. 7, 1956.
[35] *Ibid.*

To his partisans and to the country, he sounded a note of cheer and of personal reward. He asked God's blessing on partisanship, as democracy's life's blood. He reminded his supporters, including the "gallant Estes," that the right to political contest was more important than political victory. He said that during the campaign he had tried to "chart the road to a new and better America," and felt that the cause would triumph, because "America can only go forward." In his only acid touch, he hoped that "our leaders will recognize that America wants to face up squarely to the facts of today's world." Ending, he said: "A merry heart doeth good like a medicine, but a broken spirit drieth the bones. Although I lost the election, I won a grandson."[36]

Kefauver said nothing of importance. Nixon kept his counsel, but was authoritatively reported to have spent much time on Wednesday telephoning Republican party officials throughout the nation, discussing the meaning of the election for the future of the Republican party. He was not surprised that the Republicans had not recaptured the Congress; it was reported he had never given that prospect better than a fifty-fifty chance. But he was concerned to consolidate his own position with the Republican organization—a position carefully firmed up during the intensive campaigning of the weeks just past.

Stevenson forces, surveying the debacle, insisted that the election had been a "horse race" until the deterioration in the international situation. Said his Press Secretary Clayton Fritchey:

> The Administration's own failures in foreign policy, by an ironic twist, turned out to their advantage.
> The crisis alarmed the country and the election took place before people could understand its real meaning. We are convinced that this had a direct influence on the outcome of the election. Support for Mr. Eisenhower jumped from four to seven per cent in the national polls after the Israeli invaded Egypt.[37]

Labor leaders immediately saw that labor had failed to produce a decisive margin for Stevenson. They took comfort in the con-

[36] *Ibid.*
[37] *Ibid.*, Nov. 8, 1956. In this article, Russell Nixon said that Stevenson shared this view, thinking that the country was frightened and concluded it could not afford to change administrations in crisis.

gressional results and brushed off their loss of the Presidency as a personal victory for Eisenhower, but a loss for the Republican party. George Meany, President of AFL-CIO, voiced the official line for most of labor—reaffirming faith in the policy of backing "liberal, progressive candidates" and conducting vigorous political education for labor and its friends. For labor and its friends to have kept the Congress in the face of the President's majorities was little less, he said, than a political "miracle." He gave credit for the miracle to COPE. Labor interpreted the gulf between the presidential and the congressional votes to be a "mandate" for liberal domestic and international policies. Secretary of Labor James P. Mitchell, replying for the Republicans, said that the Eisenhower vote should "dispel forever the myth that the Democratic party is the party of labor."[38]

Newspapers across the country, whether for Eisenhower, for Stevenson or independent, moved to fix the election's meaning and consequences by their comment on the race and the result. With near-unanimity they perceived the outcome as a personal victory for Eisenhower. Pro-Stevenson papers pointed out that the electoral candidate preference did not necessarily extend to Mr. Nixon—although the New York *Journal-American* and the Portland *Oregonian* said it did. The pro-Stevenson papers, and some of the Eisenhower backers, noted that the vote was something less than a mandate for the Republican party. The *Atlanta Journal* questioned whether the vote meant approval of Modern Republicanism—if one took into account the outcome of the House and the Senate races. But most editorials interpreted the results as a preference for the moderate Eisenhower policies, as well as a choice between particular party standard-bearers. The *Milwaukee Journal* (Independent for Stevenson) said that the issues remained what Stevenson said they were; and "the need for vigorous, courageous, imaginative and full-time leadership has seldom been greater in our history." The *Denver Post* (Independent for Eisenhower) agreed that Eisenhower's triumph stood as a challenge to his party, and raised "the profound question of whether the Republican party as such is identifiable with the public interest. The

[38] *New York Times,* Nov. 8, 1956.

next four years provide an opportunity for Mr. Eisenhower to complete the job he tentatively started in 1953—that of infusing his party with principles, and leading it in actions that the American people feel are for the many and not just for the few."

In the Far West the *San Francisco Chronicle* summed matters thus:

> Eisenhower's concept and definition of Republicanism embody what the country desires, and those who were with Eisenhower only for the ride on his coattails have misgauged the most potent political force of this generation. A world crisis demands of the President and his Administration a new grasp of affairs.[39]

Political commentators and journalists used available returns to underscore the regional bases of the Eisenhower victory, pointing to his increased strength in the East and the South; to the failure of a farm "revolt" to throw any states to the Democrats; and to the somewhat reduced margins in California and the Pacific Northwest. They noticed Eisenhower gains among Negroes and among labor. And above all, they emphasized the ticket-splitting that came into evidence throughout the country. Walter Lippmann summarized the campaign thus:

> The campaign has been clean and decent, but not enlightening or interesting. It takes two to bring on a debate, and the President refused to be provoked into debating anything. Since there was a great contented majority behind him, he did not have to admit that there was any issue to debate. . . .
> . . . The correspondents, the commentators, and the pollsters have been essentially right in distinguishing between Eisenhower and his party. He has had an enormous vote of confidence. The Republican Party has not had one.[40]

[39] *Ibid.*
[40] *New York Herald Tribune,* Nov. 8, 1956.

13

Money and Media

POLITICAL CAMPAIGNS ARE COSTLY. So is the use of communications media. In 1956, as in previous presidential campaigns, communications media cost more than any other single class of objects for which campaigners spent money. And in 1956, as in previous presidential campaigns, the costliness of campaigning and the allegedly greater advantage possessed by Republicans over Democrats because of the former's more generous sources of funds, came into the argument of the campaign, if they did not determine its outcome.

A feature of the 1956 experience was the work of the Senate Subcommittee on Privileges and Elections dealing with campaign expenditures not after the fact, but while money was being collected and spent. On September 1, Senator Albert Gore, chairman of the subcommittee, announced his group would conduct a thorough scrutiny of election spending.

An immediate goal was to gather information pertinent to revising the inept and ineffective statutes controlling campaign spending. Another was "honest public reporting" of election finances and practices, while the voter still could decide. Gore's announced long-term goal was to "free federal elections from private subsidy." A highly plausible although unstated goal of the Democrats on the subcommittee was to demonstrate during the campaign itself the superior financial strength of the Republicans and to link the sources of giving with the interests allied with parties and candidates.

The Gore Committee held important public hearings on September 10 and 11, and on October 8, 9, and 10. The Democratic majority issued an "interim report" on November 4, while the Republican minority issued a parallel comment. The subcommittee issued also as a committee print an extensive analysis of campaign giving and spending that was never put into final form, but that stands as the single most comprehensive source of information about these matters in 1956. These moves are detailed below; they provide background to consideration of the performance of media.

The Senate Hearings

On September 10, Senator Gore opened a series of remarkable hearings—remarkable for the wealth of information they produced from a long list of knowledgeable witnesses. The hearings not only covered current estimates of who was giving, to whom, and how much, but explored in considerable depth the intricacies of campaign finance as they related to the use of television and radio.[1] The first hearings featured statements by the two party chairmen. Paul Butler demanded better control of campaign spending, so as to make impossible the control of elections merely through expenditures of money. He predicted the Democrats would not spend as much money as the Republicans, since they could not raise as much.

He also demanded free radio and television time for major party candidates. Leonard Hall opposed the free-time request on the ground that such subsidy by the electronic media might start a chain reaction that would destroy the two-party system. He revealed that the Republicans had nearly twenty times as much money in the bank as the Democrats ($646,625.22 to $35,655.54), but were trying hard to broaden the basis of their financial support.[2]

Professor Alexander Heard of the University of North Carolina had put total campaign spending at all levels in 1952 at $140 mil-

[1] *1956 Presidential and Senatorial Campaign Contributions and Practices,* Hearings Before the Senate Committee on Rules and Administration, 84 Cong. 2 sess., Pt. 1, Sept. 10 and 11, 1956 and Pt. 2, Oct. 8, 9, and 10, 1956 (1956). (Hereinafter cited as *1956 Practices.*) See also Charles A. H. Thomson, *Television, Politics, and Public Policy,* Reprint No. 25, The Brookings Institution (May 1958), pp. 371-73.

[2] *1956 Practices,* pp. 12-38, especially pp. 15, 27.

lions, and estimated this figure would rise to some $175 millions in the current campaign. He also estimated that there were from 8,000 to 10,000 organizations in the country that would be playing a relevant role in the general election campaign.[3]

The Interim Report

For whatever it might be worth to voters making up their minds in the last moments before the election, the Senate Subcommittee on Privileges and Elections issued, on November 4, an "interim staff report" dealing with its findings from two surveys, ending October 21, concerning campaign finance. As summarized in the press, the report showed that Republicans had received contributions totaling $10,000,000 while the Democrats had received but $3,700,000.[4] The committee reported contributions to labor organizations for political purposes totaling $535,000. It also reported Republican spending between January 1 and October 21 (less unreported amounts expended at county and local levels) of $7,750,000 and Democratic spending (similarly understated) of $3,887,000. It put labor-group outlays at $1,454,000, with the largest single item of $247,000 through COPE.[5]

It noted diminutions in planned spending by both parties for radio and television, and reductions in gifts from Rockefellers to Republicans. It underlined Republican "ready resources" of cash on hand near October's end of $3,678,000, compared to the Democrats' $1,091,000, suggesting that this advantage in cash position might have some corresponding advantages in campaigning. The committee emphasized its opinion that existing campaign contribution control laws were woefully inadequate.[6]

[3] *Ibid.*, pp. 76-77, 79. His discussion of the funds and motivation of campaign spending, including the role of "access" and the need for full governmental support for the campaigning process follows in the hearings.
[4] *Washington Post and Times Herald*, Nov. 5, 1956. We cite the press summaries here, as they were the visible carrier of the report's main conclusions to the voter.
[5] *Ibid.*
[6] *New York Times*, Nov. 5, 1956. The interim report showed not only that "big

Senator Gore released the report with no partisan comment, confident that the figures told an eloquent story. Even though they were of little significance in the spectrum of forces playing on the voter, Republican subcommittee member Senator Carl T. Curtis of Nebraska let out a counterblast that got little or no press attention. Said he: "I have never served on a committee which has manifested a more partisan attitude. The alleged report is full of distortions, exaggerations and is generally misleading. It is slanted for political purposes and is issued in an attempt to influence votes."[7]

In a final release for Tuesday papers, the Gore Committee upped its estimates of party receipts and spending, crediting the Republicans with contributions totaling $10,531,000, the Democrats with $3,872,000, and labor with $577,000. Total spending reflected by last-minute reports amounted to $5,985,000 by Republicans, $3,146,000 by Democrats, and $233,000 by labor groups.[8]

Presidential Campaign Spending, 1956

There is no adequate set of figures setting forth the amount of money spent for campaigning for the offices of President and Vice President in 1956. Nor in the nature of things could there be. Re-

---

business" had contributed more heavily to Republicans than to Democrats, but that the administration had received its largest support through contributions by independent groups. Some large contributors hedged their bets by giving to both sides, although the balance was usually heavily weighted in favor of the Republicans. The reported spending in behalf of Douglas McKay in Oregon was $142,290 —more than half of the total spent by "Republicans" (unclearly identified in the *Washington Post and Times Herald* account) for Senate races amounting to $316,000 of $579,000 received. The Democrats also unidentified, but presumably, as with the Republicans, meaning the Senatorial Campaign Committee, received $3,750 for Morse's campaign and spent $3,499. *Washington Post and Times Herald*, Nov. 5, 1956.

[7] Republican National Committee, Press Release, Nov. 4, 1956.

[8] *Washington Post and Times Herald,* Nov. 6, 1956. The Gore committee said the Republicans had $3,810,000 in cash on hand, the Democrats $1,144,000 and labor groups $556,000. They explained the discrepancy between these cash-on-hand figures and the preceding income-outgo figures by pointing out that the former did not reflect transfers to congressional committees, and that some political organizations do not keep balanced books!

ports of campaign spending required to be filed with the Clerk of the House of Representatives do not provide it, since expenditures of reporting units cover other races as well—and not all political units are covered. The Senate Subcommittee on Privileges and Elections did not try to make such a precise estimate. Had they tried to do so, they would have faced insoluble problems of joint cost allocation—because committees usually campaign for more than one candidate.[9]

Yet some idea of the relative magnitudes of spending for the presidential and vice-presidential offices in 1956 can be gleaned from considering the information and commentary provided by the report of the Gore committee concerning general election expenditures in 1956.[10] This report underlined the Republican edge in total funds and in support from the wealthy and the business community, as well as the near-unanimous support in funds and man power afforded the Democrats by organized labor. It dealt mostly with expenditure figures rather than with figures purportedly describing receipts and disbursements—for the very good reason that campaign finance laws and restrictions foster the proliferation of party committees and the channeling of funds from one unit to another, with each transfer of funds being counted as a receipt and a disbursement.

The unduplicated expenditure by all parties for general election purposes (not for primary or nomination campaigns) in 1956 (from Jan. 1 to Nov. 30) was put by the majority report at $33.2 million, distributed as follows:

Republican	$20,685,387
Democratic	10,977,790
Labor	941,271
Miscellaneous	581,277

Senator Curtis, in his minority views, attacked the total figures as a gross understatement of the relative contribution of labor, because the totals omitted funds spent for political "education" and

[9] See the discussion in V. O. Key, *Politics, Parties, and Pressure Groups* (4th ed., 1958), pp. 533 ff.

[10] *1956 General Election Campaigns*, Report of the Senate Committee on Rules and Administration, with tabulations and analyses on contributions and expenditures. Committee Print, 85 Cong. 1 sess. (1957). Hereinafter cited as *Gore Report*.

did not estimate in money terms labor's contribution in man power, special services, and other electioneering activities.[11] But he did not attempt to set a value on them himself. Both majority and minority agreed that the figure of $33.2 million understated total spending, because of the Gore staff's inability to get in touch with all spending units, not to mention haphazard and incomplete bookkeeping and reporting, and varying definitions of political expenditures on the part of those committees and persons who did make information available. No one seriously challenged Heard's earlier global estimate that $175 million would be spent for all 1956 races.

Some idea of the relative spending for national office purposes by the two major parties, by labor, and by miscellaneous groups[12] arises from the following comparative figures of disbursements by national level committees covering the period September 1-November 30, 1956:[13]

	Direct Expenditures	Total Expenditures
Republican	$4,396,730	$ 4,963,303
Democratic	4,523,001	4,908,912
Labor	407,350	1,331,993
Miscellaneous	260,060	327,705
Total	$9,587,141	$11,531,913

Objects of Expenditure

In 1956, as in previous campaign years, the most salient single object of campaign spending was for publicity. Specific publicity

[11] *Ibid.,* pp. 25-27.
[12] The *Gore Report* (p. 44) included under this heading the National Committee for an Effective Congress, the Christian Nationalist Crusade, the National Association of Pro America, Americans for Democratic Action, A Clean Politics Appeal, Good Government National Committee, the No Tax No War Committee, the Socialist Labor Party of America, For America, The Club, and the National Committee for T. Coleman Andrews and Thomas H. Werdel. During the eleven-month period to November 30, these groups disbursed a total of $677,200, $97,200 of it to other organizations and candidates, and the balance for direct expenditures.
[13] *Ibid.,* pp. 39-40, Tables B and E. The total figures include disbursements to other spending units. The direct expenditures give the unduplicated total of spend-

outlays by the main party committees and by labor at all levels outweighed other items of spending, as shown in the table below.[14]

	Media	Other Objects
Republicans	$ 7,838,690	$ 7,396,546
Democrats	5,642,713	4,430,770
Labor	458,870	349,016
Miscellaneous	145,794	115,672
Total	$14,086,067	$12,292,004

Both parties relied on electronic media more than in any previous campaign, at the relative expense of newspaper advertising, outdoor advertising, and printing, publication, and distribution of party literature, not to mention costs for buttons, badges, and other gadgets lumped with other forms of political communication into general administrative costs. Labor devoted a good share to radio and television, but unlike the parties, spent slightly more for printing, publication, and distribution of literature.

Television supplanted radio, the leader in 1952, as the most important single object of publicity spending. Outlays for newspaper advertising and billboards remained sizable, but only at the state and local levels.

The tables on pages 329-30 summarize spending during the campaign proper by object and by level of party organization.

---

ing by national-level agencies. The table on National Agencies (Table B) presumably includes the national committees and the congressional committees, plus any other unspecified committees operating at the national level except the senatorial committees, covered in Table E. See table p. 330 below.

[14] The *Gore Report*, p. 6, laconically identified these "other" items as "travel, maintenance of headquarters, salary and other overhead items and election-day expenses."

The table is extracted from Exhibit 2, Table A, p. 39, *Gore Report*. These figures understate the difference between spending for publicity and for other objects, because the "other" category includes expenditures partly or wholly in support of mass political communications, such as salaries of press divisions, provision of press releases, press services, and other special services in support of the publicity function—as well as omitting any allocation of costs of central management and similar general services. By the same token, they form an inadequate index of reliance on media, since the probable main impact of newspapers on political opinion comes more from news and editorials than from paid advertising, and the news columns, happily, are not for sale in America on a wide scale.

With this qualification, detail on spending for the media provides some indication of the relative emphasis given to each by the parties, and the balance of emphasis between the parties. Inspection of the breakdown between spending at the national, state, and local levels gives useful information about the relative emphasis put on the several media at those levels.

REPUBLICAN, DEMOCRATIC, AND LABOR SPENDING FOR PUBLICITY AND
OTHER OBJECTS, SEPTEMBER 1-NOVEMBER 30, 1956[a]

	Republican	Democratic	Labor	Total
TV				
National	$1,508,091	$1,681,947	$ 53,463	$3,243,501
State	1,227,743	446,082	27,046	1,700,871
Local	270,578	164,199	8,912	443,689
Total	$3,006,412	$2,292,228	$ 89,421	$5,388,061
RADIO				
National	$ 134,520	$ 320,497	$ 28,369	$ 483,386
State	635,027	180,682	5,796	821,505
Local	107,683	58,800	7,441	173,924
Total	$ 877,230	$ 559,979	$ 41,606	$1,478,815
COMBINED RADIO/TV				
National	$1,642,611	$2,002,444	$ 81,832	$3,726,887
State	1,862,770	626,764	33,842[b]	2,523,376[b]
Local	378,261	222,999	24,254[c]	625,514[c]
Total	$3,883,642	$2,852,207	$139,928	$6,875,777
NEWSPAPER AND PERIODICAL ADVERTISING				
National	$ 231,774	$ 263,714	$ 12,944	$ 508,432
State	751,843	234,907	17,569	1,004,319
Local	390,327	196,302	17,561	614,190
Total	$1,373,944	$ 694,923	$ 48,074	$2,116,941
PRINTING, PURCHASE OF LITERATURE				
National	$ 507,421	$ 861,720	$106,952	$1,476,093
State	842,028	602,362	57,334	1,501,724
Local	837,750	435,995	82,200	1,355,944
Total	$2,187,199	$1,900,076	$246,486	$4,333,761
OUTDOOR BILLBOARDS				
National	$ 49,179	$ 69,452	$ 12,385	$ 131,016
State	219,812	65,345	2,471	287,628
Local	124,914	60,710	9,526	195,150
Total	$ 393,905	$ 195,507	$ 24,382	$ 613,794
Total All Media ..	$7,838,690	$5,642,713	$458,870	$13,940,273
OTHER OBJECTS				
National	$1,965,745	$1,325,671[d]	$193,237	$3,484,653[d]
State	3,307,274[e]	1,605,914[f]	50,340	4,963,528[e,f]
Local	2,123,527[g]	1,499,185	105,439	3,728,151[g]
Total	$7,396,546	$4,430,770	$349,016	$12,176,332
Grand Total	$15,235,236	$10,073,483	$807,886	$26,116,605

[a] Data from *1956 General Election Campaigns,* Report of the Senate Committee on Rules and Administration, 85 Cong. 1 Sess. (1957), Committee Print, pp. 39-40.
[b] Includes $1,000 Radio/TV inseparable.
[c] Includes $7,901 Radio/TV inseparable.
[d] Includes $1,581 unaccounted for.
[e] Includes $61,573 unaccounted for.
[f] Includes $10 unaccounted for.
[g] Includes $2 unaccounted for.

DIRECT EXPENDITURES, NATIONAL LEVEL, SEPTEMBER 1-NOVEMBER 30, 1956[a]

Object	Republicans	Democrats	Labor	Total
TV	$1,508,091	$1,681,947	$ 53,463	$3,243,501
Radio	134,520	320,497	28,369	483,386
TV/Radio Total	$1,642,611	$2,002,444	$ 81,832	$3,726,887
News & Periodical Advertising	$ 231,774	$ 263,714	$ 12,944	$ 508,432
Printing, Purchasing and Distribution of Literature	507,421	861,720	106,952	1,476,093
Outdoor Billboards	49,179	69,452	12,385	131,016
Total All Media	$2,430,985	$3,197,330	$214,113	$5,842,428
All Other Objects	$1,965,745	$1,325,671[b]	$193,237	$3,484,653[b]
Total Direct Expenditures	$4,396,730	$4,523,001	$407,350	$9,327,081

[a] Derived from *1956 General Election Campaigns,* Report of the Senate Committee on Rules and Administration, 85 Cong. 1 sess. (1957), Committee Print, pp. 39, 40. (This combines "Senatorial Campaign Committees" with National Campaign Committees.)
[b] Includes $1,581 unaccounted for.

These tables show that at the level of national committees (including the senate and congressional campaign committees) the Democrats spent a little more than the Republicans in toto, although the Republicans spent more for "other objects." Media made the difference, as the Democrats outspent the Republicans both for radio and for television. Republican state units, however, outspent their competitors by three to one for radio and television. At the local level, the Republican predominance was less marked.

Neither party spent relatively much for newspaper and periodical advertising, concentrating such disbursements mainly at the state level and to a lesser degree at local levels. Here again the Democrats outspent their opponents at the national level; but the Republicans outspent them three to one at the state level and nearly two to one locally.

In the leaflet and pamphlet department (printing, purchase, and distribution of literature) the Democrats also outspent the Republicans at the national level, nearly two to one. Again the Republicans concentrated more heavily on the state and local levels, increasing their outlays while Democrats decreased theirs, resulting in a Republican edge of three to two.

Neither party spent much for billboards nationally—less than $50,000 by the Republicans and some $82,000 by the Democrats.

Both parties spent more at other levels, with Republicans more than doubling the Democrats' spending.

As for "other" expenditures—the heart of party organization support—the Republicans spent three dollars to the Democrats' two, and at state and local levels the gap widened to a ratio of nearly two to one.

The above figures relate to the campaign period proper, and they do not reveal an important advantage possessed (and pressed) by the Republicans that is suggested by the spending pattern for the eleven months from January through November of 1956. During the preparatory phase prior to September 1, the Republicans smartly outspent their opponents. The comparison is of interest:[15]

Period	Republican	Democratic	Labor	Miscellaneous	Total
Jan. 1-Aug. 31	$2,013,219	$ 813,385	$133,385	$319,811	$ 3,279,800
Sept. 1-Nov. 30	3,381,977	3,250,985	407,350	260,060	7,300,372
Total	$5,395,196	$4,064,370	$540,735	$579,871	$10,580,172

In sum, there was basis in 1956 as in other years for the Democratic outcry against superior Republican financial resources. The Republicans took in more money, spent more money, and better sustained their total electoral operations, when all races are considered. But the Democrats were not far behind at the national level, and in combination with their aid from labor, exceeded the Republican national total. It could not be said that the Democrats lacked substantial financial power, alone or in coalition. In contrast with the two major coalitions, the "miscellaneous" aggregation—including the minor parties as well as the Americans for Democratic Action—disposed of about 1 per cent of all political general election expenditures in 1956.[16]

Who Gave and When?

Students of party finance examine not only the totals of receipts and expenditures; they are also deeply interested in the questions

[15] *Gore Report*, Exhibit 1, p. 38. These exclude congressional and some senatorial expenditures. They are termed "other national" outlays, in distinction from "congressional" and do not include late-reported Republican "special cases" totaling $1.2 million or Democratic "special cases" of $50,000.

[16] *Ibid.*, p. 39, Table A. Since the *Gore Report* shows practically all spending by

of where the money came from; whether in big gifts or little; and from what classes of persons or interests in society. The *Gore Report*, despite the inherent biases found in the categories of analysis selected, nevertheless throws light on these points.

The vast preponderance of gifts in the amount of $500 and more went to the Republicans ($8.1 million out of a total of $10.9 million reported), and the Republicans received better than 90 per cent of such gifts originating from officers or directors of the 225 largest corporations, the 29 largest oil companies, the 10 leading radio and television stations, and 47 underwriters of bonds. All such gifts originating from officers of 37 advertising agencies went to the Republicans. And the figure of 80.7 per cent originating from officials of 17 certified airlines (lowest Republican proportion of all in these special categories) was due to the fact that Mr. R. J. Reynolds, a director of Delta airlines, gave $24,609 to the Democrats.[17]

In the field of gifts in the amount of $5,000 or more, the Republicans held their advantage, but it was not nearly so marked: they received $2,894,000 in such units, while the Democrats got $860,380 and "miscellaneous" received $55,000.[18]

Top donor turned up by the Senate Subcommittee was Lansdell K. Christie of New York City. He gave $73,164; $70,564 went to the Democrats, and the balance to a "miscellaneous" committee. Mrs. Charles S. (Joan Whitney) Payson gave $65,050 to the Republicans.[19] These figures, while substantial, fell far below the gifts of Thomas Fortune Ryan and August Belmont, who together picked up a tab for a $900,000 deficit incurred by the Democrats in 1904.[20]

In 1956 individual big givers, and givers in amounts of $500 or more provided a lower proportion of total gifts than in earlier years. The Democrats appeared again as the party relying more heavily than the Republicans on the small givers—but also as a party receiving some rather large amounts, and looking to larger

---

miscellaneous groups at the national level, their relative spending at this level is about 3 per cent of total national level spending.

[17] See Key, *Politics, Parties, and Pressure Groups*, p. 543, for the reduction of Gore data to these percentages.

[18] *Gore Report*, p. 12.

[19] *Ibid.*

[20] See Key, *Politics, Parties, and Pressure Groups*, p. 545.

rather than smaller givers as the mainstay of their financial position.[21]

Survey Research Center data for the 1956 election show that the proportion of voters who gave anything at all to political parties was very small,[22] but higher than in 1952 when givers approximated 4 per cent of respondents, or a projected figure of 3 million voters.[23]

The 1956 campaign provided little or nothing new in the way of devices for extracting money from the electorate—with two exceptions. One was the very successful "Salute to Eisenhower" closed-circuit television broadcast, that took a net of some $5 million out of Republican supporters in time to enable the three main national party committees to plan their 1956 campaign—including radio and television outlays—with complete assurance of cash in hand for essential operations.[24]

[21] While Alexander Heard demonstrated in 1952 (see his *Money and Politics,* Public Affairs Pamphlet No. 242, 1956, pp. 12-13) that 68 per cent of the receipts of 18 national-level Republican committees and 63 per cent of 15 national-level Democratic committees came from gifts in amounts of $500 or more, the Gore figures suggest that for campaign contributions at all levels, the $500 or better givers played a proportionately smaller role in 1956.

Total direct expenditures of Republicans, Democrats, and labor for the general election in 1956 of $32,604,448 were about three times as large as total gifts of $10,885,562 in amounts of $500 or over. If the total of such gifts is compared with total receipts of $48,577,049, admittedly an inflated figure, the ratio goes down to nearly one to five. Even allowing for the probability that gifts to national committees come in larger amounts than those to state and local committees, it looks as if the preponderance of the larger giver was less marked in 1956. (See *Gore Report,* pp. 6, 7, 11.) The proportion of Democratic gifts of $500 or more to combined Democratic-Labor outlays was about one to four—$2.8 million from such gifts to outlays of $11.9 million. The value of gifts to a party is partly a function of timeliness—and a preponderance of small gifts coming during the campaign itself may be less vital than the bread-and-butter support of the longer-term, better organized activities of the party for which continued big giving provides the main underwriting.

[22] See Key, *Politics, Parties and Pressure Groups* (Thomas Y. Crowell Co., 1958), pp. 545n-46n, where the percentage proportions of those who gave anything, by occupational groups, was

professional	19	unskilled workers	7
business and managerial	18	farm operator	6
white collar	7	retired	6
skilled workers	8	housewife	6

By income groups, the proportion giving varied from 1 per cent of those in the $1,000 per annum group to 33 per cent in the $10,000 or over group.

[23] Heard, *Money and Politics,* p. 12.

[24] See Charles A. H. Thomson, *Television and Presidential Politics* (1956), pp. 160n-61n.

The other exception was the joint effort at getting gifts for the parties of one's choice sponsored by the American Heritage Foundation and other public and institutional advertising minded organizations. The total receipts from this operation were very small, owing to disagreements between the two national chairmen on a joint plan of action. But it represented an initiative that got somewhat more emphasis in 1958, and that seems to offer hopes of better public recognition of the legitimacy and worth of modest political contributions.[25]

The Democrats tied a Dollars for Democrats drive directly to the costliness of radio and television. Although the receipts were modest, party officials thought that widened interest and a sense of voter loyalty might have been as valuable as the resultant cash itself.[26]

The Republicans stressed joint finance committees, operating at the state level, that would centralize (in the United Givers fashion) demands on party givers for contributions to the party cause at all levels. These committees were usually headed by large givers, able to deal on a level of parity with other large donors. Their efforts in such key states as New York were of considerable importance. In the nationwide picture, their relative importance can be seen in the fact that they raised more money from contributions by individuals and by sale of tickets to fund-raising events (dinners, luncheons, and rallies) than did any of the other committees, regular or volunteer—and their receipts from such sources ran about six times those from other committees.[27]

The relative financial importance of volunteer committees to regular committees, and of labor to other political committees, can be sensed from the balance of reported spending.[28] From these

[25] See Stephen K. Bailey, *The Condition of Our National Political Parties* (1959), pp. 11-13, 22n for further comments.

[26] According to the Democratic National Committee, it is impossible to state an exact total because there were other simultaneous fund-raising drives. It is estimated that something between $100,000 and $150,000 was probably attributable to the Dollars for Democrats campaign.

[27] See *Gore Report*, pp. 40-41. The comparable ratio for the national committees was about three to one. See also *1956 Campaign Practices*, Pt. 1, pp. 38ff, for testimony of John Hay Whitney, Chairman, United Republican Finance Committee.

[28] *Gore Report*, p. 39. The notable point of the Republican finance committees concerns their role as fund-raisers for other spending units.

figures it appears that the financial contribution of volunteer committees was considerably more important in the Democratic party than in the Republican.

REPORTED DIRECT SPENDING AND DISBURSEMENTS,
SEPTEMBER 1-NOVEMBER 30, 1956[a]

Committee Affiliation	Direct Spending	Total Disbursements
Republican		
Regular	$10,312,293	$13,112,667
Finance	2,032,471	10,104,182
Volunteer	2,890,472	3,658,024
Democratic		
Regular	8,444,979	9,739,316
Volunteer	1,628,504	2,032,907
Labor	807,886	2,162,337

[a] *Gore Report*, p. 39.

Minor Party Expenditures

The Gore committee gives only minimal information concerning minor party expenditures. The only one appearing by name was the Socialist Labor Party of America, that reported receipts of $22,800 and expenditures of $42,500 during the period January 1-November 30, 1956.[29] The so-called Constitution Party was not so identified, but its candidates were supported by three reporting groups—the National Committee for T. Coleman Andrews and Thomas H. Werdel, the National Association of Pro America, and For America.[30]

[29] *Ibid.*, p. 44.

[30] For America was founded as a nonprofit educational association in 1954; on being denied status as a tax-exempt organization on grounds of its political activities, it "went political" and carried on a sustained campaign in behalf of the following objectives: to preserve the independence of the United States (pro-Bricker Amendment, anti-Atlantic Union and World government); to preserve the solvency of the United States (opposed to foreign aid, government spending, and the income tax); to gain peace with honor through strength (by primary dependence on air power supplemented by a modern Army and Navy); to uphold States Rights; and to oppose the "drift into Socialism." See testimony of Brig. Gen. Bonner Fellers (USA, ret.), in *1956 Practices*, Pt. 2, pp. 296-98. For America voted on August 27, 1956, to support Andrews and Werdel, as "independent" candidates for President and Vice President.

The National Committee for T. Coleman Andrews and Thomas H. Werdel received $33,000 and spent $35,000 between September 11 and November 14. The National Association of Pro America received and spent just under $6,000; For America received $81,000 (almost all from individuals) and spent $81,000 during the period January 1-November 30, 1956. Nearly half of the For America outlays went for literature; the rest (some $48,000) went for "other" expenditures—headquarters overhead, salaries, etc. The National Committee spent most of its money for printed literature, buying insignificant amounts of radio and television time and billboard space.[31]

The Socialist Labor Party and the Constitution Party together were overshadowed in campaign spending and electoral activities by Americans for Democratic Action, that received $183,000 and spent $180,000 during eleven months of 1956. The great bulk of their spending ($149,000) went for "other expenditures"; their largest media outlay went for the printing and publishing and distribution of literature (some $21,000) with about $9,500 going to other organizations and candidates.[32]

Media Presentation

From the preceding look at political expenditures, it is clear that the media of mass communication stood in the forefront of importance among campaign activities in 1956.

But there is more to media presentation than what can be bought and paid for—either for time and talent and film on television, for time and talent on radio, or for advertising space in the press. Far more important both for the immediate and the longer-term presentation of politics bulk the services offered both by the electronic media and by the printing press in the course of normal news and publishing operations. Both parties recognized this situation in 1956 as before with the establishment and opera-

[31] *Gore Report,* p. 44.
[32] *Ibid.*

tion of sizable press sections and publications operations. They relied in part on house organs, as the Democrats with their *Democratic Digest,* and the Republicans, with their *Straight from the Shoulder,* tried to meet the needs and tempt the interest of the partisan-oriented. But more important were their press services and the functioning of the press system itself, in shaping the presentation of candidate, party, and issue to the electorate.

Both parties issued a sustained blast of words that in 1956, at least, tried to speak to all aspects of the campaign all the time. The editors of the nation's press filtered it through their own system of preference before placing what they had chosen in news channels open to the public.

Unfortunately for an estimate of press performance as a whole, plans laid in 1955 to make a systematic survey of the balance of political reporting in 1956 were scotched by the apprehensions of the newspaper industry. It feared that the surveyors would judge balance by mathematical comparison that would not take into account established (and usually observed) canons of newsworthiness and public interest.

One study of the treatment of the 1956 election campaign in the daily press in Pennsylvania throws useful light on the shape given to electoral news by the press operating in a politically weighty state.[33] Its authors concluded: "Results of this study provide little support for charges of a one-party press. . . . The newspapers studied gave the Republicans more space, more picture space, and better headline display, but gave the Democrats better coverage of issues. With the exception of picture space, these differences were slight."[34]

They suggest that this difference might be due to the fact that the Democrats made more news about issues. Adlai Stevenson and

[33] James W. Markham and Guido H. Stempel, III, *Pennsylvania Daily Press Coverage of the 1956 Election Campaign,* A Measurement of Performance (August 1957).

[34] *Ibid.,* p. 16. The authors comment further that the differences between space and issue percentage were so systematic that they suggested a difference in the nature of the Democratic and Republican campaigns (p. 17). It could also be suggested that such systematic differences could arise from differing perceptions of the Democratic and Republican campaigns by editors—seeing the former as a campaign of issues, the latter one of personalities.

Estes Kefauver made more speeches than did Nixon, who made many more than did Eisenhower. And in Pennsylvania at least, Harry S. Truman made many more reported speeches than any third man on the Republican presidential side. Despite retrospective opinion that the Democratic campaign bogged down badly in its late phase, *news* coverage about it did not, but was maintained evenly to the end. "Thus," they say, "the Democrats at least had the opportunity to get their message to the voters during the period of the Suez crisis."[35]

Of value in interpreting the frequently made charge that most papers are pro-Republican, is this finding: "Content seemed unaffected by the party the paper supported. The 18 Eisenhower papers, 4 neutral papers, and 2 Stevenson papers differed only slightly on the variables mentioned."[36]

Of more topical interest are the indications of the shape the press actually gave to political communication and the deviations from original intentions by the principal campaigners. As seen in the Pennsylvania press, the campaigners tended to talk about the same things, whether or not they planned to at the outset. Although the Republicans planned their campaign output around peace, progress, and prosperity, they talked about defense issues nearly three times as much as about either of the others. And in the period after Eisenhower said he had said his "last word" on the bomb issue, he and other Republican campaigners talked more about defense than about all the other issues combined.

On balance, defense was the issue most frequently mentioned, getting 25 per cent of issue references in the papers studied. Foreign policy was second with nearly 11 per cent exclusive of the 4 per cent going to Suez. Third most frequently mentioned was the issue of candidate and party ethics; this, including political invective, totaled 9 per cent of the issue references. For the Republicans, the next issue in importance was "peace and prosperity"; for the Democrats, the "farm" issue. (Democratic references to the farm issue were made the more frequent by the near-exclusive

[35] *Ibid.*, p. 23.
[36] *Ibid.*, p. 31.

preoccupation of Kefauver with it—as reported in the press columns.)

Press references revealed that communism was a dead issue in 1956—as, surprisingly enough, was the "open convention" issue that appeared to be ignored by the Democrats in the campaign period after October 1.[37]

Another study of prominence in the press, this one based on a nationwide sample accounting for about 84 per cent of the net paid daily circulation in the United States (97 per cent of Sunday circulation), dealt with comparative headlines. Press Intelligence, Inc., analyzed all headlines appearing on the front pages of 650 daily and Sunday newspapers in the United States from September 11 to November 6, 1956, inclusive. This study measured the extent to which the four presidential and vice-presidential candidates were in the focus of public attention—insofar as headline mentions on the front pages of the nation's press could put them there. Percentages of total number of mentions in these headlines, summarized by weeks, showed that Eisenhower got 50 per cent of total attention, Stevenson 36 per cent, Nixon 9, and Kefauver 5.[38]

The Republican candidates, together, got 59 per cent of the headline mentions, and the Democrats 41 per cent. Eisenhower and Nixon started strong (with 55 per cent) and got stronger, failing to gain only in one week (October 16-22) while rising to 64 per cent the total in the last week. The Republicans, on balance, got a few more "above-the-fold" headlines (those that traditionally

[37] The coding unit was the sentence; the results thus suggest that the Democrats may have used the Joe Smith reference a little more frequently than this study revealed, because it was interpolated in sentences that were referring more prominently to other points. The Democrats did keep the issue alive in part by labeling campaign vehicles the "Joe Smith" express.

[38] Eisenhower got more mentions in every week except that of October 2-8, when Stevenson and Eisenhower each got 41 per cent of the mentions. Eisenhower started with 51 per cent, dropped to 41 per cent of the headlines during the final week. Stevenson started with 39 per cent, rose to 41 per cent in the first week of October, and then declined slowly to 33 per cent in the last week. Kefauver outdrew Nixon in headline attention during the first week, but trailed him in every succeeding week. Nixon's maximum was 17 per cent in the third week of September; Kefauver never bettered his initial score. At the end of the campaign, Eisenhower and Stevenson virtually dominated headline attention, as Nixon scored but 6 and Kefauver but 3 per cent. Press Intelligence, Inc., "Headline Candidate Mentions in the 1956 Presidential Campaign" (mimeo, no date), p. 1.

signal the news of greater importance in the paper) than did their
opponents, but the Democrats got a substantial number of such
headlines too.

Eisenhower got his greatest prominence during the week of
Suez. Stevenson got his during the first two weeks in October,
when he was asking for more school aid and for an end to H-bomb
tests; attacking Eisenhower for lack of leadership; calling for a
broader health plan and attacking public-lands giveaways; and
pinpointing Nixon as the chief campaign issue. Kefauver had his
best weeks at the outset, getting mentions for advance plans for
his first tour and coverage for the first part of it. Nixon got his
greatest attention from September 18 to September 24, for advance
news of his tour, and its initial moves, notably including his praise
of Stevenson for repudiating Hiss.

Summarized, the peaks and valleys shown by this index of attention were as follows:

Candidates	Top Percentage Day's Headlines	Lowest Percentage Day's Headlines	Maximum Spread	Average[39] Advantage
Eisenhower	69	22	45	21.7
Stevenson	60	23	29	13.9
Nixon	27	0	22	
Kefauver	10	0	10	

A count of the number of days in which each candidate led his
opponent shows a substantial Republican advantage: Eisenhower
led Stevenson on 42 days, Stevenson led Eisenhower on 14, and on
1 they tied. Nixon led Kefauver on 41 days; Kefauver led Nixon on
12, and there were 4 ties.

Summarizing, one may comment that the Republicans got the
major share of this concentrated attention, but Democrats got a
good share, and each candidate got prominent attention for those
points he was most concerned to make.

And as for press performance as a whole, the judgment of Herbert Brucker still holds that the American press has developed its

[39] This is the average of the difference between the candidate's score and the
second highest candidate's score on those days on which the candidate led.

traditions and practices of objectivity and balance in reporting of the news to the point where followers of the major parties can get the news they need to permit a proper political judgment, no matter what the preferences and editorial practices of owners and managers.[40] The news and facts were there for those sufficiently motivated to search and to ponder.

This does not mean that the arrangement of press output in terms of prominence was such that he who runs and reads might hope to have an informed political judgment because of the balanced arrangement of the most salient aspects of political events. Since the available data relate chiefly to the two major parties, they leave open the question of whether the fringe parties got adequate access in 1956. Gross inspection of the nation's urban press suggests that fringe parties were underreported, but in view of their lack of color, interest, and political relevance to the electoral decision of 1956, this lack was not serious.

As for the electronic media, it has already been noted that television outstripped radio as the preferred medium for national politics. Since 1952 television extended its spread over the nation so that virtually 100 per cent of the nation's viewers could look at the political conventions and follow the major events in the ensuing campaign. Radio and television gave full coverage to the activities of the major parties. And they gave much less time to the minor parties—in particular, carrying their candidates' acceptance speeches on radio. Since these candidates had nothing of any great current or potential importance to say and the major splinter group (the Andrews-Werdel ticket) chose to conduct an off-hours, weekend campaign with no staged special events or major speeches, the nation's citizenry missed little from their spectrum of available political argument and choice.

Not even the more rabid supporters of the electronic media thought that in 1956 television or radio did much to influence the outcome of the election. Television accurately reflected a Stevenson on the attack, and thus contributed to a reshaping of his polit-

---

[40] See Herbert Brucker, *Freedom of Information* (1949), Chaps. 18 and 19, for an estimate of the effectiveness of news reporting on the political successes at the polls of Franklin D. Roosevelt. The judgment concerning the performance in the campaign of 1956 is contained in a letter to the senior author dated May 16, 1958.

ical image; and it transmitted the health and eagerness of the President, underlining the one major point at issue. Whatever the President said about being a part-time public servant, devoted to a carefully planned schedule of alternate work and recreation, was offset by his vigor and endurance when television followed him out of the White House into the far corners of the country. Those who wanted to adjudge him adequate were given ample reasons to do so. And more important, the President's appearance of energy deflated the Nixon issue.

As for Nixon himself, television and radio helped to set his new image. As for Kefauver, most of his campaigning was done out of reach of these media—in the small towns, in the byways, and on the farms. Television and radio did little to give him any momentum or public image he did not possess before his famous crime investigation—except insofar as his Rogues Gallery telecast showed him capable of rough attack. This was only partly offset by his role (with Nancy and children) of the happy family on the Democratic side, in contrast to the Republican's evocation of Ike, Mamie, and their grandchildren.

There were no innovations in the use of television in 1956 beyond certain detailed changes in style. Both the parties and the electronic journalists proved themselves more at home with the medium; and the networks in particular performed Herculean tasks of logistics as well as more than adequate tasks of news gathering and transmission at the time of the conventions.

Viewing remained high—even during some of the least newsworthy and dreariest portions of the Republican convention. The Nielsen rating of total audience for it outstripped the top entertainment shows of the week.

The total number of individual homes reached by the television and radio broadcasts of the conventions ran at about 33 million for the Democrats, and 32.8 million for the Republicans. The average audiences ran about a third of these figures. Audience amassed for speeches or other events during the campaign proper were smaller than those for the conventions or for the election's eve and result. Peak performance for the Democrats came on Wednesday, September 26, when Stevenson's speech over two networks had nearly 17 million homes tuned in on television. The following Sunday he did nearly as well, with 10.9 million on CBS and 5.8 million on NBC. Kefauver's peak came for his Rogues Gallery effort on October 20, with 11.5 million homes on television.[41]

The Republicans got their largest single audience for ex-President Hoover's five-minute appearance on October 29, which went into 13.8 million homes. Even on election eve, the Republicans had only something over 10 million viewers, and 1.6 million radio listeners. Eisenhower's peak audience came on Monday evening, October 15, with 4.1 million viewers on ABC and 6.1 million on NBC; on an earlier Monday evening, October 1, he had 9.4 million viewers plus 800,000 radio listeners over one network. Nixon got his largest audience on Friday evening, November 2, with 6.3 million television homes and 1.3 million more on radio.[42]

Inspection of audience figures for all shows indicates that the Democrats got about as many viewers, across the board, as did the Republicans. If the Republicans enjoyed any advantage from electronic media use, it came from the way they used it rather than from a net advantage in number of viewers.

A substantial majority of TV homes tuned in the election night broadcasts; a peak of 21.7 million homes was reached by one network alone. The radio reached audiences of 2.5 million (ABC), 5.5 million (CBS), 2.9 million (MBS), and 4.0 million (NBC).[43] The commentators mixed commentary with reporting to describe the curious pattern woven by the rate and distribution of election returns moving across the country from East to West—long after the decisive claims had been made by Leonard Hall and validated by a 10 P.M. edition of the *New York Times*.

As to the point of decision—1956 adds nothing to the argument whether electoral decision is necessarily made early or late, or whether electronic communications are decisive in the choice. In 1952, it appeared that the majority of voters had made their choice by the time the conventions were over. This was probably true again in 1956—but not because of anything the news media

[41] Nielsen Television-Radio Index.
[42] *Ibid.*
[43] *Ibid.*

had done. The potencies of the two candidates had been fixed in public opinion well before the conventions, and nothing in the field of action or events did anything to disturb it during the post-convention period. But this pattern did much to confirm Eisenhower could do the job. With a world in torment or a world at peace, Eisenhower was the choice. So whether the voter sought allayment for anxieties over Suez, or the chance to drift off into a world of comfortable fantasy erected on peace, prosperity, or progress, he could find fulfillment by voting for the President. And Stevenson, whatever he did offer to the voter at large or to the somewhat disappointed intellectuals, was unable to compete despite the opportunities offered him by crisis in Egypt and Hungary.

14

The Structure of the Vote

IT IS NOW IN ORDER to review the voting results; to summarize the main facts concerning the performance of major components of the electorate; and to talk briefly of ticket splitting and of coattails.

The Presidential Vote

In 1956 Dwight D. Eisenhower won by an even larger majority than in 1952, out of a slightly larger total vote.

As the figures finally came in, the President with 35.6 million votes had swept 41 states, with an electoral vote of 457 and a percentage of the total vote of 57.4. Mr. Stevenson, with 26 million, had taken 7 states, (Alabama, Arkansas, Georgia, Mississippi, Missouri, North Carolina and South Carolina) with an electoral vote of 73 and 42.0 per cent of the total vote. The balance, 0.6 per cent, went for fringe candidates—the bulk to States Rights.

The President brought Kentucky, Louisiana, and West Virginia, which were for Stevenson in 1952, into the Republican column, while Stevenson won Missouri back from the Republicans. Third parties won no electoral vote as such, although one Alabama elector, Walter F. Turner, cast his ballot for Alabama circuit judge Walter B. Jones and Governor (Senator-elect) Herman Talmadge.

The full list of candidates, their parties and the popular vote was:[1]

---

[1] Richard M. Scammon, ed., *America Votes: A Handbook of Contemporary American Election Statistics, 1956-57* (1958), pp. 1, 2.

Candidates	Party	Vote
Dwight D. Eisenhower and Richard M. Nixon	Republican	35,590,472
Adlai E. Stevenson and Estes Kefauver	Democratic	26,029,752
T. Coleman Andrews and Thomas H. Werdel	States Rights	107,929
Eric Hass and Georgia Cozzini	Socialist Labor	44,300
Enoch A. Holtwick and Edwin M. Cooper	Prohibition	41,937
Farrell Dobbs and Myra Tanner Weiss	Socialist Workers	7,797
Darlington Hoopes and Samuel H. Friedman	Socialist	2,044
Henry B. Krajewski and Anne Marie Yezo	American Third Party	1,829
Gerald L. K. Smith and Charles F. Robertson	Christian Nationalist	8

Division of the Party Vote

Since voters must use their ballots to express preference not just for party, but for issue and for candidate as well, it is impossible to determine from voting statistics as such which of the three sorts of preference are being voiced. The fact that voters can in many jurisdictions split the ballots they cast in presidential years between parties, and can give vent to candidate preference at one level while they respond to issue or party preference at another, further complicates matters. Analysts of the problem have sought to clarify matters either by interrogating panels or samples, or by interpreting election statistics on the basis of assumptions concerning the meaning of disparity between party votes cast in the same jurisdictions for different levels of office. Interpreters can put faith in the results depending on their appraisal of the adequacy, skill, and integrity of the polling processes, or on their evaluation of the assumptions.

Here we give attention to three measures of performance, on which the reader can base his own conclusions, aided by the guidance of the conclusions of certain scholars concerning the presence or effectiveness of coattails and the phenomenon of ticket splitting. We consider the relative performance of the presidential candidates of the two major parties as measured by their share of the total vote cast for presidential office, and by their share of total vote cast for the two major party candidates for that office. We add an index of the ratio between the absolute vote in 1956 and in 1952 for the office of President, chiefly as a means of casting light on areas in which Eisenhower gained or lost. And we compare the relative percentages of total party vote rolled up by the presidential and the congressional candidates of the two major parties by states for Senate races, and by congressional districts for representatives.

Given these aids, readers are left largely to their own devices to draw inferences as to the relative strengths of the parties as such. Such inferences may be shaped by a temptation to notice that the results of 1952 and 1956 may herald a trend turn in American politics—one based on unprecedented tolerance by the electorate of the control of the Executive by one party, while the Congress or one of its houses is in the control of the other.

As to the total presidential vote, the President raised his share in 1956 to 57.4 per cent of the total, as against 55.1 per cent in 1952. He made gains by this measure in 29 states, while Stevenson gained in 19. Stevenson took 42.0 per cent of the total presidential vote in 1956, compared with 44.4 per cent in 1952.

If attention is directed to the division of the total vote given to the two major parties—and the shares are roughly similar whether major party vote or total vote is considered—the President did even better. In 1956, he took 57.8 per cent of the major party vote, against 55.4 per cent in 1952, as shown in the table on page 348. He raised his margin of victory over Stevenson in 31 states, gaining 10.3 percentage points in Louisiana, 7.9 in New Jersey, 7.8 in Connecticut, and 7.4 in Rhode Island. He improved his position elsewhere by 5 percentage points or better in Alabama, Massachusetts, New Hampshire, New York, Utah, and West Virginia, thus concentrating his major gains chiefly in the Northeast.

Stevenson gained in 17 states, making his most spectacular surges in South Carolina (13.6 per cent), South Dakota (10.9 per cent), Mississippi (10.0 per cent), and North Dakota (9.6 per cent). He gained 5.7 per cent in Oregon, and 5.0 per cent in Iowa. He gained less than 5 per cent in California, Colorado, Idaho, Kansas, Minnesota, Missouri, Montana, Nebraska, Nevada, Washington and Wyoming. Thus his gains came in farming states, mountain states, and in parts of the South. In South Carolina and Mississippi, the transfer of votes from "other" parties in 1952 into the major-party lists in 1956 hurt the Republicans more than the Democrats. But elsewhere in the South, it was a consistent story of Eisenhower gains.

The table on page 348 also shows that the Republicans increased their absolute Presidential vote in 1956 over 1952 in 32 states, with

Presidential Vote, 1956 Republican Gains or Losses

State	Republican Percentage Major Party Vote[a]			Percentage Republican Absolute Vote 1956/1952
	1952	1956	Difference	
Louisiana	47.1	57.4	+10.3	107.2
New Jersey	57.5	65.4	+7.9	117.6
Connecticut	55.9	63.7	+7.8	116.5
Rhode Island	50.9	58.3	+7.4	107.1
West Virginia	48.1	54.1	+6.0	107.0
Alabama	35.2	41.1	+5.9	138.3
Utah	58.9	64.6	+5.7	111.3
New York	56.0	61.3	+5.3	110.1
New Hampshire	60.9	66.1	+5.2	106.0
Massachusetts	54.4	59.5	+5.1	107.7
Maine	66.2	70.9	+4.7	107.3
Kentucky	50.0	54.6	+4.6	115.9
Illinois	55.0	59.6	+4.6	106.5
Ohio	56.8	61.1	+4.3	107.1
Maryland	55.8	60.0	+4.2	112.2
Pennsylvania	53.0	56.6	+3.6	107.0
Delaware	51.9	55.3	+3.4	108.9
North Carolina	46.1	49.3	+3.2	103.1
Georgia	30.3	33.4	+3.1	112.1
Arizona	58.3	61.1	+2.8	116.4
Virginia	56.5	59.1	+2.6	110.7
Arkansas	43.9	46.6	+2.5	105.1
Texas	53.2	55.7	+2.5	98.2
New Mexico	55.6	58.0	+2.4	111.4
Florida	55.0	57.3	+2.3	118.0
Indiana	58.6	60.1	+1.5	103.0
Wisconsin	61.2	61.9	+0.7	97.4
Oklahoma	54.6	55.1	+0.5	91.1
Vermont	71.7	72.2	+0.5	100.7
Tennessee	50.1	50.3	+0.2	103.6
Michigan	55.8	55.8	0.0[b]	110.3
Washington	54.9	54.3	−0.6	103.5
Colorado	60.7	59.8	−0.9	103.7
Missouri	50.8	49.9	−0.9	95.2
California	56.9	55.6	−1.3	104.5
Minnesota	55.6	53.8	−1.8	94.2
Montana	59.7	57.1	−2.6	98.7
Wyoming	62.8	60.1	−2.7	92.6
Nevada	61.4	58.0	−3.4	118.9
Kansas	69.3	65.7	−3.6	90.4
Idaho	65.5	61.2	−4.3	92.2
Nebraska	69.2	65.5	−4.7	89.6
Iowa	64.2	59.2	−5.0	90.1
Oregon	60.9	55.2	−5.7	96.4
North Dakota	71.4	61.8	−9.6	81.7
Mississippi	39.6	29.6	−10.0	53.1
South Dakota	69.3	58.4	−10.9	84.3
South Carolina	49.3	35.7	−13.6	45.2
All States	55.4	57.8	+2.4	105.0

[a] Richard M. Scammon, ed., *America Votes: A Handbook of Contemporary American Election Statistics 1956-57* (1958) pp. 1-3.

[b] Michigan gave Eisenhower-Nixon a plurality of 354,000 in 1956 against 321,000 in 1952.

an over-all gain of 5 per cent. The Republican ticket made its largest gains in Alabama (38.3 per cent), Nevada (18.9 per cent), Florida (18.0 per cent), New Jersey (17.6 per cent), and Connecticut (16.5 per cent). It lost most heavily in South Carolina (54.8 per cent) and Mississippi (46.9 per cent) where the large Independent vote for Eisenhower in 1952 went into the States Rights column in 1956 (being cast for electors pledged to no presidential candidate).[2]

Turnout and Composition of the Presidential Vote

If one considers turnout as the proportion of voters to citizens of voting age, the 1956 presidential vote scored 60.4 per cent, 2.6 per cent below 1952, but the second highest in recent years. Taking turnout as the percentage of actual voters to registered voters, the figure approximates 77.4 per cent, some 3 percentage points below 1952.[3]

As to geographical composition, the Republican presidential ticket triumphed in all eight regions[4] of the country, and gained in five (New England, Middle Atlantic, East North Central, Border, and the South). The Republicans held even in the Mountain states, while the Democrats gained in the West North Central states and in the three Pacific Coast states.[5]

The Republican presidential ticket took 2,113 of the nation's

[2] See *ibid.*, pp. 211, 371.

[3] Republican National Committee, "The 1956 Elections, A Summary Report with Supporting Tables" (January 1959), p. 4 (mimeo.).

[4] The Republican study grouped the country by states into the following regions:
New England: Maine, New Hampshire, Vermont, Massachusetts, Rhode Island, Connecticut—6.
Middle Atlantic: Delaware, New Jersey, New York, Pennsylvania—4.
East North Central: Ohio, Indiana, Illinois, Michigan, Wisconsin—5.
West North Central: Minnesota, Iowa, Kansas, Nebraska, North Dakota, South Dakota—6.
Border: Kentucky, Maryland, Missouri, Oklahoma, Tennessee, West Virginia—6.
South: Alabama, Arkansas, Florida, Georgia, Louisiana, Mississippi, North Carolina, South Carolina, Texas, Virginia—10.
Mountain: Arizona, Colorado, Idaho, Montana, Nevada, New Mexico, Utah, Wyoming—8.
Pacific: California, Oregon, Washington—3.

[5] Republican National Committee, "The 1956 Elections," p. 6. The Republicans dropped from 64.0 per cent in 1952 to 59.7 per cent of the vote in the West North Central group in 1956. In the Pacific Coast states, the decline went from 57.0 to 55.3 per cent.

3,069 counties, gaining 36 over the 1952 score. They won more counties in all regions except the West North Central and Pacific Coast states.[6]

They made even deeper inroads into central cities, suburbs, and metropolitan areas, penetrating Democratic strongholds.

Eisenhower and Nixon took 25 of the 36 largest cities, including such Democratic bulwarks as Chicago, Baltimore, Milwaukee, New Orleans, Memphis, Birmingham, Toledo, and Jersey City—all of which had gone Democratic in 1952.

The tables below show the location and extent of the major Republican and Democratic achievements and gains in the big-city vote, indicating the ten cities at the top of the list in each category.[7]

Republican Percentage Gains[8]		Democratic Percentage Gains[8]	
Jersey City	15.1	Portland, Ore.	2.8
Buffalo	14.1	San Francisco	1.5
New Orleans	10.2	Detroit	1.3
Newark	9.8	Los Angeles	1.2
Rochester	8.6	Kansas City	0.4
Baltimore	7.6	Denver	0.1
Birmingham	7.5	Oakland	−0.3
Boston	6.0	Minnesota	−0.8
Chicago	5.7	Seattle	−0.8
Cincinnati	5.7	Toledo	−1.0

Republican Percentage Vote[9]		Democratic Percentage Vote[9]	
Dallas	65.7	Detroit	61.8
Buffalo	64.5	St. Louis	60.9
San Diego	63.7	Atlanta	57.8
Portland, Ore.	62.5	Philadelphia	57.0
Houston	62.3	Baltimore	54.7
Jersey City	62.3	Boston	53.6
Indianapolis	62.1	St. Paul	53.2
Rochester	62.1	Kansas City	53.1
New Orleans	58.9	Pittsburgh	52.3
San Antonio	58.5	Newark	52.2

[6] *Ibid.*, p. 7.

[7] *Ibid.*, p. 12.

[8] Gains in percentage points, comparing percentage of major party vote in 1952 with major party vote in 1956. Note that the Democrats made net gains in only six of these larger cities. In four, their performance had to be ranked according to least loss.

[9] Percentage of major party vote, 1956.

The Republicans outscored the Democrats as such in New York City by 170,000 votes, but the Democratic-Liberal Party coalition amassed 51.0 per cent of the major party vote.

In the suburbs, a growing source of Republican strength, the Republican ticket did better on the whole in 1956 than in 1952, making its most solid gains in the suburbs around Boston, Pittsburgh, Baltimore, and Chicago. But in the suburbs around Washington, D.C., the President's vote dropped most sharply (around 5 percentage points) although he took the area. And suburban areas around Los Angeles, Detroit, Cleveland, St. Louis, San Francisco, and Kansas City showed small Democratic gains, from 0.5 to 2.0 percentage points.

Increased Republican presidential strength in the cities and in the suburbs continued to threaten the Democrats in a vital sector —the metropolitan areas. In six of nine areas where the Democrats took the central city, the Republicans took the metropolitan area because of their strength in the suburbs. (Among these were the metropolitan areas of New York, Philadelphia, Cleveland, Boston, Pittsburgh, and Newark.)

Eisenhower and Nixon lost ground in some of their previously safe rural strongholds, as part of the general Republican recession in farming areas; but they found increased strength in the smaller cities and villages.

Stevenson and Kefauver made their major gains in farm areas of the North Central states from Wisconsin to Montana, as far south as Missouri. They also made gains in the Western states, although on a smaller scale. Although there was a movement away from the Republicans, there could by no means be said to have been a real farm revolt. Drought was often given as an explanation, but analysis of changes in voting in 83 counties where the Republicans dropped most sharply, showed that only 50 had been declared disaster areas.

More to the point was a diminution in farm income. Even more to the point, in considering the political impact of drought, would be the fact that Republican help in a disaster area would tend to offset the normal irrationality of voting against the administration in power when times are bad, no matter what sorts of responsibility could be assessed reasonably against the administration for the deprivation. And it is quite reasonable to suppose that there might be more political disaffection in an area that thought it was hard hit but was not so classified by those authorities responsible for bringing psychic as well as economic aid.

Gains for the Democratic presidential ticket in the farm areas were distributed as follows:

Gains of 10 per cent and over	5.0–9.9 per cent	0.1–4.9 per cent
North Dakota	Iowa	Kansas
South Dakota	Idaho	Missouri
Montana	Nebraska	Oklahoma
	Wisconsin	Illinois
	Minnesota	Tennessee
	Colorado	Michigan

The Republican ticket made gains ranging from 2.0 to 5.9 per cent in West Virginia, Arkansas, Kentucky, Alabama, Utah, Ohio, and North Carolina.[10]

The onrushing Republican presidential ticket also made gains among Negroes and most racial minorities, but Democrats rolled up an even larger proportion than usual of the Jewish vote. Eisenhower and Nixon lost the union labor vote to the Democrats, but by a smaller margin than in 1952; and they improved their showing sufficiently among the rank and file and with nonunion labor so that they shared labor's vote equally.[11]

About 3.5 million Negroes went to the polls, accounting for some 5.6 per cent of total turnout. Less than a million voted in the eleven Southern states. Fragmentary data suggest that Stevenson won among Negroes, taking from 2.1 millions to 2.3 millions of the total.[12] But Eisenhower made modest gains, as the total vote cast by Negroes for the Democratic ticket dropped substantially. The shift was much greater among Southern Negroes; as compared to an average gain of some 8.7 percentage points in ten

[10] Republican National Committee, "The 1956 Elections," p. 19.

[11] The Republicans cited Gallup and Survey Research Center data to the effect that Democrats won union labor, 52-48 per cent; the Republicans won nonunion labor, 65-35 per cent; and a Gallup poll showed that among all manual workers in 1956 the honors were easy among the presidential competitors. *Ibid.*, p. 16.

[12] Republican National Committee, "The Negro Vote" (August 1957), p. 2 (mimeo).

Northern cities, Eisenhower gained spectacularly in the Negro wards of Southern cities:

City	Percentage Points Gained
Atlanta, Ga.	54.1
Richmond, Va.	50.2
Norfolk, Va.	49.8
Durham, N.C.	47.6
Jacksonville, Fla.	40.7
Memphis, Tenn.	26.8
New Orleans, La.	13.4

One explanation offered for these results is that in areas where the Negroes had found scope and status within the Democratic party, the Republican inroads were small (the Northern cities); but where the Negroes were frozen out and Democratic leaders opposed civil rights, desegregation and other reforms sought by Negroes, the inroads were large. The visible exception to this principle was in the case of New York's 16th District, where Adam Clayton Powell's leadership seems to have swung enough votes to the Republicans to provide a 16 percentage point gain over 1952. Baltimore, on the other hand, seems to be explained clearly by the Dixiecrat orientation of the Democratic leadership.

Republican analysts credit Negro strength with making the probable difference between victory and defeat for Eisenhower in Tennessee—where the 6,000 vote plurality was well within the capability of the increased Republican vote among Negroes in Memphis alone. Similar results took place in Kentucky, benefiting Senator Thruston Morton, and in Louisiana, where the Republicans came within 38,000 votes of victory in 1952, and gained a plurality of 85,000 in 1956. Elsewhere gains among Negroes increased pluralities but were not decisive. Results in Baltimore, Chicago, and Pittsburgh suggest that Negroes, once they had decided to vote Republican, were less likely to split their tickets than were white voters.

Among "youth" (voters in the 21-29 age bracket) Eisenhower chalked up a majority for the first time since Gallup started taking polls, winning 57 per cent of their ballots.[13]

[13] Gallup release in papers dated Jan. 24, 1957.

Among Catholics, Survey Research Center data showed a 5 percentage point gain for Eisenhower and Nixon to 55 per cent over 1952.

The woman's vote again revealed a greater proportion favoring the President than among men, as 60.9 per cent of the female vote went for Eisenhower, as against 54.7 per cent of the male vote. This compared with 1952 figures of 58.1 per cent and 52.8 per cent respectively.[14]

Presidential versus Congressional Performance at the Polls

Whatever the voters thought of Eisenhower and Nixon, it was clear that they thought less, in the various political races throughout the nation, of most of the other Republican candidates. The Democrats won the Senate, 49 to 47; they won the House 233 to 201[15]—and this in the face of a clear effort by the head of the Republican ticket to get a working majority for his party.

President and Representatives

In the House races, the Republicans suffered a net loss of two seats from the 1954 count, and a net loss of 20 from the 1952 results. Republicans won 9 seats from Democrats, all in the East; but Democrats won 11 from Republicans, all (except one in Maine) in the Midwest and West.[16]

---

[14] Figures obtained from the Republican National Committee.

[15] Republican T. Millet Hand of New Jersey was re-elected in November but died on December 26, 1956. Thirty-five Senate seats were up, with 29 Senators standing for re-election (13 Democrats and 16 Republicans); 25 incumbents were re-elected, 13 of them Republicans. Three ex-Senators won short terms, two of them Republicans. Seven victors were newcomers to the Senate, two of them Republicans.

[16] The Democrats defeated Republican incumbents in the following districts: California, 11th and 29th; Iowa, 6th; Kansas, 5th; Maine, 2nd; Missouri, 7th; Mon-

Charles Press reports that in 1956 the average percentage by which Eisenhower led his congressional ticket ran from six to seven points higher than in 1944 or 1948—and in 1956 Republican congressional candidates led the President only in those districts where they had no Democratic opposition.[17]

Over-all, the story of presidential versus congressional strength is powerfully indicated by these facts: In 82 per cent of the House races the Democratic candidate ran ahead of Stevenson while Eisenhower led the Republican candidate. In the Republican party, the President ran ahead of the Republican candidate for the House of Representatives in all but 42 districts; in one district (Kentucky 8th) the President received a larger absolute vote, but tied in the percentage of the total, at 71.7 per cent. In no state did the congressional candidates collectively poll as much of a vote in that state as did the President. And in only 22 of the 42 districts did the congressional candidate outrun the President in both total votes and percentage of the total (not major party) vote cast. (See table on page 356.) The relative over-all weakness of the Republican candidates for the House is shown by the fact that according to Schattschneider's rule of thumb, a presidential margin of 57 per cent should have produced a House composed of 65 per cent of his party.[18]

In the Democratic party, in only one district—Georgia 5th—did Stevenson run ahead of the Democratic congressional candidate in percentage of the total vote; and in only nine other districts did he outpoll his congressional co-competitor in the absolute vote. (Five of these found the Democratic candidate for Congress with no opposition; their percentage was thus 100.0.) (See table on page 357.) Stevenson demonstrated superior strength in races in Alabama (8th district), Arkansas (1st, 2nd, 4th), Georgia (5th), Illinois (1st), Pennsylvania (4th) and Tennessee (4th, 6th, and 8th).

---

tana, 2nd; Nevada, at large; Oregon 2nd and 4th; and South Dakota, 1st. The Republicans defeated Democratic incumbents in the following districts: Connecticut 1st; Delaware at large; Illinois 3rd; Michigan 6th; New Jersey 6th and 14th; Pennsylvania 19th; and West Virginia 1st and 4th.

[17] Charles Press, "Voting Statistics and Presidential Coattails," *American Political Science Review*, Vol. LII (December 1958), p. 1044.

[18] *Ibid.*, pp. 1045n., 1046-47.

REPUBLICAN CANDIDATES FOR HOUSE RUNNING AHEAD OF EISENHOWER IN OWN DISTRICTS IN 1956[a]

State and District		Vote for Eisenhower and Nixon	Percentage of Total Vote	Vote for Republican House Candidate	Percentage of Total Vote
California	4th	114,783	59.5	109,188	61.9
	6th	92,836	49.0	98,683[b]	53.7
	10th	131,018	60.0	128,891	60.7
	13th	103,373	58.1	104,009[b]	59.6
	15th	94,739	54.9	97,182[b]	57.9
	18th	101,583	58.4	103,108[b]	59.3
	21st	150,895	61.0	153,679[b]	62.6
	22nd	97,317	59.2	97,317	59.8
	24th	79,645	58.1	84,120[b]	61.9
	25th	169,444	63.6	166,305	63.8
	30th	132,833	63.7	142,753[b]	66.8
Illinois	22nd	97,132	61.7	93,399	62.3
Massachusetts	1st	95,007	63.1	92,269	63.6
	5th	130,971	63.2	150,957[b]	73.3
Michigan	12th	45,922	55.6	45,721	56.3
Minnesota	1st	89,143	52.2	92,092[b]	61.5
	2nd	91,840	63.6	97,520[b]	63.8
	7th	68,306	53.6	76,271[b]	55.9
Nebraska	1st	108,486	66.4	102,012	66.9
New Jersey	1st	129,804	55.4	133,153[b]	58.3
	2nd	85,652	65.6	83,433	67.9
New York	38th	129,689	67.9	135,572[b]	71.7
	41st	97,445	61.2	99,151[b]	64.4
North Carolina	10th	90,453	62.4	89,743	62.5
North Dakota	AL	156,766	61.7	143,514	62.6
	AL			136,003	62.0
Ohio	4th	100,430	68.5	93,607	68.8
	7th	99,884	65.9	91,439	66.0
	13th	82,328	65.6	79,324	70.7
	14th	118,027	54.2	123,105[b]	58.9
	22nd	88,064	55.9	96,468[b]	66.7
	23rd	109,932	67.9	102,707	69.0
Pennsylvania	6th	89,580	50.2	90,966[b]	51.5
	22nd	85,021	56.4	85,540[b]	56.9
	27th	117,626	61.5	126,247[b]	66.0
Tennessee	1st	96,339	70.4	86,531	72.2
Virginia	10th	52,724	54.8	53,149[b]	56.2
Washington	1st	131,806	53.8	129,768	58.1
	2nd	110,151	54.7	105,975	56.0
	3rd	78,530	52.0	80,520[b]	56.5
	6th	112,530	52.3	108,014	54.0
Wisconsin	10th	59,620	56.3	67,250[b]	64.6

[a] Based on *Congressional Quarterly Almanac*, Vol. 13 (1957), pp. 145-78 with modifications by authors.

[b] Ran ahead in both percentage and absolute vote.

DISTRICTS IN WHICH STEVENSON RAN AHEAD OF
DEMOCRATIC CANDIDATE FOR CONGRESS[a]

State and District	Vote for Stevenson[b]	Percentage of Total Vote	Vote for Democratic House Candidate	Percentage of Total Vote
Alabama 8th 44,746	76.3	43,671	80.7
Arkansas 1st 33,978	59.2	25,622	[c]
2nd 24,505	59.4	19,540	[c]
4th 43,699	58.8	37,284	[c]
Georgia 5th 82,792	60.7	85,292	59.2
Illinois 1st 68,266	63.7	66,704	64.4
Pennsylvania 4th 76,534	68.5	75,374	69.1
Tennessee 4th 56,822	60.5	54,318	74.5
6th 58,123	69.6	47,098	[c]
8th 37,375	70.9	27,475	[c]

[a] From *Congressional Quarterly Almanac*, Vol. 13 (1957), pp. 144-73.

[b] In New York's 22nd, 23rd, and 24th districts there were separate Liberal and Democratic candidates for Representative. While Stevenson received votes on both tickets, in all three districts Stevenson's Democratic vote and percentage was less than that of the Democratic congressional candidate.

[c] 100.0 per cent. No Republican candidate.

President, Senators, and Governorships

From the standpoint of Eisenhower's leadership and Modern Republicanism, four of the Senate races represented clear defeats and two clear victories. Presidential supporters McKay, Langlie, Duff, and Thornton who were endorsed by the President, lost. In Washington, Magnuson overwhelmed Langlie by 249,000 votes—a margin of 22.2 per cent of the total vote for senator—in a campaign marked by as much bitterness and personal recrimination as any in the nation. In Oregon, McKay lost to maverick Morse by 61,000 votes (8.4 per cent) out of over 732,000. In Pennsylvania, Duff lost by 18,000 votes (0.4 per cent) out of over 4.5 millions. In Colorado, the Republicans lost the race and control of the Senate as Democrat Carroll bested Republican Governor Dan Thornton by 2,700 votes (0.4 per cent).

The President's men fared better in Kentucky. There Thruston Morton, not only backed by unequivocal Eisenhower support but also profiting from disaffection in Democratic ranks and a shift among Negro voters, edged out senatorial whip Earle Clements by less than 5,000 votes. John Sherman Cooper bettered his Democratic opponent by a more comfortable margin. Clear Eisenhower support accompanied the campaign of the somewhat mercurial Senator Dirksen, who won by a small margin despite Republican scandal in Illinois.

A victory for which the President could take scant credit was that of Senator Alexander Wiley of Wisconsin. Eisenhower stood aloof as Wiley fought out a primary battle with an organization-backed man and then won on his own in the final test.

For Idaho's Herman Welker, often an Eisenhower foe, neither the President's efforts nor his own were sufficient to return him to the Senate, although the winner, Frank Church, did little in his campaign to attack the President (or even the Republican slogan of partnership in power). And despite the President's clear support, Ohio's Senator George H. Bender was crushed by Democratic Governor Frank Lausche.

Only one senatorial candidate polled a higher percentage of the vote cast in his state than did the President. That was Senator Milton Young of North Dakota. (In 1952, seven senatorial candidates ran ahead of the President.) Senator Chapman Revercomb of West Virginia, running for a two-year short term, did almost as well as the President in 1956 (only to lose by a wide margin in 1958). Eisenhower ran farthest ahead of Republican senatorial candidates in Arizona, Arkansas, Idaho, Nevada, North Carolina, Ohio, Oklahoma, Utah, and Washington. In the seven senatorial races in the South, the Republicans did not have nominees in four; in the other three the GOP candidate polled better than 20 per cent only in North Carolina.

The story among the governorships ran in similar vein. Of 30 races, the Democrats won 16—but only after a court decision had invalidated enough absentee ballots in Rhode Island to bring Democrat Dennis J. Roberts in ahead of Christopher Del Sesto. The results gave the Democrats a total of 29 governors to 19 Republicans for 1957. Here again there was turnover, as Democrats defeated Republican incumbents in Washington, Oregon, Kansas,

Iowa, and Massachusetts. Republicans evicted Democrats in New Mexico, Ohio, and West Virginia.

Ticket Splitting

An election in which the presidential candidate of a party consistently outran its candidates for other offices might be explained in terms of greater popularity or campaigning effectiveness of the presidential candidate, and the total phenomenon comprehended without having to raise the issues of issue preference or party loyalty. But the case in 1956 does not admit of such simple treatment. There were too many instances in which a political unit returned a majority for the Republican candidate for President, while electing Democratic candidates for other offices—and there were also incidents in which the division of party choice went the other way.

Ticket splitting emerged as the dominant feature of the 1956 electoral results, despite the theoretical possibility that voter dropouts from participation in the nonpresidential races might account for the differences in results.[19] Press noticed that in 1956, in 82 per cent of the House races, the Democratic candidates led Stevenson, while Eisenhower led the Republican candidate for Representative. There were 127 districts that went for the President but returned Democratic representatives. In 22 of these there was no Republican candidate, so in 105 districts in which the President could have had a Republican representative, the voters turned elsewhere.

The general pattern of ticket splitting has been summarized by Campbell and Miller as follows:

> Eisenhower and Stevenson voters in the North show a generally similar pattern, although Eisenhower voters were somewhat more likely to split their ticket in both years, especially in 1956. Ticket splitting at the national level was not entirely a matter of voting for Eisenhower and a Democratic congressman; one out of every ten Stevenson voters in the North split for a Republican congress-

[19] Press, in *American Political Science Review*, pp. 1045-47.

man or senator. The Eisenhower voters in 1956 also include a small but significant number who voted an otherwise Democratic ticket, a type of splitting which was almost non-existent in the Stevenson column. In the South, however, the Eisenhower and Stevenson voters were profoundly different. If a Southern voter chose Stevenson in either 1952 or 1956 he almost certainly voted a straight Democratic ticket. If he voted for Eisenhower, he was quite unlikely to follow through with a straight Republican ticket. In both years a third or so of the Eisenhower voters in the South voted a straight Democratic ticket except for the president.[20]

They point out also that in 1956, according to their inquiries, fewer Eisenhower voters voted a straight Republican ticket than did so in 1952, noting as the reason a drop in the number of Democrats who crossed over to vote for Eisenhower. In the South, however, many more (46 versus 21 per cent) who crossed over to vote for Eisenhower in 1956 voted for a straight Republican ticket too.

Coattails

If there was ticket splitting in 1956, this was done in many districts despite clear efforts by the President not only to gain a Republican Senate and House, but to support particular Republican candidates. Eisenhower seemed to be able to get Democrats or Independents to vote for him, but not so frequently for his supporters. In some cases, too, the President was not able to keep the Republicans wholly in line. Clearly in cases of rejection, the President's positive influence, if present, was not sufficiently powerful to pull his men through. But it could have been there; and speculation will continue as to the over-all effectiveness of "coattailing" as suggested by the raw voting returns.

Commentators writing immediately after the election gave comfort and pain to those crediting presidential coattails with influence. Those noticing the re-election of Democratic majorities in both houses concluded that the coattails had failed. Others, such

[20] Angus Campbell and Warren E. Miller, "The Motivational Basis of Straight and Split Ticket Voting," *American Political Science Review*, Vol. LI (June 1957), pp. 294-95.

as the pro-Stevenson *St. Louis Post Dispatch,* reasoned that had it not been for presidential popularity, the Republicans would have done worse in congressional races than they did.[21] These general results and broad judgments cannot be decisive.

The record of the campaign showed that the President's indication of his desires was not sufficient to guarantee a majority for those he backed. Some of those he helped won; others lost. In every case where the President actively favored a candidate the President ran well ahead of him. Were his coattails helpful?

Warren Miller has clouded the classic argument that running ahead is evidence of successful coattailing[22] and the issue cannot be settled on the evidence of aggregative statistics. Campbell and Miller concluded on the evidence of their survey data collected in 1956 that there was a coattail effect,[23] but they did not estimate it as powerful or decisive.

Charles Press examined election statistics of a number of recent presidential votes (from 1946 to 1956) to see whether statewide trends or seniority might affect the relationship between congressional and presidential voting. He found these two elements had some positive correlation with differences from group averages, but did not find them wholly dependable for prediction. He suggested, moreover, that the quality of campaigning might affect the outcome. In those races with which he was personally familiar, he found that those in which the Democratic congressional candidate was an especially effective campaigner, the Republican candidate would tend to run further behind the President; in those where the Republican candidate was the more effective campaigner, he

[21] Editorial, Nov. 7, 1956. It concluded with a "well-done" for Stevenson, who had the "personal misfortune" to be pitted twice against a man whose name was a household word throughout the world. "Millions of his supporters will believe that no other Democratic nominee would have done as well against Dwight Eisenhower either time and few would have polled as many popular votes."

[22] See Warren E. Miller. "Presidential Coattails, a Study in Political Myth and Methodology," *Public Opinion Quarterly,* Vol. 19 (Winter 1955-56) pp. 353-68, where the argument is advanced that coattail effects cannot be inferred from the presence or absence of a gap between votes for candidates of the same party for different offices in the same election, since either condition is compatible with the operation or nonoperation of a coattail effect. Only survey data can clarify the matter in particular instances.

[23] Campbell and Miller in *American Political Science Review,* pp. 293-312, especially p. 310.

might run closer to the President or (in such cases as that of Representative Keating of New York in 1956) he might outrun the President. He cautiously suggested that the competitive pattern of the district might have some effect on voter motivation, especially in activating the indifferent. But he felt that the voting statistics did no more than to establish broad limits for the relationship between congressional and presidential voting, within which survey research would have to provide more precise answers.[24]

Scholars of coattails have directed their attention almost exclusively to the Republican case. There are no published studies examining the Democratic case in detail. But the observations of well-placed observers suggest that if there was a coattail effect, it was usually the other candidate who helped Stevenson. The record of the campaign contains instances in which some local candidates shunned and others sought the aid of the head of the Democratic ticket.

In the absence of more persuasive and complete poll data—a void that will be harder to fill with the passage of time—speculation and faith will continue to color the opinions of analysts on this point.

But the avidity with which campaigners sought Eisenhowerian blessing—not to mention Nixonian eloquence—stays in the record as contemporary testimony to the value placed on such support by those in the heat and uncertainty of the battle for votes.

[24] Press, in *American Political Science Review*, pp. 1048-50.

15

1956 In Perspective

THE 1956 PRESIDENTIAL CAMPAIGN did far more to confirm basic aspects of the American political process than it did to change them. The campaign repeated much of 1952. Both major parties renominated their presidential candidates—the first time that had happened in both parties in the same year since 1900. The Republicans renominated their vice-presidential candidate. Although the parties were supposed to reverse their roles of attack and defense, both of them positioned themselves on issues and appealed to most politically potent groups in similar ways. Even in differing on methods—such as partnership in power or in the degrees and kinds of aid to farmers—the parties reaffirmed the same eclectic ideals and objectives. Both parties used similar campaigning methods in both years. Neither came up with any significant changes in organization or tactics. And the voters, not to be outdone in confirmation, re-elected Eisenhower and Nixon, by a slightly greater margin.

But there were some changes, and some attempts at change that were not wholly successful. Against the pattern of repetition and confirmation, there stood out sharply the Democratic capture of both houses of Congress despite the large and increased Republican margin of victory in the presidential race. Other changes were less prominent—such as the Nixon attempt to add more statesmanship to his political image, and the Stevenson attempt to combine talking sense to the American people with a slashing style of campaigning. Efforts to rely more on television and less on barnstorming proved abortive in both parties, although the greater reach of television made campaigning by this medium all the more attractive.

Even the determinants of the voters' choice seem to have

changed relatively little. While commentators—mindful of the extent of ticket splitting and of the probable impact of foreign crisis on the voters' decisions in the last weeks—stressed that 1956 was an Eisenhower, not a Republican party victory, survey researchers have reminded us that the largest factor in voter choice was still party loyalty. Candidate preference, they found, was more weighty in 1956 than before, and looked marginally critical; but it did not exceed the great enduring current of party preference.

Issue preference was less important. Neither party was wholly successful in carrying out early intentions for emphasis on particular issues. The Democratic candidate, who had been told he must avoid foreign policy, chose to stress this field early in the campaign. The Republican candidate, who had special advantages in discussing foreign policy, insisted that the real issues were in the domestic sphere, projected himself most forcefully as a protagonist of domestic tranquillity and progress, and tried to cut off debate on the draft and on testing of hydrogen bombs by asserting in mid-campaign that he had said his "last words" on these subjects.

Neither party seemed to pinpoint issues very sharply against poll data or other evidence of shifts or stabilities in opinion. Both parties maintained activities from earlier elections that probably had little to do with the outcome in 1956 but that seemed important in appealing to special publics and in rallying the party faithful. Democrats stressed their characteristic appeals to Negroes, to Jews, and to other minorities, as well as to farmers, laborers, and other "little people." Republicans kept alive the cries of communism, corruption, and Korea that had entered political folklore as the important arguments in 1952.

Stevenson's attempt to talk seriously to varied audiences in farflung places to get widespread attention for discussion of key issues was in large part unsuccessful. This failure substantiated the agreement among most political practitioners and political scientists that a campaign is neither a feasible nor an appropriate vehicle for objective, thorough, and balanced discussion of public policy.

This failure to achieve full debate is easily understood if one considers the tremendous pressures of immediate political interest in any presidential campaign—pressures to put personality, party,

and issue in a favorable light in the immediate circumstances leading to election day. Throughout the campaign the debate on issues
was cramped by the enormously powerful forces driving national
major parties to seek majority-building consensus. Campaigners
looking for winning margins in key areas while holding existing
supporters in line do not often seek extremes on old issues or introduce uncertain new ones. They work within the existing framework of political concern and preference, as they see it or as it is
revealed by political intelligence. They appeal more than they
shape. They highlight more than they clarify.

The propaganda of both parties—platforms, speeches, films,
pamphlets, press conferences, and the rest—dealt with the same
topics and favored many of the same things. The parties differed,
however, in their reading of the so-called record. They vied in their
description of the leadership needed to bring the agreed-on world
of chiefly material progress into being. They varied in tone. The
Republicans were confident, disciplined, and hospitable to any
who would share their universal goals of peace, prosperity, and
progress. The Democrats were more shrill, flowery, and given to
partisan invective both as to personalities and as to issues.

Neither party made any significant innovations in their provi-
sions for political intelligence, although they shifted resources and
attention toward the use of private polls. Already employed in
earlier years, market research to order made great strides against
public polls in 1956. The record of outward actions suggests that
these private intelligence operations played their most weighty role
in guiding day-to-day tactical measures. Public polls have the advantage over private polls in that they can serve as evidence of
victory, and the Republicans made good use of them in the regular
campaign. Contenders for the nomination in the Democratic party
used them too. Polls were more important for revealing candidate
preference than for shaping decisions about how to deal with
issues.

While the vote reaffirmed existing leaderships, the whole campaign raised some portents. For Eisenhower, the overwhelming
electoral verdict in his favor increased for a time his optimism over
his opportunity to advance "Modern Republicanism." Stevenson's

sizable vote confirmed his position as titular leader of his party and strengthened his determination to continue fighting for the New America he envisioned and striving to interest the people in the great issues affecting their future. Nixon, as second man on the ticket, could claim at best only an ambiguous vote of confidence. But by his campaigning he clearly put many Republicans in his debt, laying up political capital on which he could draw in the intra-party struggles to come. Democrats who figured prominently in the race for their party's vice-presidential nomination—particularly Kennedy, Wagner, Gore, and Humphrey—gained thereby in national stature and received encouragement for future aspirations.

While the vote cautioned both parties to shore up evident weaknesses, neither party found this counsel weighty enough to move them to a solution of their firmly rooted internal disaffections. The Republican leadership, most powerfully based on the industrial North and East, and with its mandate thinned in Midwest and Far West, nevertheless re-emphasized its "partnership" policies despite the wish of the West for public power, and it drove ahead with its farm policies despite unrest, if not revolt, in the Midwest. Stevenson, heartened by his large vote, joined in the formation of the Democratic Advisory Council for the shaping and advocacy of policies favored by the presidential wing of his party. The Southern Democratic leaders of Congress regarded the party victory in the congressional races as clear confirmation of their views and a mandate to continue the legislative course they had been following.

Given these broad patterns of confirmation, what difference did 1956 make for the future, and what changes could be expected in 1960 and beyond?

In regard to candidates, 1956 did nothing to widen the Republican choice, or to impede the early emergence of Nixon as a man with unified organizational support and no sustained challenge for the nomination in 1960. In the Democratic party, 1956 gave impetus to Kennedy while it deflated the challenge from Kefauver and did little to alter the availability of Humphrey. Others who came into prominence in the 1956 convention and campaign were not helped much or hurt much.

As to issues, the twenty-second amendment plus the probable renomination of Nixon had more to do with the possible issue confrontations in 1960 than public response to campaign talk in 1956. The twenty-second amendment prevented renomination of President Eisenhower. Any Republican candidate succeeding him would be bound largely within the confines of the policies and performance of the Eisenhower administration. Nixon, as a close participant in both formation and execution of administration policy, would be bound more than another Republican candidate.

But this circumstance did not rule out change either in position on issues or the tone and style of the Republican candidate. The Republicans could not deal with emerging issues in 1960 by pointing to a peerless leader. That leader might be influential—if he chose to play a prominent public role—but he could not shoulder the responsibilities of highest office. The Republican candidate, whether Nixon or another, would have to combine a defense of the policies of the preceding eight years with some foreshadowing of his approach to foreseeable challenges. In the process, he would have to demonstrate his personal qualifications for leadership.

The Democratic challenger would be certain to drive issue politics into further reaches than those explored in 1956. Aspirants for the Democratic nomination in early 1960 were already denouncing the alleged lassitudes of an outwardly weak presidential style and were demanding and promising more vigorous leadership. Even in the Democratic party there were powerful forces driving toward a middle-of-the-road approach to many issues. Not all Democrats were left-wing; many of them wholeheartedly supported Eisenhower policies on public finance as well as defense. And though there were some Democrats in the Northern and Western wings of their party who felt they could win the Presidency without their Southern wing, the chances of victory seemed greater to many Democrats throughout the country if the party took stands that would allow the full organizational complement to come into play.

It seemed likely that the old issues would reverberate again— Republican talk about peace, prosperity, and progress would be silenced only by a sudden outbreak of war, an inclusive downturn, or a technological catastrophe. Democrats would protest their concern for little people and decry Republican favoritism for the powerful and the rich. But in an era of increasing challenge from abroad, and growing demands for a governmental response adequate to the strains of growth and development internally, neither party could afford to rest its case on the old issues well entrenched in political folklore.

The problems of party organization and tactics would recur. Although 1956 might have helped nationalize the language and financial organization of American party politics to a degree, it did little if anything to reduce the confederate character of the party structure. Republicans faced the problem of bolstering their strength in state governments, and especially in the burgeoning regions of the West and the somewhat disillusioned farm states. Democrats had to strengthen their positions in the metropolitan areas and themselves as a national, presidential party. In their search for balanced strength, both parties had to seek the issues, men, and tactics that would bring apathetic or disillusioned voters to a new sense of political awareness. In this, it was not certain that they would succeed, although it looked as if party involvement might appear more acceptable as well as exciting. California had Democratic clubs animated by ideological concerns; and there were signs of Republican efforts to bring intellectuals actively closer to their cause.

Future political campaigning will probably continue in its conservative, centripetal way—reinforcing rather than educating, dramatizing rather than expanding understanding of the byways of issues and their implications. Insofar as critical events occur during campaign periods, candidates, organizations, and articulate partisans will immediately give them political color. To these efforts voters can respond—not in any nice or precise way, discriminating among nuances of treatment of many issues; but in a broad and responsible choice of an aggregate that seems to give best hope of a tolerable journey into an unknown future.

What is necessary is a greater and more informed involvement of the citizen with his political fate. The electoral process is one of many means whereby the interested citizen may affect the course of democratic politics and of public policy. The vote itself is important; but the communications surrounding the campaigning process may be even more important insofar as they help set the tone and framework within which responsible officials carry the course of the nation forward. Campaigning can take place on many planes, and the seeking of votes is always subject to the threat if not reality of a Gresham's law. There is no way of repealing such a law or declaring it unconstitutional. It can only be devalued in practice, by a political system in which voters discern and punish shabby practices.

Thus a main task for campaigners, candidates, and parties for the future is to see that the dignity of the voter—his intelligence and the worth of his role—is fully respected. Demonstration of such genuine respect can offset the cynical images associated with huckstering—if the public relations fraternity by regulating its own practices will reduce the load, and if parties themselves will insist on high professional standards from the media and opinion managers they consult. The parties might even forego the temptation to reply to the propaganda of the opposition by claiming their foes are dominated by hidden or not-so-hidden persuaders. Politics contains cynicisms enough on all sides without adding this pot-versus-kettle contest in denigration.

In the context of a politics of respect, Stevenson's effort to "talk sense" to the voter made sense. His understandable failure was not merely a failure to amass a majority; it was a failure to hold to his high standards of political discussion under the stresses of the campaign. In the same vein, Eisenhower's failure was a failure to use his unexampled popularity and influence to galvanize his nation into a genuine, not merely a verbal crusade. In the context of a turbulent as well as a rewarding future, 1956 was a failure—although not a fatal one. Its governing conditions are gone. Both parties must envisage challenges and opportunities for the future. Insofar as they do so, the electoral struggles of 1960 and beyond will play a more vital role in a politics that hopefully will involve a larger, better educated, more concerned electorate than that which basked through the summer and fall of 1956. Such an outcome is not inevitable; such things can never be so. But modern communications, organization, and other forces making for community offer the opportunity. Both the electorate and the parties have roles to play if it is to be seized.

Index

DATE DUE
